ROBERT SOUTHEY
LIVES OF LABOURING-CLASS POETS

ROBERT SOUTHEY LIVES OF LABOURING-CLASS POETS

Edited by Tim Fulford

First published 2024
by Routledge
4 Park Square, Milton Park, Abingdon, Oxon OX14 4RN

and by Routledge
605 Third Avenue, New York, NY 10158

Routledge is an imprint of the Taylor & Francis Group, an informa business

© 2024 selection and editorial matter, Tim Fulford; individual owners
retain copyright in their own material.

The right of Tim Fulford to be identified as the author of the editorial
material, and of the authors for their individual chapters, has been
asserted in accordance with sections 77 and 78 of the Copyright, Designs
and Patents Act 1988.

All rights reserved. No part of this book may be reprinted or reproduced
or utilised in any form or by any electronic, mechanical, or other
means, now known or hereafter invented, including photocopying and
recording, or in any information storage or retrieval system, without
permission in writing from the publishers.

Trademark notice: Product or corporate names may be trademarks
or registered trademarks, and are used only for identification and
explanation without intent to infringe.

British Library Cataloguing-in-Publication Data
A catalogue record for this book is available from the British Library

ISBN: 978-1-032-45087-2 hbk
ISBN: 978-1-003-43134-3 ebk

DOI: 10.4324/9781003431343

Typeset in Times New Roman
by Apex CoVantage, LLC

TO
JOHN GOODRIDGE,
EDITOR, SCHOLAR, ENTHUSIAST, FRIEND

CONTENTS

Acknowledgements	ix
List of Abbreviations	x

	Editorial Introduction	1
1	**Southey's Review of James Grant Raymond, *The Life of Thomas Dermody, Interspersed with Pieces of Original Poetry, The Annual Review*, 5 (1806), 382–397**	40
2	**Southey's Account of the Life of Henry Kirke White, from *The Remains Of Henry Kirke White*, 2 vols (London, 1807)**	59
3	**Southey's Review of Samuel F. B. Morse, *Amir Khan, and other Poems: the Remains of Lucretia Maria Davidson*, *The Quarterly Review*, 41 (1829), 289–301**	89
4	**Southey's Introduction to *Attempts in Verse, by John Jones, an Old Servant: with Some Account of the Writer, Written by Himself: and an Introductory Essay on the Lives and Works of Our Uneducated Poets* (London, 1831)**	101
	Stephen Duck	*140*
	James Woodhouse	*152*
	John Bennet	*156*
	Ann Yearsley	*157*
	John Frederick Bryant	*161*
	An Account of John Jones's Life Written by Himself	*174*
5	**Southey's Review of Eliza Bray, *Fables, and other Pieces in Verse, by Mary Maria Colling, The Quarterly Review*, 47 (1832), 81–103**	179

vii

CONTENTS

Appendix I: Correspondence Concerning the Lives	202
Appendix II: Reviews of and Comments on the Lives	211
Appendix III: The Poems of John Jones	232
Endnotes	305
Index	325

ACKNOWLEDGEMENTS

I am grateful to all in the family of Southey scholars; their work has made this edition possible. In particular, my fellow editors of Southey's prose works, Carol Bolton, Tom Duggett, Jonathan Gonzalez, and Cristina Flores Moreno have shared their enthusiasm, their insights, and their frustrations. Lynda Pratt, Ian Packer have encouraged me and shared their detailed knowledge of Southey. Ian Mackenzie provided invaluable help tracing and translating classical sources. Julia Carlson listened, queried, and bore with me. John Goodridge inspired the book by his friendship and improved it by his editorial and critical input; he has enabled all my study of neglected poets by his ground-breaking work in recovering labouring-class poets for our study and enjoyment.

ABBREVIATIONS

CLRS	*The Collected Letters of Robert Southey*, gen ed. Lynda Pratt, Tim Fulford and Ian Packer. Romantic Circles Electronic Edition, 2009-ongoing
Life and Correspondence	*The Life and Correspondence of Robert Southey*, ed. C. C. Southey, 6 vols (London, 1849–50)
New Letters	*New Letters of Robert Southey*, ed. Kenneth Curry, 2 vols (New York and London, 1965)
RSLPW	Robert Southey, *Later Poetical Works 1811–38*, gen. eds. Tim Fulford and Lynda Pratt, 4 vols (London, 2012)
RSPW	Robert Southey, *Poetical Works 1793–1810*, gen. ed. Lynda Pratt, 5 vols (London, 2004)
Warter	*Selections from the Letters of Robert Southey*, ed. John Wood Warter, 4 vols (London, 1856)

EDITORIAL INTRODUCTION

Southey's publications on labouring-class poets – gathered together here for the first time – were foundational. Before him, almost no one had thought to discuss such poets together, let alone explore the conditions in which their poetry was composed, written down, published, and marketed.[1] Just as Samuel Johnson brought metaphysical poetry into being by writing critical *Lives of the Poets*, Southey created labouring-class poetry in the public mind by placing the verse in the context of the versemakers' biographies.[2] The effect of this was manifold: the material conditions of being a poet in the different social classes came into sharp focus; individual writers were recovered from neglect and their work revalued; poetry was democratized because the status of ordinary people's verse was raised. As Poet Laureate, Southey was at the heart of the literary and political establishment; that he was paying detailed attention to lower-class poetry meant that it could no longer simply be dismissed with condescension. Reading Milton and Pope could no longer mean ignoring or despising Kirke White and Yearsley. Southey argued for plebeian poets' merits and gave readers the means to appreciate those merits; in the process, he exposed conventional taste as the expression of class prejudice.

Collecting reviews, biographies, letters, and introductions, this book shows that Southey's commitment to plebeian writing spanned his career. It demonstrates him discovering and recovering labouring-class poets – including several little-known women writers – by most of the means at his disposal as a professional man of letters: he advised poets on their drafts, reviewed their publications, wrote their biographies, and collected and edited their verse; he also solicited subscriptions on their behalf and used his influence with publishers to get them into print. The effect of this career-long involvement was to expand the canon of poetry and to increase the number of perspectives, experiences, and dictions that it included. It was to enable labouring-class writers to do what Wordsworth aimed to achieve in his lyrical ballads – to show that 'men who do not wear fine cloaths' can 'feel (and write) deeply.'[3]

Southey did not use the term 'labouring-class poet' – though all the poets he discussed were from the so-called lower orders: farmworkers, servants, milkmaids, and artisans, with a sprinkling of apprentice shopkeepers and clerks. Nor did he use the hackneyed 'peasant poet' tag, with its associations of class inferiority and rural

DOI: 10.4324/9781003431343-1

simplicity.[4] As he first showed, most of these poets were in fact not farmhands but tradesmen – in particular, shoemakers – people whose sedentary, repetitive jobs allowed them to listen, to read, and to compose while they worked. 'Uneducated poets' was the term used in the title of the book he published in 1831, *Attempts in Verse, by John Jones, an Old Servant: with Some Account of the Writer, Written by Himself: and an Introductory Essay on the Lives and Works of Our Uneducated Poets*. But this was more his publisher's choice than his own. 'Self-taught' was the term that Southey used to designate the poets he respected for educating themselves in poetry (and other discourses) so well that they could write with sophistication and control. He respected them because, as he described, the work required for artisans and 'mechanics' to teach themselves was enormous, indeed heroic. Such people typically lacked libraries, were poorly schooled, were busy at work, and had little money. Often, he showed, their efforts had been recognized by educated people who had assisted them with books, with education, and with funds. He himself assisted them privately, when asked, by advising them on their poetry and by helping them get to university. He also made it his task, as a professional writer with influence over publishers, to promote their work by writing favourable reviews in respected journals and by creating accessible yet accurate collections of their verse: he edited the poetry of Thomas Chatterton and Henry Kirke White for the posthumous editions that established their reputations,[5] with proceeds going to the poets' families. The biography that he attached to the latter emphasized the Herculean labour in self-education undertaken by Kirke White – a butcher's boy, stocking loom knitter and lawyer's clerk by background – while also asserting the quality of his poems in their own right. Kirke White, he showed, had mastered a difficult art. Vindication, rather than condescension, was his motive.

Overall, Southey's discussions reveal a three-part hierarchy. Foremost were the 'self-taught,' 'self-instructed,' and 'self-educated' poets who achieved high literary standards. These poets included many whose reputations he assisted in raising (in fact, the majority of the notable plebeian poets of the early nineteenth century) – Thomas Chatterton, Henry Kirke White, Robert Bloomfield, Ebenezer Elliot, Herbert Knowles, James Montgomery, and Allan Cunningham. He thought that they had 'natural genius' – an innate ability – but had striven to improve it by study of their art. Other instances of this kind of poet were, he wrote,

> Mr. Struthers of Glasgow – whose 'Sabbath' exhibits many of the best *graces* of composition and versification, in company with the more precious graces of natural genius, and a deeply devotional spirit: he also, though practising a humble trade, has obviously made poetry, as an art, the subject of elaborate study. But we may instance Charles Crocker, the humble Chichester shoemaker, and Robert Millhouse, the weaver of Nottingham, as men, who having the poetic feeling, have acquired its utterance, and made themselves acquainted with the forms and diction of poetry by sedulously availing themselves of those means of instruction, which, living as they have done in large towns, were within their reach. Mr. Crocker

tells us that he carefully studied an English grammar; and that he attended a lecture of Mr. Thelwall's on Milton and Shakspeare, and learned from it far more of the art of versification than he could possibly have acquired by reading; for the lecturer examined the structure of Milton's verses, and entered minutely into the nature of the feet of which they are composed.

He tells us also, that he hired books from a circulating library; and purchased the poems of Milton, Cowper, Goldsmith, Collins, and others; committed much of them to memory, and used to repeat them when at work.

(see following, p. 191)

If Southey here lays out the kind of self-education in literary technique that won his respect, he did not, however, require it to be a matter of learning to work within the conventions of the polite verse of the day as practised by classically educated gentlemen. Southey was himself attacked for deliberately breaching these conventions; his poetry was identified as a radical assault on the supposedly eternal canons of taste.[6] He did not expect the labouring-class poets whom he supported to submerge their original voice in approved diction, topics, and forms any more than he did, but he did wish them to know what they were doing and why – to understand how their work differed from convention and to control the relationships of sound, imagery, syntax, rhythm, and stanza form. Such poets, he thought, deserved support in entering the professional classes – though preferably not as full-time authors, since, as he knew from personal experience, consistently making a living from the pen was extremely difficult. It was, in his opinion, better to be a clerk, a priest, or a tradesman who published, since, as he remarked when advising Allan Cunningham (1784–1842) on his draft poem 'The Maid of Elvar':

Crowded as this age is with candidates for public favour, you will find it infinitely difficult to obtain a hearing. The booksellers look blank upon poetry, for they know that not one volume of poems out of a hundred pays its expenses; and they know also how much more the immediate success of a book depends upon accidental circumstances than upon its intrinsic merit. They of course must look to the chance of profit as the main object. If this first difficulty be overcome, the public read only what it is the fashion to read; and for one competent critic – one equitable one – there are twenty coxcombs who would blast the fortunes of an author for the sake of raising a laugh at his expense.

Do not, therefore, rely upon your poetical powers as a means of bettering your worldly condition. This is the first and most momentous advice which I would impress upon you. If you can be contented to pursue poetry for its own reward, for the delight which you find in the pursuit, go on and prosper. But never let it tempt you to neglect the daily duties of life, never trust to it for profit, as you value your independence and your peace. To trust to it for support is misery and ruin.

(Southey to Cunningham, 10 July 1819 (*CLRS*, 3329))

EDITORIAL INTRODUCTION

Here we can detect a certain ambivalence: Southey both wanted the expanding public sphere to be enriched by published poetry from the lower classes and also, for their own sakes, to save poor poets from dependence on professional writing in a busy market likely to bring them poverty and failure. Hence, he advised Cunningham to pursue poetry for its own sake – advice which was taken in that Cunningham continued to earn his bread as a clerk of works in the studio of the fashionable sculptor Francis Chantrey (who had himself come from a very modest background as the son of a small farmer).

Second in Southey's hierarchy were 'uneducated' poets – people from the lower classes who had not self-educated or been taught to any great degree but whose naïve verses contained some evidence of natural genius and moral worth. Southey supported the work of poets whom he put in this category (writers such as John Jones (b. 1774) and Mary Colling (1804–53)) by organising subscription editions of their work with the intention of bringing them a deserved, one-off financial reward. He did not, however, think that they had the potential to have a career as a writer or as a member of the professional classes: not for them a career in the church or as a bookseller or editor. It was best for such poets that they remain in their original occupation – perhaps as a domestic servant – pursuing poetry as a hobby that brought them and their friends contentment and self-worth, in the manner of a Sunday painter today. If this sounds restrictive, Southey's primary motivation was not snobbery, though he did harbour some reactionary fears of an egalitarian society in which servants rose beyond their station. He was chiefly motivated by the desire to protect these poets, still less equipped for professional authorship than their more strongly self-instructed brethren, from reliance on a fickle reading public for their income. He himself had never been able to support his family from the proceeds of publishing poetry, nor had his friends Coleridge and Wordsworth. The case of Robert Bloomfield (1766–1823), whose work Southey greatly admired, was also salient. Initially a huge seller, Bloomfield had given up working as a shoemaker, depended on his royalties, and ended desperately poor. John Clare's later descent into poverty and the madhouse, which Southey did not live to see, would not have surprised him.

In the third sub-category were uneducated poets who wrote for purposes of social climbing – egotistical men whose vanity led them to assume that their poetry, however naïve and however bad, deserved to win them instant status and who expected established poets to use their influence to achieve this for them: these were poetasters and hacks. Southey instanced, with wry mock-exasperation, James Barnfield and John Alford (see pages 193–95 for Alford's brazen self-advertisements).

Southey's conceptualization of labouring-class poetry came about in response to several interrelated social contexts. From circa 1800, developments in print culture and the book market altered the conditions of access to publication. The price of paper, which in the eighteenth century made up half to two-thirds the cost of a book, fell because of the industrialisation of textile manufacture: cloth was cheaper and more widespread, and therefore so were the old rags from which paper was made, until, in the 1860s, wood pulp paper became available, further lowering the price. In the 1810s, the stereotype and the Fourdrinier continuous papermaking machine mechanised printing, making large print runs possible and further reducing production costs per publication (Bloomfield's bestselling *Collected Poems* (1809) was one of the first poetry volumes to be reprinted via stereotype). And then there was a major development in the reproduction of images: from the 1820s it became possible to engrave images on steel plates, rather than the traditional copper ones. Far harder, steel held the lines of the burin much longer: thousands of pulls of an engraving could now be made instead of hundreds. In consequence, heavily illustrated literary annuals, anthologies which Southey called 'picture books for grown children,' could be purchased cheaply (*Life and Correspondence*, V, 339). They became the fashion: in 1829, *The Keepsake* featured snippets of verse, some by labouring-class poets (including Clare and James Hogg), that were now subservient to the illustrations. It sold over 20,000 copies. Wordsworth's collections of poetry, by contrast, were selling by the hundred.

With the technological changes came changes in bookselling as publishers tried to win sales by feeding the tastes of the middle classes, which they helped to shape. The expanding 'reading public' (a newly conceptualised body in the early nineteenth century) was increasingly urban and suburban but still connected to the countryside: as a result, not only did books circulate more widely, but newspapers, journals, and magazines also sprang up and found their way around the realm. Bloomfield, Kirke White, and Cunningham, for example, first read and then published poetry in magazines. As for book publication, in the eighteenth century, a poet from the 'lower orders' might appear in print if in receipt of patronage from a local nobleman keen to show he protected 'genius' among the lower classes who worked on his estates. Or a plebeian poet might appear in a volume published by subscription as an act of charity. But by 1800, matters had begun to change, as the success of Bloomfield showed. Bloomfield was a farm boy and then an urban artisan who composed his Georgic poem *The Farmer's Boy* in his head whilst making shoes. Though patronised by a great landowner – the third Duke of Grafton – as a man of genius from his estates, Bloomfield was helped into print neither by this connection nor by subscriptions but by a literary gentleman who was an experienced magazine poet and by a businessman who was the literary editor of a magazine. Capel Lofft and Thomas Hill prepared Bloomfield's poem for book publication by the magazine's publisher – Vernor and Hood. Jointly, they adopted an astute marketing strategy, not only branding the poet as a 'farmer's boy' – appealing to readers' pastoral and maternal sentiment – but also issuing the book in different formats at different prices. When it became an enormous seller – the bestselling poetry book until Scott's *Lay of the Last Minstrel* – it was clear that labouring-class poets could be hot commercial property and that they need not appear under the cover of a noble patron or a subscription list of charitable gentlefolk.

It was in this increasingly commercial publishing culture that Southey himself became a professional author, making a precarious living (with additional support from wealthy friends and then from a state pension). He made it his role, as an expert insider who had come from a poor, shopkeeping, lower-class family, to advise prospective authors on their manuscripts and to assist them into print – just as Lofft and Hill had Bloomfield. Thus, he could promote poetry from people whose background resembled his own that would otherwise have remained in draft or gone unnoticed. And he offered counsel to outsiders about the nature of the market – how small were the chances for anyone, let alone a poet from the lower classes who lacked connections among literary men, to achieve long-term financial success. His publications about labouring-class writing were both a guide to and a warning about a commercial yet unreliable market that, he saw, was no longer primarily shaped by aristocratic patrons or wealthy subscribers. He wrote in response to what he expected, in the present publishing climate, to be the commercial success of a tiny few and the commercial failure of the vast majority. But he also foresaw that conditions would change, making it still harder for labouring-class poets to come to notice. In this context, his *Lives* are acts of commemoration – as if he wanted to identify and describe a dying species before it became extinct in a print culture that had already been saturated by 'peasant poets' and that increasingly valued informational prose over imaginative verse. Education, he wrote, meant that the plebeian poetry

> is not so rare as it has been deemed to be: that it is becoming less so in every generation, because wherever it exists it is now called forth by the wide extension of education (such as it is), and by the general diffusion of books; and that as it becomes common the conventional value which it has hitherto borne will, like that of precious stones, be necessarily abated. This may be a humiliating lesson, but it is a wholesome one; and many there are for whom it will be well if they receive it, and lay it to heart in time.
>
> (see p. 100)

Here, Southey's point is that there will be fewer uneducated, naïve poets in the future because, even in the poorer classes, education in poetry will be prevalent: there will thus be more educated poets, from all classes. As educated poets from the poorer classes become more common, they will be less of a cultural phenomenon – less like Bloomfield had been – and thus less likely to seem exceptional in the competitive book market: 'it will be one consequence of general education and the diffusion of cheap books, that more poems will be written, and fewer published,' and thus 'imitative power will be so commonly called forth, that it will no longer be mistaken for an indication of genius' (see p. 190). The social danger for poor poets is thus that in trying to be professional writers, they enter a packed field in which the once-efficacious unique selling point (the 'peasant poet' image used to market Bloomfield and Clare) is no longer effective; they are unlikely to prosper. Those who do succeed will do so simply as educated authors – their class origin bringing them no rarity value, although it may still inflect what and how they write. This situation effectively came about – much later than Southey expected – after 1945, when universal free secondary education, means-tested free higher education, and cheap paperback books enabled scores of working-class children to develop into adult authors. Seamus Heaney and Tony Harrison were the most successful poets from the lower classes, but not because labouring-class poets were rare, collectable phenomena per se, or even because their poetry uniquely uncovered the condition of being from the labouring class. They stood out from other, imitative poets (both labouring-class and middle-class) because of their combination of genius and education. Southey saw poets such as Kirke White as heralds of such a future: they achieved by their own astonishing efforts a technical competence that mass education would one day normalise and added to it a distinctive original voice.

Southey's opinion changed subtly as the prospect neared of a Whig reform of parliament that would enfranchise formerly voteless men of the lower classes. From the mid-1820s, attempts gathered pace to educate the labouring classes through Mechanics' Institutes, National Schools, and the Society for the Diffusion of Useful Knowledge. In 1829 and 1831, Southey intervened in the debate precipitated by this so-called 'March of Intellect,' about which he remained deeply sceptical. In his *Sir Thomas More: or, Colloquies on the Progress and Prospects of Society* and *Introductory Essay on the Lives and Works of Our Uneducated Poets* (1829/1831), he was suspicious that the kind of education being promoted would lead to a utilitarian society based on economic individualism and laissez-faire liberalism – what Marx later termed *capitalism*. Knowledge, he feared, was being defined as useful only if it advanced a notion of 'progress' in which happiness was equated with the acquisition of wealth. Anticipating Dickens's creation of Gradgrind, he opposed a kind of learning that devalued all aspects of knowledge except an accumulation of facts that promoted a society of 'getting and spending.'[7] There would, he worried, be no education in literature that engaged the mind and the feelings – that sought to understand the human for its own sake (what we now call the humanities). Artisans would learn mechanics; tradesmen would learn economics: denied exposure to poetry, fewer and fewer of them would become plebeian poets. He feared that there would be political consequences too: labourers trained by this kind of education would learn to demand their economic advancement; this demand would be rejected by the governing classes, leading to revolution and civil war. His vision of education was, instead, one that involved the church, through religious schools, teaching loyalty, duty, morality, and self-discipline as it imparted knowledge. In this way, he hoped, knowledge would create emotional and intellectual bonds to the historical nation as embodied in its traditions and institutions (cf. what is called in the USA 'civics'). Thus, he welcomed and assisted into print self-taught writers who, against the social odds, might be able to educate themselves into a career in one of the national institutions – principally the church. Their poetry would accompany their profession as a cleric giving moral advice and spiritual succour, rather than being their profession in itself. Thus, too, he welcomed and circulated the poetry of uneducated servants that expressed, in what he viewed as naively written verse, the emotional depth and moral values that were absent from the utilitarian, practical mass education now being formulated. Neither group would promote class conflict or demand political revolution; nor would they show knowledge to be chiefly a means to social and economic advancement.

Pitched against the prospect of extinction, Southey's accounts of labouring-class poets are valuable today not least for the picture they give of ordinary lives. They reveal the material circumstances in which poor, ill-educated people lived; they uncover the means by which such people encountered poetry and became writers. They do not condescendingly assume, as commentators often did, that 'uneducated' poets simply spontaneously 'warble[d their] wood notes wild'[8] – spouting the verse that natural genius endowed them with. On the contrary, they delineate a process of acculturation to versemaking – encounters with poems that led people to emulation (e.g. reading magazine verse, or hearing ballads and tavern songs, or coming across a tattered volume owned by a fellow worker). Southey details the variety of life circumstances that led the poets to pursue poetry and to which, in turn, becoming a poet led. In the process, he creates an extremely vivid and, for the times, rather rare body of social and literary history, portraying exactly how it was to be, for instance, a maker of clay pipes and how such a maker became a rhymester. Effectively, Southey anticipates by 150 years the 'history from below' that Marxist historians engaged in after World War II. Unlike Victorian social historians such as Henry Mayhew and Charles Booth, he does not investigate the poor in order to anonymise them into occupational groups, to generalise about their condition, to reform their culture or rectify their behaviour. His aim is to counter the Whig assumption that 'history' is a record of central, progressive trends, a teleology leading to the enlightened liberal society epitomised by contemporary middle-class Britain (albeit susceptible of further progress via reform). The 'March of Intellect,' in his sceptical view, has no time to explore and no space to validate lives, actions, and discourses that it judges not to be illustrative of these progressive trends: they are dismissed as unimportant byways and dead ends. His *Lives*, on the contrary, exemplify his humanistic version of history; they celebrate humanity in its variety, describing beggars and cobblers in as much loving detail as most biographers described statesmen and kings. Ordinary people's feelings and actions are the focus, but Southey is not ideologically driven to write history as a narrative of working-class heroes and victims. He celebrates the quirky, the odd, and the comic as well as the hardworking martyr to a desire for self-advancement. As Wordsworth sought to do in *Lyrical Ballads*, Southey seeks to develop our feelings and understandings by sympathetically rendering the details of the extraordinary within the ordinary. Whereas Wordsworth is sober and tragic, Southey values ordinary people's eccentric, inventive, and unusual lives, celebrating the vagaries of people who do not remain within the conventional norms of their position – whether social position or gender position (women writers) or age position (he is fascinated by juvenile prodigies). There's no explicit ideology of self-improvement governing this. Unlike Samuel Smiles,

Southey doesn't produce biographies of lower-class writers in order to preach self-help to the lower orders, nor is his purpose to teach readers to be content with their lot (although he does wish to protect 'uneducated' poets from attempting social advancement by becoming professional authors – a path likely to be disastrous in most cases). If there is a moral purpose, it is to learn about humanity in its complexity and thus see society, both past and present, to be teeming, various, and resistant to simple generalizations.[9] Implicit in this approach is a conservative resistance to the reformist schemes of middle-class intellectuals and upper-class governors: these Southey thought dangerously simplistic and top-down. There is also an incipient meritocratic humanism in that it is by sympathetically representing ordinary people's efforts and foibles that Southey educates himself and his readers. In line with this, he explicitly identifies poetry writing and poetry reading as morally improving, not because poetry inculcates a particular set of doctrines, but because it educates the feelings, and he assumes that such an education is in itself productive of virtue. In effect, his lives of labouring-class poets both argue for and attempt to exemplify literary study as a development of mind and a communication of feeling.

Southey was berated for these arguments in *The Edinburgh Review* (see Appendix II) in an article that epitomises the kind of thinking he opposed – the reviewer poured scorn on the idea that writing and reading poetry would make a labourer a better person than 'one who discovers a bent for calculation or mechanics.' Arguing against patronage and charity being given to the poor – whether poets or not – the reviewer adopted the chilling lingo of the liberal lawmakers who organised social policy in terms derived from Adam Smith's 'laws' of economic supply and demand. Certain that he spoke the language of universal reason, he declared that:

> True rational humanity would not willingly see any one dependent upon the capricious bounty of another. Unable to reverse that general law, which prescribes labour as the lot of man, it endeavours to direct the labour of the poor into a channel where they may claim a recompense from the exigencies of others, and not from their compassion. It would endow them with a right to receive assistance, instead of teaching them to supplicate for alms.

This statement was a single step away from the ideology that enabled the New Poor Law, which created faceless and humiliating workhouses as 'assistance' to people whose labour (in an era of starvation wages) brought in insufficient income to support them. Depersonalisation, bureaucracy, the 'rational' justifying the interests of those who benefitted from the laissez-faire capitalism that depended on cheap labour and that pretended that the 'direction' of the poor's labour into a 'channel' that benefited others was an impersonal, natural law. Unsurprisingly, the reviewer saw poetry as outside the 'general law' – that is, unimportant to the society he wanted, in which labourers needed to be taught to become economically productive. He hoped that Southey would, in the future, 'rather teach them to cultivate pursuits which are more in harmony with their daily habits, and to prefer the useful to the ornamental.'

Southey rejected the useful/ornamental opposition. His arguments about poetry and the labouring classes are early shots in the intense debate about class, culture, society, and education that polarized Victorian Britain and led to an uneasy alliance between working-class Chartist campaigners for the enfranchisement of the poor and former revolutionaries such as Wordsworth and Coleridge. Southey and his fellow Lake Poets, though now conservatives, asserted the full humanity of labouring-class people and resisted policies that subjected them, and their culture, to impersonal regulation and incarceration if no longer viewed as economically productive in the terms valued by legislators. They attacked the capitalist ideology that lay behind these policies, undermining its claim to be rational and historically valid. Later, J. S. Mill would echo some of their arguments as he threw off the shackles of the utilitarianism in which he had been raised. Matthew Arnold would also fight, in their name, for education to value poetry as a means of cultivating feelings and morals rather than teaching the economically 'useful.' In the twentieth century, F. R. Leavis developed Arnold's arguments before Raymond Williams redirected them in a critique designed to make both capitalists and Marxists revalue the meaning of culture. Williams's comments on what he saw as the Romantics' pioneering discourse place Southey at the start of this contest about culture, class, and humanity:

> The emphasis on a general common humanity was evidently necessary in a period in which a new kind of society was coming to think of men as merely a specialised instrument of production. The emphasis on love and relationship was necessary not only within the immediate suffering but against the aggressive individualism and primarily economic relationships which the new society embodied. Emphasis on the creative imagination, similarly, may be seen as an alternative construction of human motive and energy, in contrast with the assumptions of the prevailing political economy.[10]

****

Southey's *Lives*

Throughout his biographical narratives, Southey is concerned with how labouring-class people come to write, and how they fashion a life as a poet. Thomas Dermody (1775–1802) was the first to receive Southey's detailed scrutiny (and to be represented in this collection). Reviewing in 1806 *The Life of Thomas Dermody* by J. G. Raymond, Southey portrayed this Irish juvenile writer as a negative example – a lesson in how not to be a labouring-class poet. Dermody ran away from home as a boy and thereafter subsisted on his wits. The son of an alcoholic rural schoolmaster, he knew enough Latin and Greek to be able to impress the

EDITORIAL INTRODUCTION

literati of Dublin and thereby escape being a street child. Booksellers and theatre craftsmen gave him lodging, impressed by his prodigious ability to make rhymes. Literary gentlemen provided clothing and schooling, only to find that Dermody ran away rather than study. Noblemen and women became his patrons and paid for his poetry to be published, although he repeatedly squandered their benefactions on drink and 'low company.' Southey chronicled these events with little imaginative sympathy for someone who must have been a disturbed and displaced child who had learned not to trust adults. But his exasperation at Dermody's dishonest and self-indulgent conduct was formative: it made him see what he did approve of in a poor poet dependent on patrons, whether or not that poet was a boy prodigy. What Dermody conspicuously lacked, Southey prized: studiousness, diligence, application to the art of poetry. Failing to exert himself, not only did Dermody die early, a malnourished alcoholic exploited by his drinking companions, but he also missed the opportunity to develop an original body of writing. He was, Southey was sure, simply a mimic adept at copying others' poetic style. He lacked a voice or a subject matter of his own. He wasted his potential just as he betrayed his helpers; the poverty of his life was matched by the paucity of his writing.[11]

Having formed his view by assessing Dermody, Southey next produced an anthology that was intended to expand the canon of English poets that was currently being created by the publication of multi-volume collections of poets such as that introduced by Samuel Johnson's *Lives*,[12] another selected and introduced by Robert Anderson,[13] and in particular a collection of Early English poets selected by George Ellis.[14] Southey's *Specimens of the Later English Poets: With Preliminary Notices*, 3 vols (London, 1807), expressed his belief that poets from obscure, lower-class walks of life should be revived and read. Unlike Johnson, Anderson, and Ellis, he included a number of labouring-class women poets, as well as men who had previously been omitted. The result was to put English poetry of the last hundred years on a new footing. And while many of the *Lives* that Southey included were brief, the poems and excerpts that were included of each writer served to pique readers' interest and invite them to go back to the original publications. Among Southey's roster are a number of poets studied today, of whom he is one of the earliest scholars. Mary Barber, Thomas Blacklock, Michael Bruce, John Cunningham, Robert Dodsley, Stephen Duck, William Falconer, Constantia Grierson, Henry Jones, and Mary Leapor all figure in the *Specimens*. Jones is condemned, like Dermody, for his feckless, drunken life; Leapor, by contrast, is praised for her efforts to teach herself:

> The father of this extraordinary young woman, was gardener to Judge Blencowe. Her education was suitable to the poverty of her origin; she was merely taught to read and write. At first her parents encouraged her propensity to poetry; but afterwards fearful that it might be prejudicial to her well doing in the world, they endeavoured by every means to prevent her future indulging it. Her perseverance conquered.

11

EDITORIAL INTRODUCTION

Her life was however very short, and her talents not known till she could reap no benefit from fame. Two volumes of her Poems were printed, 1748 and 1751.

(*Specimens*, II, 91)

Blacklock is also commended for perseverance, which, in his case, enabled him to overcome the double disadvantage of being born into a labouring-class family and of going blind when a boy.

[T]his calamity was counterbalanced by an acute and comprehensive mind, and an amiable disposition; he acquired an early taste for poetry, by hearing it from his father's readings; as he advanced in age, he acquired the Latin, Greek, and French languages, and a knowledge of Philosophy; his poems are very extraordinary productions, and demonstrate the power of genius, to overcome obstacles, which even nature has thrown in its way; the combined powers of his other senses, and the ideas he received through them, enabled him to form such associations, as that of sight would have assisted to supply him with, and it very seldom occurs in reading his works, that any trace of the deficiency of this sense can be discovered.

(*Specimens*, III, 357)

The poet about whom Southey is most vehement is Thomas Chatterton. Building on his 1803 edition of Chatterton's posthumous *Collected Poems* (1803), Southey now placed his fellow Bristol poet at the centre of his mission to widen the canon beyond the narrow limits of gentlemen's class-derived taste. His brief *Life of Chatterton* makes clear his animus against gentlemanly critics and patrons: he claims they were unfit to appreciate Chatterton's achievements and accuses them of neglect.

Chatterton's sad story is well known; his life the wonder, his death the disgrace of his country. That a boy of seventeen years should have afforded a subject for dispute to the first criticks and scholars of his time is scarcely to be credited: who then shall believe that this prodigy of nature should be left a prey to indigence and famine! Scorned by those who envied him, and not understood by those who pretended to patronize him, the very efforts of his genius were made a plea for attacking his moral character; and inferences were unjustly drawn from his successful imitation of ancient manuscripts, that he would not scruple to commit the crime of forgery.

This malicious insinuation, invented only to justify the odious neglect with which he was treated, met its refutation in his death, which was innocent to all the world, except himself. Hunger itself did not tempt him to the violation of any social duty, and he closed his short life, unstained by any crime, the probable guilt of which was imputed to him by avarice and envy.

(*Specimens*, II, 420)

Having put these recent poets on the map, Southey wrote an extended biography of the still more recently deceased prodigy Henry Kirke White (1785–1806; the second text collected here). This *Life* introduced the posthumous edition of Kirke White's writings that Southey produced for the benefit of Kirke White's family – *The Remains of Henry Kirke White . . . with an Account of His Life* (1807). It proved to be the single most important biography of any labouring-class poet, surpassing in significance even the biographical sketch compiled by Capel Lofft to preface Bloomfield's *Farmer's Boy*. Whereas Lofft depicted Bloomfield, who was over 30 years old, as the callow country boy he had been when first he came to London, thereby appealing to readers' protective sentiment, Southey portrayed how Kirke White developed from a precocious child into a brilliant and learned, if unstable, man who was killed by overwork and illness aged 21. He stressed self-education rather than proffered infantilisation. And this proved still more effective than Lofft's narrative, which had helped Bloomfield's poems sell 25,000 copies before 1813 – an enormous number for the period – but was rejected by the poet, who replaced it as soon as he had power to do so. And it could not secure Bloomfield popularity in later life: by 1822, he found it difficult to secure the sort of advances from publishers that would support his family (Southey was consulted on how best to relieve his poverty). Bloomfield's work underwent a revival after his death, and he ultimately became one of the ten bestselling poets of the nineteenth century. Southey's *Life of Kirke White* made its subject another of this top ten and established him as a major cultural icon in Britain and America. Kirke White's *Remains* went through eleven editions in 17 years before copyright was broken in 1824. After that, dozens more collections followed from over 20 different publishers before 1900. Kirke White's work was on the shelves of readers all over Britain and America, and he attained a near-mythical reputation, before and then alongside Keats. Indeed, Keats was viewed in his terms as a Romantic youth whose sensitivity (the mark of his genius) left him unable to survive the study he imposed on himself as he tried to succeed in the harshly competitive world that he aspired to join. Kirke White, in Southey's hands, first embodied the figure of the juvenile genius so insightful into his own gift and into the world at large that he foresaw his early death and imagined being among the English poets after it, just as Keats later did. Keats's friends, it turns out, had introduced him to Southey's edition of his predecessor, hence the borrowings from Kirke White's verse that appear in his odes and sonnets.[15]

Southey had first spotted Kirke White's potential in 1804 when reviewing *Clifton Grove*, the collection Kirke White had published with Vernor and Hood with the help of Lofft and Hill – the team that had published Bloomfield. Southey compared the poems favourably with those of the young Pope and Chatterton.[16] He then came across a patronising treatment of the volume in *The Monthly Review*[17]

EDITORIAL INTRODUCTION

and wrote to Kirke White commiserating and offering his help in advancing his ambition to study at Cambridge.[18] Kirke White was helped to gain a place there by the support of the evangelical clerics, only to die before graduating, his health destroyed by sleep deprivation and by tuberculosis. Southey was then asked if he might create an edition of his writings from the surviving manuscripts. Inspecting these, he was astonished at how much had been achieved by a young man who had so recently been working as a factory operative:

> These papers (exclusive of the correspondence) filled a box of considerable size. Mr. Coleridge was present when I opened them, and was, as well as myself, equally affected and astonished at the proofs of industry which they displayed. Some of them had been written before his hand was formed, probably before he was thirteen. There were papers upon law, upon electricity, upon chemistry, upon the Latin and Greek languages, from their rudiments, to the higher branches of critical study, upon history, chronology, divinity, the fathers, &c. Nothing seemed to have escaped him. His poems were numerous; among the earliest, was a sonnet addressed to myself, long before the little intercourse which had subsisted between us, had taken place. Little did he think, when it was written, on what occasion it would fall into my hands. He had begun three tragedies when very young; one was upon Boadicea, another upon Iñez de Castro: the third was a fictitious subject. . . . Much of his time, latterly, had been devoted to the study of Greek prosody: he had begun several poems in Greek, and a translation of the Samson Agonistes. I have inspected all the existing manuscripts of Chatterton, and they excited less wonder than these.
>
> (*Remains of Henry Kirke White*, I, 51)

Undoubtedly, Southey saw something of his own boyhood self in both Chatterton and Kirke White. He, too, had been a city boy from an impoverished tradesman's family; he, too, had been a lonely lad who read and wrote, for amusement, epic poetry of the chivalric era. He paid tribute to Chatterton by compiling the first collected edition of his work,[19] thus helping to promote the image of the boy genius from the humble background – the prodigy tragically ignored by the world and cut off by death. Now he repeated the mythmaking process with Kirke White, not least because Kirke White seemed a paragon of industry and honesty whose death was not his fault, save that he had weakened his constitution by overwork so that it was the more vulnerable to the consumption that killed him. Thus, whereas Chatterton had, it appeared, committed suicide,[20] Kirke White's death was tragically undeserved. Unlike Dermody, who had squandered his talent, wasted the help given him, and ruined his health by drinking, Kirke White had been too dedicated for his own good. His death was a cruel warning of the dangers of too fanatical a devotion to self-advancement through learning, noble though that devotion was and, in more moderate doses, exemplary. Kirke White was in fact the opposite of Dermody: a moral exemplar of the virtues of hard work to all young people who were not born to privilege, he was also a monitory lesson about proper limits. Kirke White made self-advancement into the professional classes seem a possible goal, only to expire from exhaustion before it was reached. It was this dual lesson to be drawn from his case, as well as his talent, that Southey emphasised throughout the *Life*. And he stressed that Kirke White's self-conscious meditations on his commitment to studying and to poetry-writing, and on the price he paid for this commitment, were among the most impressive qualities of his verse. This poet from the labouring classes did not merely write about his labour, as Bloomfield and Stephen Duck had become renowned for doing; he wrote about his inner thoughts, hopes, and fears – pondering the costs of self-education and of verse-making and reflecting on the prospect of death like a latter-day Thomas Gray and like the present-day Wordsworth. Kirke White became, in Southey's *Life*, a Romantic poet avant la lettre – a distinctly modern poet in that his subject was, to a great extent, himself.

The effect of Southey's *Life* was more to glamorise than to warn. Burn-out seemed a price worth paying for such prophetic insight into one's own self and into the human condition more widely. Better to die tragically young through dedication to one's art than slowly to rust – as Percy Shelley said of John Keats and Robert Browning implied of Wordsworth.[21] Both Shelley and Browning knew Kirke White's story and had his verse by heart. Whitman, too, as late as the 1880s, saw Kirke White as the epitome of the poet too sensitive to endure life's shocks and buffets, although he thought – as Byron also had when considering Kirke White and Keats – that poets should be more manly and robust.[22]

It was, Southey found, harder to be manly and robust when born to poverty or to a labouring-class culture in which one did not fit: not only was the route to literariness harder, and likely to alienate one from one's fellows and family, but the chances of becoming sick were also much higher. Sensitivity, both mental and physical, tended to come with the territory. In 1808, he received a letter from a 28-year-old unpublished poet named Ebenezer Elliott. Elliott was the son of a Calvinist preacher and ironmaster who found neither hellfire sermons nor factory work to his taste. A lonely boy who had suffered from smallpox and later endured depression, Elliott had skipped school in favour of the typically female recreations of country walking and collecting wildflowers. Botanising, flower-painting, and reading became his hobbies – he later recalled that he taught himself to love and write poetry from a collection of poets including Milton, Young, and Shenstone that his father happened to inherit. These hobbies sustained him while working for little pay in the family foundry to learn the iron trade. He married in 1806 but, despite devoting his wife's marriage portion to the business, found that its financial difficulties continued, hastening his father's death. It went bankrupt in the post-war crash of 1816. Reaching out from this difficult milieu, Elliott wrote to the man known as the supporter of Kirke White's advancement from a background

EDITORIAL INTRODUCTION

of labour in shop and mill. Southey counselled him not to depend on income from publishing his poems.

> Poetry is the worst article in the market; – out of fifty volumes which may be published in the course of a year, not five pay the expense of publication: and this is a piece of knowledge which authors in general purchase dearly, for in most cases these volumes are printed at their risk.
>
> From that specimen of your productions which is now in my writing desk, I have no doubt that you possess the feeling of a poet, and may distinguish yourself; but I am sure that premature publication would eventually discourage you. You have an example in Kirke White; – his Clifton Grove sold only to the extent of the subscription he obtained for it; and the treatment which it experienced drove him, by his own account, almost to madness. My advice to you is, to go on improving yourself, without hazarding any thing: you cannot practise without improvement. . . . Try the newspapers. Send what you think one of your best short poems (that is, any thing short of 100 lines) to the Courier or the Globe. If it is inserted send others, with any imaginary signature. If they please nobody, and nobody notices them for praise, nobody will for censure, and you will escape all criticism. If, on the contrary, they attract attention, the editor will be glad to pay you for more, – and they still remain your property, to be collected and reprinted in whatever manner you may think best hereafter.
>
> (Southey to Elliott, 13 October 1808; *CLRS* 1519)

Southey also offered to organise a subscription edition, if Elliott insisted on book publication. Elliott then sent him the poem 'The Soldier's Love,' and Southey, having read it, advised against publication in a letter that was disarmingly frank in that it admitted that his own early narrative poems had been full of faults. Anything but condescending, Southey reassured his tyro correspondent that he had himself made the mistakes that he hoped Elliott would now be able to avoid:

> [N]o young man can possibly write a good narrative poem, – tho I believe he cannot by any <other means> so effectually improve himself as by making the attempt. I myself published one at the age of one & twenty, – it made a reputation for me, – not so much by its merits as because it was taken up by one party, & abused by another, almost independently of its merits or demerits, at a time when party spirit was more violent than it is to be hoped it ever will be again. What has been the consequence of this publication? that the poem from beginning <to end> was full of incorrect language, & errors of every kind, that all the weeding of years could never weed it clean, – & that <many> people at this day rate me not according to the standard of my present intellect but by what it was fourteen years ago.
>
> (Southey to Elliott, 3 February 1809; *CLRS* 1573)

Southey also noted that, in a bigger and more competitive public sphere, 'criticism is conducted upon a different plan from what it was when [he] commenced [his] career.' Elliott's poem would attract 'venomous' 'malice & ridicule' (as Kirke White's first collection had).

Elliott was grateful, and numerous letters were exchanged over the following decade as Southey and Elliott compared ideas about prosody and narrative structure, sent each other books, and gave tips for reading; Elliott became confident enough to refer to the 'unaccountable clinks' in the prosody of Southey's *Curse of Kehama* (Southey took this in good part) (Southey to Elliott, 7 February 1811; *CLRS* 1866). The two men met in 1823, and Southey then helped Elliott's son gain a scholarship at Cambridge. Southey welcomed each of the volumes that Elliott published, praising some, criticising others, recommending he reduce ornamentation and adopt a plainer style. In 1831, Elliott finally succeeded in doing so (in effect throwing off the influence of Southey's earlier verse at Southey's behest) when he published, anonymously, his *Corn Law Rhymes*. These radical poems, written in the manner of *Lyrical Ballads*, took up the cause of the exploited mechanics, artisans, and labourers, dramatizing their suffering, depicting their poverty, protesting at their exploitation, and hinting at armed rebellion if parliament were not reformed so as to enfranchise them. The now-conservative Southey was shocked at the near endorsement of violent action (so reminiscent of his own radical poems of 1794), though he noted that he, too, had been drawing attention to labourers' poverty. But he was strongly impressed by the poems' quality. He told a correspondent:

> You may probably have seen the *Corn Law Rhymes*, which were brought into notice as the poems of an operative. I detected the author by internal evidence – not of the politics but of the poetry: and happen to know what extraordinary pains he has been taking for more than twenty years in studying poetry as an art.[23]

Wordsworth was impressed, too, and later said, 'None of us have done better than he has in his best. . . . Elliott has a fine eye for nature. He is an extraordinary man.'[24] Now with an independent, forceful, and original voice, Elliott had learned from his apprenticeship and become the most striking example of Southey's mentorship and encouragement bearing fruit.

Elliott was not the only poor young writer who sought Southey's help in the wake of *The Remains of Henry Kirke White*. In 1810, Southey was approached by two poets concerning their efforts to publish the posthumous poems of their friend, a bank clerk in Bristol named William Roberts. Southey took up the case, writing to Kirke White's brother, John Neville White, seeking a subscription to the proposed volume:

> I want your assistance in a business in which I am sure it will interest you to give it. A youth of Bristol, by name William Roberts, died

EDITORIAL INTRODUCTION

of consumption about two years ago, at the age of nineteen. He was employed in a bank, and his salary, 70/. a year (I believe), was materially useful in assisting towards the support of his father and mother, and a grandmother, and one only sister. The family had known better days . . . and one calamity following another, has reduced them very greatly. Yet still there remains that feeling which, if I call it pride, it is only for want of a better word to express something noble in its nature. William was a youth of great genius, and a few days before his death he bequeathed his poems in trust to his two intimate friends to be published for the benefit of his sister, that being all he had to bequeath, and his passionate desire (like that of Chatterton) was to provide for her. You must remember that at that time he did not foresee the subsequent distresses of his father and mother. These friends were a young physician of the name of Hogg, settled somewhere near London, and James, a banker of Birmingham, an acquaintance of mine, the author of that sweet poem upon the Otaheitean Girl, of which some stanzas were quoted in the third Quarterly Review. James has arranged the poems and letters of the poor fellow for the press, and will draw up a biographical memoir. He has consulted me upon the subject, and the plain statement which I have here made of the circumstances has interested me very deeply. . . . My opinion is that great things might have been done by William Roberts; that every one will acknowledge this; but that his Remains will not obtain a general sale. Of Henry's I foresaw the success as much as such a thing could be foreseen. But Roberts has left nothing so good as Henry's best pieces; in fact he died younger, and was precluded from the possibility of advancing himself as Henry did, in choosing a learned profession because his salary was wanted at home. . . .

My hope is that such a sum may be raised as will be sufficient to place Eliza Roberts in a situation respectably to support herself and her parents. I do not yet know what extent the publication will run to, but as soon as this is settled, I will beg you to *beg* subscriptions.

(Southey to John Neville White, 11 March 1810; *CLRS* 1757)

What Southey does not say here is that it was he who got the volume placed with Longmans, his usual publishers. Although he did not himself write Roberts's *Life*, he was responsible for making it public. The volume, *Poems and Letters by the Late William Isaac Roberts*, was clearly modelled on his *Remains of . . . Kirke White*, including as it did a prefatory biography, letters, and poems. The biography depicted a life of drudgery —12-hour days as a clerk in a bank — the kind of office job that was then becoming common for the first time and that Charles Lamb, Charles Dickens, and Herman Melville showed to be

18

EDITORIAL INTRODUCTION

soul-destroying. Nevertheless, like Kirke White, Roberts found time to study every evening:

> The value of Roberts's application to his intellectual improvement, can only be duly appreciated by considering that it never detained him from severer duties, and that his attendance at the bank was uniform, and generally from nine in the morning until eight or nine at night. He would then come home faint and weary with his daily labour, and after the refreshment of tea, which was his favourite beverage, he would retire to his chamber, and there recruit his spirits by composition or reading. Late, however, as he might be thus employed, he never failed during the summer to resume his studies at an early hour in the morning. A walk before breakfast with one or two select friends, was nevertheless an indulgence that he occasionally allowed himself.
>
> *(Poems and Letters, p. xv)*

Roberts's poems were derivative, but at least one seemed prophetic of his own death and of the grief and loneliness it would bequeath to his sister.

> O'er many a wild, o'er many a wave.
>   My solitary path has been;
> Alas! and is a brother's grave,
>   My mournful journey's closing scene?
>
> My heart had hoped one joy to prove,
>   Tho' fate of many has bereft me;
> Had fondly hoped a brother's love,
>   To cheer this drooping heart, was left me.
>
> But hoped in vain! – no more renew'd
>   Is love's embrace or friendship's vow;
> The wreath of death in tears bedew'd.
>   Is all that I can give thee now.
>
> 'Farewell! Farewell' – tho' fate denied
>   To clasp thee living to my breast;
> Still will I kneel thy tomb beside,
>   And weeping, hail thy peaceful rest!
>
> *(Poems and Letters, p. 12)*

The whole publishing strategy repeated what Southey had done both for Kirke White and for Chatterton – save that seeking subscribers guaranteed a sale

EDITORIAL INTRODUCTION

even if the poetry was not of strong interest. That Southey devoted so much energy to it shows his commitment to assisting young men who reminded him of his young self – or at least helping their families if they had already died. It also shows his continuing fascination by the intellectual culture of lower- and lower-middle-class Bristol – his own city, Chatterton's, and also that of William Bryan, the millenarian prophet whose life he wrote in 1806.[25] He would add the biography of the poets John Frederick Bryant and Ann Yearsley in 1831.

By 1816, his support of Kirke White and Roberts had made Southey a port of call for young and poor writers hoping for a route towards publication. In that year, he received a letter from a schoolboy called Herbert Knowles seeking advice on a graveyard poem written in Kirke White's macabre manner. Southey replied on the same day, telling Knowles that he 'never saw clearer proofs of feeling & power in the verses of a young Poet' but that the poem was not yet ready to be published (to Knowles, 27 October 1816; *CLRS* 2855). He offered to help Knowles reach university and wrote to his schoolmaster as to how best to do so. Finding that Knowles's relations had become impoverished and were no longer able to pay for him, he himself pledged £10 per annum to support Knowles at Cambridge and also canvassed others' backing (see his letter to Grosvenor Charles Bedford, 20 November 1816, *CLRS* 2866). He succeeded in getting the poet, banker, and socialite Samuel Rogers to offer £10 p.a., while Lord Spencer, with whom Rogers had been staying, pledged the same amount. These funds sufficed. Knowles, on hearing the news, responded in a letter to Southey expressing his thanks but also his anxiety that he might be expected to repeat the scholarly feats that Kirke White had performed at university.[26] Knowles declared that he had neither the knowledge nor the stamina of Kirke White and that efforts to compete would kill him. Evidently, he had read Southey's *Life* and feared that he was being positioned as the new Kirke White – the youthful genius who would make good on the career that had escaped his predecessor at the eleventh hour. Having attracted the support that reading the *Remains* had led him to seek, Knowles was now worried about its consequences: was he strong enough to play the part of prodigy, protégé, and phenomenon of self-advancement through poetry?

As it turned out, Knowles was not. Consumption killed him, as it had Roberts and Kirke White. He did not even live long enough to go up to Cambridge. Southey paid tribute to his unfulfilled potential – and showed his determination that poor people's verse should, if of merit, reach the public – by including Knowles's 'The Three Tabernacles' under the revised title 'Lines Written in the Churchyard of Richmond, Yorkshire' in his article 'Cemeteries and Catacombs of Paris' in *The Quarterly Review*.[27] He wrote:

> The reader will remember that they are the verses of a school-boy, who had not long been taken from one of the lowest stations in life, and he will

EDITORIAL INTRODUCTION

then judge what might have been expected from one who was capable of
writing with such strength and originality upon the tritest of all subjects.

LINES
WRITTEN IN THE CHURCHYARD
OF
RICHMOND, YORKSHIRE,
BY
HERBERT KNOWLES

'It is good for us to be here: if thou wilt, let us make
here three Tabernacles, one for Thee, and one for Moses,
and one for Elias.' – Matthew, xvii. 4.

1.

Methinks it is good to be here,
If thou wilt, let us build: but for whom?
   Nor Elias nor Moses appear,
But the shadows of eve that encompass the gloom,
The abode of the dead and the place of the tomb.

2.

Shall we build to Ambition? Oh, no!
Affrighted he shrinketh away:
   For see, they would pin him below,
In a small narrow cave, and begirt with cold clay,
To the meanest of reptiles a peer and a prey.

3.

To Beauty? Ah, no! she forgets
The charms which she wielded before;
   Nor knows the foul worm that he frets
The skin which but yesterday fools could adore
For the smoothness it held, or the tint which it wore.

4.

Shall we build to the purple of Pride,
The trappings which dizen the proud?
   Alas! they are all laid aside:
And here's neither dress nor adornment allowed,
But the long winding-sheet, and the fringe of the shroud.

EDITORIAL INTRODUCTION

5.

To Riches? Alas! 'tis in vain.
Who hid, in their turns have been hid:
   The treasures are squandered again.
And here in the grave are all metals forbid
But the tinsel that shone on the dark coffin-lid.

6.

To the pleasures which Mirth can afford?
The revel, the laugh, and the jeer?
   Ah! here is a plentiful board,
But the guests are all mute as their pitiful cheer,
And none but the worm is a reveller here.

7.

Shall we build to Affection and Love?
Ah, no! they have withered and died,
   Or fled with the spirit above.
Friends, brothers, and sisters are laid side by side,
Yet none have saluted, and none have replied.

8.

Unto sorrow? The dead cannot grieve.
Not a sob, not a sigh meets mine ear,
   Which compassion itself could relieve!
Ah, sweetly they slumber, nor hope, love, nor fear,
Peace, peace is the watch-word, the only one here.

9.

Unto death, to whom monarchs must bow?
Ah, no! For his empire is known,
   And here there are trophies enow.
Beneath the cold dead, and around the dark stone,
Are the signs of a sceptre that none may disown.

10.

The first tabernacle to HOPE we will build,
And look for the sleepers around us to rise!
   The second to FAITH, which insures it fulfill'd;
And the third to the LAMB of the great sacrifice,
Who bequeathed us them both when he rose to the skies.

EDITORIAL INTRODUCTION

In the same year as he published Knowles's poem – 1819 – Southey received an enquiry from Allan Cunningham, then 35 years old. Cunningham was a poor Scot by background. He had been an apprentice stonemason, but his interest in collecting ballads from local singers had brought him the friendship of James Hogg and Walter Scott. He was a clerk in London by 1819, when he asked Southey how he might improve and bring to press his poem 'The Maid of Elvar.' Southey's advice was technical and candid:

> It is no easy task, Mr. Cunningham, to answer a letter like yours. I am unwilling to excite hopes which are but too likely to end in severe disappointment; and equally unwilling to say anything which might depress a noble spirit. The frankest course is the best. Patience and prudence are among the characteristic virtues of your countrymen: the progress which you have made proves that you possess the first in no common degree; and if you possess a good share of the latter also, what I have to say will neither be discouraging nor useless.
>
> Your poem contains incurable defects, but not such as proceed from any want of power. You have aimed at too much, and failed in the structure of the story, the incidents of which are impossible for the time and place in which they are laid. This is of little consequence if you are of the right mould. Your language has an original stamp, and could you succeed in the choice of subjects, – I dare not say that you would obtain the applause of which you are ambitious, – but I believe you would deserve it.
>
> Let me make myself clearly understood. In poetry, as in painting, and music, and architecture, it is far more difficult to design than to execute. A long tale should be everywhere consistent, and everywhere perspicuous. The incidents should depend upon each other, and the event appear like the necessary result, so that no sense of improbability in any part of the narration should force itself upon the hearer. I advise you to exercise yourself in shorter tales, – and these have the advantage of being more to the taste of the age.
>
> (Southey to Cunningham, 10 July 1819; *CLRS* 3329)

Cunningham took this counsel in that he did publish shorter tales, *Traditional Tales of the English and Scottish Peasantry* (1822) and *The Songs of Scotland, Ancient and Modern* (1825). Southey commended his work in his *Introductory Essay to the Lives and Works of Our Uneducated Poets*, having, in 1829, contributed an 'Epistle from Robert Southey, Esq. to Allan Cunningham' to *The Anniversary* (a literary annual that Cunningham was editing). This poem fondly commemorated the two men's friendly conversation in London. Here was a case, then of a relationship in which an established poet had advised an aspiring poet now becoming one of mutual respect between peers.

In 1829, Southey published some of the reflections to which over 20 years of being the supporter of Kirke White and then of other labouring-class and juvenile

23

poets had given rise. These reflections appeared in a review in the *Quarterly* of an American edition of the work of a prodigy who had died young – *Amir Khan, and other Poems: the Remains of Lucretia Maria Davidson*. This review constitutes the third item in this collection. Davidson had been a precocious girl in an impoverished family. Substituting for her invalid mother, she had also performed most of the domestic duties of the household, the family being unable to afford a servant. Like Kirke White, she had read and written ferociously, depriving herself of sleep. With the aid of a benefactor who had seen her verse, she was sent to school but then had to return home, having lost weight and become ill and weak. She died in 1825, of anorexia or consumption or both, aged 17. Her *Remains* were then published by a family friend, Samuel Morse, on the model of Kirke White's – an editorial preface, a biographical memoir, and an extensive selection of her nearly 300 surviving manuscript poems. The rationale echoed Southey's in editing Kirke White and Chatterton: she was, Morse declared, a 'child of genuine poetic feeling,' both dutiful and pious, and a prodigy as promising as Milton had been at the same age (pp. iii-v).

Southey's review reflected upon Davidson's biography so as to define the necessary conditions for successful self-education in a child in poor circumstances. He was against young poets being directed to what adults judged to be useful or proper reading:

> Much history she had also read, both sacred and profane; 'the whole of Shakspeare's, Kotzebue's, and Goldsmith's dramatic works; (oddly consorted names!) and many of the popular novels and romances of the day:' of the latter, she threw aside at once those which at first sight appeared worthless. As for what is called directing the taste of youthful genius, this is so much more likely (we had almost said so sure) to be injurious rather than useful, that in a case like this it is fortunate when an ardent mind is left to itself, and allowed, like the bee, to suck honey from weeds and flowers indiscriminately. The vigorous mind, like the healthy stomach, can digest and assimilate coarse food.
>
> (see p. 90)

Davidson led him to generalise about child geniuses' brilliance and seemingly inevitable tendency to pursue knowledge in an 'intellectual fever' that isolated and exhausted them. He concluded that 'in our own language, except in the cases of Chatterton and Kirke White, we can call to mind no instance of so early, so ardent, and so fatal a pursuit of intellectual advancement.' Like the 'marvellous boy[s],'[28] she drove herself close to madness:

> Her application was incessant; and its effects on her constitution, already somewhat debilitated by previous disease, became apparent in increased nervous sensibility. Her letters at this time exhibit the two extremes of feeling in a marked degree. They abound in the most sprightly or most

EDITORIAL INTRODUCTION

gloomy speculations, bright hopes and lively fancies, or despairing fears and gloomy forebodings.

(see p. 96)

Davidson was, in repeating the course of her English predecessors, demonstrating that burnout was almost inevitable among unsupported child poets who were treated as prodigies. Southey wished his review to warn against such treatment, fearing that his *Life of Kirke White* may have been at least partly responsible, because it had been mistakenly read as a glamourisation of doomed youth: He declared:

> The story of Kirke White should operate not more as an example than a warning; but the example is followed and the warning overlooked. Stimulants are administered to minds which are already in a state of feverish excitement. Hot-beds and glasses are used for plants which can only acquire strength in the shade; and they are drenched with instruction, which ought to drop as the rain and distil as the dew.

(see p. 97)

Reviewing Davidson's life and works evidently concentrated Southey's mind on the appropriate conditions in which plebeian poets could flourish and avoid burnout, for it was in a work written at the same time (and published in 1831) that he laid out his arguments in detail – thus producing the first full-scale discussion of labouring-class poetry in general. *Attempts in Verse, by John Jones, an Old Servant: with Some Account of the Writer, Written by Himself: and an Introductory Essay on the Lives and Works of Our Uneducated Poets* (the fourth item in this collection) began in the same way that his involvement with Elliott, Roberts, and Knowles had begun. Southey received a letter from John Jones, a servant in a Yorkshire family, requesting that he advise on some manuscript poems. Southey did so and, thinking the poems naïve but indicative of an original eye for nature and of the writer's moral virtue, offered to organise a subscription edition. The idea was to benefit Jones and his family, although he was not a skilled-enough poet for a commercial publication to succeed or to make a career by writing. He was, in the distinction that Southey introduced, an 'uneducated' rather than 'self-taught' poet. Southey solicited friends and literary gentlefolk successfully and used his influence with John Murray, the publisher, so that the volume did appear, with Jones's poems (reproduced here in Appendix III) following an introduction by Southey. That introduction grew as Southey composed it, so that Murray retitled the book to give it precedence (an action that embarrassed Southey because it might seem patronising to Jones). But Murray had astutely realised that reflections on plebeian poetry by the Poet Laureate and biographer of Kirke White (as well as of such famous lower-middle-class Englishmen as Nelson and Wesley) would give the book wider and more long-lasting interest than Jones's verse. It was in the introduction that Southey formulated his distinction between uneducated and

25

self-taught poets and laid out the conditions in which labouring-class poets found their way to print. It was there, too, that he discussed the likely effects on the publication of labouring-class poetry of the drive to educate the 'lower orders.' But that was not all. The introduction unfolded into biographies of some of the most prominent labouring-class poets of the last 200 years. It became a history of the genre, the *Lives* of these poets illustrating typical conditions of production and consumption while outlining the various risks and rewards of being a plebeian poet at different historical junctures. Each of the *Lives* sympathetically rehabilitated a largely forgotten writer and their work while also depicting the culture in which they flourished – and/or failed. None of the writers chosen appeared in the standard collections of writers that were currently establishing the canon – neither in Johnson's *Lives* nor in Anderson's British poets. Southey was, in effect, creating an alternative, lower-class canon.

The first writer covered was the seventeenth-century 'water poet' John Taylor, then almost completely forgotten and still today obscure. Southey's long and loving treatment of Taylor's self-promoting life and writings expresses his determination that quirkiness and eccentricity should be chronicled as a record of the variousness of human invention and the value of humour. It also reveals his admiration of poetic chutzpah – of a chancer's ability to use his talent for rhyme not only to win him sympathetic and remunerative audiences but also to erect himself into a verse commentator on many aspects of the times that are normally omitted from print because thought trivial. This was historically valuable, Southey implied, and the biography suggests his fascination by the culture of the era, in which a former waterman (ferryman) with a gift for telling amusing stories in verse could wine and dine not only with Ben Jonson but also with many of the King's favourite courtiers and office-holders. Southey was attracted by a culture in which the institutionalised gap between nobleman and commoner, and rich and poor, was bridgeable, in a way unlikely in his own time, by the benevolent egotism of Taylor's poems, which described unlikely journeys undertaken for bets and featured ludicrous incidents as well as boasting of his drinking exploits. In this culture, the labouring-class man could reinvent himself, via a capacity to stage both his life and his writings in a series of comic exploits, as a companion of the highest-ranking aristocrats and the foremost poets. Taylor's verse – plain-speaking, witty, digressive – bespoke a time in which poetry was not alienated from the direct expression of thought and feeling in speech: neither poetic diction nor codes of politeness had overtaken it. T. S. Eliot's 'dissociation of sensibility,' supposedly setting in after this period, is anticipated here; Eliot's is a later formulation of the rediscovery of seventeenth-century literature and culture that began with the Romantics. Southey, with Coleridge, was also an early rediscoverer of John Donne; like Charles Lamb, he also brought back to notice the plain-speaking poetry of George Wither and Charles Cotton.

If the seventeenth century represents a somewhat golden age in Southey's history, the next labouring-class poet he discusses is shown to have lived in a more familiar, fallen world – one of tighter borders and a greater gap between

EDITORIAL INTRODUCTION

classes. This, however, was partly a matter of geography. Stephen Duck was a rural labourer in a village; unlike the urban ferryman and sailor Taylor, he did not come to writing amid a culture of social and physical mobility. Peasants were bound to the spot, Southey suggests, and shows that the strength of Duck's early verse was the opposite of Taylor's. Duck chronicled the round of rural labour with an insider's knowledge of how it felt on the body and in the mind to one whose life was organised by it. Southey praised him for more than verisimilitude, moreover. After carefully detailing his self-education reading Shakespeare, Seneca, Ned Ward, and *The Spectator* – books a friend happened to have brought from London to Duck's village – Southey pointed out Duck's acquisition of 'command of language and . . . skill in versification,' saying of 'The Thresher's Labour' that 'the truth of the description is not its only merit, for there are passages in it which would have done no discredit to more celebrated names' – and then excerpting those passages at length. On this basis, Southey attacked Jonathan Swift for his contemptuous epigram that insisted on returning Duck the poet to peasant status:

> From *threshing* corn, he turns to *thresh* his brains,
> For which her Majesty allows him *grains*;
> Tho' 'tis confest, that those who ever saw
> His poems, think them all not worth a *straw*.
> Thrice happy Duck, employed in threshing *stubble*!
> Thy toil is lessen'd, and thy profits double

(see p. 150)

Southey insists that the patronage Duck received from the Queen, after a friend of Pope encouraged him and brought his work to notice, was merited. He became a priest and was given a country parish – as Southey had hoped Kirke White and Knowles would be given – and Southey refutes notions that this preferment was inappropriate. He will not let snobbery at Duck's lack of gentlemanly education prevail. He is certain that Duck's

> character, his inclination, and his abilities, were alike suited to this way of life; and he is said to have been much followed as a preacher, not only while novelty and his reputation were likely to attract congregations, but as long as he lived.

(see p. 151)

Equally, Southey refuses to ascribe Duck's death by suicide to the 'transition from a life of great bodily labour to a sedentary one, and to excess in study.' This poet is absolutely not a lesson in the dangers of raising the poor above their station: 'till [his] malady occurred he had been a useful parish priest, and approved himself every way worthy of the patronage which had been bestowed upon him' for about 30 years. The cause was probably, Southey speculated, 'accidental, or constitutional' (see p. 151).

27

EDITORIAL INTRODUCTION

Arguing that Duck was not a great poet and knew himself not to be, Southey depicts him as an example of self-education producing merited self-advancement – to the benefit of the locality – because in the relatively small and static social world of the early eighteenth century, gentlemanly and royal patronage was able to foster those who deserved it. Patronage was not, that is, spoilt for choice by the sheer number of candidates vying for attention, as in the more-populous, better-educated social world of the 1830s. Nor were patrons then so remote from their country estates or so decadent that they failed to pay attention to people of merit in their area. Whereas Kirke White had been kept waiting by the Duchess of Devon-shire, who Southey lambasted for frivolity, and Bloomfield had been abandoned by the fourth Duke of Grafton, Duck had been properly promoted: he was 'a mod-est, diligent, studious, good man; and the patronage which he obtained is far more honourable to the spirit of his age, than the temper, which may censure or ridicule it, can be to ours' (see p. 152). If not as golden an age as the early seventeenth century, the early eighteenth was still, in Southey's opinion, a more propitious era to be a labouring-class poet than was his own period.

James Woodhouse (1735–1820), the next poet to receive Southey's attention, is the first of the shoemaker poets discussed.[29] Southey traces his versemaking not to a vague spirit visiting a natural genius but to a painstaking and gradual process of self-teaching and labouring. Having read only magazines, Woodhouse

> used to work with a pen and ink at his side, while the [cobbler's] last was in his lap; – the head at one employ, the hands at another; and when he had composed a couplet or a stanza, he wrote it on his knee.
>
> (see p. 153)

Being an artisan, with a repetitive task in a small workshop where one was master of one's movements, rather than a mechanic feeding an engine or a field hand gov-erned by a farmer, Woodhouse had space and (barely) time for composition. The gentleman poet William Shenstone, who lived nearby, gave Woodhouse access to his grounds and his library, and there Woodhouse learned 'some of the artifices of versification.' Southey, however, judged that this learning did not lead to an original style in which the poet's specific experience was articulated: polish, para-doxically, led to a certain dullness.

> A process, indeed, is observable, both in the verses of Woodhouse and Stephen Duck, which might be looked for, as almost inevitable: they began by expressing their own thoughts and feelings, in their own lan-guage; all which, owing to their stations in life, had a certain charm of freshness as well as truth; but that attraction passes away when they begin to form their style upon some approved model, and they then pro-duce just such verses as any person, with a metrical ear, may be taught to make by a receipt.
>
> (see p. 155)

28

EDITORIAL INTRODUCTION

Here was a test of merit by which to judge a self-taught poet: was he or she valuable only because they had a class-based perspective and diction that did not appear in gentlemanly verse, or could they retain their individuality when they learned more of the art of poetry? Southey thought that Woodhouse could not, but he seems to have been ignorant of the later poems that Woodhouse published as *Love Letters to My Wife* (1804) and, anonymously, as *The Life and Lucubrations of Crispinus Scriblerus* (1815).

Woodhouse's biography is followed by that of another shoemaker, John Bennet (1737–1803) of Woodstock, from whose *Poems on Several Occasions* (1774) Southey extracts some passages of sharp social observation. He then passes on to the *Life* of his fellow Bristol poet, Ann Yearsley (1753–1806), telling her story from the biography written by her patron, the evangelical writer, educationalist, and poet Hannah More. Despite desperate poverty, Yearsley had, we learn, managed to read *Paradise Lost* and *Night Thoughts*, some of Shakespeare's plays, and a translation of Virgil's *Georgics*. Southey respectfully summarises More's efficiency in winning subscribers for Yearsley's poems and deals even-handedly with the dispute over control of the profits that led to More's and Yearsley's acrimonious separation and to the blackening of Yearsley's name as an ingrate. Since More was still alive when he wrote, he could hardly suggest she had been highhanded in refusing to allow Yearsley to control the proceeds of her own labour. More's paternalism prevented her from viewing Yearsley as a potential equal as a professional author. She wished her to remain a grateful, obliged domestic servant. Southey relates Yearsley's later career as one of financial disappointment and reports local rumours that 'she was deranged for some time before her death.' If so, he reasoned, it was probably because

that such an effect would be wrought upon a highly sensitive mind by embarrassments, disappointments, the sense of supposed injuries, and the perpetual consciousness that her powers, not having been kindlily developed, had failed to produce, what, under favourable circumstances, they could not have failed to bring forth.

(see p. 161)

He excerpted two powerful passages from the poems, which in general he found not to have fulfilled the potential Yearsley showed before coming under, and then losing, More's tutelage, but noted that:

Flourishing reputations (of the gourd tribe) have been made by writers of much less feeling and less capability than are evident in these lines. Ann Yearsley, though gifted with voice, had no strain of her own whereby to be remembered, but she was no mocking-bird.

(see p. 161)

Faint praise perhaps, but praise nonetheless for a poet whose brief vogue had not led to a successful career or kept her from poverty. Remembering her 25 years

EDITORIAL INTRODUCTION

after her death, Southey at least began the process of taking a female labouring-class poet seriously. In this respect, he was ahead of his time: it was not until the late twentieth century that feminist critics began to study women poets of the Romantic era in detail. Yearsley would finally attain a collected scholarly edition of her writings in 2014.[30]

Southey stayed in Bristol for the next biography, of the clay-pipe maker and singing poet John Frederick Bryant (1753–1791) – a man whose shop, not far from Southey's father's, he had often passed on the way to school. Here, Southey's sense of the former proximity of two writers' lives that had subsequently diverged so drastically reminded him that, had it not been for the munificence of his rich uncle, he himself might have been in similar circumstances to Bryant. He narrates Bryant's peripatetic and extremely poor life at length, drawing on the autobiography with which Bryant prefaced his *Verses* – published from his shop in Long Acre, London, 1787. He quotes Bryant to the effect that his passion for reading interfered with the labour he was required to do in the family workshop:

> Natural philosophy, and particularly astronomy, began at this time to be the favourite subject of my contemplation; but while my mind was busy, endeavouring to explain the mechanism of terrestrial nature, or soaring among the stars, the labour of my hands turned out to little amount; the less so, as I was extraordinarily slow and awkward at my work, even when I did my best and set my mind most upon it, which I believe was owing to the very great dislike I ever had to the business.
>
> (see p. 163)

He shows that Bryant was so poor that his only means of travelling was on foot and that, to pay for food and lodging en route, he was forced to sell his Bible, his hat, and items of the clothing he stood up in. Bloomfield had recorded the same of itinerant journeymen in his manuscript concerning his shoemaking work-mates.[31] Clare's journey out of Essex, made without money,[32] was not out of the ordinary among poor labourers. Nor were the other adventures to which poverty condemned Bryant – but Southey's detailed rehearsal of them served to draw aspects of poor people's lives to middle-class readers' attention. Bryant left Bristol for London to become a sailor but found that hands were not wanted; he then

> led a precarious life, sometimes in his old employ, then as a labourer at Woolwich, where they were digging foundations for the barracks; there he was disabled by the ground falling in upon him, and consequently discharged. He then got into work sometimes with a tobacco-pipe-maker at Woolwich, who was a Bristol man, sometimes as a jobber in the rope-grounds, and when both occupations failed, he attended on the quays, and now and then got a job at the cranes; but there were at that time so many men of all descriptions out of employ, that if there was a job for four or five men to perform, there were generally twenty to

30

scramble for it; and not being so good a scrambler as many of his competitors, he could not earn a bare subsistence, so that he was obliged to part with every thing he could possibly spare, and was once so hard put to it as to go without a morsel of food from Saturday afternoon till Monday night.

(see p. 165)

He was then a bricklayer's labourer, and a sailor, and then having been discharged unfit, press-ganged into the navy – a fate he escaped by joining the press-gang itself. Returning to Bristol, he took up pipe-making again in his now-dead father's workshop but scarcely made a living. What transformed his fortune was his ability to rhyme. He found, during a desperate journey from Wales, where he had failed to establish a shop, that his ability to sing, and to invent songs, enabled him to dine and board in inns 'scot-free.' A chance encounter in an inn with a travelling gentleman gave him a chance not only to sing for his supper but also to send some of his songs for further perusal. That gentleman and his friends organised a subscription edition of the verse and enabled Bryant to set up shop in London as a stationer and bookseller. Southey clearly approved of their conduct, so like his own, and he showed by excerpting passages that, although Bryant had little self-education, he produced not only tavern songs but also a sonnet on his own labour and a moving prayer: he could write in different genres.

In conclusion, Southey pointed up a moral about patronage and about poetic value that was aimed at critics who dismissed labouring-class poets because they lacked the excellence of those who had been better educated:

When we are told that the thresher, the milkwoman, and the tobacco-pipe-maker did not deserve the patronage they found, – when it is laid down as a maxim of philosophical criticism that poetry ought never to be encouraged unless it is excellent in its kind, that it is an art in which inferior execution is not to be tolerated, – a luxury, and must therefore be rejected unless it is of the very best, – such reasoning may be addressed with success to cockered and sickly intellects, but it will never impose upon a healthy understanding, a generous spirit, or a good heart.

(see p. 173)

This reasoning justified Southey promoting the poems of Jones, the Yorkshire servant who had approached him for advice, and whose verse followed the *Introductory Essay on the Lives and Works of Our Uneducated Poets*. As others had done for Bryant, Yearsley, Duck, and Woodhouse, and as he himself had done for Kirke White and Roberts, he was now assisting a deserving poet by publishing a subscription edition (see Appendix I for his letters concerning Jones). He also, however, reminded readers that some labouring-class poets were excellent enough to stand alone, needing no patronage as 'uneducated' authors of 'inferior' but worthy verse, although they might deserve help when exposed to the vagaries of the book market:

> I do not introduce Robert Bloomfield here, because his poems are worthy of preservation separately, and in general collections; and because it is my intention one day to manifest at more length my respect for one whose talents were of no common standard, and whose character was in all respects exemplary. It is little to the credit of the age, that the latter days of a man whose name was at one time so deservedly popular, should have been past in poverty, and perhaps shortened by distress, that distress having been brought on by no misconduct or imprudence of his own.
>
> (see p. 172)

While the *Introductory Essay on the Lives and Works of Our Uneducated Poets* was Southey's major contribution to the recovery of labouring-class writers and to the expansion of the literary canon, it was not his last. In 1832, *The Quarterly Review* carried his anonymous review of a book he had helped bring into being, *Fables, and other Pieces in Verse, by Mary Maria Colling*. Colling (1804–1853) was a domestic servant of a neighbour of a middle-class novelist who had herself sought Southey's advice on her work – Eliza Bray (1790–1883). Southey corresponded with Bray (see Appendix I), suggesting she should base her romances on the local tales and legends of her region, Dartmoor, instead of setting them in Europe. He organized publication of the long letters narrating these local tales that she then wrote him at his request. Her *A Description of the Part of Devonshire Bordering on the Tamar and the Tavy* (1836) became a major written source for Devonian and Cornish folklore. While encouraging Bray, Southey took the opportunity to bring another woman writer into print, via Bray's good offices as interlocutor, biographer, and gatherer of the verse fables that Colling had been producing. As with Jones, his motive was to benefit a morally worthy naïve poet – an 'uneducated' poet – whose work showed originality and freshness, even if not sophisticated. He did not wish the publication to enable Colling to launch a literary career, and he assured readers that Colling herself did not wish this either: she was happy as a servant to a benevolent 'master.' Her poetry was an example of what Southey was sure was generally true – versemaking and versereading was a civilizing influence in its own right rather than a means to money and fame. Poetry and painting should, he concluded,

> be cultivated for their own sake, not with a view to popular applause, – for the pleasure which they impart within their own circle, – for the moral and intellectual improvement which is obtained in the pursuit, – and they contribute then, in no slight degree, to adorn society, and to increase the sum of its innocent and beneficial enjoyments. 'Poetry,' says Mackenzie, in one of his youthful letters, 'let the prudence of the world say what it will, is, at least, one of the noblest amusements. Our philanthropy is

almost always increased by it. There is a certain poetic ground on which we cannot tread without feelings that mend the heart; and many who are not able to reach the Parnassian heights, may yet advance so near as to be bettered by the air of the climate.'

(see p. 190)

This is an appealing, if somewhat sunny, vision, and it is not undermined, even if it is cast into shadow, by what later happened to Colling. She found that her employer exerted enough mastery to prevent new editions of her book from being published (to Eliza Bray's chagrin). She was not able to control her own printed writing, while, at the same time, her new status as the darling of the local gentry attracted resentment from other servants. As so often, the labouring-class writer was left with restricted agency and caught between patrons and peers. The resultant frustration may have been one of the causes of the mental illness that led to her confinement for a while, as it was in Clare's case and may have been in Yearsley's.

****

Collectively, Southey's writings on labouring-class poets demonstrate a groundbreaking commitment to democratising the canon by reviving writers who had been neglected because of their class position and their supposed lack of education. He also includes women poets, at a time when very few beyond bluestocking gentlewomen were attended to. Not only does he bring Yearsley, Davidson, Colling (and Bray) into notice, but he also makes apparent the material circumstances in which they, as women, struggled to write – domestic service – the male expectation that women would do all the household and family work – economic dependence on men. Likewise the lives led by poor men – these, too, are evoked with respect and an understanding as to how they shape the verse and the versemaker's career. Southey is a social as well as literary historian.

He is also a creator of a cultural icon, by glamourizing the child genius who aspires to class advancement and literary greatness only to die young, prophesying his own demise in a society he sees as indifferent to him. Placing Chatterton, Kirke White, Knowles, and Davidson in this category, he forms a literary tradition, just as he also does with plebeian poets, by creating a roster of *Lives* that bring not just particular poets but a particular kind of poetry to notice. Public awareness of labouring-class poetry as a valuable tradition begins with him – as does the argument that this tradition is subject to changing conditions of labour, education, and publication. The days of professional authorship for a mass readership would indeed present new opportunities and difficulties for the labouring-class writer, as Southey saw, making the old mixture of local patronage and publication-by-subscription a niche, or retro, activity – albeit one he continued in specific cases.

While Southey has carefully formulated arguments – against professional authorship in the new market, against new utilitarian definitions of knowledge and schemes of education, and for poetry writing and reading as civilizing influences and disinterested explorations of what it is to be human – his work also has facets of which he appears to be less conscious. He shows, but does not thematise, that labouring-class poets are, at least in part, shaped by their particular work. Farmworker poets – Duck, Woodhouse, Yearsley – are shown to be less mobile because of their work on the land and thus less able to self-educate and more dependent on the patronage of a local gentleman or woman. But within the relatively static social world of the old country estate, that patronage was often effective. Within the city occupied by urban artisans, it is less so. Taylor and Bryant are itinerant workers and become poets by learning from contact with the numerous people they meet, rather than by one patron's encouragement. Bloomfield, shoemaking in London, is enlightened by the circulation of magazines and arrival of workmates who bring him new knowledge and new books. Between the lines, Southey is more excited by the lives and work of these relatively mobile, or mobilized, poets than he is by the farmworkers and domestic servants who are limited by their confining labour to a smaller range of experience and education. He prefers the comic self-fashioning of such men of the world to the pious and moral observations of Jones and Colling, although he specifically endorses those observations. He also appreciates the poets' ability to write – a learnt ability – about other things than their own labour: his ideal labouring-class poet learns to make his verse a supple medium for encountering a varied and various world; s/he is not merely valued as a documentary source on what it is like to be a thresher or a milkmaid. Thus, he semi-idealises a time when, supposedly, a plebeian poet and wit such as Taylor could socialize with nobleman and courtiers – or even go on a diplomatic mission abroad – over the more rigidly hierarchical and divided class structure of the eighteenth and nineteenth centuries.

Darker aspects of plebeian poets' lives are more prevalent than first appears. Southey makes it strongly apparent that depending on authorship for income is madness for any poet: he depicts the print culture of his times as a fashion-driven, capitalist market that consumes its children. But less stridently, he also reveals various costs of being, or trying to be, a poet from the labouring classes. For servants such as Jones and Colling, recognition risks arousing resentment from employers who suspect the new author of having his head turned, and from fellow servants who are envious of the attention received. The now-published author may grow discontented with being at others' beck and call yet be unable without gentlemanly patronage to continue publishing. Amateur status does not, in these circumstances, translate into free agency or respite from a contest for authority over words and deeds. Woodhouse's relationship with his patron, the poet Elizabeth Montagu, for whom he worked as a bailiff and steward, was a prickly one, although Southey does not discuss it. Evidently, Yearsley clashed with her gentlewoman patron, Hannah More, in part because More expected her to remain in the servant class after publishing and be grateful. Southey registers these tensions but does not explicitly allow them to spoil his fantasy of servants happily publishing while remaining cheerfully in service – what Tim Burke calls his 'dream of a sub-professional space in which writerly skill is accorded status and value but is not vulnerable to the fluctuations of the market economy and does not endanger the internal economy of the writer's identity.'[33] That internal economy, Southey implies, is in fact more vulnerable than he states. As he adds to the story of Kirke White's mental crises those of Davidson, Duck, and Yearsley, an outline begins to appear of a buried anxiety that is not just about burnout from over-studying but also depression from alienation. Perhaps, the cumulative evidence suggests, the breakdown of patronage relationships endured by Woodhouse, Yearsley, and Bloomfield is almost inevitable and leaves the poet both without support from 'above' and isolated from his or her original labouring-class community. Patron-power and patron-trauma are spectres stalking Southey's narrative. Indeed, it comes to seem that Southey attempts to create safe zones – help into the learned professions for poor young men who successfully self-educate and one-off subscriptions for those who will remain in the labouring or servant classes – because he is haunted by more than the main danger he distinctly warns about. Not just the danger of foundering as an author making his living from the fickle market; not even just the danger of burning out under the pressure of study and ambition. Also the danger of the breakdown of the patron and mentor relationship; the danger of class-based contempt of the kind Swift and Byron displayed; the danger of envy from labouring-class peers and resentment from employers; the danger of losing a stable social position and, with it, a stable identity. 'We poets in our youth begin in gladness; / But thereof come in the end despondency and madness,' wrote Wordsworth with Chatterton in mind. Charles Lamb, a poor clerk from an impoverished family, as well as a budding poet and friend of Coleridge and Southey, had been confined in a madhouse in 1796. Southey himself had suffered a nervous breakdown in 1799 under the pressure, when isolated from his family and his few remaining friends, of trying to publish fast enough to make a living from his pen.

A final ghost in the text is related to Southey's fear that educating the exploited labouring classes in economics and politics without also cultivating their feelings of loyalty and morality would lead them to making (not unjustified) demands for equality that, if refused by the self-interested higher classes, would be followed by an explosive revolution. That ghost is scarcely visible, appearing only when a brief mention of John Thelwall is made. It is the ghost of radical poets, many of whom had been Southey's friends or allies in his revolutionary youth. Thelwall, the political orator and poet tried for treason in 1794, when Southey wrote his revolutionary play *Wat Tyler*, had remained an acquaintance for many years – but his verse is absent from Southey's *Lives*. So is William Hone, the poet whose satires on monarch and minsters led the government to prosecute him in 1817 for blasphemous libel. Southey had feared the power of Hone's poetry to stir up the 'mob' and had called for journalists like him to be imprisoned. But Southey later became Hone's cordial correspondent and contributed to Hone's collection of folklore. Yet Hone and his political parodies were also missing from Southey's *Lives* – as was Thomas Spence, the advocate of the redistribution of land who rallied supporters in verse. Southey had himself, in 1793 and 1794, been an advocate of the abolition of landed

EDITORIAL INTRODUCTION

property. Among more recent labouring-class radicals, Richard Carlile, poet, journalist, and publisher of both Hone and (against Southey's will) *Wat Tyler*, was also conspicuous by his absence. Disruptors of the status quo were not welcome. Southey had brought into being a tradition of labouring-class poetry, but it was a tradition purged of democrats, radicals, and revolutionaries.

Notes

1 A notable predecessor was Joseph Spence (1699–1768), Oxford Professor of Poetry, who had taken a keen interest in 'natural' poets, including Stephen Duck, his account of whom is a key source. Southey went a great deal further, moving away from the 'primitive natural genius' that was the primary model for Spence.

2 It should be noted that some labouring-class poets had begun to understand themselves as a brethren, if not a tradition: 'By the end of the century certain key figures – notably Chatterton and Burns – had attained iconic significance . . . , and one labouring-class poet could address another as "brother bard and fellow labourer": Labouring-class poetry was thus a distinctive tradition in the eighteenth-century both on its own and on others' terms, and in some ways it forms an alternative literary history, alongside and overlapping with the more familiar, canonical one.' John Goodridge, *Introduction to Eighteenth-Century English Labouring-Class Poets 1700–1800*, 3 vols, gen. eds. John Goodridge and Simon Kövesi (London, 2003), I.

3 Wordsworth, letter to Charles James Fox, 14 January 1801; *The Letters of William and Dorothy Wordsworth: the Early Years 1787–1805*, ed. Ernest De Selincourt, rev. Chester L. Shaver (Oxford, 1967), p. 315.

4 'The phenomenon of the "peasant-poet" was perceived as a species of natural genius, a kind of home-grown noble savage, whose poetry miraculously emerged from a rustic lifestyle, specifically without benefit of formal training and thus untainted with classicism or learned sophistry.' *History of British Working Class Literature*, ed. John Goodridge and Bridget Keegan (Cambridge, 2017), p. 4.

5 Nick Groom states of the former: 'This edition was then the canonical Chatterton for the Romantic period (Wordsworth and Coleridge were both subscribers to the edition), and was of enormous influence in presenting for the first time the dizzying extent of Chatterton's literary achievements.' Nick Groom, 'With Certain Grand Cottleisms': Joseph Cottle, Robert Southey and the 1803 Works of Thomas Chatterton,' *Romanticism*, 15 (2009), 225–38 (p. 226).

6 Three long reviews by the self-appointed but powerful arbiter of traditional, gentlemanly taste were especially perceptive about and dismissive of the challenge that Southey's poetic innovations posed: Francis Jeffrey reviewed *Thalaba the Destroyer* in *The Edinburgh Review*, 1 (October 1802), 63–83, reprinted in *Robert Southey: The Critical Heritage*, ed. Lionel Madden (London and Boston, 1972), pp. 68–90. He reviewed *Madoc* in *The Edinburgh Review*, 7 (October 1805), 1–29. He reviewed *The Curse of Kehama* in *The Edinburgh Review*, 17 (1811), 429–65, declaring that Southey spoilt his 'lofty principles' and 'tenderness of heart' by the 'perversity of his manifold affectations,' 'wilful deformities,' and 'irregularity of measure' (p. 452), meaning that he, like his fellow Lake poets, 'wage[d] a desperate war on the established system of public taste and judgement' (p. 434).

7 From line 2 of Wordsworth's sonnet 'The world is too much with us.'

8 Milton on Shakespeare from 'L'Allegro,' line 134.

9 On Southey's historiography, see Esther Wohlgemut, 'Southey, Macaulay and the Idea of a Picturesque History,' *Romanticism on the Net*, 32–33 (2003/4), www.erudit.org/en/journals/ron/1900-v1-n1-ron769/009261ar/ and the Editor's Introduction to Southey's

EDITORIAL INTRODUCTION

Sir Thomas More: or, Colloquies on the Progress and Prospects of Society (1829), ed. Tom Duggett (London, 2018).

10 R. Williams, *Culture and Society* (London, 1958), p. 42.

11 For modern assessments of Dermody's poetry, see Stephen Dornan, 'Thomas Dermody, Robert Burns and the Killeigh Cycle,' *Scottish Studies Review*, 6 (2005), 9–21; 'Thomas Dermody's Archipelagic Poetry,' *European Romantic Review*, 21 (2010), 409–23, Jim Kelly, *Ireland and Romanticism: Publics, Nations and Scenes of Cultural Production* (New York, 2011), pp. 1–10; Julia Wright, '"Sons of Song": Irish Literature in the Age of Nationalism,' *Romantic Poetry*, ed. Angela Esterhammer (Amsterdam, 2002), pp. 333–54.

12 Samuel Johnson's *Lives of the Most Eminent English Poets* (1779–81) was commissioned to preface a multi-volume anthology of poets, which eventually ran to 56 volumes, far exceeding the number of poets of whom Johnson had written biographies.

13 Anderson's *Complete Edition of the Poets of Great Britain* (London and Edinburgh, 1795).

14 George Ellis, *Specimens of the Early English Poets*, 3 vols (London, 1801).

15 On the effect of Kirke White on Keats's poetry and reputation, see Tim Fulford, 'Kirke White and Keats,' https://kirkewhitecom.wordpress.com/kirke-white-and-keats/.

16 *The Annual Review*, 2 (1803), 552–54 (p. 554).

17 43 (February 1804), 218.

18 See Southey's letter to Kirke White of 18 May 1804, *CLRS* 942. See also his letters to Kirke White's brother John Neville White: 20 December 1806, *CLRS* 1245; 7 April 1807, *CLRS* 1304.

19 See note 4.

20 The assumption that Chatterton's death was caused by suicide rather than an accidental overdose has been questioned by modern scholars. See the entry for Chatterton in the *ODNB*, by Nick Groom.

21 Shelley in 'Adonais' and Browning in 'The Lost Leader.'

22 Shelley's response to Kirke White is discussed by Nora Crook, 'An Inheritor of Unfulfilled Renown: Kirke White and Shelley'; Browning's memory of Kirke White by Joe Phelan, 'Robert Browning and Henry Kirke White'; Whitman's by Tim Fulford, 'Kirke White in America: Transcendentalism – Bryant and Whitman,' all in https://kirkewhitecom. wordpress.com. In 1821, after Shelley had suggested that Keats had been killed by a bad review in *The Quarterly*, Byron told him 'Kirke White was nearly extinguished in the same way – by a paragraph or two in "the Monthly" – Such inordinate sense of censure is surely incompatible with great exertion': *Byron's Letters and Journals*, ed. Leslie A. Marchand, 13 vols (London, 1973–1994), VIII, 163.

23 *New Letters*, II, 375 (letter of 29 March 1832).

24 Henry Crabb Robinson, *Diary, Reminiscences, and Correspondence* (London, 1870; 1872), II, 171.

25 Southey recalled, 'Bryan I knew personally, & heard from his own lips his history, & his explanation of the system of Brothers.' In *Letters from England*, Southey gives in detail Bryan's story. A copperplate printer and engraver, and a Quaker, and then a prophetic healer in Bristol, Bryan, after experiencing a vision, went in 1789 with John Wright to join the Society of Illuminés at Avignon, where, in that post-Swedenborgian, semi-Masonic group, he received spiritual communications informing him of the coming of a prophet and the imminent millennium. Returning later in the year, Bryan lived in London. In 1793, he was at first suspicious of the claims of the new millenarian preacher Richard Brothers to be a prophet and, he told Southey, took a knife to a meeting, intending to stab him. However, he was impressed by Brothers and, by 1795, had become one of his advocates, as he revealed in his *A Testimony of the Spirit of Truth concerning Richard Brothers . . . in an address to the people of Israel, &c., to the gentiles called Christians, and all other gentiles. With some account of the manner of*

EDITORIAL INTRODUCTION

the Lord's gracious dealing with his servant W. Bryan (London, 1795). Southey's life of William Bryan can be found in his *Letters from England by Don Manuel Espriella* (1807). *See Robert Southey and Millenarianism: Documents Concerning the Prophetic Movements of the Romantic Era*, ed. Tim Fulford. http://romantic-circles.org/editions/southey_prophecy/HTML/Espriella.html

26 Knowles to Southey, 28 December 1816, in *Life and Correspondence*, IV, 223–26.

27 21 (April 1819), 359–98 (396–98).

28 'I thought of Chatterton, the marvellous boy, / The sleepless soul that perished in its pride,' from stanza 7 of Wordsworth's 'Resolution and Independence.'

29 On the numerous shoemaking poets, see Bridget Keegan, 'Cobbling Verse: Shoemaker Poets of the Long Eighteenth Century,' *The Eighteenth Century*, 42 (2001), 195–217.

30 *The Collected Works of Ann Yearsley*, ed. Kerri Andrews, 3 vols (London, 2014).

31 Bloomfield's manuscript account of the lives of his shoemaking workmates is held at BL Add. MS 28265.

32 Clare's narrative of his journey out of an Essex asylum to Helpston is included in *John Clare by Himself*, ed. Eric Robinson and David Powell (New York, 2002), pp. 257–65.

33 Tim Burke, 'Southey's Anti-Professional Fantasy: Writing for Pleasure and the Uneducated Poet,' *Romanticism*, 17 (2011), 63–76 (p. 70).

Further Reading

Andrews, Kerri, *Ann Yearsley and Hannah More, Patronage and Poetry* (London and Brookfield, VT, 2013).

———, (gen. ed.), 'New Directions on Mary Leapor and Ann Yearsley', *Tulsa Studies in Women's Literature* 34 (2015).

Batt, Jennifer, *Class, Patronage, and Poetry in Hanoverian England: Stephen Duck, the Famous Threshing Poet* (Oxford, 2020).

Binfield, Kevin and William J. Christmas (eds.), *Teaching Labouring-Class British Literature of the Eighteenth and Nineteenth Centuries* (New York, 2018).

Bloomfield, Robert, *The Letters of Robert Bloomfield and His Circle*, ed. Tim Fulford and Lynda Pratt, associate editor John Goodridge, Romantic Circles Electronic Editions (2012). www.rc.umd.edu/editions/bloomfield_letters/

———, *The Collected Writings of Robert Bloomfield*, ed. Tim Fulford, John Goodridge, and Sam Ward, Romantic Circles Electronic Editions (2019). https://romantic-circles.org/editions/bloomfield_poems/index.html

Bridgen, Adam J., 'Patronage, Punch-Ups, and Polite Correspondence: The Radical Background of James Woodhouse's Early Poetry', *Huntington Library Quarterly*, 80 (2017), 99–134.

Capp, Bernard, *The World of John Taylor the Water Poet 1578–1753* (Oxford, 1994).

Christmas, William J., *The Lab'ring Muses: Work, Writing, and the Social Order in English Plebeian Poetry, 1730–1830* (Newark and London, 2001).

Ellinghausen, Laurie, 'The New Bourgeois Hero: The Self-presentation of John Taylor "The Water Poet"', in *Labor and Writing in Early Modern England, 1567–1667* (Aldershot, 2008), pp. 93–120.

Ferguson, Moira, *Eighteenth-Century Women Poets: Nation, Class, and Gender* (Albany, 1995).

Fulford, Tim, 'To "Crown with Glory the Romantick Scene": Robert Bloomfield's "To Immagination" and the Discourse of Romanticism', *Romanticism*, 15 (2009), 181–200.

Fulford, Tim and John Goodridge (eds.), 'New Essays on Robert Bloomfield', *European Romantic Review*, 31 (2020).

Fulford, Tim and Debbie Lee, 'The Jenneration of Disease: Vaccination, Romanticism and Revolution', *Studies in Romanticism*, 39 (2000), 139–63.

Goodridge, John, *Rural Life in Eighteenth-Century English Poetry* (Cambridge, 1995).

———, 'John Clare and Eighteenth-Century Poetry: Pomfret, Cunningham, Bloomfield', *Eighteenth Century: Theory and Interpretation*, 42 (2001), 264–78.

———, (gen. ed.), *Eighteenth-Century English Labouring-Class Poets*, 3 vols (London, 2003).

———, *John Clare and Community* (Cambridge, 2012).

Goodridge, John and Bridget Keegan (eds.), *Robert Bloomfield: The Inestimable Blessing of Letters* (essay collection, online publication, Romantic Circles Praxis series, 2012).

Goodridge, John and Bridget Keegan (eds.), *A History of British Working Class Literature* (New York, 2017).

Goodridge, John and Bridget Keegan, 'Land, Labor, Literature', in Sarah Eron, Nicole Aljoe, and Suvir Kaul (eds.), *The Routledge Companion to Eighteenth-Century Literatures in English* (London, 2024).

Keegan, Bridget, *British Labouring-Class Nature Poetry, 1730–1837* (Basingstoke, 2008).

Kirke White, Henry, *The Collected Poetry of Henry Kirke White*, ed. Tim Fulford (Liverpool, 2024) (Editor's Introduction).

Landry, Donna, *The Muses of Resistance: Laboring-Class Women's Poetry in Britain, 1739–1796* (Cambridge, 1990).

McEathron, Scott, 'Wordsworth, Lyrical Ballads, and the Problem of Peasant Poetry', *Nineteenth-Century Literature*, 54 (1999), 1–26.

Sales, Roger, 'Poor Relations: Writing in the Working Class 1770–1835', in *The Penguin History of Literature: The Romantic Period*, ed. David B. Pirie (London, 1994), pp. 259–88.

Unwin, Rayner, *The Rural Muse: Studies in the Peasant Poetry of England* (London, 1954).

Van-Hagen, Steve, 'Patrons, Influences, and Poetic Communities in James Woodhouse's *The Life and Lucubrations of Crispinus Scriblerus*', in Ileana Baird (ed.), *Social Networks in the Long Eighteenth Century: Clubs, Salons and Textual Coteries* (Newcastle upon Tyne, 2014), pp. 309–33.

White, Simon, 'Rethinking the History of the Wye: Robert Bloomfield's "Banks of Wye"', *Literature and History*, 16 (2007), 46–58.

———, *Robert Bloomfield, Romanticism and the Poetry of Community* (Aldershot and Burlington, VT, 2007).

White, Simon, John Goodridge and Bridget Keegan (eds.), *Robert Bloomfield: Lyric, Class, and the Romantic Canon* (Lewisburg, PA, 2006).

Williams, Raymond, *The Country and the City* (Oxford, 1973).

Woodhouse, James, *The Life and Lucubrations of Crispinus Scriblerus, A Selection*, ed. Steve Van-Hagen (Cheltenham, 2005).

Yearsley, Ann, *The Collected Works of Ann Yearsley*, ed. Kerri Andrews, 3 vols (London, 2014).

1

SOUTHEY'S REVIEW OF JAMES GRANT RAYMOND[1]

The Life of Thomas Dermody, Interspersed with Pieces of Original Poetry,
The Annual Review, 5 (1806), 382–397

Perhaps no memoirs ever appeared more dishonourable to the person of whom they treat, and more honourable to the age in which he lived, than those of Thomas Dermody.

He was the son of an Irish schoolmaster, at Ennis, in the county of Clare, where he was born on the 17th of January, 1775. His father must have been a man of considerable learning and considerable ability, or he could not, whatever had been the natural talents of the boy, have made him so good a scholar, as, in his ninth year, to act as Greek and Latin usher in the school. At ten years of age he produced a Monody upon the death of a younger brother, which thus begins:

> What dire misfortune hovers o'er my head?
> Why hangs the salt dew on my aching eye?
> Why doth my bosom pant, so sad, so sore.
> That was full blithe before?
> Bitter occasion prompts the untimely sigh;
> Why am I punish'd thus, ye angels! Why?
> A shepherd swain like me, of harmless guise,
> Whose sole amusement was to feed his kine.
> And tune his oaten pipe the livelong day, –
> Could he in aught offend th' avenging skies.
> Or wake the red-wing'd thunderbolt divine?
> Ah! no: of simple structure was his lay;
> Yet unprofan'd with trick of city art.
> Pure from the head, and glowing from the heart. –
> Thou dear memorial of a brother's love.
> Sweet flute, once warbled to the list'ning grove,
> And master'd by his skilful hand.
> How shall I now command

SOUTHEY'S REVIEW OF *THE LIFE OF DERMODY*

The hidden charms that lurk within thy frame.
Or tell his gentle fame?
Yet will I hail, unmeet, his star-crown'd shade;
And beck his rural friends, a tuneful throng,
To mend the uncouth lay, and join the rising song.
Ah! I remember well yon oaken arbour gay.
Where frequent at the purple dawn of morn,
Or 'neath the beetling brow of twilight grey.
We sate, like roses twain upon one thorn,
Telling romantic tales, of descant quaint,
Tinted in various hues with fancy's paint:
And I would hearken, greedy of his sound.
Lapt in the bosom of soft ecstacy.
Till, lifting mildly high
Her modest frontlet from the clouds around,
Silence beheld us bruise the closing flow'rs.
Meanwhile she shed her pure ambrosial show'rs.

This is certainly a wonderful production for a boy of ten years old; it shows also the character as well as the prematurity of his talents. He was a young mocking bird.

Nicholas Dermody, the father, was addicted to drunkenness, the sin which most easily besets a man of learning and ability, who is condemned to pass his life among the ignorant, and in pursuits inadequate to his powers. Ale and tobacco are all that such men can enjoy in common with their associates, and they become sots from sympathy. His example was fatal to his son. He contracted a love of alehouse company, and of the lowest sensual gratifications, which made his whole life a series of follies and calamities, and brought him at an early age, to the grave.

About the end of his tenth year without giving the least intimation to his father, the boy set off for Dublin, with a single change of linen in his pocket, a couple of shillings, and the second volume of Tom Jones, which he often said, determined him on this adventure.[2]

'While pleasingly contemplating the scenes which his fancy suggested, he soon beguiled a great extent of ground, for desire gave additional vigour to his exertions. At last he recollected that it would be proper for him to look about for a lodging: but no token of any such retreat could he discover, except the languid glimmer of a lone cottage standing in a dark avenue, and to this he turned with the utmost speed.

As soon as he entered the wretched hut, he discovered a corpse in the middle of the floor, on a few unshaped boards, which were intended for a coffin; at the foot of which sat five children sobbing and murmuring, while an emaciated female hung over the head of it in silent grief. Dermody stood during some minutes amazed; and was on the point of retiring from a spectacle which to him was equally distressing and mysterious, when the woman, lifting up an eye of heaviness and of the meekest resignation, beckoned him to a seat near the hearth, where some expiring embers cast a melancholy gleam. She again sunk into her former state: and uttered several incoherent speeches, which he could not distinctly hear; but from which he gathered that she was grandmother to the little mourners, that she had seen happy days though now in misery and want, and that the person deceased was her daughter. This dismal scene deeply affected Dermody and, wiping the tear from his eye, he put his hand into his pocket, gave one of his shillings (the half of all his worldly store) to the old woman, and with a sigh of sympathy took his leave. He had not walked many yards from the door, before he returned with the excuse of having left his cane but in reality to gratify the finest feelings of humanity, by pressing *his last* shilling into the hands of the unfortunate and aged woman.

Careless of repose, he once more took the road, and proceeded on his journey; till he came to the ruins of an old monastery, within whose dilapidated walls he determined to await the dawn of day.

He had not long taken his stand in this dark abode, when his ears were suddenly assailed by a deep and sonorous voice, chanting the antiquated air of Lillabullero.[3] This quick transition, in the gloom of night, from grief to merriment, gave a pleasing turn to his reflections: and he instantly darted from the monastery, and quickly overtook the jovial minstrel; who proved to be no less a personage than the parish-clerk, in his return from a neighbouring fair, exercising his lungs in the manner described above, to keep aloof "the dapper elves and swart babes"[4] of darkness; who owe a particular grudge to the pillars of the church. He also continually whirled a cudgel round his whole body, as if to secure it in a kind of magical circle. Dermody courteously saluted him, and in a short time they became intimate. Some minutes parted agreeably: the parish-clerk rapidly conversing on matters of state, matters of mirth, and lastly, on matters of religion; till, on a sudden, in the midst of a copious harangue, he sprung down a narrow lane to the right, wishing his companion a pleasant journey, flourishing his cudgel, and singing aloud his favourite tune of Lillabullero.

The darkness of the night, the whimsicality of the parish-clerk, the affecting scene of the cottagers, the uncertainty of finding a second retreat till morning, and the recollection that his flight must alarm his father, depressed his spirits to a degree under which he must have sunk, had he not been relieved by the sound of another human voice, – which fortunately proved to be a carrier's with whom he was acquainted, who was now pursuing his journey to the metropolis.

Being almost overwhelmed with fear, he candidly told his tale to the honest carrier, who, with a warmth and generosity always to be found in the heart of an Irish peasant, shared his homely morsel with the young traveller; and, by giving him a short ride now and then, enabled him, though so scantily provided, to accomplish a journey of above a hundred and forty English miles (the distance from Ennis to Dublin).'

He had procured a letter of recommendation from one of his acquaintances to an eminent apothecary in College Green, which he did not produce till he had waited two or three days about the town; living upon the sale of his second shirt. When that little supply was gone, he made his way to College Green with the letter, which as may be naturally expected, proved of no service; and the boy without a friend or a penny, strolled about the streets of Dublin. He went, however, the right way to work, by displaying his talents to those who would listen to him at book-stalls, or at petty bookseller's shops. In one of these walks, he stopped at a stall, and taking up a book, was observed by the owner below, who, as poor Dermody's forlorn appearance excited no expectation of his intending to *buy*, hastened up the steps for the purpose of watching his property. He found him reading a Greek author, and having satisfied himself that the boy understood it, asked him down into the cellar, and made him partake of the humble dinner which had just been placed upon the table. Dermody told his story, and the man who had some value for learning, and some kindness in his nature, engaged him to stay with him, and teach his son Latin. But if tutorship would have contented him, he might have remained at home with his father; disputes arose, he grew wary, and declared his intention of leaving his situation. His good-natured employer pitied the boy, and recommended him to one Lynch, a dealer in his own line, but in somewhat easier circumstances, who at that time kept a little secondhand shop in Stephen-street, and wanted a lad to stand behind the counter.[5] Here he went; his qualifications were extolled by the poor cellar-tradesman, and Lynch, on his part, did not fail to mention them to the students of the college who frequented his shop. This situation also he soon quitted, and once more walked the streets: he stopt as usual, to read Greek at a bookstall, and was noticed by Dr. Houlton,[6] who then held a medical appointment under the Irish Government. The Doctor took him home to dinner, and was so astonished at his acquirements, that he desired him to take up his abode with him, till some situation could be obtained for the prosecution of his studies.

With this gentleman he remained about ten weeks. The account of him during that time, is written by Dr. Houlton, and contains ample and almost wonderful proofs of his learning and ready talents; it also shows the germs of his ungovernable and wayward character. The Doctor was now obliged to leave Dublin, and the friend with whom he meant to have consulted on the means of procuring Dermody some suitable situation, and who would have taken him under his protection, went to England. He therefore gave him money and dismissed him, at a time, when, he says, if my business in the country had not compelled me to part with him, I am inclined to think he would soon have separated himself from me. Dermody seemed to feel no regret at the separation. The money in his pocket consoled him, in a few days he wasted the whole, and then roved about the streets by day, and begged the meanest shelter during the night.

While he was at Dr. Houlton's, a scene-painter, by name Coyle, who belonged to the Dublin theatre, was employed in painting the Doctors house. Dermody became acquainted with him, and now in his distress often strolled to his house. At last, when he could no longer dissemble the truth, he confessed to Coyle that he had left his shirt for the payment of his last lodging, and had slept four nights in the streets.

'My wife,' says this worthy man, 'released it, and made him a pallet-bed on the floor; at which he was pleased and grateful. I was then out of employment at the theatre; and as my wife kept no servant, she made him a substitute to go on her common errands. His pride was silently hurt at this office but he said little. The circumstance of my being out of employment, made the situation of the boy more unpleasant: I thought him rather a burden, and wished him to get another home; but could not find it in my heart in turn him out. He had scarcely any clothes, his shoes were worn out, and for some time he went barefooted. I was again engaged at the theatre; and being very busy, I could not go home to my meals: Mrs. Coyle therefore sent him every morning with my breakfast. I always observed his pride: he refused to go to the theatre, as he considered himself above the common rank. I was not angry with him: I said nothing, and was sorry to see him hurt by it. At length he grew familiar, went on messages, warmed my size-pots at the theatre, told merry tales, and wrote verses on the walls with chalk.

While he was thus employed in the painting-room, as superintendant of the glue, oil, and colour-pots, Mr. Cherry,[7] now of Drury-lane theatre, with great rapture brought one morning into the green-room a poem, written, as he said, by a most surprising boy then in the house. The subject of it was highly agreeable and entertaining to the performers: being a sarcastic comparison between Mr. Daly,[8] patentee of the Theatre Royal, and Mr. Astley,[9] manager of the equestrian theatre, in which the feats of the latter were humourously and satirically enlarged upon. The description which Mr. Cherry gave of the boy, together with the merit of the composition, raised among the performers the greatest curiosity to see him; and, led on by Cherry, they rushed from the green-room to the place where the painter and his wonderful attendant were at work. If their astonishment was excited on hearing the poem read, it was now increased tenfold at the sight of the author. Infantine in appearance, and clad in the very garb of wretchedness; with a meagre, half-starved, but intelligent countenance; a coat much too large for him, and the shoulders and arms seen naked through it; without waist-coat, shirt, or stockings; with a pair of breeches made for a full-grown person, coiled and ragged, reaching to his ancles; his uncovered toes thrust through a pair of old slippers without heels, almost of the magnitude of Kamskatka[10] snow-shoes; his hair clotted with glue, and his face and almost naked body smeared and disfigured with paint of different colours, black, blue, red, green, and yellow: – thus in amazement stood before them, with a small pot of size[11] in one hand, and a hair-brush in the other, the translator of Horace, Virgil, and Anacreon! – Each of the performers felt a sympathetic glow of tenderness for the wretched boy, and each seemed anxious to administer to his necessities. Among the number was Mr. Owenson;[12] a gentleman conspicuous for his domestic attachments, and distinguished by his humanity. In him Dermody found a benefactor: he treated him with tenderness, received him into his family with affection, clothed, and became a second parent to him.'

Mr. Owenson was one of the best and steadiest of the many steady and good friends whom it was Dermody's fortune to meet with.[13] The plan which he formed for this extraordinary boy was to get him an introduction to the college: a distant relation of his, Dr. Young, afterwards Bishop of Clonfert, was then one of the senior fellows, and Professor of Natural Philosophy.[14] To him he took Dermody in his rags, in one hand, and a specimen of his poetry in the other. The Doctor was equally astonished and delighted. When he perceived that the boy hung back, as if ashamed, he placed him on a chair by his aide, and exclaimed, 'By Jove, you are fit to sit by the side of a king.' He offered to superintend his studies, and complete him for college, and gave him a Homer, a Greek Lexicon, a Horace, and Murray's Logic.[15] On receiving this last work, Dermody said with a downcast look, 'Sir, I think I should not like this; for any one of common sense and little knowledge can quibble without studying to quibble.' It was settled that he should come to Dr. Young three days in the week.

'Unfortunately for Dermody, the studies which he now entered upon with Dr. Young, were neither suited to his genius nor his disposition; and at last became so repugnant to him, that he would often with tears lament the mental drudgery into which he had been thrown, and the loss of those caresses he once enjoyed in the arms of the muses. For some time, however, he duly attended; but as often as possible he would sculk from what he called scholastic torture, and spend his hours in playing with his adopted sisters, or in writing sonnets appropriate to the familiar incidents of their happy home. His aversion to this mode of instruction still increasing, became at last so powerful, that he absented himself entirely from his studies, without giving the least previous information either to Mr. Owenson or to Dr. Young. Chance, however, one day brought those gentlemen together; and Mr. Owenson, being anxious to hear what progress Dermody had made under so great a master, began to question the doctor about his pupil, but to his great surprise was informed that he had attended only once during a period of four weeks. Dr. Young, being hitherto ignorant of the cause, naturally concluded his absence was occasioned by the adoption of some more commodious arrangement for his closer application, and that it was consequently with the knowledge and approbation of his patron. His astonishment on being told the contrary, was evident and interesting. He loved the boy; and had passed over many of his youthful irregularities, in the hope that a little experience would amend them: but this deviation from rectitude was of too great a magnitude to be treated with lenity. The more he considered the circumstance, the greater pain it gave him; and the glow of his friendly resentment brought forth this emphatic exclamation: "By Jove! my good friend," having his hand upon his heart, "I fear all is not right *here*." His feelings were too sensibly affected to enter into the investigation of any immediate or remote cause of such delinquency; and they separated.'

He had no sooner lost this friend, than Mr. Owenson found another for him, and introduced him to the Reverend Gilbert Austin,[16] who kept a school of high repute in Dublin, and with that liberality which it was ever Dermody's good fortune to find, undertook to instruct him; he was to return to his meals and bed at Mr. Owenson's, but the distance being found inconvenient, Mr. Austin took him into his own house, introduced him to his friends, and by their advice opened a subscription for his education and support, which was liberally patronized. He also selected and printed at his own expence, a small collection of his poems, stating in the preface that the author had not yet attained his thirteenth year.[17] As the advertisement is dated March, 1789, there is either some error in the dates, or Dermody had represented himself as younger than he really was.

This brought him into great fame. It became the rage of the day to have the 'little poet' at all parties of consequence. Lady Charlemont,[18] Lady Maurice Gore,[19] Lady Crofton,[20] and the Duke of Leinster[21] were among his patrons. Mr. Austin placed in the Bank at onetime an hundred and fifty pounds, to be portioned out at his discretion for the support and education of his ward, and the floating subscriptions, many of which were annual, enabled him, after he had been about three months in the family, to place him as a boarder in a contiguous house inhabited by one Aickbourne, a glass manufacturer.[22] This man was a violent Methodist, he endeavoured to convert Dermody, and his zeal was requited with some unlucky jokes which the son of the tabernacle did not forget, and had soon too good an opportunity to revenge.

Nothing could wean Dermody from his passion for low company. He got acquainted with a rascally drawing-master,[23] who wished to get the business of Mr. Austin's school, and persuaded him to show Mr. Austin a drawing of a flower, as his own performance, after receiving only three lessons. Irish conspiracies, of whatever kind, are usually defeated by some egregious folly in the parties concerned. The drawing-master did not remember that the thing was impossible: Dermody was accused of falshood, he persisted in his story: the proof was easy, materials were brought, and he was desired to copy the drawing. Upon the consequent detection, he was immediately ordered from the parlour to the kitchen, and then kept in disgrace. In this resentment, he wrote four lines, in which the families of his patron and patroness were severely ridiculed. Aickborne, the Methodist, found these lines, and carried them to Mr. Austin, in the hope of ruining the boy. Mr. Austin, in an intemperate and inexcusable fit of anger, destroyed the poems which he had collected for publication, returned to the subscribers the whole of the money which he had received for his support and education, shut his doors against him, and turned him out once more upon the world.

'He was now in a more lamentable condition than when he first arrived in the metropolis. His faults were blazoned forth by every one, and distorted into a thousand aggravated forms. He was forsaken and pointed at as a monster of ingratitude – none would listen to his vindication; all ears and all hearts were closed against him; while the Methodist who effected his ruin was applauded for his upright conduct, and ratified himself by seeing a helpless boy of thirteen years of age thrown an unpitied outcast from society, for writing, in a moment of passion, four mirthful lines against his benefactor! Wherever he appealed, he was treated with scorn and neglect; and to make his situation still more pitiable, his steadfast friend Mr. Owenson was at this time in a distant part of the country, and his amiable wife no more.[24] His hopes of immediate relief from that quarter being thus frustrated, he took courage and wrote the following letter to the Secretary at War; who, considering his youth and forlorn condition, humanely administered to his necessities.

SOUTHEY'S REVIEW OF *THE LIFE OF DERMODY*

To Sackville Hamilton, Esq,[25] *Dublin Castle*

Sir,

Ever sensible of your bounty and patronage, I beg leave to defend myself in your favour. Mr. Austin has been pleased to return the money received from gentlemen for my benefit, on account of my leaving his house. You may suppose that I was culpable for misconduct: in a certain degree I acknowledge it; but, good heaven! did I deserve so heavy a punishment? The occasion of my writing the few silly lines for which I have suffered so severely, was derived from my being kept in the kitchen, and made to open Mr. Austin's gate. If I chose, I might be a companion for servants without applying for that treatment to him. I hope sir, you will consider that I am as *poor* now as when you first afforded me your protection, and consequently in need of that money which you were pleased to give me. I am sure no gentleman will be capable of taking back his money, which he gave with benevolence. These things which I have mentioned are known to all the young gentlemen of the school. I should be sorry to gain the title of *ungrateful*, but I must defend myself in the impartial eyes of those who have been my kind benefactors.

I have the honour of being, sir, your humble servant,

Thomas Dermody

October, 18, 1799

Unquestionably the punishment was heavier than the offence. Worthless he was, utterly and irreclaimably worthless, but this had not yet been proved; it might have been foreseen, but who shall condemn and punish upon foresight? Mr. Austin might have withdrawn his protection, that Dermody deserved: all beyond this was unjust. Dermody was more excusable for his offence, than this gentleman for the manner in which he resented it.

The boy thus deserted, made the best use of his talents, commenced writer for a newspaper, and thus supported himself till Mr. Owenson arrived in Dublin. That excellent man received him with sorrow indeed, but also with affection, and after some time procured for him the protection of Mr. Atkinson,[26] since Judge Advocate for Ireland, and the effectual patronage of the Countess Dowager of Moira,[27] whose name never should be mentioned without honour. This munificent patroness adopted him, and placed him under the care of Mr. Boyd,[28] the translator of Dante, at Killeagh, with whom he remained two years, and added French and Italian, and some little Spanish to his acquirements. If it had been possible to serve Dermody, his better star was now presiding. Lady Moira would have continued her bounty till he had been qualified for some honourable profession, and settled in it. But he would not be served, he pestered her with letters insisting on being removed from Mr. Boyd's, and permitted to seek his fortune in London; till wearied out at last, Lady Moira sent him ten guineas that he might follow his own pursuits; saying, that as he had thought proper to withdraw himself from her direction and protection, in a manner equally ungracious and absurd, that was the last favour he was ever to expect from her, or any of her family.

Dermody's moral habits had received no improvement at Killeagh. The precepts and the example of Mr. Boyd were wasted upon him, and he lost no opportunity of degrading his nature, by associating with alehouse acquaintance. It appears by his writings during these two years, that Burns[29] was become a favourite object of his imitation. Men of talents, who employ those talents in praise of drunkenness and debauchery, little know the evil they do, and the heavy, heavy sin for which they are accountable. Of these associates he took his farewell, and set out for Dublin. His money was soon gone, and his main means of support came from the bounty of Mr. Owenson, by whose interest he was enabled to publish his poems, and by whose exertions obtained from them considerable relief. It was still this gentleman's hope, that Dermody would have grace enough to enter the college; but the die was cast! while it was possible by begging money to indulge himself in all sordid and disgraceful gratifications, this wretched boy was contented.

The patronage which he received was very great. Never did a people more cordially and more generously encourage what they believed to be genius in a countryman, than the Irish in this instance. Mr. Grattan[30] quoted passages from one of his poems, in the Irish House of Commons, and introduced him with strong recommendations to many persons of taste and fortune. Mr. Flood,[31] it is said, honoured him with his particular friendship while he lived, and suggested to him a plan for a poem on the British Constitution. This fragment of Mr. Flood's is too curious to be omitted.

> Exordium: something like the beginning of Paradise Lost, but suited to the subject of the British constitution and its reform.
>
> Read Macaulay's History of England.[32] Describe from its earliest beginning, the dawn of liberty, or strugglings of those champions of the people. Describe the ages of superstition: the tyranny of the first William. Paint the law of conquest as the most wicked. Shew monarchy, with a few exceptions, from William downward, in its truest colours: the people in the most wretched state of slavery and ignorance. Paint superstition and popery: and shout in her ear, that that religion was the established one when monarchy was in its full power. The reign of John, &c.: the contending nobles, and the power of the pope in those days, strong subjects for your muse. Monarchy and the nobility (which is Aristocracy) waging their wars; but still the people in an abject state of slavery to both, and tuns of their blood spilt in the cause where king and nobles were fighting for power.
>
> Then the wars of York and Lancaster; all for kingly power: the same blood shed, but still the people in abject slavery. Run through the whole constitutional history; the aspiring characters down to Harry the Eighth: but above all take care that the outlines of your historical painting be true. The Reformation; the throwing off the papal yoke: that being the first

dawn of English liberty. Harry's character as drawn by Mrs. Macaulay; indeed all the characters as drawn by her: also queen Elizabeth, and Mary queen of Scots; those are openings for the finest feelings of your muse. From Elizabeth's death, the entire throwing off the papal yoke; Martin Luther, and John Calvin: at those times the British constitution gradually advancing. Then the bigoted James the First: the political characters of that reign. Then Charles the First: a wide field for your muse. Cromwell, though a devil, an instrument, under Providence, of much good: his character; magnanimity. The state of the nation, and the character of the people, till the arrival of George the First. H. Flood.

On such a theme, says Mr. Raymond, what might not the fervour of youthful and approved genius have accomplished? There is no reason to believe that Dermody could have accomplished any thing valuable upon any subject; his poetry does not exhibit the slightest mark of originality; he was a mocking-bird who could combine the notes of others with a song which should partake so much of all, as to be unlike any one – but he had no note of his own. He never displays feeling; how should he when his whole life evinces that he had none? – and never discovers a thinking mind. But had he really possessed the supereminent genius, which they who mistake talents for genius, attributed to him, on such a subject as this which Mr. Flood proposed, he must have failed. No swan could make its way along the river of Oblivion, with such a dead weight upon her neck.

There was not a man of letters in Ireland who did not notice Dermody. Percy,[33] Preston,[34] Walker,[35] Sterling,[36] Tighe, all encouraged him.

'His introduction to Mr. Edward Tighe[37] was as singular as it was ludicrous. Mr. Tighe, being in the habit of frequenting an eminent bookseller's in College-green, was one day as he left the shop, accosted by a ragg'd boy, who told him that he had just left a letter of introduction at his house, and waited upon him by the desire of a gentleman who was his particular and intimate friend. Mr. Tighe, doubting perhaps the truth of his story, desired him in a very rough tone to go about his business, and walked on without giving the circumstance any further consideration. But as he ascended the steps to knock at his door, he perceived Dermody close behind him; who loudly asserted his innocence, and added that he had taken the liberty of following him home for the purpose of convincing him that he had not told a falsehood. Mr. Tighe being of rather an irritable temper, began to treat him as an impostor; and was on the point of knocking him down with his cane, when fortunately the servant appeared at the door. Dermody used no attempt to assuage the choler of his furious assailant, but made the best of his way from him by flight. The letter convinced Mr. Tighe of his error; and, generously conceiving he was bound to atone for the injury he had done, he dispatched the servant with the utmost speed to bring Dermody back. The latter had by this time nearly reached the bottom of the street; when turning round, and perceiving the servant making huge strides towards him (for the purpose, as his fears informed him, of giving him the bastinado),[38] he set off with increased velocity, nor was he convinced that his apprehensions were grounded till he had been thus *run down* after a long chase.

When he returned, Mr. Tighe apologized for the error he had committed, and assured him that he would make every reparation for the alarm he had occasioned him. As the letter informed Mr. Tighe that the bearer was a poet, the first part of the interview produced only some frivolous questions and answers incident to such an introduction; but at length in an unlucky moment Mr. Tighe, thinking that the boy was merely gifted with the knack of rhyming, asked him if he had gone through his Latin Accidence. This so enraged Dermody that he snatched his hat from the table, and without much ceremony left the house. During the early part of their conversation, Dermody had received a pamphlet written by Mr. Tighe, which was to be the subject of a copy of verses: it had luckily been put into his pocket before the last fatal question; but from the fury and indignation that blazed in his countenance when he darted from the room, Mr. Tighe supposed that an everlasting separation had taken place. He was deceived; the following day Dermody made his appearance, with the pamphlet written by Mr. Tighe in one hand, and his own poem in the other; when, to the great astonishment of that gentleman, instead of a panegyric on his book, a keen and pointed satire was presented. He had the liberality to applaud the poem, and reward the author: he presented him with five guineas, a snuff-coloured suit of clothes, and a cocked hat, the formidable eccentricity of which surpassed that of "ancient Pistol."[39] The hat and suit were by Mr. Tighe's desire as a lesson of economy, to be worn without alteration: and Dermody, to the no small amusement of his friends, for some time figured away in these sober and antiquated habiliments; the breeches being tied below the calf of the leg, the waistcoat lapelled to his knees, the skirts of the coat dangling at his heels, and the hat with a significant and solemn slouch covering both his ears.'

Mr. Tighe was a whimsical, but useful and steady friend. His temper, naturally irritable, was not improved by a complication of bodily infirmities; he really admired Dermody, and wished to serve him, but as he often had occasion to reprove him for his misconduct, he generally, before he could reach the end of his lecture, became so irritated, that his utterance was almost choaked, and oaths and broken sentences came rattling out in confusion. Dermody on these occasions, would depart in dudgeon, and appear no more till Mr. Tighe sent for him. At length he disappeared, and was not heard of for many months, when absolute want brought him from the disgraceful haunts in which he had been wallowing; his first application was to Mr. Tighe, who sent him money, and the following letter.

'Notwithstanding your ungrateful conduct to Mr. Owenson, Mr. Austin, and that universally honoured and esteemed lady the Countess of Moira, I am endeavouring to form schemes for your living and advantage. You must, I conclude, become an author by profession, or an actor, or both. In either of those characters one can assist you.

The stage is open to you, if you have talent; and the press is equally so.

I have two grand and favourite objects for this enquiry: 1. the diminution of drams of all sorts, which destroy the people in every sense; 2. the rearing, and employing in industry, orphan children of both sexes, in order to produce an uncontaminated race. If you can by your pen assist these great objects in prose or verse, you will do great credit to yourself, benefit the public, and create the means of living. Byrne or Moore[1] shall purchase your works: and the first may be entitled 'The Devil's Gift for 1793; consisting of Epigrams, Ballads, and comical Essays.'

Edward Tighe.

This was his last communication with this gentleman, whose friendship he seems to have renounced because he was incapable of bearing his just reproof. As he advanced in his career of debauchery, all shame seemed to be leaving him. He applied to the Countess of Moira, who secretly instructed a bookseller to print at her expence, anything which he might offer; but refused him any immediate supplies, with great propriety: for what availed it, to administer relief to-day, to one whose profligacy, not his misfortunes, would make him equally in need of it tomorrow?

His next resource was to turn political writer; and he produced a pamphlet called 'The Rights of Justice,'[40] in which, by taking the republican side, he entirely destroyed the last lingering sparks of affection and good-will towards him, which many of his friends still retained. Mr. Raymond is anxious to convince the reader that he became a revolutionist from distress, and not from principle: he had unfortunately no reason to fear that poor Dermody would ever be suspected of principle. Sinking from bad to worse, he now lived by begging, wrote mean petitions, and carried them himself to people of rank. Still his good fortune continued. Lord Kilwarden,[41] upon whom he had written a panegyric, found him out in his garret, took him home to dinner in his rags, and sent him back at night dead drunk, with five guineas in his pocket. There was some excuse for this, as he had of late been scantily fed, and a little wine overpowered him. Lord Kilwarden actually engaged apartments for him in the college, and promised to furnish them, to defray the whole of his expences there, and to allow him thirty pounds a year, that he might appear with respectability. No – he would not consent to this arrangement, but retired to his alehouses and his garrets, and trusted to charity for food.

To trace the whole series of his follies, would be to transcribe Mr Raymond's very interesting book. At length he determined to go to London, but before he could put this design in execution, he was *crimped*,[42] and safely lodged in a tender. *Crimping* was at this time practiced in Ireland with unparalleled atrocity. Dermody was a fit subject to be sent to serve the King as a vagabond, but kidnapping, whether in Africa or Europe, is equally abominable, and ought not to be winked at, much less encouraged. From this situation Mr White released him. He entered into the service not long after, and was then bought out by Mr Emerson;[43] and in a few weeks enlisted as a private soldier in the 108th regiment. This last act he endeavoured to conceal, but Mr Atkinson saw and recognized him on Usher's Island,[44]

---

1 [Southey's note:] Two respectable booksellers. [Patrick Byrne (1740/41–1814) and James Moore (fl. 1786–1803). Both had premises on College Green, Dublin.]

near Lady Moira's mansion.[45] After seeking to avoid him in vain, Dermody said, it was his own free and voluntary act, and that he was resolved to try his fortune in other climates as a soldier.

The Earl of Granard,[46] who commanded the regiment, was well known to Mr. Atkinson. Lady Moira, though she had justly given Dermody up, still kept an anxious eye upon him, wishing rather than hoping for any favourable change of conduct. A consultation was held at her house, and it was agreed, that the most probable method of reclaiming him would be to let him remain some time in the ranks, and be by degrees advanced, if his conduct deserved it. This was a wise plan. His conduct was now irreproachable: he was successively made corporal and serjeant, and going to the continent under Lord Moira, was by him appointed to a second-lieutenancy in the waggon corps. While lying at Southampton, he could not refrain from his favourite vice of drunkenness; but on the continent he behaved well, and his friends began to hope and expect a thorough reformation. He received several dangerous wounds, and on the reduction of this army, was put upon half-pay. Full of hope, and having a new character to begin with, he once more determined to appear upon the public theatre, and went to London, where Lord Moira[47] placed him in the house of Mr Faulder,[48] the bookseller in Bond-street. It had been happier for Dermody, if his noble friends had not so soon credited his reformation, (a thing always to be slowly believed, except it be accomplished by the strong influence of religious enthusiasm), and had procured him another military situation upon actual service; he could not then have yielded to his vices, and his talents might have become useful.

In London he soon relapsed into his old habits. Lord Moira was compelled to withdraw his bounty, and he commenced a second career of shame. Those with whom he now associated, were of the lowest order of society, and instead of preserving for the day of want the last liberal donation of his noble patron, he joined in their ruinous debaucheries and wasted it: – then half starved and half naked, took shelter at last in a garret with an Irish cobler, in Strutton-ground, Westminster. In this state of distress, he found out Mr Raymond, who for four years lost sight of him, and given him up as dead. This gentleman clothed him, and by his wise active friendship, and that of Mr Allingham,[49] Dermody might still have been saved if he would. Never did man's good angel make so many efforts to rescue him from perdition! They made him collect some of his poems, and write more, and on Mr. Allingham's recommendation, Messrs. Vernor and Hood[50] gave him a 'liberal sum' for them, which relieved him from immediate embarrassment, and enabled him for some time to live at ease.

At this time he had once more many friends, but nothing could make him forsake his friend the Irish cobler, and his poisonous habits of vulgar profligacy. The following anecdote will amuse our readers.

'Among those to whom the friendship of Mr. Allingham had introduced Dermody, was Mr. Johnson, now an officer in the regiment commanded by the Earl of Moira. This gentleman, who was himself a votary of the muses, became very soon attached to Dermody; and frequently meeting him at the chambers of

Mr. Allingham, would rally him on the uncouth mode in which he dressed himself and appeared in public. One day business brought him at an early hour to the apartments of his friend, who had likewise gone out sooner than usual; when, to his great astonishment, he found Dermody on the steps of the door, almost in a state of nakedness, and offensively dirty.

Mr Johnson, in an authoritative tone, desired Dermody to follow him. He obeyed: and the march finished on the banks of the New River, at a tavern near Sadler's Wells, where this gentleman lodged. As they approached the door, Mr. Johnson with great caution commanded a halt; but in a low voice, that none might hear him and observe his companion. After surveying the fortifications, the order was given to ascend quickly, and take possession of a back room which overlooked the river, up one pair of stairs. The commander followed; and having shut the door, and fanned himself a little with his hat, as if safe from the danger of the field and sure of his prisoner, he told him with a loud voice to strip to the skin. To Dermody the shouts of real war had not been so dreadful: he almost fancied that he was to be made a sacrifice to the god of battle. However, he obeyed his superior; who, leaving Dermody to disrobe himself, went to order a scrubbing brush, soap, towels, and a large tub of water. The appearance of this last article gave the poet a cold tremor: he was plunged in, and purified. Not less joy did Dermody feel when released from the terrors of his immersion, than did young Ammon,[51]

> When Glory, like the dazzling eagle, stood
> Perch'd on his beaver in the Granic flood.[52]

A clean and fashionably frilled shirt, with appropriate stockings, shoes, breeches, neckcloth, waistcoat and coat, were speedily brought from Mr. Johnson's wardrobe; and as they happened to fit him, he was, with the aid of the village barber, quickly metamorphosed from a ragged mendicant of Parnassus, into a fashionable modern gentleman.

The old habiliments were now with much disdain thrown from the window, upon the bank of the river: and a comfortable supper having been by this time put upon the table, the two friends sat down to enjoy by a snug fire "the feast of ducklings and the flow of soul."[53] The cloth had not long been removed, before they perceived by the faint light of the moon, a number of persons wandering up and down the bank of the river.

Soon afterwards torches were brought, and stuck at short distances from each other; in order, it appeared, that the object of their search might be more easily discovered: and a dragging-iron being plunged into the river, shewed that they were in pursuit of a dead body. The stillness of the evening, the twinkling lights glancing on the smooth surface of the water, and the anxiety and grief pictured in every countenance, made the scene awful and interesting. Tale after tale was brought to the tavern, and each messenger varied in his report. One saw the unfortunate person wandering distractedly on the banks of the river, another saw him plunge into it; one saw him floating on the surface of the water; another, by the light of the torches, perceived him at the bottom: now he was found, and now he was not: now appeared one who had seen the body taken from the river and now the discarded garments of Dermody, the unconscious cause of this alarm and anxiety, were brought to the tavern. At a late hour, the populace gradually dispersed; some shedding tears, and others heaving only a sigh of sympathy, at the hapless fate of the wretched man who they supposed had by despair been driven to destroy himself. The dread that the general pity might be changed into resentment, alone hindered the two friends, who had witnessed the whole scene through the window, from declaring themselves the innocent authors of this unfounded alarm; for they were not at all inclined to laugh at so serious a mistake, nor to sport with the feelings which were so interestingly conspicuous in every countenance.'

Lord Moira though he had withdrawn his patronage from this miserable man, seldom slighted his applications for relief. He received from him occasionally very considerable sums, and also from Mr. Bragge Bathurst,[54] Mr. Hiley Addington,[55] and the present Lord Sidmouth.[56] No man of letters in this country ever received so much from the bounty of the rich and the great. He now also addressed some flattering lines to Sir James Bland Burges, upon his admirable poem of Richard the First,[57] and from him he received in return that liberality which he seems to have obtained from everyone to whom he was made known, and in every instance to have abused.

Sir James encouraged him to print a second volume of poems, opened a subscription for their publication, and also recommended him to the Literary Fund, who gave him ten pounds, which was 'entrusted to the care of Mr. Baker,[58] their collector, for the purpose of providing decent clothing for him.' Within a week after he had appeared in his new clothes, Sir James Bland Burges hearing a violent altercation in his hall, went out to learn the cause of it, and found Dermody there, struggling with two of his servants, who were endeavouring to prevent him from forcing his way into the house. He was in rags, was covered with mud (in which it appeared he had just been rolled), had a black eye, and a broken head, from which the blood trickled down his breast, and was so drunk that he could scarcely speak. His account was that he had pawned his new clothes, after which he had been arrested, and carried to a spunging-house, where he had been drinking with the bailiffs, and writing a poem. This poem as soon as he had finished it, he wished to take to Sir James, but they would not let him; he had watched his opportunity, and slipt off: but they overtook him, and he was obliged to fight his way, in which he had succeeded. He then gave Sir James the poem, which proved to be the *Extravaganza*[59] one of his very best, and which, says Mr. Raymond, though it might add fresh honour to the first writer in our language, was thus produced in the midst of intemperance and brutality, by a wretch in a state of intoxication, and lost to every feeling of decency and shame. This debt was paid by Sir James, who from this time was pestered continually with begging letters, one after another, for Dermody had long since lost all sense of shame, and was not to be deterred by denial, from repeating his mean solicitations. In like manner, he wearied out the Literary Fund, continuing to beg, till they would no longer give.

This wretched man meantime was paying the heavy price of his profligacy. The wretches with whom he associated, considered him as a sort of wild beast, whom they had caught, and of whom they were to make the most they could; they contrived to make him their vassal, and to render him obedient by the dread of punishment. The little food which he required was purchased and provided by them, a running account was kept against him, and of course he was always brought in debtor.

'They found this plan too profitable to adopt any other; and by keeping him always in debt, they kept him always in dread. Whenever he received a win of money, he honestly brought it to his landlord, who always (as he termed it) "carried it to the account;" and when money was wanted and Dermody had none to give, the request was in general followed by an arrest, which frequently turned out a very profitable speculation. The fear of a prison made him importune his friend, who never suffered him to languish in confinement; and as those who had occasioned his embarrassments were his messengers during such periods, they consequently obtained a knowledge of his patron; and turned the kind benevolence intended to relieve him, into a source of emolument to themselves.

The natural consequence of thoughtlessness and dissipation is dependancy as Dermody had in his exigencies no other means of support than what these associates were pleased to afford him he conceived himself bound when fortune smiled upon him, not only to discharge his debts of this description, but to bestow some signal mark of favour for the kindness thus conferred upon him while penny-less. These returns varied, according as the obligations he laboured under were weighty or trivial: without any consideration of the motive which occasioned them. At one time he might be seen in his garret in company with his hosts the cobler and his wife, and some attic lodger of equal consequence, regaling on a goose which his industry had roasted by a string in his own apartment: while the pallet-bed, which stood in a corner, was strewed with various vegetables; the fire-side decorated with numerous foaming pots of porter; and the cobler's work-stool, boot-leg, lapstone, &c. were commodiously placed as seats. On another occasion, in some neighbouring ale-house, entertaining the same personages with the various rarities which resorts of this description generally afford: where as the astonished guests, enveloped in clouds of smoke, sat listening with rapture to the eloquence of Dermody, the host was to be discovered in the back ground applauding with one hand, while his other dextrously scored an additional item to the bill; which, if Dermody could not discharge it during the following day, was at once put into the hands of some pettifogging practitioner of the law, and the unfortunate debtor appeared in the evening through the bars of a spunging-house, like Bajazut in his iron cage.[60]

A singular circumstance of this kind occurred while Dermody lodged at a mean public-house in Portpool-lane.[61] The author had received a very melancholy epistle from him, in which he deplored his want of proper clothes to visit Mr. Addington in, as he had been requested to do on something material

SOUTHEY'S REVIEW OF *THE LIFE OF DERMODY*

concerning the publication of his Ode to Peace, which in a few days after made its appearance.[62] Business of some consequence prevented the author from attending on him at the time mentioned; and some days having passed before leisure permitted him to supply the things required, so he went one evening to apologize for his apparent neglect, and to mention that the necessary articles were ready. On entering the house his ears were assailed by violent plaudits and huzzas, which appeared to issue from the attic story. Having little curiosity to inquire into the cause of these extraordinary rejoicings he only requested to see Dermody. The good woman of the house quickly dispatched a messenger to give the proper information: and the author was soon ushered into a room at the top of which sat Dermody in a new suit of clothes, surrounded by half a score of the landlord's smoking-acquaintances; the table strewed with tobacco, pipes, and a plentiful flow of wine and spirits; and the sideboard loaded with bottles, the late contents of which had left the members of this elevated society in a state of equal jollity and confusion.

The entrance of the author damped the joy of the meeting; and Dermody, who well knew that the look which accompanied his appearance in the room was a just rebuke for the impropriety of *his* conduct, began to frame an apology; which being little attended to, he flew into a rage, and repeated the following lines:

> When wit's wild flashes wreathe a smile.
> Dimpling on Bacchus' blushy cheek;
> Or when, gaunt sorrow to beguile,
> Outrageous peals of humour break;
>
> If then, all furrrow'd o'er with frown.
> With mad-cap jollity at odds,
> You strike each quaint chimera down,
> A fiend amid the laughing Gods;
>
> Go to the tabernacle clan,
> Who drone devotion through the nose,
> And hide with pray'r *the inward man*;
> I herd not with such imps as those.
>
> If your pure palate is so nice,
> That ev'n in frolic's festive hour
> You can't endure a little vice.
> To sweeten life's eternal sour;
>
> 'Fore heav'n! you'll find no saint in me,
> From *passion's* furnace glowing hot
> And as for prim hypocrisy,
> Hypocrisy! I know her not.[63]

It was however, soon discovered that the honourable Mr. Bragge, had presented him with the clothes, as well as the money which was thus imprudently lavished upon vipers whose rapacious appetites could they have by that means derived equal gratification, would have preyed on his vitals.'

His last patron was Mr. Addington, who not only relieved his wants, but endeavoured to correct his errors, condescended to advise him, and would have essentially served him had it been possible to serve Dermody. He instructed Mr. Hatchard the bookseller to print and publish the volume of his poems which were now preparing for the press; and this he did when fully convinced of the incurable profligacy of this poor wretched man.[64] The scene was soon to close, – no constitution could long hold out against such excesses; he became consumptive, 'his fatal illness rendered his days and nights heavy and burthensome,' and it was hoped that these distresses would be alleviated by the 'profits arising from the sale of the work:' but these were scarcely sufficient to alleviate in the smallest degree his accumulating distresses. Lord Moira, Sir James Bland Burges, and Mr. Smith[65] of Dublin being acquainted by Mr. Raymond with his situation, each sent him ten guineas. He withdrew, making a last effort, from the perpetual persecution of his accursed associates, and took shelter in a miserable cottage near Sydenham, that he might die in peace. From hence he wrote to Mr. Raymond, who with Mr. Allingham went to him. They procured him every immediate comfort which his situation required and admitted, took a good lodging for him and engaged a careful nurse, left money for his use, and departed, meaning to return the next morning, and remove him to his new apartment, but he expired that evening, July 15th, 1802.

Thus terminated the miserable and disgraceful life of Thomas Dermody. That he was not possessed of real genius we must again repeat, – none of his productions indicating any real feeling, or any strong powers of thought: but for readiness and prematurity of imitative talents he is probably unexampled. He could compose as rapidly as another could transcribe: the poems which he had written before he was fourteen would fill ten volumes of a moderate size! Who would not have regretted if a man of such prodigious promise had perished for want of patronage?

The complaint that genius goes unrewarded, in which men who suspect themselves of genius are so fond of indulging, is generally ill founded. Chatterton did not wait till he could be known;[66] and in almost every other instance, the men in question would have died upon dunghills sooner as the fit consequence of their worthlessness, if the talents which they possessed had not reprieved them. There are other persons who are fond of maintaining that poetical genius leads to extravagance and profligacy and is connected with it: on such men it would be idle to bestow an argument; they seek to depreciate a gift which they do not possess, and calumniate what they envy. In the case of Dermody this however may be remarked, that to his talents he was indebted not only for all the numerous friends whom they procured him, and for all the bounty which he received; but also for those lucid intervals in a life of madness which kept his soul alive, and prevented him from sinking into utter brutality: – for a sense of what was right

SOUTHEY'S REVIEW OF *THE LIFE OF DERMODY*

which preserved him from committing crimes against others as well as himself, and for hours of silent anguish and frequent regret and repentance, which however unavailing in this world, it is to be hoped have not proved wholly so.

After the account which we have extracted we need not say that this is a very interesting book, – in every respect highly honourable to Mr. Raymond both as an author and as a man.

2

SOUTHEY'S ACCOUNT OF THE LIFE OF HENRY KIRKE WHITE

from *The Remains Of Henry Kirke White,*
2 vols (London, 1807)

It fell to my lot to publish, with the assistance of my friend Mr. Cottle, the first collected edition of the works of Chatterton,[67] in whose history I felt a more than ordinary interest, as being a native of the same city, familiar from my childhood with those great objects of art and nature by which he had been so deeply impressed, and devoted from my childhood with the same ardour to the same pursuits. It is now my fortune to lay before the world some account of one whose early death is not less to be lamented as a loss to English literature, and whose virtues were as admirable as his genius. In the present instance there is nothing to be recorded but what is honourable to himself, and to the age in which he lived; nothing to be regretted, but that one so ripe for heaven should so soon have been removed from the world.

Henry Kirke White, the second son of John and Mary White,[68] was born in Nottingham, March 21st, 1785. His father is a Butcher; his mother, whose maiden name was Neville, is of a respectable Staffordshire family.

From the years of three till five, Henry learnt to read at the school of a Mrs. Garrington; whose name, unimportant as it may appear, is mentioned, because she had the good sense to perceive his extraordinary capacity, and spoke of what it promised with confidence. She was an excellent woman, and he describes her with affection in his poem upon Childhood. At a very early age his love of reading was decidedly manifested; it was a passion to which every thing else gave way. 'I could fancy,' says his eldest sister, 'I see him in his little chair, with a large book upon his knee, and my mother calling, "Henry, my love, come to dinner;" which was repeated so often without being regarded, that she was obliged to change the tone of her voice before she could rouse him.' When he was about seven, he would creep unperceived into the kitchen, to teach the servant to read and write; and he continued this for some time before it was discovered that he had been thus laudably employed. He wrote a tale of a Swiss emigrant, which was probably his first composition, and gave it to this servant, being shamed to show it to his mother. The consciousness of genius is always at first accompanied with this diffidence; it

DOI: 10.4324/9781003431343-3

59

is a sacred solitary feeling. No forward child, however extraordinary the promise of his childhood, ever produced any thing truly great.

When Henry was about six, he was placed under the Rev. John Blanchard, who kept, at that time, the best school in Nottingham.[69] Here he learnt writing, arithmetic, and French. When he was about eleven, he one day wrote a separate theme for every boy in his class, which consisted of about twelve or fourteen. The master said he had never known them write so well upon any subject before, and could not refrain from expressing his astonishment at the excellence of Henry's. It was considered as a great thing for him to be at so good a school, yet there were some circumstances which rendered it less advantageous to him than it might have been. Mrs. White had not yet overcome her husband's intention of breeding him up to his own business; and by an arrangement which took up too much of his time, and would have crushed his spirit, if that 'mounting spirit' could have been crushed, one whole day in the week, and his leisure hours on the others were employed in carrying the butcher's basket. Some differences at length arose between his father and Mr. Blanchard, in consequence of which Henry was removed.

One of the ushers, when he came to receive the money due for tuition, took the opportunity of informing Mrs. White what an incorrigible son she had, and that it was impossible to make the lad do any thing. This information made his friends very uneasy; they were dispirited about him, and had they relied wholly upon this report, the stupidity or malice of this man would have blasted Henry's progress for ever. He was, however, placed under the care of a Mr. Shipley,[70] who soon discovered that he was a boy of quick perception, and very admirable talents; and came with joy, like a good man, to relieve the anxiety and painful suspicions of his family.

While his school-masters were complaining that they could make nothing of him, he discovered what Nature had made him, and wrote satires upon them. These pieces were never shown to any, except his most particular friends, who say that they were pointed and severe. They are enumerated in the table of Contents to one of his manuscript volumes, under the title of School-Lampoons; but, as was to be expected, he had cut the leaves out and destroyed them.

One of his poems written at this time, and under these feelings, is preserved.

On Being Confined to School,
One Pleasant Morning in Spring.
Written at the age of thirteen.

THE morning sun's enchanting rays
Now call forth every songster's praise;
Now the lark with upward flight,
Gayly ushers in the light;
While wildly warbling from each tree,
The birds sing songs to Liberty.

But for me no songster sings,
For me no joyous lark up-springs;
For I, confin'd in gloomy school,
Must own the pedant's iron rule,
And far from sylvan shades and bowers,
In durance vile must pass the hours;
There con the scholiast's dreary lines
Where no bright ray of genius shines,
And close to rugged learning cling,
While laughs around the jocund spring.

How gladly would my soul forego
All that arithmeticians know,
Or stiff grammarians quaintly teach,
Or all that industry can reach,
To taste each morn of all the joys
That with the laughing sun arise;
And unconstrain'd to rove along
The bushy brakes and glens among;
And woo the muse's gentle power,
In unfrequented rural bower.
But, ah! such heav'n-approaching joys
Will never greet my longing eyes;
Still will they cheat in vision fine,
Yet never but in fancy shine.

Oh, that I were the little wren,
That shrilly chirps from yonder glen!
Oh, far away I then would rove,
To some secluded bushy grove;
There hop and sing with careless glee,
Hop and sing at liberty;
And till death should stop my lays,
Far from men would spend my days.

About this time his mother was induced, by the advice of several friends, to open a Ladies' Boarding and Day School, in Nottingham, her eldest daughter having previously been a teacher in one for some time.[71] In this she succeeded beyond her most sanguine expectations, and Henry's home comforts were thus materially increased, tho' it was still out of the power of his family to give him that education, and direction in life, which his talents deserved and required.

It was now determined to breed him up to the hosiery trade, the staple manufacture of his native place, and at the age of fourteen he was placed in a stocking-loom, with the view, at some future period, of getting a situation in a hosier's warehouse.

During the time that he was thus employed, he might be said to be truly unhappy; he went to his work with evident reluctance, and could not refrain from sometimes hinting his extreme aversion to it; but the circumstances of his family obliged them to turn a deaf ear.[1] His mother, however, secretly felt that he was worthy of bet-

---

1 [Southey's note:] His temper and tone of mind at this period, when he was in his fourteenth year, are displayed in this extract, from an address to Contemplation.

> Thee do I own, the prompter of my joys,
> The soother of my cares, inspiring peace;
> And I will ne'er forsake thee.—Men may rave,
> And blame and censure me, that I don't tie
> My ev'ry thought down to the desk, and spend
> The morning of my life in adding figures
> With accurate monotony; that so
> The good things of the world may be my lot,
> And I might taste the blessedness of wealth:
> But, Oh! I was not made for money getting;
> For me no much respected plum awaits,
> Nor civic honour, envied—For as still
> I tried to cast with school dexterity
> The interesting sums, my vagrant thoughts
> Would quick revert to many a woodland haunt,
> Which fond remembrance cherish'd, and the pen
> Dropt from my senseless fingers as I picturd,
> In my minds eye, how on the shores of Trent
> I erewhile wander'd with my early friends
> In social intercourse. And then I'd think
> How contrary pursuits had thrown us wide,
> One from the other, scatter'd o'er the globe;
> They were set down with sober steadiness,
> Each to his occupation. I alone,
> A wayward youth, misled by Fancy's vagaries,
> Remain'd unsettled, insecure, and veering
> With ev'ry wind to ev'ry point o' th compass.
> Yes, in the Counting House I could indulge
> In fits of close abstraction;—yea, amid
> The busy bustling crouds could meditate,
> And send my thoughts ten thousand leagues away
> Beyond the Atlantic, resting on my friend.
> Aye, Contemplation, ev'n in earliest youth
> I woo'd thy heavenly influence! I would walk
> A weary way when all my toils were done,
> To lay myself at night in some lone wood,
> And hear the sweet song of the nightingale.
> Oh, those were times of happiness, and still
> To memory doubly dear; for growing years
> Had not then taught me man was made to mourn;
> And a short hour of solitary pleasure,
> Stolen from sleep, was ample recompence
> For all the hateful bustles of the day.

ter things; to her he spoke more openly; he could not bear, he said, the thought of spending seven years of his life in shining and folding up stockings; he wanted *something to occupy his brain*, and he should be wretched if he continued longer at this trade, or indeed in any thing except one of the learned professions. These frequent complaints, after a year's application, or rather misapplication (as his brother says) at the loom, convinced her that he had a mind destined for nobler pursuits. To one so situated, and with nothing but his own talents and exertions to depend upon, the Law seemed to be the only practicable line. His affectionate and excellent mother made every possible effort to effect his wishes, his father being very averse to the plan, and at length, after overcoming a variety of obstacles, he was fixed in the office of Messrs. Coldham and Enfield, attornies and town-clerks of Nottingham.[72] As no premium could be given with him, he was engaged to serve two years before he was articled, so that though he entered this office when he was fifteen, he was not articled till the commencement of the year 1802.

On his thus entering the law, it was recommended to him by his employers, that he should endeavour to obtain some knowledge of Latin. He had now only the little time which an attorney's office, in very extensive practice, afforded; but great things may be done in 'those hours of leisure which even the busiest may create,'[2] and to his ardent mind no obstacles were too discouraging. He received some instruction, in the first rudiments of this language, from a person who then resided at Nottingham under a feigned name, but was soon obliged to leave it, to elude the search of government, who were then seeking to secure him. Henry discovered him to be Mr. Cormick, from a print affixed to a continuation of Hume and Smollet, and published, with their histories, by Cooke. He is, I believe, the same person who wrote a life of Burke.[73] If he received any other assistance it was

---

    My op'ning mind was ductile then, and plastic,
    And soon the marks of care were worn away,
    While I was swayed by every novel impulse,
    Yielding to all the fancies of the hour.
    But it has now assum'd its character,
    Mark'd by strong lineaments, its haughty tone,
    Like the firm oak, would sooner break than bend.
    Yet still, oh Contemplation! I do love
    To indulge thy solemn musings; still the same
    With thee alone I know to melt and weep,
    In thee alone delighting. Why along
    The dusky tract of commerce should I toil,
    When with an easy competence content,
    I can alone be happy; where with thee
    I may enjoy the loveliness of nature,
    And loose the wings of Fancy!—Thus alone
    Can I partake of happiness on Earth,
    And to be happy here is man's chief end,
    For to be happy he must needs be good.

2 [Southey's note:] Turner's Preface to the History of the Anglo Saxons. [Sharon Turner, *History of the Anglo Saxons*, 4 vols (London, 1799–1805), I, preface].

very trifling; yet, in the course of ten months, he enabled himself to read Horace with tolerable facility, and had made some progress in Greek, which indeed he began first. He used to exercise himself in declining the Greek nouns and verbs, as he was going to and from the office, so valuable was time become to him. From this time he contracted a habit of employing his mind in study during his walks, which he continued to the end of his life.

He now became almost estranged from his family; even at his meals he would be reading, and his evenings were entirely devoted to intellectual improvement. He had a little room given him, which was called his study, and here his milk supper was taken up to him, for to avoid any loss of time, he refused to sup with his family, though earnestly intreated so to do, as his mother already began to dread the effects of this severe and unremitting application. The law was his first pursuit, to which his papers show he had applied himself with such industry, as to make it wonderful that he could have found time, busied as his days were, for any thing else. Greek and Latin were the next objects; at the same time he made himself a tolerable Italian scholar, and acquired some knowledge both of the Spanish and Portugueze. His medical friends say that the knowledge he had obtained of chemistry was very respectable. Astronomy and electricity were among his studies; some attention he paid to drawing, in which it is probable he would have excelled. He was passionately fond of music, and could play very pleasingly by ear on the piano-forte, composing the bass to the air he was playing; but this propensity he checked, lest it might interfere with more important objects. He had a turn for mechanics, and all the fittings up of his study were the work of his own hands.

At a very early age, indeed soon after he was taken from school, Henry was ambitious of being admitted a member of a Literary Society, then existing in Nottingham, but was objected to on account of his youth; after repeated attempts, and repeated failures, he succeeded in his wish, through the exertions of some of his friends, and was elected. In a very short time, to the great surprise of the Society, he proposed to give them a Lecture, and they, probably from curiosity, acceded to the proposal. The next evening they assembled, he lectured upon Genius, and spoke extempore for above two hours, in such a manner, that he received the unanimous thanks of the Society, and they elected this young Roscius[74] of oratory their Professor of Literature. There are certain courts at Nottingham, in which it is necessary for an attorney to plead; and he wished to qualify himself for an eloquent speaker, as well as a sound lawyer.

With the profession in which he was placed, he was well pleased, and suffered no pursuit, numerous as his pursuits were, to interfere in the slightest degree with its duties. Yet he soon began to have higher aspirations, and to cast a wistful eye toward the universities, with little hope of ever attaining their important advantages, yet probably not without some hope, however faint. There was at this time a magazine in publication, called the Monthly Preceptor,[75] which proposed prize themes for boys and girls to write upon; and which was encouraged by many schoolmasters, some of whom, for their own credit, and that of the important institutions in which they were placed, should have known better than to encourage it. But in schools, and in all practical systems of education, emulation is made the main spring, as if there were not enough of the leaven of disquietude in our natures, without inoculating it with this dilutement – this *vaccine virus* of envy. True it is that we need encouragement in youth; that though our vices spring up and thrive in shade and darkness, like poisonous fungi, our better powers require light and air; and that praise is the sunshine, without which genius will wither, fade, and die, or rather in search of which, like a plant that is debarred from it, will push forth in contortions and deformity. But such practices as that of writing for public prizes, of publicly declaiming, and of enacting plays before the neighbouring gentry, teach boys to look for applause instead of being satisfied with approbation, and foster in them that vanity which needs no such cherishing. This is administering stimulants to the heart, instead of 'feeding it with food convenient for it;'[76] and the effect of such stimulants is to dwarf the human mind, as lap-dogs are said to be stopt in their growth, by being dosed with gin. Thus *forced*, it becomes like the sapling which shoots up when it should be striking its roots far and deep, and which therefore never attains to more than a sapling's size.

To Henry, however, the opportunity of distinguishing himself, even in the Juvenile Library, was useful; if he had acted with a man's foresight, he could not have done more wisely than by aiming at every distinction within his little sphere. At the age of fifteen, he gained a silver medal for a translation from Horace; and the following year a pair of twelve inch globes, for an imaginary Tour from London to Edinburgh. He determined upon trying for this prize one evening when at tea with his family, and at supper he read to them his performance, to which seven pages were granted in the magazine, though they had limited the allowance of room to three. Shortly afterwards he won several books for exercises on different subjects. Such honours were of great importance to him; they were testimonies of his ability, which could not be suspected of partiality, and they prepared his father to regard with less reluctance that change in his views and wishes which afterwards took place.

He now became a correspondent in the Monthly Mirror,[77] a magazine which first set the example of typographical neatness in periodical publications, which has given the world a good series of portraits, and which deserves praise also on other accounts, having among its contributors some persons of extensive erudition, and acknowledged talents. Magazines are of great service to those who are learning to write; they are fishing boats, which the Buccaneers of Literature do not condescend to sink, burn, and destroy; young poets may safely try their strength in them, and that they should try their strength before the public, without danger of any shame from failure, is highly desirable. Henry's rapid improvement was now as remarkable as his unwearied industry. The pieces which had been rewarded in the Juvenile Preceptor, might have been rivalled by many boys; but what he produced a year afterwards, few men could equal. Those which appeared in the Monthly Mirror attracted some notice, and introduced him to the acquaintance of Mr. Capel Lofft, and of Mr. Hill, the proprietor of the work, a gentleman who is himself a lover of English literature, and who has probably the most copious collection of English poetry in existence.[78] Their encouragement induced him, about the close of the year 1802, to prepare a little volume of poems for the press. It was his hope that this publication might either, by the success of its sale, or the notice which it might excite, enable him to prosecute his studies at college, and fit himself for the Church. For though so far was he from feeling any dislike to his own profession, that he was even attached to it, and had indulged a hope that one day or other he should make his way to the Bar: a deafness, to which he had always been subject, and which appeared to grow progressively worse, threatened to preclude all possibility of advancement; and his opinions, which had at one time inclined to deism, had now taken a strong devotional bias.

Henry was earnestly advised to obtain, if possible, some patroness for his book, whose rank in life, and notoriety in the literary world, might afford it some protection. The days of dedications are happily well nigh at an end; but this was of importance to him, as giving his little volume consequence in the eyes of his friends and townsmen. The Countess of Derby[79] was first applied to, and the manuscript submitted to her perusal. She returned it with a refusal, upon the ground that it was an invariable rule with her never to accept a compliment of the kind: but this refusal was couched in language as kind as it was complimentary, and he felt more pleasure at the kindness which it expressed, than disappointment at the failure of his application: a 2£ note was inclosed as her subscription to the work. The Margravine of Anspach[80] was also thought of. There is among his papers the draught of a letter addressed to her upon the subject, but I believe it was never sent. He was then recommended to apply to the Dutchess of Devonshire.[81] Poor Henry felt a fit repugnance at courting patronage in this way, but he felt that it was of consequence in his little world, and submitted; and the manuscript was left, with a letter, at Devonshire House, as it had been with the Countess of Derby. Some time elapsed, and no answer arrived from her Grace; and as she was known to be pestered with such applications, apprehensions began to be entertained for the safety of the papers. His brother Neville[82] (who was now settled in London), called several times; of course he never obtained an interview; the case at last became desperate, and he went with a determination not to quit the house till he had obtained them. After waiting four hours in the servant's hall, his persever-ance conquered their idle insolence, and he got possession of the manuscript. And here he, as well as his brother, sick of 'dancing attendance' upon the great, would have relinquished all thoughts of the dedication; but they were urged to make one more trial; – a letter to her Grace was procured, with which Neville obtained audi-ence, wisely leaving the manuscript at home; and the Dutchess, with her usual good nature, gave permission that the volume should be dedicated to her. Accordingly her name appeared in the title page, and a copy was transmitted to her in due form, and in its due Morocco livery, of which no notice was ever taken. Involved as she was in an endless round of miserable follies, it is probable that she never opened the book; oth-erwise her heart was good enough to have felt a pleasure in encouraging the author. Oh, what a lesson would the history of that heart hold out!

Henry sent his little volume to each of the then existing Reviews, and accompa-nied it with a letter, wherein he stated what his disadvantages had been, and what were the hopes which he proposed to himself from the publication; requesting from them that indulgence of which his productions did not stand in need, and which it might have been thought, under such circumstances, would not have been withheld from works of less promise. It may be well conceived with what anxiety he looked for their opinions, and with what feelings he read the following article in the Monthly Review for February, 1804.

The circumstances under which this little volume is offered to the public, must, in some measure, disarm criticism. We have been informed that Mr. White has scarcely attained his eighteenth year, has hitherto exerted himself in the pursuit of knowledge under the discouragements of penury and misfortune, and now hopes, by this early authorship, to obtain some assistance in the prosecution of his studies at Cambridge. He appears, indeed, to be one of those young men of talents and application who merit encouragement; and it would be gratifying to us, to hear that this publication had obtained for him a respectable patron, for we fear that the mere profit arising from the sale cannot be, in any measure, adequate to his exigencies as a student at the university. A subscription, with a statement of the particulars of the author's case, might have been calculated to have answered his purpose; but, as a book which is to 'win its way' on the sole ground of its own merit, this poem cannot be contemplated with any sanguine expectation. The author is very anxious, however, that critics should find in it something to commend, and he shall not be disappointed; we commend his exertions, and his laudable endeavours to excel; but we cannot compliment him with having learned the difficult art of writing good poetry.

Such lines as these will sufficiently prove our assertion:

'Here would I run, a vis'onary *Boy*,
When the hoarse thunder shook the vaulted *Sky;*
And, fancy led, beheld the Almighty's form,
Sternly *careering* in the eddying storm.'

If Mr. White should be instructed by Alma-mater, he will, doubtless, produce better sense, and better rhymes.[83]

I know not who was the writer of this precious article. It is certain that Henry could have no personal enemy; his volume fell into the hands of some dull man, who took it up in an hour of ill humour, turned over the leaves to look for faults, and finding that *Boy* and *Sky* were not orthodox rhymes, according to his wise creed of criticism, sat down to blast the hopes of a boy, who had confessed to him all his hopes and all his difficulties, and thrown himself upon his mercy. With such a letter before him, (by mere accident I saw that which had been sent to the Critical Review),[84] even though the poems had been bad, a good man would not have said so; he would have avoided censure if he had found it impossible to bestow praise.[85] But that the reader may perceive the wicked injustice, as well as the cruelty of this reviewal, a few specimens of the volume, thus contemptuously condemned because *Boy and Sky* are used as rhymes in it, shall be inserted in this place.

TO THE HERB ROSEMARY.[3]

1.

Sweet scented flower! who art wont to bloom
On January's front severe:
And o'er the wintery desert drear
To waft thy waste perfume!
Come, thou shalt form my nosegay now,
And I will bind thee round my brow,
And as I twine the mournful wreath,
I'll weave a melancholy song,
And sweet the strain shall be, and long,
The melody of death.

2.

Come, funeral flow'r! who lov'st to dwell
With the pale corse in lonely tomb,
And throw across the desert gloom
A sweet decaying smell.
Come press my lips, and lie with me
Beneath the lowly Alder tree,
And we will sleep a pleasant sleep,
And not a care shall dare intrude
To break the marble solitude,
So peaceful, and so deep.

3.

And hark! the wind-god as he flies,
Moans hollow in the Forest-trees,
And sailing on the gusty breeze
Mysterious music dies.
Sweet flower, that requiem wild is mine,
It warns me to the lonely shrine,
The cold turf altar of the dead;
My grave shall be in yon lone spot,
Where as I lie, by all forgot,
A dying fragrance thou wilt o'er my ashes shed.

---

3 [Southey's note:] The Rosemary buds in January – it is the flower commonly put in the coffins of the dead.

TO THE MORNING.

Written during Illness.

Beams of the day-break faint! I hail
Your dubious hues, as on the robe
Of night, which wraps the slumbering globe,
I mark your traces pale.
Tired with the taper's sickly light,
And with the wearying, numbered night,
I hail the streaks of morn divine:
And lo! they break between the dewy wreathes
That round my rural casement twine;
The fresh gale o'er the green lawn breathes,
It fans my feverish brow, – it calms the mental strife,
And cheerily re-illumes the lambent flame of life,

The Lark has her gay song begun,
She leaves her grassy nest,
And soars 'till the *unrisen sun*
Gleams on her speckled breast.
Now, let me leave my restless bed,
And o'er the spangled uplands tread.
Now thro' the custom'd wood-walk wend;
By many a green lane lies my way,
Where high o'er head the wild-briers bend,
'Till on the Mountain's summit grey,
I sit me down, and mark the glorious dawn of day.

Oh Heaven! the soft refreshing gale
It breathes into my breast,
My sunk eye gleams, my cheek so pale
Is with new colours drest,
Blythe Health! thou soul of life and ease!
Come thou too, on the balmy breeze,
Invigorate my frame:
I'll join, with thee, the buskind chace,
With thee the distant clime will trace,
Beyond those clouds of flame.

Above, below, what charms unfold
In all the varied view;
Before me all is burnish'd gold,
Behind the twilight's hue.

The mists which on old Night await,
Far to the West, they hold their state,
They shun the clear, blue face of Morn;
Along the fine cerulean sky
The fleecy clouds successive fly,
While bright prismatic beams their shadowy folds adorn.

And hark! the Thatcher has begun
His whistle on the eaves,
And oft the Hedger's Bill is heard
Among the rustling leaves.
The slow team creaks upon the road,
The noisy whip resounds,
The driver's voice, his carol blythe,
The Mower's stroke, his whetting scythe,
Mix with the morning's sounds.

Who would not rather take his seat,
Beneath these clumps of trees,
The early dawn of day to greet,
And catch the healthy breeze,
Than on the silken couch of sloth,
Luxurious to lie;
Who would not from life's dreary waste,
Snatch when he could, with eager haste,
An interval of joy!

To him, who simply thus recounts
The morning's pleasures o'er,
Fate dooms, ere long, the scene must close
To ope on him no more.
Yet Morning! unrepining still
He'll greet thy beams awhile,
And, surely thou, when o'er his grave
Solemn the whisp'ring willows wave,
Wilt sweetly on him smile.
And the pale Glow-worm's pensive light,
Will guide his ghostly walks in the drear moonless night.

An author is proof against reviewing, when, like myself, he has been reviewed above seventy times; but the opinion of a reviewer upon his first publication, has more effect, both upon his feelings and his success, than it ought to have, or would have, if the mystery of the *ungentle craft* were more generally understood. Henry wrote to the Editor, to complain of the cruelty with which he had been treated. This remonstrance produced the following answer in the next month.

Monthly Review, March, 1804.[86]

ADDRESS TO CORRESPONDENTS. In the course of our long critical labours, we have necessarily been forced to encounter the resentment, or withstand the lamentations of many disappointed authors: but we have seldom, if ever, been more affected than by a letter from Mr. White of Nottingham, complaining of the tendency of our strictures on his poem of Clifton Grove, in our last number. His expostulation is written with a warmth of feeling in which we truly sympathize, and which shall readily excuse, with us, some expressions of irritation: but Mr. White must receive our most serious declaration, that we did 'judge of the book by the book itself;' excepting only, that from his former letter, we were desirous of mitigating the pain of that decision which our public duty required us to pronounce. We spoke with the utmost sincerity, when we stated our wishes for patronage to an unfriended man of talents, for talents Mr. White certainly possesses, and we repeat those wishes with equal cordiality. Let him still trust, that, like Mr. Giffard, (see Preface to his Translation of Juvenal), some Mr. Cookesley may yet appear, to foster a capacity which endeavours to escape from its present confined sphere of action;[87] and let the opulent inhabitants of Nottingham reflect, that some portion of that wealth which they have worthily acquired by the habits of industry, will be laudably applied in assisting the efforts of mind.

Henry was not aware that reviewers are infallible. His letter seems to have been answered by a different writer; the answer has none of the common-place and vulgar insolence of the criticism; but to have made any concession would have been admitting that a review can do wrong, and thus violating the fundamental principle of its constitution.

The poems which had been thus condemned, appeared to me to discover strong marks of genius. I had shewn them to two of my friends, than whom no persons living better understand what poetry is, nor have given better proofs of it; and their opinion coincided with my own. I was fully convinced of the injustice of this criticism, and having accidentally seen the letter which he had written to the reviewers, understood the whole cruelty of their injustice. In consequence of this I wrote to Henry, to encourage him: told him that though I was well aware how imprudent it was in young poets to publish their productions, his circumstances seemed to render that expedient, from which it would otherwise be right to dissuade him, advised him therefore, if he had no better prospects, to print a larger volume by subscription, and offered to do what little was in my power to serve him in the business. To this he replied in the following letter:

I dare not say all I feel respecting your opinion of my little volume. The extreme acrimony with which the Monthly Review (of all others the most important), treated me, threw me into a state of stupefaction; I regarded all that had passed as a dream; and thought I had been deluding myself into an idea of possessing poetic Genius, when in fact I had only the longing, without the *afflatus.* I mustered resolution enough, however, to write spiritedly to them: their answer, in the ensuing number, was a tacit acknowledgment that they had been somewhat too unsparing in their correction. It was a poor attempt to salve over a wound wantonly, and most ungenerously inflicted. Still I was damped, because I knew the work was very respectable, and therefore could not, I concluded, give a criticism *grossly* deficient in equity – the more especially, as I knew of no sort of inducement to extraordinary severity. Your letter, however, has revived me, and I do again venture to hope that I may still produce something which will survive me.

With regard to your advice and offers of assistance, I will not attempt, because I am unable to thank you for them. To-morrow morning I depart for Cambridge, and I have considerable hopes that, as I do not enter into the university with any sinister or interested views, but sincerely desire to perform the duties of an affectionate and vigilant pastor, and become more useful to mankind, I therefore have hopes, I say, that I shall find means of support *in the University*. If I do not, I shall certainly act in pursuance of your recommendations: and shall, without hesitation, avail myself of your offers of service, and of your directions.

In a short time, this will be determined; and when it is, I shall take the liberty of writing to you at Keswick, to make you acquainted with the result.

I have only one objection to publishing by subscription, and I confess it has weight with me. It is, that in this step, I shall seem to be acting upon the advice, so unfeelingly and contumeliously given by the Monthly Reviewers, who say what is equal to this – that had I gotten a subscription for my poems, before their merit was known, I might have succeeded: provided, it seems, I had made a *particular statement of my case;* like a beggar, who stands with his hat in one hand, and a full account of his cruel treatment on the coast of Barbary, in the other, and so gives you his penny sheet for your sixpence, by way of half-purchase, half-charity.

I have materials for another volume, but they were written principally while Clifton Grove was in the press, or soon after, and do not now at all satisfy me. Indeed, of late, I have been obliged to desist, almost entirely, from converse with the dames of Helicon. The drudgery of an attorney's office, and the necessity of preparing myself, in case I should succeed in getting to College, in what little leisure I could boast, left no room for the flights of the imagination.

I have stated that his opinions were, at one time, inclining towards deism; it need not be said on what slight grounds the opinions of a youth must needs be founded: while they are confined to matters of speculation, they indicate, whatever their eccentricities, only an active mind; and it is only when a propensity is manifested to such principles as give a sanction to immorality, that they show something wrong at heart. One little poem of Henry's remains, which was written in this unsettled state of mind. It exhibits much of his character, and can excite no feelings towards him, but such as are favourable.

MY OWN CHARACTER

Addressed (during illness) to a Lady

Dear Fanny, I mean, now I'm laid on the shelf,
To give you a sketch-aye, a sketch of myself.
'Tis a pitiful subject, I frankly confess,
And one it would puzzle a painter to dress;
But however, here goes, and as sure as a gun,
I'll tell all my faults like a penitent nun;
For I know, for my Fanny, before I address her,
She wont be a cynical father confessor.
Come, come, 'twill not do! put that curling brow down,
You can't, for the soul of you, learn how to frown.

Well, first I premise, its my honest conviction,
That my breast is a chaos of all contradiction;
Religious – Deistic – now loyal and warm;
Then a dagger-drawn Democrat hot for reform;
This moment a fop – *that*, sententious as Titus;
Democritus now, and anon Heraclitus;
Now laughing and pleas'd, like a child with a rattle;
Then vex'd to the soul with impertinent tattle;
Now moody and sad, now unthinking and gay,
To all points of the compass I veer in a day.

I'm proud and disdainful to Fortune's gay child,
But to poverty's offspring submissive and mild;
As rude as a Boor, and as rough in dispute;
Then as for politeness – oh! Dear – I'm a brute!
I shew no respect where I never can feel it;
And as for contempt, take no pains to conceal it.
And so in the suite, by these laudable ends,
I've a great many foes, and a very few friends.

And yet, my dear Fanny, there are who can feel
That this proud heart of mine is not fashion'd of steel.
It can love, (can it not?) – it can hate, I am sure;
And its friendly enough, tho' in friends it be poor.
For itself tho' it bleed not, for others it bleeds;
If it have not *ripe* virtues, I'm sure it's the *seeds*;
And tho' far from faultless, or even so-so,
I think it may pass, as our worldly things go.

Well, I've told you my frailties without any gloss;
Then as to my virtues, I'm quite at a loss!

I think I'm devout, and yet I can't say,
But in process of time I may get the wrong way.
I'm a *general lover*, if that's commendation,
And yet can't withstand, *you know whose* fascination,
But I find that amidst all my tricks and devices,
In fishing for virtues, I'm pulling up vices;
So as for the *good*, why if I possess it,
I am not yet learned enough to express it.

You yourself must examine the lovelier side,
And after your every art you have tried,
Whatever my faults, I may venture to say
Hypocrisy never will come in your way.
I am upright, I hope; I am downright, I'm clear;
And I think my worst foe must allow I'm sincere,
And if ever sincerity glow'd in my breast,
'Tis now when I swear ——————— * *

About this time Mr. Pigott,[88] the curate of St. Mary's, Nottingham, hearing what was the bent of his religious opinions, sent him, by a friend, Scott's Force of Truth,[89] and requested him to peruse it attentively, which he promised to do. Having looked at the book, he told the person who brought it to him, that he could soon write an answer to it; but about a fortnight afterwards, when this friend enquired how far he had proceeded in his answer to Mr. Scott, Henry's reply was in a very different tone and temper. He said, that to answer that book was out of his power, and out of any man's, for it was founded upon eternal truth; that it had convinced him of his error; and that so thoroughly was he impressed with a sense of the importance of his maker's favour, that he would willingly give up all acquisitions of knowledge, and all hopes of fame, and live in a wilderness, unknown, till death, so he could insure an inheritance in heaven.

A new pursuit was thus opened to him, and he engaged in it with his wonted ardour. 'It was a constant feature in his mind,' says Mr. Pigott, 'to persevere in the pursuit of what he deemed noble and important. Religion, in which he now appeared to himself not yet to have taken a step, engaged all his anxiety, as of all concerns the most important. He could not rest satisfied till he had formed his principles upon the basis of christianity, and till he had begun in earnest to think and act agreeably to its pure and heavenly precepts. His mind loved to make distant excursions into the future and remote consequences of things. He no longer limited his views to the narrow confines of earthly existence; he was not happy till he had learnt, to rest and expatiate in a world to come. What he said to me when we became intimate, is worthy of observation: that, he said, which first made him dissatisfied with the creed he had adopted, and the standard of practice which he had set up for himself, was the *purity of mind* which he perceived was every where inculcated in the Holy Scriptures, and required of every one who would become a successful candidate for future blessedness. He had supposed that morality of conduct was all the purity required; but when he observed that purity of the very *thoughts* and *intentions* of the soul also, was requisite, he was convinced of his deficiencies, and could find no comfort to his penitence, but in the atonement made for human frailty by the Redeemer of mankind, and no strength adequate to his weakness, and sufficient for resisting evil, but the aid of God's spirit, promised to those who seek them from above in the sincerity of earnest prayer.'

From the moment when he had fully contracted these opinions, he was resolved upon devoting his life to the promulgation of them; and therefore to leave the Law, and, if possible, place himself at one of the Universities. Every argument was used by his friends to dissuade him from his purpose, but to no effect; his mind was unalterably fixed; and great and numerous as the obstacles were, he was determined to surmount them all. He had now served the better half of the term for which he was articled; his entrance and continuance in the profession had been a great expence to his family; and to give up this lucrative profession, in the study of which he had advanced so far, and situated as he was, for one wherein there was so little prospect of his obtaining even a decent competency, appeared to them the height of folly or of madness. This determination cost his poor mother many tears, but determined he was, and that by the best and purest motives. Without ambition he could not have existed, but his ambition now was to be eminently useful in the ministry.

It was Henry's fortune, through his short life, as he was worthy of the kindest treatment, always to find it. His employers, Mr. Coldham and Mr. Enfield, listened with a friendly ear to his plans, and agreed to give up the remainder of his time, though it was now become very valuable to them, as soon as they should think his prospects of getting through the University were such as he might reasonably trust to; but till then, they felt themselves bound, for his own sake, to detain him. Mr. Piggott, and Mr. Dashwood,[90] another clergyman, who at that time resided in Nottingham, exerted themselves in his favour: he had a friend at Queen's College, Cambridge,[91] who mentioned him to one of the Fellows of St. John's,[92] and that gentleman, on the representations made to him of Henry's talents and piety, spared no effort to obtain for him an adequate support.

As soon as these hopes were held out to him, his employers gave him a month's leave of absence, for the benefit of uninterrupted study, and of change of air, which his health now began to require. Instead of going to the sea coast, as was expected, he chose for his retreat the village of Wilford, which is situated on the banks of the Trent, and at the foot of Clifton Woods.

These woods had ever been his favourite place of resort, and were the subject of the longest poem in his little volume, from which, indeed, the volume was named. He delighted to point out to his more intimate friends the scenery of this poem; the islet to which he had often forded when the river was not knee deep; and the little boat wherein he had sate for hours, and sometimes all day long, reading or writing, or dreaming with his eyes open. He had sometimes wandered in these woods till night far advanced, and used to speak with pleasure of having once been overtaken there by a thunder storm, at midnight, and watching the lightning over the river and the vale towards the town.

In this village his mother procured lodgings for him, and his place of retreat was kept secret, except from his nearest friends. Soon after the expiration of the month, intelligence arrived that the plans which had been formed in his behalf had entirely failed. He went immediately to his mother: 'all my hopes,' said he, 'of getting to the University are now blasted; in preparing myself for it, I have lost time in my profession; I have much ground to get up, and as I am determined not to be a *mediocre* attorney, I must endeavour to recover what I have lost.' The consequence was, that he applied himself more severely than ever to his studies. He now allowed himself no time for relaxation, little for his meals, and scarcely any for sleep. He would read till one, two, three o'clock in the morning; then throw himself on the bed, and rise again to his work at five, at the call of a *Larum*, which he had fixed to a Dutch clock in his chamber. Many, nights he never laid down at all. It was in vain that his mother used every possible means to dissuade him from this destructive application. In this respect, and in this only one was Henry undutiful, and neither commands, nor tears, nor intreaties could check his desperate and deadly ardour. At one time she went every night into his room, to put out his candle; as soon as he heard her coming up stairs, he used to hide it in a cupboard, throw himself into bed, and affect sleep while she was in the room; then when all was quiet, rise again and pursue his baneful studies.

'The night,' says Henry, in one of his letters, 'has been every thing to me; and did the world know how I have been indebted to the hours of repose, they would not wonder that night-images are, as they judge, so ridiculously predominant in my verses.' During some of these midnight hours he indulged himself in complaining, but in such complaints that it is wished more of them had been found among his papers.

ODE
ON DISAPPOINTMENT.

1.

Come, Disappointment, come!
Not in thy terrors clad;
Come in thy meekest, saddest guise;
Thy chastening rod but terrifies
The restless and the bad.
But I recline
Beneath thy shrine,
And round my brow resign'd, thy peaceful cypress twine.

2.

Tho' Fancy flies away
Before thy hollow tread,
Yet Meditation in her cell,

Hears, with faint eye, the ling'ring knell,
That tells her hopes are dead;
And tho' the tear
By chance appear,
Yet she can smile and say, my all was not laid here.

3.

Come, Disappointment, come!
Tho' from hope's summit hurl'd,
Still, rigid Nurse, thou art forgiven,
For thou severe wert sent from heaven,
To wean me from the world;
To turn my eye
From vanity,
And point to scenes of bliss that never, never die.

4.

What is this passing scene?
A peevish April day!
A little sun – a little rain,
And then night sweeps along the plain,
And all things fade away.
Man (soon discuss'd)
Yields up his trust,
And all his hopes and fears lie with him in the dust.

5.

Oh, what is Beauty's power?
It flourishes and dies;
Will the cold earth its silence break,
To tell how soft, how smooth a cheek,
Beneath its surface lies?
Mute, mute is all
O'er beauty's fall,
Her praise resounds no more when mantled in her pall.

6.

The most belov'd on earth,
Not long survives to-day;
So music past is obsolete,
And yet 'twas sweet, 'twas passing sweet,
But now 'tis gone away.

Thus does the shade,
In memory fade,
When in forsaken tomb the form belov'd is laid.

7.

Then since this world is vain,
And volatile and fleet,
Why should I lay up earthly joys,
Where rust corrupts and moth destroys,
And cares and sorrows eat!
Why fly from ill,
With anxious skill,
When soon this hand will freeze, this throbbing heart be still.

8.

Come, Disappointment, come!
Thou art not stern to me;`
Sad Monitress! I own thy sway,
A votary sad in early day,
I bend my knee to thee.
From sun to sun,
My race will run,
I only bow and say, My God, thy will be done!

On another paper are a few lines, written probably in the freshness of his disappointment.

I dream no more – the vision flies away,
And Disappointment * * * *
There fell my hopes – I lost my all in this,
My cherish'd all of visionary bliss.
Now hope farewell, farewell all joys below;
Now welcome sorrow, and now welcome woe.
Plunge me in glooms * * * *

His health soon sunk under these habits; he became pale and thin, and at length had a sharp fit of sickness. On his recovery, he wrote the following lines in the church-yard of his favourite village:

LINES WRITTEN IN WILFORD CHURCH-YARD,

On recovery from Sickness.

Here would I wish to sleep. This is the spot
Which I have long mark'd out to lay my bones in;

SOUTHEY'S LIFE OF KIRKE WHITE

Tir'd out and wearied with the riotous world,
Beneath this yew I would be sepulchred.
It is a lovely spot! The sultry sun,
From his meridian height, endeavours vainly
To pierce the shadowy foliage, while the zephyr
Comes wafting gently o'er the rippling Trent,
And plays about my wan cheek. 'Tis a nook
Most pleasant; – Such a one perchance did Gray
Frequent, as with the vagrant muse he wanton'd.
Come, I will sit me down and meditate,
For I am wearied with my summers walk;
And here I may repose in silent ease;
And thus, perchance, when life's sad journey's o'er,
My harass'd soul, in this same spot, may find
The haven of its rest – beneath this sod
Perchance may sleep it sweetly, sound as death.
I would not have my corpse cemented down
With brick and stone, defrauding the poor earth worm
Of its predestined dues; no, I would lie
Beneath a little hillock, grass o'ergrown,
Swath'd down with oziers, just as sleep the cotters.
Yet may not *undistinguish'd* be my grave,
But there at eve may some congenial soul
Duly resort, and shed a pious tear,
The good man's benizon – no more I ask.
And oh! (if heavenly beings may look down
From where, with cherubim inspir'd, they sit,
Upon this little dim-discover'd spot,
The earth), then will I cast a glance *below*
On him who thus my ashes shall embalm;
And I will weep too, and will bless the wanderer,
Wishing he may not long be doom'd to pine
In this low-thoughted world of darkling woe,
But that, ere long, he reach his kindred skies.
Yet, 'twas a silly thought – as if the body,
Mouldering beneath the surface of the earth,
Could taste the sweets of summer scenery,
And feel the freshness of the balmy breeze!
Yet nature speaks within the human bosom,
And, spite of reason, bids it look beyond
His narrow verge of being, and provide
A decent residence for its clayey shell,
Endeard to it by time. And who would lay
His body in the city burial place,
To be thrown up again by some rude Sexton,

And yield its narrow house another tenant,
Ere the moist flesh had mingled with the dust;
Ere the tenacious hair had left the scalp,
Expos'd to insult lewd, and wantonness!
No, I will lay me in the *village* ground;
There are the dead respected. The poor hind,
Unletter'd as he is, would scorn to invade
The silent resting place of death. I've seen
The labourer, returning from his toil,
Here stay his steps, and call his children round,
And slowly spell the rudely sculptur'd rhymes,
And, in his rustic manner, moralize.
I've mark'd with what a silent awe he'd spoken,
With head uncover'd, his respectful manner,
And all the honours which he paid the grave,
And thought on cities, where ev'n cemeteries,
Bestrew'd with all the emblems of mortality,
Are not protected from the drunken insolence
Of wassailers profane, and wanton havock.
Grant Heav'n, that here my pilgrimage may close!
Yet, if this be deny'd, where'er my bones
May lie – or in the city's crouded bounds,
Or scatter'd wide o'er the huge sweep of waters,
Or left a prey on some deserted shore
To the rapacious cormorant, yet still,
(For why should sober reason cast away
A thought which soothes the soul) – yet still my spirit.
Shall wing its way to these my native regions,
And hover o'er this spot. Oh, then I'll think
Of times when I was seated 'neath this yew
In solemn rumination; and will smile
With joy that I have got my long'd release.

His friends are of opinion that he never thoroughly recovered from the shock which his constitution had sustained. Many of his poems indicate that he thought himself in danger of consumption; he was not aware that he was generating or fostering in himself another disease, little less dreadful, and which threatens intellect as well as life. At this time youth was in his favour, and his hopes, which were now again renewed, produced perhaps a better effect than medicine. Mr. Dashwood obtained for him an introduction to Mr. Simeon, of King's College,[93] and with this he was induced to go to Cambridge. Mr. Simeon, from the recommendation which he received, and from the conversation he had with him, promised to procure for him a Sizarship at St. John's, and to supply him with 30l. annually, of which, it afterwards appeared, 20l. were from Mr. Wilberforce,[94] and the remainder from himself. His brother Neville promised twenty, and his mother, it was hoped, would be able to allow fifteen or twenty more. With this, it was thought, he could go through College. If this prospect had not been opened to him, he would probably have turned his thoughts towards the orthodox dissenters.

On his return to Nottingham, the Rev. – Robinson,[95] of Leicester, and some other friends, advised him to apply to the Elland Society[96] for assistance, conceiving that it would be less oppressive to his feelings to be dependant on a Society, instituted for the express purpose of training up such young men as himself, (that is, such in circumstances and opinions) for the ministry, than on the bounty of an individual. In consequence of this advice, he went to Elland, at the next meeting of the Society, a stranger there, and without one friend among the members. He was examined, for several hours, by about five and twenty clergymen, as to his religious views and sentiments, his theological knowledge, and his classical attainments. In the course of the enquiry, it appeared that he had published a volume of poems; their questions now began to be very unpleasantly inquisitive concerning the nature of these poems, and he was assailed by queries from all quarters. It was well for Henry that they did not think of referring to the Monthly Review for authority. My letter to him happened to be in his pocket; he luckily recollected this, and produced it as a testimony in his favour. They did me the honour to say that it was quite sufficient, and pursued this part of their inquiry no farther. Before he left Elland, he was given to understand that they were well satisfied with his theological knowledge; that they thought his classical proficiency prodigious for his age, and that they had placed him on their books. He returned little pleased with his journey. His friends had been mistaken; the bounty of an individual calls forth a sense of kindness, as well as of dependance: that of a Society has the virtue of charity perhaps, but it wants the grace. He now wrote to Mr. Simeon, stating what he had done, and that the beneficence of his unknown friends was no longer necessary: but that gentleman obliged him to decline the assistance of the Society, which he very willingly did.

This being finally arranged, he quitted his employers in October, 1804. How much he had conducted himself to their satisfaction, will appear by this testimony of Mr. Enfield, to his diligence and uniform worth. 'I have great pleasure,' says this gentleman, 'in paying the tribute to his memory, of expressing the knowledge which was afforded me, during the period of his connection with Mr. Coldham and myself, of his diligent application, his ardour for study, and his virtues and amiable disposition. He very soon discovered an unusual aptness in comprehending the routine of business, and great ability and rapidity in the execution of every thing which was entrusted to him. His diligence and punctual attention were unremitted, and his services became extremely valuable a considerable time before he left us. He seemed to me to have no relish for the ordinary pleasures and dissipations of young men; his mind was perpetually employed, either in the business of his profession, or in private study. With his fondness for literature, we were well acquainted, but had no reason to offer any check to it, for he never permitted the indulgence of his literary pursuits to interfere with the engagements of business.

81

The difficulty of hearing, under which be laboured, was distressing to him in the practice of his profession, and was, I think, an inducement, in cooperation with his other inclinations, for his resolving to relinquish the law. I can, with truth, assert that his determination was matter of serious regret to my partner and myself.'

Mr. Simeon had advised him to *degrade for* a year, and place himself, during that time, under some scholar. He went accordingly to the Rev. Grainger,[97] of Winteringham, in Lincolnshire, and there, notwithstanding all the intreaties of his friends, pursuing the same unrelenting course of study, a second illness was the consequence. When he was recovering, he was prevailed upon to relax, to ride on horseback, and to drink wine; these latter remedies he could not long afford, and he would not allow himself time for relaxation, when he did not feel its immediate necessity. He frequently, at this time, studied fourteen hours a day; the progress which he made in twelve months was indeed astonishing; when he went to Cambridge, he was immediately as much distinguished for his classical knowledge, as his genius; but the seeds of death were in him, and the place to which he had so long looked on with hope, served unhappily as a hot house to ripen them.[4]

During his first term, one of the University Scholarships became vacant, and Henry, young as he was in College, and almost self-taught, was advised, by those who were best able to estimate his chance of success, to offer himself as a competitor for it. He past the whole term in preparing himself for this, reading for College subjects in bed, in his walks, or, as he says, where, when, and how he could, never having a moment to spare, and often going to his tutor without having read at all. His strength sunk under this, and though he had declared himself a candidate, he was compelled to decline; but this was not the only misfortune. The general College examination came on; he was utterly unprepared to meet it, and believed that a failure here would have ruined his prospects for ever. He had only about a fortnight to read what other men had been the whole term reading. Once more he exerted himself beyond what his shattered health could bear; the disorder returned, and he went to his tutor, Mr. Catton, with tears in his eyes, and told him that he could not go into the Hall to be examined. Mr. Catton, however, thought his success here of so much importance, that he exhorted him, with all possible earnestness, to hold out the six days of the examination. Strong medicines were given him, to enable him to support it, and he was pronounced the first man of his year. But life was the price which he was to pay for such honours as this, and Henry is not the first young man to whom such honours have proved fatal. He said to his most intimate friend, almost the last time he saw him, that were he to paint a picture of Fame, crowning

---

4 [Southey's note:] During his residence in my family, says Mr. Grainger, his conduct was highly becoming, and suitable to a Christian profession. He was mild and inoffensive, modest, unassuming, and affectionate. He attended, with great cheerfulness, a Sunday School, which I was endeavouring to establish in the village, and was at considerable pains in the instruction of the children; and I have repeatedly observed, that he was most pleased, and most edified, with such of my sermons and addresses to my people, as were most close, plain, and familiar. When we parted, we parted with mutual regret, and by us his name will long be remembered with affection and delight.

a distinguished under-graduate, after the Senate-house examination, he would represent her as concealing a Death's-head under a mask of beauty.

When this was over he went to London; London was a new scene of excitement, and what his mind required was tranquillity and rest. Before he left College he had become anxious concerning his expences, fearing that they exceeded his means. Mr. Catton perceived this, and twice called him to his rooms to assure him of every necessary support, and every encouragement, and to give him every hope. This kindness relieved his spirits of a heavy weight, and on his return he relaxed a little from his studies, but it was only a little. I found among his papers the day thus planned out: – 'Rise at half past five. Devotions and walk till seven. Chapel and breakfast till eight. Study and Lectures till one. Four and a half clear reading. Walk, &c. and dinner, and Woollaston, and chapel, to six. Six to nine, reading – three hours. Nine to ten, devotions. Bed at ten.'

Among his latest writings are these resolutions:

> I will never be in bed after six. I will not drink tea out above once a week, excepting on Sundays, unless there appear some good reason for so doing. I will never pass a day without reading some portion of the Scriptures. I will labour diligently in my mathematical studies, because I half suspect myself of a dislike to them. I will walk two hours a day, upon the average of every week.

Sit mihi gratia addita ad hæc facienda.[98]

About this time, judging by the hand writing, he wrote down the following admonitory sentences, which, as the paper on which they are written is folded into the shape of a very small book, it is probable he carried about with him as a manual.

1   Death and judgment are near at hand.
2   Though thy bodily part be now in health and ease, the dews of death will soon sit upon thy forehead.
3   That which seems so sweet and desirable to thee now, will, if yielded to, become bitterness of soul to thee all thy life after.
4   When the waters are come over thy soul, and when in the midst of much bodily anguish, thou distinguishes the dim shores of Eternity before thee, what wouldest thou not give to be lighter by this one sin!
5   God has long withheld his arm; what if his forbearance be now at an end? Canst thou not contemplate these things with the eyes of Death? Art thou not a dying man, dying every day, every hour?
6   Is it not a fearful thing to shrink from the summons when it comes? To turn with horror and despair from the future being? Think what strains of joy and tranquillity fall on the ear of the saint who is just swooning into the arms of his Redeemer; what fearful shapes, and dreadful images of a disturbed conscience, surround the sinner's

bed, when the last twig which he grasped fails him, and the gulph yawns to receive him.

7   Oh, my soul, if thou art yet ignorant of the enormity of sin, turn thine eyes to the man who is bleeding to death on the cross! see how the blood, from his pierced bands, trickles down his arms, and the more copious streams from his feet run on the accursed tree, and stain the grass with purple! Behold his features, though scarcely animated with a few remaining sparks of life, yet how full of love, pity, and tranquillity! A tear is trickling down his cheek, and his lip quivers. He is praying for his murderers! O, my soul! it is thy Redeemer – it is thy God! And this too for Sin – for Sin? and wilt thou ever again submit to its yoke?

8   Remember that the grace of the Holy Spirit of God is ready to save thee from transgression. It is always at hand: thou canst not sin without wilfully rejecting its aid.

9   And is there real pleasure in Sin? Thou knowest there is not. But there is pleasure . . . pure and exquisite pleasure, in holiness. The Holy Ghost can make the paths of religion and virtue, hard as they seem, and thorny, ways of pleasantness and peace, where though there be thorns, yet are there also roses, and where all the wounds which we suffer in the flesh, from the hardness of the journey, are so healed by the balm of the spirit that they rather give joy than pain.

The exercise which Henry took was no relaxation, he still continued the habit of studying while he walked; and in this manner, while he was at Cambridge, committed to memory a whole tragedy of Euripides. Twice he distinguished himself in the following year, being again pronounced first at the great College examination, and also one of the three best theme writers, between whom the examiners could not decide. The College offered him, at their expence, a private tutor in mathematics during the long vacation; and Mr. Catton, by procuring for him exhibitions to the amount of 66l. per annum, enabled him to give up the pecuniary assistance which he had received from Mr. Wilberforce and Mr. Simeon. Never, perhaps, had any young man, in so short a time, excited such expectations; every University honour was thought to be within his reach; he was set down as a medallist, and expected to take a senior wrangler's degree: but these expectations were poison to him; they goaded him to fresh exertions when his strength was spent. His situation became truly miserable; to his brother, and to his mother, he wrote always that he had relaxed in his studies, and that he was better; always holding out to them his hopes, and his good fortune; but to the most intimate of his friends, (Mr. Maddock),[99] his letters told a different tale: to him he complained of dreadful palpitations – of nights of sleeplessness and horror, and of spirits depressed to the very depth of wretchedness, so that he went from one acquaintance to another, imploring society, even as a starving beggar intreats for food. During the course of this summer, it was expected that the Mastership of the Free-School at Nottingham would shortly become vacant. A relation of his family was at that time mayor of the town; he suggested to them what an advantageous situation it would be for Henry, and offered to secure for him the necessary interest. But though the salary and emoluments are estimated at from 4 to 600l. per annum, Henry declined the offer; because, had be accepted it, it would have frustrated his intentions with respect to the ministry. This was certainly no common act of forbearance in one so situated as to fortune, especially as the hope which he had most at heart, was that of being enabled to assist his family, and in some degree requite the care and anxiety of his father and mother, by making them comfortable in their declining years.

The indulgence shown him by his College, in providing him a tutor during the long vacation, was peculiarly unfortunate. His only chance of life was from relaxation, and home was the only place where he would have relaxed to any purpose. Before this time he had seemed to be gaining strength; it failed as the year advanced: he went once more to London to recruit himself, – the worst place to which he could have gone: the variety of stimulating objects there hurried and agitated him, and when he returned to College, he was so completely ill, that no power of medicine could save him. His mind was worn out, and it was the opinion of his medical attendants, that if he had recovered, his intellect would have been affected. His brother Neville was just at this time to have visited him. On his first seizure, Henry found himself too ill to receive him, and wrote to say so; he added, with that anxious tenderness towards the feelings of a most affectionate family which always appeared in his letters; that he thought himself recovering; but his disorder increased so rapidly, that this letter was never sent; it was found in his pocket after his decease. One of his friends wrote to acquaint Neville with his danger: he hastened down; but Henry was delirious when he arrived. He knew him only for a few moments, the next day sunk into a state of stupor; and on Sunday, October 19th, 1806, it pleased God to remove him to a better world, and a higher state of existence.

****

The will which I had manifested to serve Henry, he had accepted as the deed, and had expressed himself upon the subject in terms which it would have humbled me to read, at any other time than when I was performing the last service to his memory. On his decease, Mr. B. Maddock addressed a letter to me, informing me of the event, as one who had professed an interest in his friend's fortunes. I enquired, in my reply, if there was any intention of publishing what he might have left, and if I could be of any assistance in the publication; this led to a correspondence with his excellent brother, and the whole of his papers were consigned into my hands, with as many of his letters as could be collected.

These papers (exclusive of the correspondence) filled a box of considerable size. Mr. Coleridge was present when I opened them, and was, as well as myself, equally affected and astonished at the proofs of industry which they displayed. Some of them had been written before his hand was formed, probably before he was thirteen. There were papers upon law, upon electricity, upon chemistry, upon the Latin and Greek languages, from their rudiments, to the higher branches of critical study, upon history, chronology, divinity, the fathers, &c. Nothing seemed to have escaped him.

His poems were numerous; among the earliest, was a sonnet addressed to myself, long before the little intercourse which had subsisted between us, had taken place. Little did he think, when it was written, on what occasion it would fall into my hands. He had begun three tragedies when very young; one was upon Boadicea, another upon Iñez de Castro:[100] the third was a fictitious subject. He had planned also a History of Nottingham. There was a letter upon the famous Nottingham election, which seemed to have been intended, either for the newspapers, or for a separate pamphlet. It was written to confute the absurd stories of the Tree of Liberty, and the Goddess of Reason; with the most minute circumstances, and a not improper feeling of indignation against so infamous a calumny; and this came with more weight from him, as his party inclinations seem to have leaned towards the side which he was opposing. This was his only finished composition in prose. Much of his time, latterly, had been devoted to the study of Greek prosody: he had begun several poems in Greek, and a translation of the Samson Agonistes. I have inspected all the existing manuscripts of Chatterton,[101] and they excited less wonder than these.

Had my knowledge of Henry terminated here, I should have hardly believed that my admiration and regret for him could have been increased; but I had yet to learn that his moral qualities, his good sense, and his whole feelings, were as admirable as his industry and genius. All his letters to his family have been communicated to me without reserve, and most of those to his friends. A selection from these are arranged in chronological order, in these volumes, which will make him his own biographer, and lay open to the world as pure, and as excellent a heart, as it ever pleased the Almighty to warm with life. Much has been suppressed, which, if Henry had been, like Chatterton, of another generation, I should willingly have published, and the world would willingly have received; but in doing honour to the dead, I have been scrupulously careful never to forget the living.

It is not possible to conceive a human being more amiable in all the relations of life. He was the confidential friend and adviser of every member of his family; this he instinctively became; and the thorough, good sense of his advice is not less remarkable than the affection with which it is always communicated. To his mother, he is as earnest in beseeching her to be careful of her health, as he is in labouring to convince her that his own complaints were abating; his letters to her are always of hopes, of consolation, and of love. To Neville he writes with the most brotherly intimacy, still, however, in that occasional tone of advice which it was his nature to assume, not from any arrogance of superiority, but from earnestness of pure affection. To his younger brother he addresses himself like the tenderest and wisest parent; and to two sisters, then too young for any other communication, he writes to direct their studies, to enquire into their progress, to encourage, and to improve them. Such letters as these are not for the public, but they to whom they are addressed will lay them to their hearts like relics, and will find in them a saving virtue, more than ever relics possessed.

With regard to his poems, the criterion for selection was not so plain; undoubtedly many have been chosen which he himself would not have published, and some few which, had he lived to have taken that rank among English poets, which would assuredly have been within his reach, I also should then have rejected among his posthumous papers. I have, however, to the best of my judgment, selected none which does not either mark the state of his mind, or its progress, or discover evident proofs of what he would have been, if it had not been the will of Heaven to remove him so soon. The reader, who feels any admiration for Henry, will take some interest in all these remains, because they are his; he who shall feel none, must have a blind heart, and therefore a blind understanding. Such poems are to be considered as making up his history. But the greater number are of such beauty, that Chatterton is the only youthful poet whom he does not leave far behind him,

While he was under Mr. Grainger, he wrote very little; and when he went to Cambridge, he was advised to stifle his poetical fire, for severer and more important studies; to lay a billet on the embers until he had taken his degree, and then he might fan it into a flame again. This advice he followed so scrupulously, that a few fragments, written chiefly upon the back of his mathematical papers, are all which he produced at the University, The greater part, therefore, of these poems, indeed nearly the whole of them, were written before he was nineteen. Wise as the advice may have been which had been given him, it is now to be regretted that he adhered to it, his latter fragments bearing all those marks of improvement which were to be expected from a mind so rapidly and continually progressive. Frequently he expresses a fear that early death would rob him of his fame; yet short as his life was, it has been long enough for him to leave works worthy of remembrance. The very circumstance of his early death gives a new interest to his memory, and thereby new force to his example. Just at that age when the painter would have wished to fix his likeness, and the lover of poetry would delight to contemplate him, in the fair morning of his virtues, the full spring blossom of his hopes, – just at that age hath death set the seal of eternity upon him, and the beautiful hath been made permanent. To the young poets who come after him, Henry will be what Chatterton was to him; and they will find in him an example of hopes, with regard to worldly fortune, as humble; and as exalted in all better things, as are enjoined equally by wisdom and religion, by the experience of man, and the word of God. And this example will be as encouraging as it is excellent. It has been too much the custom to complain that genius is neglected, and to blame the public when the public is not in fault. They who are thus lamented as the victims of genius, have been, in almost every instance, the victims of their own vices; while genius has been made, like charity, to cover a multitude of sins, and to excuse that which in reality it aggravates. In this age, and in this country, whoever deserves encouragement, is, sooner or later, sure to receive it. Of this Henry's history is an honourable proof. The particular patronage which he accepted, was given as much to his piety and religious opinions, as to his genius: but assistance was offered him from other quarters. Mr. P. Thomson, (of Boston, Lincolnshire), merely upon perusing his little volume, wrote to know how he could serve him; and there were many friends of literature who were ready to have afforded him any support which he needed, if he had not been thus provided. In the University he received every encouragement which he merited, and from Mr. Simeon, and his tutor Mr. Catton, the most fatherly kindness.

'I can venture,' says a Lady of Cambridge, in a letter to his brother, 'I can venture to say, with certainty, there was no member of the University, however high his rank or talents, who would not have been happy to have availed themselves of the opportunity of being acquainted with Mr. Henry Kirke White. I mention this to introduce a wish, which has been expressed to me so often by the senior members of the University, that I dare not decline the task they have imposed upon me; it is their hope that Mr. Southey will do as much justice to Mr. Henry White's limited wishes, to his unassuming pretensions, and to his rational and fervent piety, as to his various acquirements, his polished taste, his poetical fancy, his undeviating principles, and the excellence of his moral character; and that he will suffer it to be understood that these inestimable qualities had not been unobserved, nor would they have remained unacknowledged. It was the general observation, that he possessed genius without its eccentricities.'

Of this fervent piety, his letters, his prayers, and his hymns, will afford ample and interesting proofs. I must be permitted to say, that my own views of the religion of Christ Jesus differ essentially from the system of belief which he had adopted; but, having said this, it is, indeed, my anxious wish to do full justice to piety so fervent. It was in him a living and quickening principle of goodness, which sanctified all his hopes, and all his affections; which made him keep watch over his own heart, and enabled him to correct the few symptoms, which it ever displayed, of human imperfection.

His temper had been irritable in his younger days, but this he had long since effectually overcome: the marks of youthful confidence, which appear in his earliest letters, had also disappeared, and it was impossible for man to be more tenderly patient of the faults of others, more uniformly meek, or more unaffectedly humble. He seldom discovered any sportiveness of imagination, though he would very ably, and pleasantly, rally any one of his friends for any little peculiarity; his conversation was always sober, and to the purpose. That which is most remarkable in him, is his uniform *good sense*, a faculty perhaps less common than genius. There never existed a more dutiful son, a more affectionate brother, a warmer friend, nor a devouter christian. Of his powers of mind it is superfluous to speak; they were acknowledged wherever they were known. It would be idle too to say what hopes were entertained of him, and what he might have accomplished in literature. These volumes contain what he has left, immature buds, and blossoms shaken from the tree, and green fruit; yet will they evince what the harvest would have been, and secure for him that remembrance upon earth for which he toiled.

3

SOUTHEY'S REVIEW OF SAMUEL F. B. MORSE[102]

Amir Khan, and other Poems: the Remains of Lucretia Maria Davidson, Who Died at Plattsburgh, N. Y., August 27, 1825, Aged Sixteen Years and Eleven Months. With a Biographical Sketch, New York, 1829, *The Quarterly Review,* 41 (1829), 289–301

Lucretia Maria Davidson was born September 27, 1808, at Plattsburgh, on Lake Champlain. She was the second daughter of Dr. Oliver Davidson, and Margaret his wife. Her parents were in straitened circumstances, and it was necessary, from an early age, that much of her time should be devoted to domestic employments: for these she had no inclination, but she performed them with that alacrity which always accompanies good will; and, when her work was done, retired to enjoy those intellectual and imaginative pursuits in which her whole heart was engaged. This predilection for studious retirement she is said to have manifested at the early age of four years. Reports, and even recollections of this kind, are to be received, the one with some distrust, the other with some allowance; but when that allowance is made, the genius of this child still appears to have been as precocious as it was extraordinary. Instead of playing with her schoolmates, she generally got to some secluded place, with her little books, and with pen, ink, and paper; and the consumption which she made of paper was such as to excite the curiosity of her parents, from whom she kept secret the use to which she applied it. If any one came upon her retirement, she would conceal or hastily destroy what she was employed upon; and, instead of satisfying the enquiries of her father and mother, replied to them only by tears. The mother, at length, when searching for something in a dark and unfrequented closet, found a considerable number of little books, made of this writing-paper, and filled with rude drawings, and with strange and apparently illegible characters, which, however, were at once seen to be the child's work. Upon closer inspection, the characters were found to consist of the printed alphabet; some of the letters being formed backwards, some sideways, and there being no spaces between the words. These writings were decyphered, not without much difficulty; and it then appeared that they consisted of regular verses,

DOI: 10.4324/9781003431343-4

generally in explanation of a rude drawing, sketched on the opposite page. When she found that her treasures had been discovered, she was greatly distressed, and could not be pacified till they were restored; and as soon as they were in her possession, she took the first opportunity of secretly burning them. For it had not been in fear of discouragement or prohibition from her parents that she had concealed her childish compositions; but because there is a sensitiveness in true genius which shrinks at first, as if instinctively, from exposure. Where there is no indication of this intellectual modesty, there is but too much reason for apprehending that the moral sense to which it is akin, is wanting also.

These books having thus been destroyed, the earliest remaining specimen of her verse is an epitaph, composed in her ninth year, upon an unfledged robin, killed in the attempt at rearing it. The editor has not thought proper to insert it: such things are invaluable, as relics, to those who knew and loved the departed; but, from public curiosity it is always better that they should be withheld. When she was eleven years of age, her father took her to see the decorations of a room in which Washington's birthday was to be celebrated. Neither the novelty nor the gaiety of what she saw attracted her attention; she thought of Washington alone, whose life she had read, and for whom she entertained the proper feelings of an American; and as soon as she returned home, she took paper, sketched a funeral urn, and wrote under it a few stanzas, which were shown to her friends. Common as the talent of versifying is, any early manifestation of it will always be regarded as extraordinary by those who possess it not themselves; and these verses, though not otherwise remarkable, were deemed so surprising for a child of her age, that an aunt of hers could not believe they were original, and hinted that they might have been copied. The child wept at this suspicion, as if her heart would break; but as soon as she recovered from that fit of indignant grief, she indited a remonstrance to her aunt, in verse, which put an end to such incredulity.

Proud as her parents were of so hopeful a child, they never attempted to impede her in her endeavours to improve herself; and all the time that could be spared from her indispensable domestic avocations was given to reading. We are told that, before she was twelve years of age, she had read most of the standard English poets – a vague term, excluding, no doubt, much that is of real worth, and including more that is worth little or nothing, and yet implying a wholesome course of reading for such a mind. Much history she had also read, both sacred and profane; 'the whole of Shakspeare's, Kotzebue's,[103] and Goldsmith's[104] dramatic works; (oddly consorted names!) and many of the popular novels and romances of the day:' of the latter, she threw aside at once those which at first sight appeared worthless. As for what is called directing the taste of youthful genius, this is so much more likely (we had almost said so sure) to be injurious rather than useful, that in a case like this it is fortunate when an ardent mind is left to itself, and allowed, like the bee, to suck honey from weeds and flowers indiscriminately. The vigorous mind, like the healthy stomach, can digest and assimilate coarse food. This girl is said to have observed every thing: 'frequently she has been known to watch the storm, and the retiring clouds, and the rainbow, and the setting sun, for hours.'

SOUTHEY'S REVIEW OF *LUCRETIA DAVIDSON*

An English reader is not prepared to hear of distress arising from straitened circumstances in America – the land of promise, where there is room enough for all, and employment for every body. Yet even in that new country, man, it appears, is born not only to those ills which flesh is heir to, but to those which are entailed upon him by the institutions of society. Lucretia's mother was confined by illness to her room and bed for many months; and this child, then about twelve years old, instead of profiting under her mother's care, had in a certain degree to supply her place in the business of the family, and to attend, which she did dutifully and devotedly, to her sick bed. At this time, a gentleman who had heard much of her verses, and expressed a wish to see some of them, was so much gratified on perusing them, that he sent her a complimentary note, enclosing a bank-bill for twenty dollars. The girl's first joyful thought was that she had now the means, which she had so often longed for, of increasing her little stock of books; but, looking towards the sick bed, tears came in her eyes, and she instantly put the bill into her father's hands, saying, 'Take it, father; it will buy many comforts for mother; I can do without the books.'

To relate this anecdote as an extraordinary instance of duty or sensibility, would be as unfitting as to leave it untold. If there had been no such outward manifestation, the inward grace must have been wanting; but it may well be conceived how these parents must have doated upon such a child, whose person, moreover, was as beautiful as her disposition and her mind. Yet there were friends, as they are called, who remonstrated with them on the course they were pursuing in her education, and advised that she should be deprived of books, pen, ink, and paper, and rigorously confined to domestic concerns. Her parents loved her both too wisely and too well to be guided by such counsellors, and they anxiously kept the advice secret from Lucretia, lest it should wound her feelings – perhaps, also, lest it should give her, as it properly might, a rooted dislike to these misjudging and unfeeling persons. But she discovered it by accident, and its effect upon her was such as could little have been foreseen: instead of exciting resentment, it produced acquiescence in the prudential reasons which had been urged, and a persevering effort of self-denial, the greatest which could be made. Without declaring any such intention, she gave up her pen and her books, and applied herself exclusively to household business, for several months, till her body as well as her spirits failed. She became emaciated, her countenance bore marks of deep dejection, and often, while actively employed in domestic duties, she could neither restrain nor conceal her tears. The mother seems to have been slower in perceiving this than she would have been had it not been for her own state of confinement; she noticed it at length, and said, 'Lucretia, it is a long time since you have written any thing.' The girl then burst into tears, and replied, 'O mother, I have given that up long ago.' 'But why?' said her mother. After much emotion, she answered, 'I am convinced from what my friends have said, and from what I see, that I have done wrong in pursuing the course I have. I well know the circumstances of the family are such, that it requires the united efforts of every member to sustain it; and since my eldest sister is now gone, it becomes my duty to do every thing in my power to lighten the cares of my parents.' On this occasion, Mrs. Davidson acted with equal discretion and tenderness; she advised her to take a middle course, neither to forsake her favourite pursuits, nor devote herself to them, but use them in that wholesome alternation with the everyday business of the world, which is alike salutary for the body and the mind. 'She therefore occasionally resumed her pen, and seemed comparatively happy.'

Let no parent wish for a child of precocious genius, nor rejoice over such a one without fear and trembling! Great endowments, whether of nature or of fortune, bring with them their full proportion of temptations and dangers; and perhaps in the endowments of nature the danger is greatest because there is most at stake. In most cases it seems as if the seeds of moral and intellectual excellence were not designed to bring forth fruits on earth, but that they are brought into existence and developed here only for transplantation to a world where there shall be nothing to corrupt or hurt them, nothing to impede their growth in goodness, and their progress toward perfection. This is a consideration which may prepare the parent's heart, or console it. Such a plant was Lucretia Davidson. Under the most favourable circumstances, and with the most judicious culture, it seems hardly possible that she could have been reared; an intellectual fever seems to have gathered strength with her growth, and all things tended unhappily to feed rather than to allay it; privations and difficulties on the one hand, indulgence and excitement on the other; an indulgence not to be censured, and yet if to be blamed, excusable, because it was the only indulgence that could be shown here, and an excitement less the effect of misjudging kindness, than of causes over which prudence could have no control. If there had been some who would have debarred her from all intellectual pursuits, and have brought down her spirit, her hopes and aspirations, to the low level of her condition in life, there were (and could not but be) others who wondered at her as a prodigy, and took pleasure in encouraging her to the exertion and display of her gift of verse. How this operated may be seen in some lines, not otherwise worthy of preservation than for the purpose of showing how the promises of reward affect a mind like hers. They were written in her thirteenth year.

> Whene'er the muse pleases to grace my dull page,
> At the sight of *reward*, she flies off in a rage;
> Prayers, threats, and intreaties I frequently try,
> But she leaves me to scribble, to fret, and to sigh.
>
> She torments me each moment, and bids me go write,
> And when I obey her she laughs at the sight;
> The rhyme will not jingle, the verse has no sense,
> And against all her insults I have no defence.
>
> I advise all my friends who wish me to write,
> To keep their rewards and their gifts from my sight,
> So that jealous Miss Muse won't be wounded in pride,
> Nor Pegasus rear till I've taken my ride.

SOUTHEY'S REVIEW OF *LUCRETIA DAVIDSON*

Let not the hasty reader conclude from these rhymes that Lucretia was only what any child of early cleverness might be made by forcing and injudicious admiration. In our own language, except in the cases of Chatterton and Kirke White,[105] we can call to mind no instance of so early, so ardent, and so fatal a pursuit of intellectual advancement.

'She composed with great rapidity; as fast as most persons usually copy. There are several instances of four or five pieces on different subjects, and containing three or four stanzas each, written on the same day. Her thoughts flowed so rapidly, that she often expressed the wish that she had two pair of hands, that she might employ them to transcribe. When "in the vein," she would write standing, and be wholly abstracted from the company present and their conversation. But if composing a piece of some length, she wished to be entirely alone; she shut herself into her room, darkened the windows, and in summer placed her Æolian harp in the window': (thus, by artificial excitement, feeding the fire that consumed her.)

'In those pieces on which she bestowed more than ordinary pains, she was very secret; and if they were, by any accident, discovered in their unfinished state, she seldom completed them, and often destroyed them. She cared little for any of her works after they were completed: some, indeed, she preserved with care for future correction, but a great proportion she destroyed: very many that are preserved, were rescued from the flames by her mother. Of a complete poem, in five cantos, called "Rodri," and composed when she was thirteen years of age, a single canto, and part of another, are all that are saved from a destruction which she supposed had obliterated every vestige of it.

She was often in danger, when walking, from carriages, &c., in consequence of her absence of mind. When engaged in a poem of some length, she has often forgotten her meals. A single incident, illustrating this trait in her character, is worth relating. She went out early one morning to visit a neighbour, promising to be at home to dinner. The neighbour being absent, she requested to be shown into the library. There she became so absorbed in her book, standing, with her bonnet unremoved, that the darkness of the coming night first reminded her that she had forgotten her meals, and expended the entire day in reading.' – pp. 18, 20.

She was peculiarly sensitive to music. There was one song (it was Moore's Farewell to his Harp)[106] to which she 'took a special fancy;' she wished to hear it only at twilight – thus, with that same perilous love of excitement which made her place the wind-harp in the window when she was composing, seeking to increase the effect which the song produced upon a nervous system, already diseasedly susceptible; for it is said, that whenever she heard this song she became cold, pale, and almost fainting; yet it was her favourite of all songs, and gave occasion to these verses, addressed, in her fifteenth year, to her sister.

When evening spreads her shades around,
And darkness fills the arch of heaven;
When not a murmur, not a sound
To Fancy's sportive ear is given;

SOUTHEY'S REVIEW OF *LUCRETIA DAVIDSON*

When the broad orb of heaven is bright,
And looks around with golden eye;
When Nature, softened by her light,
Seems calmly, solemnly to lie:

Then, when our thoughts are raised above
This world, and all this world can give,
Oh, Sister! sing the song I love,
And tears of gratitude receive.

The song which thrills my bosom's core,
And, hovering, trembles half afraid,
Oh, Sister! sing the song once more
Which ne'er for mortal ear was made.

'Twere almost sacrilege to sing
Those notes amid the glare of day;
Notes borne by angels' purest wing,
And wafted by their breath away.

When, sleeping in my grass-grown bed,
Shouldst thou still linger here above,
Wilt thou not kneel beside my head,
And, Sister! sing the song I love?

To young readers it might be useful to observe, that these verses in one place approach the verge of meaning, but are on the wrong side of the line: to none can it be necessary to say, that they breathe the deep feeling of a mind essentially poetical. The most gratifying reward that an author can receive, is to know that his writings have strengthened the weak, stablished the wavering, given comfort to the afflicted, and obtained the approbation of the wise and the good; but simply to have been the means of imparting innocent pleasure to a simple and innocent heart, is itself neither a light nor an unworthy gratification; and we think well enough of Mr. Moore's better nature, to hope and expect that, when he knows how this melody of his affected this young earthly angel, he will not let her remain 'without the meed of some melodious tear.'

The extreme sensitiveness of her frame might have occasioned sufficient apprehension for the probable consequence, even if it had not been dangerously excited both by her own habits, and the attention of which she was the conscious as well as constant object. She complains thus, in her fifteenth year, of frequent and violent head-aches.

Head-ache! thou bane to Pleasure's fairy spell!
Thou fiend! thou foe to joy! I know thee well;

Beneath thy lash I've writhed for many an hour;
I hate thee, for I've known, and dread thy power.

Even the heathen gods were made to feel
The aching torments which thy hand can deal;
And Jove, the ideal king of heaven and earth,
Owned thy dread power, which called stern Wisdom forth.

Wouldst thou thus ever bless each aching head,
And bid Minerva make the brain her bed,
Blessings might then be taught to rise from woe,
And wisdom spring from every throbbing brow.

But always the reverse to me, unkind,
Folly for ever dogs thee close behind:
And, from this burning brow, her cap and bell
Forever jingle Wisdom's funeral knell.

More than once, too, her verses breathe something like a desire and an anticipation of death:

TO A STAR
(*Written in her Fifteenth Year*)

Thou brightly glittering Star of Even –
Thou gem upon the brow of Heaven!
Oh! were this fluttering spirit free,
How quick 't would spread its wings to thee!

How calmly, brightly, dost thou shine,
Like the pure lamp in Virtue's shrine;
Sure the fair world which thou may'st boast
Was never ransomed, never lost.

There, beings pure as Heaven's own air,
Their hopes, their joys, together share;
While hovering angels touch the string,
And seraphs spread the sheltering wing.

There, cloudless days and brilliant nights,
Illumed by Heaven's refulgent lights;
There, seasons, years, unnoticed roll,
And unregretted by the soul.

Thou little sparkling Star of Even –
Thou gem upon an azure Heaven!
How swiftly will I soar to thee,
When this imprisoned soul is free!

'Her desire of knowledge increased as she grew more capable of appreciating its worth;' and she appreciated much beyond its real worth the advantages which girls derive from the ordinary course of female education. 'Oh!' she said one day to her mother, 'that I only possessed half the means for improvement which I see others slighting! I should be the happiest of the happy.' A youth whom nature has endowed with diligence and a studious disposition has, indeed, too much reason to regret the want of that classical education which is wasted upon the far greater number of those on whom it is bestowed; but, for a girl who displays a promise of genius like Lucretia, and who has at hand the Bible and the best poets in her own language, no other assistance can be needed in her progress than a supply of such books as may store her mind with knowledge. Lucretia's desire of knowledge was a passion which possessed her like a disease. 'I am now sixteen years old,' she said, 'and what do I know? Nothing! – nothing, compared with what I have yet to learn. Time is rapidly passing by: that time usually allotted to the improvement of youth; and how dark are my prospects in regard to this favourite wish of my heart!' At another time she said – 'How much there is yet to learn! – If I could only grasp it at once!' In October 1824, when she had just entered upon her tenth year, a gentleman, then on a visit at Plattsburgh, saw some of her verses – was made acquainted with her ardent desire for education, and with the circumstances in which she was placed; and he immediately resolved to afford her every advantage which the best schools in the country could furnish. This gentleman has probably chosen to have his name withheld, being more willing to act benevolently than to have his good deeds blazoned; and yet, stranger as he needs must be, there are many English readers to whom it would have been gratifying, could they have given 'a local habitation and a name.'[107] When Lucretia was made acquainted with his intention, the joy was almost greater than she could bear. As soon as preparations could be made, she left home, and was placed at the 'Troy Female Seminary,' under the instruction of Mrs. Willard.[108] There she had all the advantages for which she had hungered and thirsted; and, like one who had long hungered and thirsted, she devoured them with fatal eagerness. Her application was incessant; and its effects on her constitution, already somewhat debilitated by previous disease, became apparent in increased nervous sensibility. Her letters at this time exhibit the two extremes of feeling in a marked degree. They abound in the most sprightly or most gloomy speculations, bright hopes and lively fancies, or despairing fears and gloomy forebodings. In one of her letters from this seminary, she writes thus to her mother: 'I hope you will feel no uneasiness as to my health or happiness; for, save the thoughts of my dear mother and her lonely life, and the idea that my dear father is slaving himself, and wearing out his very life, to earn a subsistence for his family – save these thoughts (and I can assure you, mother, they come not seldom), I am happy. Oh! how often I think, if I could have but one-half the means I now expend, and be at liberty to divide that half with mamma, how happy I should be! cheer up and keep good courage.' In another, she says: 'Oh! I am so happy, so contented now, that every unusual movement startles me. I am constantly afraid that something will happen to mar it.' Again, she says: 'I hope the expectations of my friends will not be disappointed: but I am afraid you all calculate upon *too much.* I hope not, for I am not capable of much. I can study and be industrious; but I fear I shall not equal the hopes which you say are raised.' The story of Kirke White should operate not more as an example than a warning; but the example is followed and the warning overlooked. Stimulants are administered to minds which are already in a state of feverish excitement. Hot-beds and glasses are used for plants which can only acquire strength in the shade; and they are drenched with instruction, which ought to drop as the rain and distil as the dew – as the small rain upon the tender herb, and as the shower upon the grass.

It is to be wished that Mr. Morse had inserted part of her letters in these Remains, and to be hoped that he will do so in a future edition. During the vacation, in which she returned home, she had a serious illness, which left her feeble and more sensitive than ever. On her recovery she was placed at the school of Miss Gilbert, in Albany; and there, in a short time, a more alarming illness brought her to the very borders of the grave. Before she entered upon her intemperate course of application at Troy, her verses show that she felt a want of joyous and healthy feeling – a sense of decay. Thus she wrote to a friend, who had not seen her since her childhood:

And thou hast mark'd in childhood's hour
The fearless boundings of my breast,
When fresh as summer's opening flower,
I freely frolick'd and was blest.

Oh say, was not this eye more bright?
Were not these lips more wont to smile?
Methinks that then my heart was light,
And I a fearless, joyous child.

And thou didst mark me gay and wild,
My careless, reckless laugh of mirth;
The simple pleasures of a child,
The holiday of man on earth.

Then thou hast seen me in that hour,
When every nerve of life was new,
When pleasures fann'd youth's infant flower,
And Hope her witcheries round it threw.

That hour is fading; it has fled;
And I am left in darkness now,
A wanderer tow'rds a lowly bed,
The grave, that home of all below.

Young poets often affect a melancholy strain, and none more frequently put on
a sad and sentimental mood in verse than those who are as happy as an utter want
of feeling for any body but themselves can make them. But in these verses the feeling was sincere and ominous. Miss Davidson recovered from her illness at Albany
so far only as to be able to perform the journey back to Plattsburgh, under her
poor mother's care. 'The hectic flush of her cheek told but too plainly that a fatal
disease had fastened upon her constitution, and must ere long inevitably triumph.'
She however dreaded something worse than death, and while confined to her bed,
wrote these unfinished lines, the last that were ever traced by her indefatigable
hand, expressing her fear of madness.

There is a something which I dread,
It is a dark, a fearful thing;
It steals along with withering tread,
Or sweeps on wild destruction's wing.

That thought comes o'er me in the hour
Of grief, of sickness, or of sadness;
'Tis not the dread of death, – 'tis more,
It is the dread of madness.

Oh! may these throbbing pulses pause
Forgetful of their feverish course;
May this hot brain, which burning, glows
With all a fiery whirlpool's force,

Be cold, and motionless, and still
A tenant of its lowly bed;
But let not dark delirium steal –

The stanzas with which Kirke White's fragment of the 'Christiad' concludes,
are not so painful as these lines.[109] Had this however been more than a transient
feeling, it would have produced the calamity which it dreaded: it is likely, indeed,
that her early death was a dispensation of mercy, and saved her from the severest
of all earthly inflictions; and that same merciful Providence which removed her
to a better state of existence, made these apprehensions give way to a hope and
expectation of recovery, which, vain as it was, cheered some of her last hours.
When she was forbidden to read it was a pleasure to her to handle the books which
composed her little library, and which she loved so dearly. 'She frequently took

them up and kissed them; and at length requested them to be placed at the foot of her bed, where she might constantly see them,' and anticipating a revival which was not to be, of the delight she should feel in re-perusing them, she said often to her mother, 'what a feast I shall have by-and-bye.' How these words must have gone to that poor mother's heart they only can understand who have heard such like anticipations of recovery from a dear child, and not been able, even whilst hoping against hope, to partake them.

When sensible at length of her approaching dissolution, she looked forward to it without alarm; not alone in that peaceful state of mind which is the proper reward of innocence, but in reliance on the divine promises, and in hope of salvation through the merits of our blessed Lord and Saviour. The last name which she pronounced was that of the gentleman whose bounty she had experienced, and towards whom she always felt the utmost gratitude. Gradually sinking under her malady, she passed away on the 27th of August 1825, before she had completed her seventeenth year. Her person was singularly beautiful; she had 'a high, open forehead, a soft black eye, perfect symmetry of features, a fair complexion, and luxuriant dark hair. The prevailing expression of her face was melancholy. Although, because of her beauty as well as of her mental endowments, she was the object of much admiration and attention, yet she shunned observation, and often sought relief from the pain it seemed to inflict upon her, by retiring from the company.'

'That she should have written so voluminously as has been ascertained,' says the editor of these remains, 'is almost incredible. Her poetical writings which have been collected, amount in all to two hundred and seventy-eight pieces of various length; when it is considered that among these are at least five regular poems of several cantos each, some estimate may be formed of her poetical labours. Besides there were twenty-four school exercises, three unfinished romances, a complete tragedy, written at thirteen years of age, and about forty letters, in a few months, to her mother alone. To this statement should also be appended the fact, that a great portion of her writings she destroyed. Her mother observes, "I think I am justified in saying that she destroyed at least one-third of all she wrote."

'Of the literary character of her writings,' says the editor, 'it does not, perhaps, become me largely to speak; yet I must hazard the remark, that her defects will be perceived to be those of youth and inexperience, while in invention, and in that mysterious power of exciting deep interest, of enchaining the attention and keeping it alive to the end of the story; in that adaptation of the measure to the sentiment, and in the sudden change of measure to suit a sudden change of sentiment; a wild and romantic description; and in the congruity of the accompaniment to her characters, all conceived with great purity and delicacy, – she will be allowed to have discovered uncommon maturity of mind, and her friends to have been warranted in forming very high expectations of her future distinction.'

This may seem high praise: yet in these 'immature buds, and blossoms shaken from the tree, and green fruit,'[110] there was as fair a promise of future excellence as ever genius put forth. But it is not from the intrinsic value of these poor remains that the interest arises with which this little volume cannot but be perused. We have entered into no account of the longer poems which it contains, nor selected from the smaller pieces any except a few of those which are transcripts of the authoress's individual feelings; for youthful poetry must always be imitative, and that which is least faulty is far from being the most hopeful. Indeed, wherever imitative talent exists in the highest degree creative genius has rarely, if ever, been found to co-exist. In these poems there is enough of originality, enough of aspiration, enough of conscious energy, enough of growing power, to warrant any expectations, however sanguine, which the patron, and the friends, and parents of the deceased could have formed; nor can any person rise from the perusal of such a volume without feeling the vanity of human hopes. But those hopes are not vain which look beyond this world for their fulfilment. Knowing, as we know, that not a particle of matter can be destroyed, how surely, then, may we conclude that this which is demonstrated in material existencies is true of spiritual things; that love, and generous feelings, and noble thoughts, and holy desires, are not put off when we put off mortality; but that, inhering in our immortal nature, they partake its immortality, and constitute in their fruition a part of that happiness which our Almighty and All-merciful Father has appointed for all his creatures who do not wilfully renounce their birthright! This is a consolation which reason suggests, which philosophy approves, which scripture warrants, and on which the understanding and the heart may rest.

To those parents who may have the fearful charge of a child like Lucretia Davidson, these memoirs will have a deep and painful interest. They clearly indicate the danger, but afford no clue to the means of averting it. It is as perilous to repress the ardour of such a mind as to encourage it. The Quaker discipline, which, for the majority of women, is the best of which experience has ever been made, produces deplorable effects upon those whose constitution of mind is too sensitive. The difficulty is to indulge such a mind without pampering it; to regulate it, without forcing it from its natural and proper bent. The first step toward this is, that we should ourselves estimate mental endowments not too highly, but at their just worth; and then teach others, in whom the dawn of genius appears, that the gift is not so rare as it has been deemed to be: that it is becoming less so in every generation, because wherever it exists it is now called forth by the wide extension of education (such as it is), and by the general diffusion of books; and that as it becomes common the conventional value which it has hitherto borne will, like that of precious stones, be necessarily abated. This may be a humiliating lesson, but it is a wholesome one; and many there are for whom it will be well if they receive it, and lay it to heart in time.

4

SOUTHEY'S INTRODUCTION TO *ATTEMPTS IN VERSE*

by John Jones, an Old Servant: with Some
Account of the Writer, Written by Himself: and
an Introductory Essay on the Lives and Works of
Our Uneducated Poets (London, 1831)

Being at Harrowgate with my family in the summer of 1827, I received there the following letter:

Sir,
The person who takes the liberty of addressing you is a poor, humble, uneducated domestic, who, having attempted the stringing together a few pieces in verse, would be happy in the possession of your opinion of them.

Living in a family, Sir, in which there are fourteen children, I have devoted but little time exclusively to their construction, they having been chiefly composed when in the exercise of my domestic duties, and frequently borne on my memory for two or three weeks before I had leisure to ease it of its burthen.

Seeing in a Leeds paper, Sir, that you were at Harrowgate, I avail myself of the opportunity it affords me of soliciting the favour of your perusal of them, as well, Sir, from a conviction that I should be satisfied with your opinion, as that, from the kindness of your nature, you would forgive me if I intruded upon you what you could not in justice foster with your approval.

Should it be your pleasure to inspect them, Sir, I shall be happy in sending them to you; and though it may not suit your present convenience, they might, in your possession, Sir, await a more favourable opportunity.

The last of my humble attempts, Sir, occurred to me from seeing a lady of the family collecting the crumbs from the breakfast-table, and putting them by to await the coming of a little red-breast, who never failed to solicit them at the window during the winter months; and as it has just fallen from among some papers in which I placed it two or three months ago, not having room to insert it in my book, it suggested the idea of sending it as a specimen; and though, Sir, I can hardly hope that my poor little Robin possesses any trait of beauty worthy of your admiration, I do hope, Sir, that its harmless simplicity will obtain for me your pardon for the liberty I have taken in thus addressing you, and with that hope, Sir, I subscribe myself

DOI: 10.4324/9781003431343-5

101

SOUTHEY'S INTRODUCTION TO *ATTEMPTS IN VERSE*

Your most respectful
      and most dutiful servant,
            John Jones.

At W. S. Bruere's, Esq.
Kirkby Hall, near Catterick,
Tuesday, 19th June.

THE RED-BREAST

Sweet social bird with breast of red,
  How prone's my heart to favour thee!
Thy look oblique, thy prying head,
  Thy gentle affability;

Thy cheerful song in winter's cold,
  And, when no other lay is heard,
Thy visits paid to young and old,
  Where fear appals each other bird;

Thy friendly heart, thy nature mild,
  Thy meekness and docility,
Creep to the love of man and child,
  And win thine own felicity.

The gleanings of the sumptuous board,
  Conveyed by some indulgent fair,
Are in a nook of safety stored,
  And not dispensed till thou art there.

In stately hall and rustic dome,
  The gaily robed and homely poor
Will watch the hour when thou shalt come,
  And bid thee welcome to the door.

The Herdsman on the upland hill,
  The Ploughman in the hamlet near,
Are prone thy little paunch to fill,
  And pleased thy little psalm to hear.

The Woodman seated on a log
  His meal divides atween the three,
And now himself, and now his dog,
  And now he casts a crumb to thee.

SOUTHEY'S INTRODUCTION TO *ATTEMPTS IN VERSE*

For thee a feast the Schoolboy strews
    At noontide, when the form's forsook;
A worm to thee the Delver throws,
    And Angler when he baits his hook.

At tents where tawny Gipsies dwell,
    In woods where Hunters chase the hind,
And at the Hermit's lonely cell,
    Dost thou some crumbs of comfort find.

Nor are thy little wants forgot,
    In Beggar's hut or Crispin's stall;
The Miser only feeds thee not,
    Who suffers ne'er a crumb to fall.

The Youth who strays, with dark design,
    To make each well-stored nest a prey,
If dusky hues denote them thine,
    Will draw his pilfering hand away.

The Finch a spangled robe may wear,
    The Nightingale delightful sing,
The Lark ascend most high in air,
    The Swallow fly most swift on wing,

The Peacock's plumes in pride may swell,
    The Parrot prate eternally,
But yet no bird man loves so well,
    As thou with thy simplicity.

Sir Joseph Banks[111] used pleasantly to complain that tortoise-shell tom-cats were the plague of his life, because every ignorant man or woman who happened to possess one, favoured him with the first offer of it, at fifty, or perhaps an hundred guineas below what, upon the faith of vulgar opinion, they believed to be the established price of so great a curiosity. For this flattering preference Sir Joseph was indebted to the high rank in the scientific world which he so deservedly held and filled so worthily: it was a tribute to his station and his character. Authors, and especially poets, who send their works for my perusal and opinion and advice thereon, have been as much the plague of my life as the tom-tortoise-shells were of his. Mr. George Coleman[112] has no sinecure in his office of Licenser for the Stage; alas! the office[113] which has thus been thrust upon me is a sine-salary, and the business itself is of a more ungracious kind. Two circumstances have drawn upon me this persecution; the publication of Henry Kirke White's Remains,[114] and the appointment which I have the honour to hold of Poet Laureate, . . . the Poet

103

SOUTHEY'S INTRODUCTION TO *ATTEMPTS IN VERSE*

Laureate being supposed by many persons to be a sort of Lord Chancellor in Literature, a Lord Keeper of the King's taste, and to have the literary patronage of the public and the state at his disposal. The appointment itself has not exposed me to more sarcasms, as pungent as they have been new, concerning sack and sackbut,[115] than this opinion has produced suitors to the High Court of Poetry over which I am supposed to preside. Know all men by these presents, that the Poet Laureate receiveth no allowance of sack; (the more's the pity!) and that any application to him in that, or any other capacity, for poetical preferment, from aspirant sons of song, might as well be addressed to the Man in the Moon.

Little likelihood then, certain readers will think, should there seem to have been, that Mr. John Jones would obtain such an answer to his application as he hoped for. But if there be some who think thus, many others I am sure there are whom it will not surprise to know, that the incipient displeasure which such a communication may be expected to excite, gave way as I perused his letter, and was completely dispelled by the verses: the former pleased me because of its simple humility; and in the latter, with all their imperfections, I saw something of Cunningham's vein, or of Cotton's, a man of higher powers, whom Cunningham followed.[116] I read them to my wife and daughters, and to a lady of our party, whose approbation in the case of my own writings has long been to me an earnest of the only approbation which I am desirous to obtain, . . . that of the wise, the gentle, and the good.[117] They were pleased with the natural images and the natural feeling in these poor verses; and they were pleased, also, that instead of returning a discouraging reply and thus preventing any farther trouble to myself, I told my humble applicant he might send me his book, warning him, however, against indulging in any expectation that such poems would be found generally acceptable in these days; . . . the time for them was gone by, and whether the public had grown wiser in these matters or not, it had certainly become less tolerant and less charitable.

Accordingly, the manuscript was sent me, and with it the letter which follows.

Kirkby Hall, near Catterick, 23d June

Sir,
I feel greatly obliged to you for your kindness in condescending to take the trouble of perusing my poor bits of verses. I am only fearful, Sir, that, even in your own expectations, you will not be gratified. Mine, Sir, have never been of a very sanguine nature. Had I been so fortunate as to come under your notice twenty years ago, your advice and encouragement might have made something better of me; but I am now, Sir, on the wrong side of fifty, and having never met with encouragement, and being generally very actively employed, I have not had leisure to seek for ideas, but only endeavoured to arrange those that came voluntarily, and that at times, Sir, when I have been too busily engaged to make a happy disposal of them. Consequently, Sir, my productions have been very

limited, but from having had a little more leisure the last year, I have added several little pieces to my stock. Being on the Continent a few years, Sir, I attempted a long piece, which I intended denominating The Maid of the Wye, and under great difficulties I persevered in it for some time; but we were a large family in a small house, Sir, and from the repeated solicitations of some little favourites of the family, and from the noisy clamour of several Flemish maid-servants, and other causes, I became so disgusted with it that I gave it up, and could never again resume it. I have copied some passages of it into my book, the rest is destroyed; those you will find, Sir, entitled, A Fanciful Description of a Passage down the Wye; Fragments; and, I believe, all that run in the same metre, are parts of it. Should it be your opinion, Sir, that by weeding out a few of the worst pieces, and, if their faults were pointed out to me, correcting others, it would not be too contemptible to solicit a subscription for, I might as well, Sir, avail myself of any little benefit it might afford me; but if otherwise, Sir, I must beg of you not to let your kindness get the better of your judgement; for though I have had the bringing up of a family under circumstances which have subjected me to great difficulties, the struggle I trust is over, and if it has left me poor, Sir, my anxiety in respect to worldly prosperity is greatly diminished. It may be some gratification to your benevolent heart, Sir, to know that the interest you take in promoting the wishes of such an inferior being as myself, excites my gratitude; and when I tell you, Sir, that I have been upwards of twenty years in my present service, and that I possess the good wishes of every family it has been my lot to serve, I hope, Sir, it will impress you with a favourable opinion of my character. Believe me, Sir, I feel myself.

Your much obliged and most dutiful Servant,

John Jones

This letter did not diminish the favourable opinion which I had formed of the writer from his first communication. Upon perusing the poems I wished they had been either better or worse. Had I consulted my own convenience, or been fearful of exposing myself to misrepresentation and censure, I should have told my humble applicant that although his verses contained abundant proof of a talent for poetry, which, if it had been cultivated, might have produced good fruit, they would not be deemed worthy of publication in these times. But on the other hand, there were in them such indications of a kind and happy disposition, so much observation of natural objects, such a relish of the innocent pleasures offered by nature to the eye, and ear, and heart, which are not closed against them, and so pleasing an example of the moral benefit derived from those pleasures, when they are received by a thankful and thoughtful mind, that I persuaded myself there were many persons who would partake, in perusing them, the same kind of gratification which I had felt. There were many, I thought, who would be pleased at seeing how much intellectual enjoyment

SOUTHEY'S INTRODUCTION TO *ATTEMPTS IN VERSE*

had been attained in humble life, and in very unfavourable circumstances; and that this exercise of the mind, instead of rendering the individual discontented with his station, had conduced greatly to his happiness, and if it had not made him a good man, had contributed to keep him so. This pleasure should in itself, methought, be sufficient to content those subscribers who might kindly patronize a little volume of his verses. . . . Moreover, I considered that as the Age of Reason had commenced, and we were advancing with quick step in the March of Intellect, Mr. Jones would in all likelihood be the last versifyer of his class; something might properly be said of his predecessors, the poets in low life, who with more or less good fortune had obtained notice in their day; and here would be matter for an introductory essay, not uninteresting in itself, and contributing something towards our literary history. And if I could thus render some little service to a man of more than ordinary worth, (for such upon the best testimony Mr. Jones appeared to be,) it would be something not to be repented of, even though I should fail in the hope (which failure, however, I did not apprehend) of affording some gratification to 'gentle readers:' for readers there still are, who, having escaped the epidemic disease of criticism, are willing to be pleased, and grateful to those from whose writings they derive amusement or instruction.

It is evident that there could be no versifyers of this class in early times. The language of a Saxon thane was not more cultivated than that of the churl on his estate; indeed, the best as well as earliest of our Anglo-Saxon poets was in the lowest condition of freemen, and was employed as a night-herdsman when he composed his first verses. The distinction between the language of high and low life could not be broadly marked, till our language was fully formed, in the Elizabethan age: then the mother tongue of the lower classes ceased to be the language of composition; that of the peasantry was antiquated, that of the inferior citizens had become vulgar. It was not necessary that a poet should be learned in Greek and Latin, but it was that he should speak the language of polished society.

Another change also, in like manner widening the intellectual distinctions of society, had by that time taken place. In barbarous ages the lord had as little advantage over his vassal in refinement of mind as of diction. War was his only business; and war, even in the brightest days of chivalry, tended as surely to brutalize the feelings of the chiefs, and render their hearts callous, as the occupations of husbandry did to case-harden and coarsen the hind and the herdsman; but when arts and luxuries (of that allowable kind for which a less equivocal term is to be desired) had found their way from cloisters into courts and castles, an improvement as well of intellect as of manners, rapidly ensued. Then, also, the relations of states became more complicated, and courts in consequence more politic: the minds of the great grew at the same time more excursive and more reflecting; and in the relaxation which they sought in poetry, something more was required than the minstrels afforded in their lays, whether of ribaldry or romance. Learning being scarce, they who possessed a little were proud of exhibiting in their writings the extent of that small stock;

SOUTHEY'S INTRODUCTION TO *ATTEMPTS IN VERSE*

and the patrons whom they courted, and who themselves were in the same stage of intellectual culture, were flattered at being addressed in a strain which must have been unintelligible to the multitude. When literature revived, the same kind of pleasure which had just before been given by a pedantic vocabulary, was produced by classical allusions, and imitations of ancient, or of Italian writers. The language then improved so suddenly, that it changed more in the course of one generation than it had done in the two preceding centuries; Elizabeth, who grew up while it was comparatively barbarous, lived to see it made capable of giving adequate expression to the loftiest conceptions of human imagination. Poets were then, perhaps, more abundant than they have been in any subsequent age until the present: and, as a necessary consequence of that abundance, all tricks of style were tried, and all fantasticalities of conceit abounded; they who were poets by imitative desire or endeavour, putting forth their strength in artificial and ambitious efforts, while the true poets held the true course, . . . though the best of them did not always escape from what had thus been made the vice of their age.

The circumstances, therefore, of low breeding and defective education were so unfavourable, that the first person who, in a certain degree overcame them, obtained great notoriety, and no inconsiderable share of patronage. This was John Taylor, the Water-Poet, a man who has long been more known by name than by his writings.[118] He was born in Gloucestershire, but at what place none his biographers have stated in their scanty notices, nor has he himself mentioned in the volume entitled, 'All the Works of John Taylor, the Water Poet, being sixty-three in number, collected into one Volume by the Author, with sundry new Additions, corrected, revised, and newly imprinted, 1630.' The book, though in height that of a modern quarto, would be catalogued among folios, for its shape; it is in fact neither, but of a nondescript size which may be called sexto, the sheet being folded into six leaves. It contains something more than 600 pages, in three series of paging, more than two-thirds consisting of verse closely printed and in double columns. Taylor lived twenty-four years after the publication of this volume, and published a great deal more; and though in this collection, (which is all that I have had opportunity of perusing,) there is some ribaldry and more rubbish, there is, nevertheless, so much which repays the search, that I wish the remainder of his works had been in like manner collected.

Young Taylor had an odd schoolmaster, upon whom some of his neighbours played a scurvy jest; the poor man was fond of new milk, and went to market for the purpose of buying a milch cow; but being short-sighted, and perhaps in other respects better qualified to deal with books than men, the seller, in sport it may be believed rather than roguery, sold him a bull, . . . which poor 'Master Green, being thus overseen,' drove contentedly home, and did not discover the trick till he had called the maid to milk it. What happened to the pail in consequence called forth a memorial in four lines from his pupil, which was probably John's first attempt in verse. In other respects he was by his own account no very hopeful scholar: in

107

SOUTHEY'S INTRODUCTION TO *ATTEMPTS IN VERSE*

that part of the poem called Taylor's Motto, which he entitles, 'My Serious Cares and Considerations,' he says –

> I was well entered, forty winters since,
> As far as possum in my accidence;
> And reading but from possum to posset,
> There I was mired and could no further get,
> Which when I think upon with mind dejected,
> I care to think how learning I neglected.

Having thus stuck fast in the thorns and brambles of the Latin grammar, he was taken from school and bound apprentice to a Thames waterman, perhaps as soon as he could handle an oar. The occupation is likely to have been his own choice, for it was well suited to his bold, hardy, and at that time, idle disposition; in those days, too, it was a thriving one, and gave employment to more men than any other trade or calling in the metropolis. Taylor, indeed, says, that 'the number of watermen and those that lived and were maintained by them, and by the only labour of the oar and scull, betwixt the bridge of Windsor and Gravesend, could not be fewer than forty thousand.' There may be some exaggeration in this; but when this assertion was made, the company was overstocked with hands; the circumstances which had occasioned its great growth and prosperity having changed. The first cause of its decline was the long peace which this country enjoyed under James I.: the Thames had been in time of war the great nursery for the navy; the watermen were at continual demand for the Queen's service, 'as in duty bound,' and good service they had done in all Elizabeth's wars. 'Every summer 1500 or 2000 of them were employed' in her ships, 'having but nine shillings and fourpence the month, apiece, for their pay; and yet they were able then to set themselves out like men, with shift of apparel, linen and woollen, and forbear charging of their prince for their pay, sometimes six months, nine months, twelve months, sometimes more; for then there were so few watermen, and the one half of them being at sea, those that staid at home had as much work as they would do.' To their good fortune, also, for a while, the players at that time 'began to play on the Bankside (Southwark) and to leave playing in London and Middlesex, for the most part.' There were three companies playing there at once, 'besides the bear-baiting;' and 'then there went such great concourse of people by water, that the small number of watermen remaining at home were not able to carry them, by reason of the court, the terms, the players, and other employments; so that they were enforced and encouraged (hoping that this golden stirring world would have lasted ever) to take and entertain men and boys.' Owing to this establishment of the three theatres on the Bankside, the company of watermen was increased more than half. But peace came, and the men who had been employed at sea returned to their old trade upon the river; and as misfortunes seldom come singly, (for a misfortune to the watermen peace was,) two of the three sets of players removed from the Surrey side to the Middlesex one, and there played 'far remote from the Thames, so that every day in the week they drew unto them 3000 or 4000 people that were used to spend their monies by water.' This reduced the watermen to great distress, and in 1613 they petitioned the King that the players might not be allowed to have a playhouse in London, nor within four miles of it, on that side the river; 'the reasons that moved us unto it,' says Taylor, 'being charitably considered, make the suit seem not only reasonable, but past seeming most necessary to be sued for, and tolerable to be granted.' He was selected by the company to deliver the petition and follow the business, which he did at the cost of seven pounds two shillings, for 'horse-hire, horse-meat, and man's meat, expended in two journies to Theobalds,[119] one to Newmarket,[120] and two to Royston,'[121] before he could get the petition referred to the commissioners for suits. A counter-petition was presented by his Majesty's players, who said, that the watermen might just as reasonably propose to remove the Exchange, the walks in St. Paul's, or Moorfields, to the Bankside, for their own profit, as to confine them to it; 'but our extremities and cause,' says Taylor, 'being judiciously pondered by the honourable and worshipful commissioners, Sir Francis Bacon[122] very worthily said, that so far forth as the public weal was to be regarded before pastimes, or a serviceable, decaying multitude before a handful of particular men, or profit before pleasure, so far was our suit to be preferred before their's.' A day was appointed for determining the business; but before it came, the chief commissioner, Sir Julius Cæsar, was made Master of the Rolls,[123] by which means the commission was dissolved, and the case never came to a farther hearing. Had it proceeded, another proof would probably have been given, notwithstanding Bacon's opinion, that the convenience of the great public when opposed to any part of that public, must ultimately prevail, even though the convenience gained should be trifling, and the injury sustained by the minor part of the most serious nature. Within our own memory, shoe-strings have prevailed over buckles in despite of ridicule, and covered buttons over metal ones in defiance of pains and penalties, in each case to the great detriment of what had been a flourishing branch of our manufactures. But the watermen were unreasonable in requiring that the Londoners, in that best age of the English drama, should, whenever they went to the play, be put to the discomfort and charged with the expense of crossing and recrossing the water; and that the players should be confined to the Bankside, where bad weather must so materially have affected their receipts.

Taylor complains in another of his pamphlets, that he and many thousands more were 'much impoverished and hindered of their livings' by the proclamations which from time to time were issued, requiring the gentry to retire from the capital into their own countries. In certain despotic governments the sovereigns are said to have pursued the evil policy of keeping their nobles about the court, for the purpose of lessening their influence in the provinces, and rendering them dependent upon court favour and state employments, by involving them in habitual expenses beyond what their patrimonial revenues could support. No such erroneous views either of their own or the public interest were entertained by the kings of England; but this opposite policy, which required the landed proprietors to reside during the greater part of the year upon their own estates, seems, like the acts that were enforced against new buildings about London, to have originated in a prudent desire of keeping down both the size and population of the metropolis, because of the plague, visitations of which were then so frequent and so dreadful. This deprived the watermen of good part of their employ; and Taylor complains that his 'poor trade,' which had already suffered so much, was undone when hackney coaches came into use. The decay of what had once been a thriving occupation allowed him to engage in adventures which he might have been too wise to have undertaken if his fortune had been more prosperous.

But before this unfavourable change in his circumstances was felt, he had become known as the Water-Poet. His own account of the manner in which he took to the rhyming trade, may be understood to mean, that he was led to it by an imitative impulse, to his own surprise, and not very early in life.

> I that in quiet, in the days of yore,
> Did get my living at the healthful oar,
> And with content did live, and sweat, and row,
> Where, like the tide, my purse did ebb and flow;
> My fare was good, I thank my bounteous Fares,
> And pleasure made me careless of my cares.
> The watry element most plentiful,
> Supplied me daily with the oar and scull;
> And what the water yielded, I with mirth
> Did spend upon the element of earth.
> Until at length a strange poetic vein,
> As strange a way possest my working brain:
> It chanced one evening on a reedy bank,
> The Muses sat together in a rank,
> Whilst in my boat I did by water wander,
> Repeating lines of Hero and Leander.[124]
> The triple Three[125] took great delight in that,
> Call'd me ashore, and caused me sit and chat,
> And in the end, when all our talk was done,
> They gave to me a draught of Helicon,
> Which proved to me a blessing and a curse,
> To fill my pate with verse, and empt my purse.

These lines seem also to confess, that though he 'left no calling for this idle trade,' he had in some degree neglected one. It is, indeed, apparent, that he was a boon companion, neither unconscious of the wit and ready talents which he possessed, nor diffident of them; and though in his grammatical studies he had stuck at posset, he had been in a very good school for improving the sort of ability with which Nature had endowed him. Even as late as Dr. Johnson's days, a license of wit (if wit it may be called) was allowed to all persons upon the river, which would not have been tolerated any where else. Fluency in this sort of speech he could not choose but learn; and his vocation also brought him into conversation with persons of all descriptions, the best as well as the worst, especially when the theatres were on the Bankside. Moreover, he was not a mere freshwater sailor; he

SOUTHEY'S INTRODUCTION TO *ATTEMPTS IN VERSE*

had seen service enough to have entitled him to call himself an old seaman, if that denomination had in those days sounded more respectably than his own; for he had made no fewer that sixteen voyages in the Queen's ships, and was in the expeditions under Essex at Cadiz and the Azores.[126] And no other occupation could have offered him such opportunities for reading as invited him in the intervals of chance leisure, even on his busiest days; in fact, he was a diligent reader; and although it was because of his low birth, low station, and want of regular education, that he obtained notice at first for his productions, there are many in these days who set up, not alone for simple authors in prose or rhyme, but as critics by profession, upon a much smaller stock of book-knowledge than Taylor the Water-Poet had laid in. Hear his account of his own studies!

> I care to get good books, and I take heed
> And care what I do either write or read;
> Though some through ignorance, and some through spite,
> Have said that I can neither read nor write.
> But though my lines no scholarship proclaim,
> Yet I at learning have a kind of aim;
> And I have gathered much good observations,
> From many human and Divine translations.

*****

> The Poet –[1] *Quid*, (or Ovid if you will,)
> Being in English, much hath helpt my skill.
> And Homer too, and Virgil I have seen,
> And reading them I have much bettered been.
> Godfrey of Bulloyne, well by Fairfax done;
> Du Bartas, that much love hath rightly won;
> Old Chaucer, Sidney, Spenser, Daniel, Nash, –
> I dipt my finger where they used to wash.
> As I have read these poets I have noted
> Much good, which in my memory is quoted.

> Of histories I have perused some store,
> As no man of my function hath done more.
> The Golden Legend I did overtoss,
> And found the gold mixt with a deal of dross.
> I have read Plutarch's Morals and his Lives,
> And like a bee suckt honey from those hives.
> Josephus of the Jews, Knowles of the Turks,

---

1 [Southey's note:] Some jest is, I suppose, intended, which I cannot explain; – or, perhaps, it is pretended, to fill up the line.

SOUTHEY'S INTRODUCTION TO *ATTEMPTS IN VERSE*

> Marcus Aurelius, and Guevara's works;
> Lloyd, Grimstone, Montaigne, and Suetonius,
> Agrippa, whom some call Cornelius,
> Grave Seneca and Cambden, Purchas, Speed,
> Old monumental Fox and Holinshed;
> And that sole Book of Books which God hath given,
> The blest eternal Testaments of Heaven,
> That I have read, and I with care confess,
> Myself unworthy of such happiness.

The subject of his reading is one which he was evidently pleased with referring to, though he took care to ground his best claims for indulgence upon his 'natural art.' Wherefore, he says, –

> do I take a scholar's part,
> That have no ground or axioms of art;
> That am in poesy an artless creature,
> That have no learning but the Book of Nature,
> No academical poetic strains,
> But homespun medley of my motley brains.

The first person who patronised him he addresses as 'the Right Worshipful and my ever respected Mr. John Moray, Esquire:'[127] – probably, the same 'Mr. John Murray, of the bed-chamber to the king,' whom Bacon calls his very good friend. Taylor has addressed this sonnet to him, and prefixed it to the earliest of his multifarious productions:

> Of all the wonders this vile world includes,
> I muse how flattery such high favours gain;
> How adulation cunningly deludes
> Both high and low, from sceptre to the swain.
> But if that thou by flattery couldst obtain
> More than the most that is possest by men,
> Thou canst not tune thy tongue to falsehood's strain;
> Yet with the best canst use both tongue and pen.
> Thy sacred learning can both scan and ken
> The hidden things of Nature and of Art.
> 'Tis thou hast raised me from Oblivion's den,
> And made my muse from obscure sleep to start.
> Unto thy wisdom's censure I commit
> This first-born issue of my worthless wit.

This first-born had an odd name; he called it, in Tayloric style, 'Taylor's Water-Work; or the Sculler's Travels from Tyber to Thames; with his boat laden with a

SOUTHEY'S INTRODUCTION TO *ATTEMPTS IN VERSE*

Hotch-potch, or gallimaufrey of Sonnets, Satires, and Epigrams. With an inkhorn disputation betwixt a Lawyer and a Poet; and a quarterne of new catched Epigrams, caught the last fishing-tide; together with an addition of Pastoral Equivoques, or the Complaint of a Shepherd. Dedicated to neither Monarch nor Miser, Keaser nor Caitiff, Palatine nor Plebeian, but to great Mounsier Multitude, alias All, or Every One.'

The manner in which he published his books, which were separately of little bulk, was to print them at his own cost, make presents of them, and then hope for 'sweet remuneration' from the persons whom he had thus delighted to honour. This mode of publication was not regarded in those days so close akin to mendicity as it would now be deemed; pecuniary gifts of trifling amount being then given and accepted, where it would now be deemed an insult to offer and a disgrace to receive them. The method, however, did not always answer, and Taylor complains to this effect, though rather for others than for himself. He says, –

> Yet to excuse the writers that now write,
> Because they bring no better things to light,
> 'Tis because Bounty from the world has fled;
> True Liberality is almost dead:
> Reward is lodged in dark oblivion deep,
> Bewitch'd, I think, into an endless sleep;
> That though a man in study take great pains,
> And empt his veins and pulverize his brains,
> To write a poem well, which being writ
> With all his judgement, reason, art, and wit,
> He at his own charge print, and pay for all,
> And give away most free and liberal,
> Two, three, or four, or five hundred books,
> For his reward he shall have – nods and looks;
> That all the profit a man's pains shall get,
> Will not suffice one meal to feed a cat.
> Yet noble Westminster, thou still art free,
> And for thy bounty I am bound to thee;
> For hadst not thou and thy inhabitants,
> From time to time, relieved and help'd my wants,
> I had long since bid poetry adieu;
> And therefore still my thanks shall be to you.
> Next to the Court in general, I am bound
> To you, for many friendships I have found.
> There, when my purse hath often wanted bait
> To fill or feed it, I have had receit.

Ben Jonson is one of the persons to whom he declares himself 'much obliged for many undeserved courtesies received from him, and from others by his favour.'[128]

113

And in a Dedication to Charles I. he says, 'My gracious Sovereign, your Majesty's poor undeserved servant, having formerly oftentimes presented to your Highness many such pamphlets, the best fruits of my lean and steril invention, always your princely affability and bounty did express and manifest your royal and generous disposition; and your gracious father, of ever-blessed and famous memory, did not only like and encourage, but also more than reward the barren gleanings of my poetical inventions.' His Funeral Elegy, which he calls 'A Living Sadness, duly consecrated to the Immortal Memory' of this 'all-beloved sovereign Lord, the Peerless Paragon of Princes,' concludes with these lines, addressed to all who read the poem.

> I boast not; but his Majesty that's dead
> Was many times well pleased my lines to read,
> And every line, word, syllable, and letter,
> Were by his reading graced and made better;
> And howsoever they were, good or ill,
> His bounty showed he did accept them still.
> He was so good and gracious unto me,
> That I the vilest wretch on earth should be,
> If for his sake I had not writ this verse,
> My last poor duty to his royal hearse.
> Two causes made me this sad poem write;
> The first my humble duty did invite,
> The last, to shun that vice which doth include
> All other vices, foul ingratitude.

The Earl of Holdernesse was one of his good patrons, and moved King James to bestow a place upon him.[129] What this place was does not appear in his writings, nor have his biographers stated: one office, which must have been much to his liking, he held at the Tower, by appointment of Sir William Wade;[130] it was that of receiving for the lieutenant his perquisite of 'two black leathern bottles or bombards of wine,' (being in quantity six gallons,) from every ship that brought wine into the river Thames, a custom which had continued at that time more than 300 years. This was a prosperous part of Taylor's life, and if he did not write like Homer in those days, it was not for any failure in drinking like Agamemnon. He says –

> Ten years almost the place I did retain,
> And gleaned great Bacchus' blood from France and Spain;
> Few ships my visitation did escape,
> That brought the sprightful liquor of the grape:
> My bottles and myself did oft agree,
> Full to the top, all merry came we three!
> Yet always 'twas my chance, in Bacchus' spite,
> To come into the Tower unfox'd, upright.

SOUTHEY'S INTRODUCTION TO *ATTEMPTS IN VERSE*

But the spirit of reform was abroad: the merchants complained that the bottles were made bigger than they used to be, and 'waged law' with the lieutenant; and had it not been for the Wine-Poet's exertions, in finding and bringing into court those witnesses, who could swear to the size of the bottles for fifty years, they would have carried their cause. Poor Taylor was ill-rewarded for his services; no sooner had he established the right, than the office which he had held was put to sale, and he was discharged because he would not buy it. 'I would not,' he says, 'or durst not, venture upon so unhonest a novelty, it being sold indeed at so high a rate, that whoso bought it must pay thrice the value of it.'

> O bottles, bottles, bottles, bottles, bottles!
> Plato's divine works, nor great Aristotle's,
> Did ne'er make mention, that a gift so royal
> Was ever bought and sold!

He alludes to a loss of a different kind, in his 'Navy of Ships and other vessels that have the art to sail by land as well as by sea,' the names of these vessels being the Lord-ship, the Scholarship, the Lady-ship, the Goodfellow-ship, the Apprentice-ship, the Court-ship, the Friend-ship, the Fellow-ship, the Footman-ship, the Horse-manship, the Surety-ship, the Wor-ship, and the Woodman-ship. In this tract there is some wholesome satire, and abundance of wit. The ship which he had been unlucky enough to embark in in this fleet, was the Surety-ship, of which he says, 'she is so easy to be boarded, that a man need not trouble his feet to enter her, or use any boat to come to her, – only a dash with a pen, the writing of a man's name, passing his word, or setting his mark (though it be but the form of a pair of pot-hooks, a cross, a crooked billet, or a M for John Thompson,)[131] any of these facile ways hath shipt a man into the Surety-ship during his life, and his heirs after him; and though the entrance into her be so easy, yet she is so full of impertinent and needy courtesy, that many men will lend a hand into her, with more fair intreaties, requests, and invitations, than are commonly used to a mask at the court, or a groce of gossips in the country; and being once entered, a tenpenny nail, driven to the head, may as soon scape out of an oaken post, as a man may get ashore again. She is painted on the outside with vows and promises; and within her are the stories of the tattered Prodigal, eating husks with the swine, the picture of Niobe, with Alecto, Tisiphone, and Megæra, dancing *lac-rymæ*;[132] her arms are a goose-quill or pen couchant, in a sheep-skin field sable; the motto above, *Noverint universi*;[133] the supporters, an usurer and a scrivener; the crest, a woodcock; the mantles, red wax, with this other motto beneath, sealed and deliv-ered. This ship hath the art to make parchment the dearest stuff in the world; for I have seen a piece little bigger than my two hands that hath cost a man a thousand pounds. I myself paid a hundred pounds once for a small rotten remnant of it. She is rigged most strangely; her ropes and cables are conditions and obligations; her anchors are leases forfeited; her lead and line are mortgages; her main-sails are interchangeable indentures; and her top-sails, bills and bonds; her small shot are arrests and actions; her great ordnance are extents, outlawries, and executions.'

Taylor's productions would not have been so numerous if he had not gained something by them. If any celebrated person died, he was ready with an elegy, and this sort of tribute always obtained the acknowledgment in expectation of which it was offered. But it is evident, that he delighted in acquiring knowledge, and took pleasure in composition for its own sake, as in the exercise of a talent which he was proud to possess. His Memorial of all the English monarchs, from Brute to King Charles, was probably composed as much for this motive as to impress upon his own memory the leading facts of English history; then a set of miserable portraits cut in wood, without the shadow of resemblance till we come to bluff King Henry VIII., fitted it for popular and perhaps for profitable sale. It is, probably, from this bald and meagre chronicle in rhyme, which, for the subject, is likely to have been more common than any other of his tracts, that the commonly expressed opinion of his writings has been drawn, as if they were wholly worthless, and not above the pitch of a bellman's verses.[134] But a more injurious opinion has seldom been formed; for Taylor had always words at will, and wit also when the subject admitted of its display. His account of the Books in the Old and New Testament,[135] is in the same creeping strain. The best specimen of his historical verses is entitled God's Manifold Mercies in the Miraculous Deliverance of our Church of England, from the year 1565 until this present 1630, particularly and briefly described. This is in a series of what some late writers have conveniently called quatorzains,[2] to distinguish them from sonnets of proper structure: they are introduced thus:

> There was a Bull in Rome was long a breeding,
> Which Bull proved little better than a Calf;
> Was sent to England for some better feeding,
> To fatten in his Holiness' behalf.
> The virtues that this Beast of Babel had
> In thundering manner was to bann and curse;
> Rail at the Queen as it were raging mad;
> Yet, God be thanked, she was ne'er the worse.
> The goodly sire of it was impious Pius;
> He taught it learnedly to curse and bann;
> And to our faces boldly to defy us
> It madly over England quickly ran.
> But what success it had, read more and see,
> The fruits of it here-underwritten be.

'This bull did excommunicate and curse the queen; it deposed her from her crown; it proclaimed her an heretic; it cursed all such as loved her; it threatened

---

2 [Southey's note, referring to Wordsworth's sonnet sequence *Ecclesiastical Sketches* (1822):] It is remarkable, that Mr. Wordsworth should have cast his Ecclesiastical Sketches in a form so nearly similar. The coincidence (for I know Mr. Wordsworth had never seen Taylor's works, nor heard of this portion of them) may seem to show the peculiar fitness of this form for what may be called memorial poetry.

SOUTHEY'S INTRODUCTION TO *ATTEMPTS IN VERSE*

damnation to all subjects as durst obey her; and it promised the kingdom of heaven to those that would oppose and kill her.'

He goes through the series of treasons which the bull produced, down to the Gunpowder-plot, and concludes with this Thanksgiving.

> And last of all, with heart and hands erected,
> Thy Church doth magnify thy name, O Lord!
> Thy Providence preserved, thy Power protected.
> Thy planted Vine, according to thy word.
> My God! what shall I render unto Thee,
> For all thy gifts bestowed on me always?
> Love and unfeigned thankfulness shall be
> Ascribed for thy mercies, all my days.
> To Thee, my Priest, my Prophet, and my King,
> My Love, my Counsellor and Comforter,
> To Thee alone, I only praises sing,
> For only Thou art my Deliverer.
> All honour, glory, power, and praise, therefore,
> Ascribed be to Thee for evermore.

These are no mean verses. Indeed, in every General Collection of the British Poets there are authors to be found, whose pretensions to a place there are much feebler than what might be advanced on behalf of Taylor the Water Poet. Sometimes he has imitated the strongly-marked manner of Josuah Silvester:[136] sometimes, George Wither's[137] pedestrian strain; in admiring imitation of which latter poet, (and not with any hostile or envious feeling, as has somewhere been erroneously stated,) he composed a piece which he called Taylor's Motto, the Motto, (which is his only opposition to Wither) being, Et habeo, et careo, et curo.[138] There is in Wither, when in his saner mind and better mood, a felicity of expression, a tenderness of feeling, and an elevation of mind, far above the Water Poet's pitch;[139] nevertheless, Taylor's Motto is lively, curious, and characteristic, as well of the age as of the writer. It contains about fourteen hundred lines; and he tells us,

> This book was written (not that here I boast),
> Put hours together, in three days at most;
> And give me but my breakfast, I'll maintain
> To write another ere I eat again;
> But well, or ill, or howsoe'er it's penn'd,
> Like it as you list; and so, I make an
> > END.

He has imitated Chaucer in a catalogue of birds,[140] which though mostly a mere catalogue, has some sweet lines in it: and in other places he enumerates the names

SOUTHEY'S INTRODUCTION TO *ATTEMPTS IN VERSE*

of rivers, the variety of diseases, and, more curiously and at greater length, the different trades and callings which were exercised in his days. Like poor Falconer,[141] he made use also of his nautical vocabulary in verse.

> You brave Neptunians, you saltwater crew,
> Sea-ploughing mariners, I speak to you:
> From hemp you for yourselves and others gain
> Your spritsail, foresail, topsail, and your main,
> Top, and top-gallant, and your mizen abaft,
> Your coursers, bonnets, drablers, fore and aft,
> The sheets, tacks, boliens,[142] braces, halliers,[143] tyes,
> Shrouds, ratlings, lanyards, tackles, lifts, and gies,
> Your martlines, ropeyarns, gaskets, and your stays,
> These for your use, small hemp-seed up doth raise:
> The buoy-rope, boat-rope, quest-rope, cat-rope, port-rope,
> The bucket-rope, the boat-rope, long or short rope,
> The entering-rope, the top-rope, and the rest,
> Which you that are acquainted with know best:
> The lines to sound within what depth you slide,
> Cables and hausers, by which ships do ride:
> All these, and many more than I can name,
> From this small seed, good industry doth frame.
> Ships, barks, hoys, drumlers, craires, boats, all would sink,
> But for the ocum caulk'd in every chink.
> The unmatched loadstone, and best figured maps,
> Might show where foreign countries are (perhaps);
> The compass (being rightly toucht) will show
> The thirty-two points where the winds do blow;
> Men with the Jacob's staff, and Astrolobe
> May take the height and circuit of the globe:
> And sundry art-like instruments look clear
> In what horizon, or what hemisphere
> Men sail in through the raging ruthless deep,
> And to what coast, such and such course to keep;
> Guessing by the Arctic or Antarctic star,
> Climates and countries being ne'er so far.
> But what can these things be of price or worth,
> To know degrees, heights, depths, east, west, south, north.
> What are all these but shadows and vain hopes,
> If ships do either want their sails or ropes?
> And now ere I offend, I must confess
> A little from my theme I will digress;
> Striving in verse to show a lively form
> Of an impetuous gust or deadly storm.

SOUTHEY'S INTRODUCTION TO *ATTEMPTS IN VERSE*

Where, uncontrolled, Hyperborean blasts
Tears all to tatters, tacklings, sails, and masts;
Where boisterous puffs of *Eurus'*[144] breath did hiss,
And 'mongst our shrouds and cordage widely whiz;
Where thundering *Jove*, amidst his lightning flashing,
Seem'd overwhelmed with *Neptune's* mountain dashing;
Where glorious *Titan* hid his burning light,
Turning his bright meridian to black night;
Where blustering *Eole*[145] blew confounding breath,
And thunder's fearfull larum threatened death;
Where skies and seas, hail, wind, and slavering sleet,
As if they all at once had meant to meet
In fatal opposition, to expire
The world, and unto *Chaos* back retire.
Thus, while the Winds' and Sea's contending gods,
In rough robustious fury are at odds,
The beaten ship, tost like a forceless feather,
Now up, now down, and no man knowing whither:
The topmast some time tilting at the moon,
And being up doth fall again as soon,
With such precipitating low descent,
As if to hell's black kingdom down she went.
Poor ship that rudder on no steerage feels,
Sober, yet worse than any drunkard reels,
Unmanaged, guideless, too and fro she wallows,
Which (seemingly) the angry billows swallows.

A STORM

Midst darkness, lightning, thunder, sleet, and rain,
Remorseless winds and mercy-wanting main,
Amazement, horror, dread from each man's face
Had chased away life's blood, and in the place
Was sad despair, with hair heaved up upright,
With ashy visage, and with sad affright,
As if grim death with his all-murdering dart,
Had aiming been at each man's bloodless heart.
Out cries the master, 'Lower the topsail, lower!'
Then up aloft runs scrambling three or four,
But yet for all their hurly burly hast,
Ere they got up, down tumbles sail and mast.
'Veer the main-sheet there,' then the master cried,
'Let rise the fore-tack, on the larboard side:
Take in the fore-sail, yare, good fellows, yare,

Aluffe at helm there, – ware, no more, beware,
Steer south-south-east there, I say ware no more,
We are in danger of the leeward shore,
Clear your main-brace, let go the bolein there,
Port, port the helm hard, Romer, come no near.
Sound, sound, heave, heave the lead, what depth, what depth?'
'Fathom and a half, three all.'
Then with a whiff, the winds again do puff,
And then the master cries 'Aluff, aluff,
Make ready the anchor, ready the anchor, hoa,
Clear, clear the boigh-rope, steddy, well steer'd so;
Hale up the boat; in sprit-sail there afore,
Blow wind and burst, and then thou wilt give o'er.
Aluff, clap helm a-lee, yea, yea, done, done,
Down, down alow, into the hold quick run.
There's a plank sprung, something in hold did break,
Pump-bullies, carpenters, quick stop the leak.
Once heave the lead again, and sound abaffe.'
'A shafnet less, seven all.'
'Let fall the anchor then, let fall,
Man, man the boat, a woat hale, up hale,
Top your main yard a port, veer cable alow,
Go way a-head the boat there hoe, dee row,
Well pumpt, my hearts of gold, who says amends,
East and by south, west and by north she wends,
This was a weather with a witness here,
But now we see the skies begin to clear,
To dinner, hey, and let's at anchor ride,
Till wind grows gentler, and a smoother tide.'

'*I think,*' he pursues in prose, '*I have spoken Heathen Greek, Utopian, or Bermudian, to a great many of my readers in the description of this storm, but indeed I wrote it only for the understanding mariner's reading. I did it three years since, and could not find a better place than this to insert it, or else must have lain in silence.*'

In this prose postcript Taylor alludes to some epitaphs in gibberish upon Tom Coryat the Odcombian,[146] whose harmless eccentricities made him the butt of all wits and witlings, his contemporaries. Sometimes he amused himself with verses of grandiloquous nonsense, – not that kind of nonsense which passes for sense and sublimity with the poet himself, and is introduced as such to the admiration of the world by some literary master of the ceremonies; – but honest right rampant nonsense.

Think'st thou a wolf thrust through a sheepskin glove,
Can make me take this goblin for a lamb?
Or that a crocodile in barley-broth
Is not a dish to feast Don Belzebub?

SOUTHEY'S INTRODUCTION TO *ATTEMPTS IN VERSE*

Give me a medlar in a field of blue
Wrapt up stigmatically in a dream,
And I will send him to the gates of Dis,
To cause him fetch a sword of massy chalk
With which he won the fatal Theban field
From Rome's great mitred metropolitan.

Among his exhibitions of metre are some sonnets, as he calls them, composed upon one rhyme: one little piece in which all the lines rhyme upon *Coriat*, and another in which *crudities* is the keyword, – levelled against the same poor inoffensive humourist, who, ridiculous as he was, and liked to make himself, is nevertheless entitled to some respect for his enterprising spirit, his perseverance, and his acquirements; and to some compassion for his fate. It may be more worthy of notice, that Hudibrastic rhymes[147] are to be found in the Water-Poet's works: there may be earlier specimens, and probably are, for Taylor possessed an imitative rather than inventive talent; but this is the earliest that I have seen.

Whether from this itch of imitation, or the love of adventure, or want of other employment, and the desire of gain, Taylor engaged at different times in expeditions which were characterised by some singularity, or some difficulty, and even danger. Such undertakings were not uncommon at that time. His 'loving friend,' Samuel Rowlands,[148] in some verses addressed to him upon his, 'Sculler's Travels from Tiber to Thames,' enumerates some of those which had attracted most notice.

Ferris gave cause of vulgar wonderment,
When unto Bristow[3] in a boat he went:
Another with his sculler ventured more,
That rowed to Flushing from our English shore:
Another did devise a wooden whale
Which unto Calais did from Dover sail:
Another with his oars and slender wherry
From London unto Antwerp o'er did ferry:
Another, maugre fickle fortune's teeth,
Rowed hence to Scotland and arrived at Leith.

These were all wagering adventures. The first which Taylor undertook (in the year 1616) he published an account of, with this title, 'Taylor's Travels, three weeks, three days, and three hours' observations, from London to Hamburg, in Germany, amongst Jews and Gentiles; with descriptions of Towns and Towers, Castles and Citadels, artificial Gallowses and natural Hangmen, dedicated for the present to the absent Odcombian knight errant, Sir Thomas Coriat, Great Britain's

---

3 [Southey's note:] A tract describing this adventure, and the honours with which the adventurers were entertained at Bristol, is noted in that very valuable repository of literary information, the British Bibliographer, vol. ii. [*The Most Dangerous Adventure of R. Ferris, A. Hill and W. Thomas, Who Went in a Boat by Sea from London to Bristol* (1590). *The British Bibilographer*, compiled by Sir Egerton Brydges and Joseph Haaslewood, was published in four volumes between 1810 and 1814.]

121

SOUTHEY'S INTRODUCTION TO *ATTEMPTS IN VERSE*

Error, and the world's Mirror.' He had a brother settled in a town which he calls Buckaburgh, in the earldom of Schomberg;[149] and the motive for this journey was to visit him: but he thought it might be turned to some account also, by finding persons who would receive money from him, and pay him back a larger sum if he performed the specified journey, and returned from it. I have to thank him for the story of Roprecht the Robber,[150] which I found in his account of this journey. It seems that he made a second to the same country, but there is only a bare intimation of this in the collected volume of his works. His third undertaking was to travel on foot from London to Edinburgh, 'not carrying any money to or fro; neither begging, borrowing, or asking meat, drink, or lodging.' This he performed in 1618, and published an account of it in verse and prose, entitled 'The Pennyless Pilgrimage, or the Moneyless Perambulation of John Taylor, alias the King's Majesty's Water-Poet.' 'This journey,' says he, 'was undertaken, neither in imitation or emulation of any man, but only devised by myself, on purpose to make trial of my friends, both in this kingdom of England and that of Scotland, and because I would be an eye-witness of divers things which I had heard of that country. And whereas many shallow-brained critics do lay an aspersion on me that I was set on by others, or that I did undergo this project either in malice or mockery of Master Benjamin Jonson, I vow, by the faith of a Christian, that their imaginations are all wild; for he is a gentleman to whom I am so much obliged, for many undeserved courtesies that I have received from him, and from others by his favour, that I durst never to be so impudent or ingrateful, as either to suffer any man's persuasions, or mine own instigation, to make me to make so bad a requital for so much goodness.'[151]

The undertaking was no very arduous one, for he was at that time a well-known person: he counted (as appears by his own words) on his friends upon the road; he carried, in his tongue, a gift which, wherever he might be entertained, would be accepted as current payment for his entertainment; and moreover, he had his man to accompany him, and a sumpter-beast well victualled for the journey.

> There in my knapsack to pay hunger's fees,
> I had good bacon, bisket, neat's tongue, cheese,
> With roses, barberries, of each conserves,
> And mithridate that vigorous health preserves;
> And, I intreat you take these words for no lies,
> I had good aquavita, rosasolies,
> With sweet ambrosia, the gods' own drink,
> Most excellent gear for mortals, as I think;
> Besides I had both vinegar and oil.

Thus provided he set forth, baiting and lodging as he went with friend or acquaintance, or at the cost or invitation of good-natured strangers. He says

> I made my legs my oars, and rowed by land.

But he, and probably his man too, had been more used to ply their arms than their legs, for they were poor pedestrians; and had nearly foundered by the time they

SOUTHEY'S INTRODUCTION TO *ATTEMPTS IN VERSE*

reached Daventry. It had been a wet and windy day, and meeting with something like Tom Drum's entertainment[152] from the hostess of the Horse-shoe in that town, who had 'a great wart rampant on her snout,' they were fain

> to hobble seven miles more,
> The way to Dunchurch, foul with dirt and mire,
> Able, I think, both man and horse to tire:
> On Dunsmore-heath, a hedge doth then enclose
> Grounds on the right-hand, there I did repose.
> Wit's whetstone, Want, then made us quickly learn,
> With knives to cut down rushes and green fern,
> Of which we made a field-bed in the field,
> Which sleep and rest and much content did yield.
> There with my mother Earth I thought it fit
> To lodge. –
> My bed was curtained with good wholesome airs,
> And being weary, I went up no stairs;
> The sky my canopy; bright Phoebe shin'd;
> Sweet bawling Zephyrus breath'd gentle wind;
> In heaven's star-chamber I did lodge that night,
> Ten thousand stars me to my bed did light.
> There barricadoed with a bank lay we,
> Below the lofty branches of a tree.
> There my bedfellows and companions were,
> My man, my horse, a bull, four cows, two steer;
> But yet for all this most confused rout,
> We had no bed-staves, yet we fell not out.
> Thus Nature, like an ancient free upholster,
> Did furnish us with bedstead, bed, and bolster;
> And the kind skies (for which high Heaven be thanked!)
> Allowed us a large covering, and a blanket.

Proceeding the next day 'through plashes, puddles, thick, thin, wet, and dry,' he reached Coventry, and was there entertained two or three days by Dr. Holland, the once well-known Philemon, who used, in translation, more paper and fewer pens than any other writer before or since; and who 'would not let Suetonius be Tranquillus.'[153] After leaving him, he was welcomed at Lichfield by an acquaintance, who offered him money also, which it was against the bond to accept, and supplied him with 'good provant.' The next day's was no pleasant journey.

> That Wednesday I a weary way did pass,
> Rain, wind, stones, dirt, and dabbling dewy grass,
> With here and there a pelting scattered village,
> Which yielded me no charity or pillage;

SOUTHEY'S INTRODUCTION TO *ATTEMPTS IN VERSE*

For all the day, nor yet the night that follow'd,
One drop of drink I am sure my gullet swallow'd.
At night I came to a stony town call'd Stone,
Where I knew none, nor was I known of none.
I therefore through the streets held on my pace,
Some two miles farther, to some resting place.
At last I spied a meadow newly mowed,
The hay was rotten, the ground half o'er-flowed:
We made a breach and entered, horse and man,
There our pavilion we to pitch began,
Which we erected with green broom and hay,
To expel the cold and keep the rain away;
The sky all muffled in a cloud 'gan lower,
And presently there fell a mighty shower,
Which without intermission down did pour
From ten at night until the morning's four.
We all this time close in our couch did lie,
Which being well compacted kept us dry.

Sir Urien Legh[154] entertained him with right old hospitality at Adlington, near Macclesfield, from the Thursday-night till Monday-noon, – having him at his own table; though Taylor had not 'shifted a shirt' since he left London. Sir Urien gave him a letter to his kinsman, Edmund Prestwitch,[155] a good esquire, near Manchester; there he was lodged and fed, and shaved, and his horse (for the second time) shod; and for this gentleman's sake he was sumptuously entertained by the people of Manchester, Mr. Prestwitch sending a man and horse to guide him, and bear his expenses through the county. But his recommendation sufficed in lieu of all charges at Manchester: the kindness which he there experienced, Taylor thus relates:

Their loves they on the tenter-hooks did rack,
Roast, boiled, baked, too-too-much, white, claret, sack;
Nothing they thought too heavy, or too hot,
Cann followed cann, and pot succeeded pot.
Thus what they could do, all they thought too little,
Striving in love the traveller to whittle.
We went into the house of one John Pinners,
(A man that lives amongst a crew of sinners,)
And there eight several sorts of ale we had,
All able to make one stark drunk, or mad.
But I with courage bravely flinched not,
And gave the town leave to discharge the shot.
We had at one time set upon the table,
Good ale of Hyssop (twas no Esop-fable):
Then had we ale of Sage, and ale of Malt,

SOUTHEY'S INTRODUCTION TO *ATTEMPTS IN VERSE*

And ale of Wormwood that could make one halt;
With ale of Rosemary, and of Bettony,
And two ales more, or else I needs must lie.
But to conclude this drinking aley tale,
We had a sort of ale called Scurvy ale.
Thus all these men at their own charge and cost
Did strive whose love should be expressed most;
And farther to declare their boundless loves,
They saw I wanted, and they gave me, gloves.

The hostess, also, of the Eagle and Child,[156] had his shirts and bands washed, and gave him twelve silk points. The same recommendation procured him a good reception at Preston, where he tarried three days, and protests that he never saw a town more wisely governed by the law. 'Kind Master Thomas Banister,'[157] the mayor, spent much cost and charge upon him, and rode with him at his departure two miles on his way.

There by good chance I did more friendship get,
The under-shriefe of Lancashire we met,
A gentleman that loved and knew me well,
And one whose bounteous mind doth bear the bell.
There, as if I had been a noted thief,
The Mayor delivered me unto the Shriefe;
The Shriefe's authority did much prevail,
He sent me unto one that kept the jail.
Thus I, perambulating poor John Taylor,
Was given from Mayor to Shriefe, from Shriefe to Jailor.
The Jailor kept an inn, good beds, good cheer,
Where, paying nothing, I found nothing dear,
For the under-shriefe, kind Master Covill[158] named,
(A man for house-keeping renowned and famed,)
Did cause the town of Lancaster afford
Me welcome, as if I had been a lord.

Master Covill sent a man with him to Sedbergh, which was two days' journey, and they scarcely missed an alehouse on the way, so liberal was the guide of his master's money. The next stage was to Master Edmund Branthwaite's, at Carling Hill.[159] Branthwaite escorted him to Orton, where Master Corney,[160] 'a good true divine,' was his host; and Master Corney sent a man with him 'o'er dale and down, who lodged and boarded him at Peereth (Penrith) town.' There he found a volunteer guide for Carlisle; but two miles wide of that city Sir John Dalstone[161] entertained him. One might have hoped in these parts for a happy meeting between John Taylor and Barnabee, of immortal memory; indeed, it is likely that the Water-Poet and the Anti-Water-Poet were acquainted, and that the latter may

125

have introduced him to his connections hereabout, Branthwaite being the same name as Brathwait, and Barnabee's brother having married a daughter of this Sir John Dalstone.[162] He makes his acknowledgments also to Sir Henry Curwen,[163] for good offices at Carlisle. Adam Robinson, who had been mayor of that city the preceding year,[164] provided him with a guide to Edinburgh, which, of the many helps upon his journey, was the greatest. Having crost the border, he then proceeds with his narrative in prose.

He waded the Esk and the Annan, and reached Moffatt in one day from Carlisle – 'the weariest day's journey that ever he footed.' The next day brought him one-and-twenty miles to a sorry village called Blithe; 'but I was blithe myself,' he says, 'to come to any place of harbour or succour; for since I was born I never was so weary, or so near being dead with extreme travel. I was foundered and refoundered of all four; and for my better comfort, I came so late, that I must lodge without doors all night, or else in a farmhouse where the good wife lay in child-bed, her husband being from home, her own servant maid being her nurse; a creature naturally compacted and artificially adorned with an incomparable homeliness.' Hence it was but fifteen miles to Edinburgh, in which 'wished, long-expected, ancient, famous city,' he came to take rest on the 13th of August, having started from London on the 14th of July.

'I entered like Pierce Pennyless,[165] altogether moneyless, but, I thank God, not friendless; for, being there, for the time of my stay, I might borrow – if any man would lend; spend – if I could get; beg – if I had the impudence; and steal – if I durst adventure the price of a hanging. But my purpose was to house my horse, and to suffer him and my apparel to lie in durance, or lavender, instead of litter, till such time as I could meet with some valiant friend that would desperately disburse. Walking thus down the street, (my body being tired with travel, and my mind attired with moody, muddy, Moor-ditch melancholy,) my contemplation did devoutly pray, that I might meet one or other to prey upon, being willing to take any slender acquaintance of any map whatsoever; viewing and circumviewing every man's face I met, as if I meant to draw his picture; but all my acquaintance was *non est inventus*:[166] (pardon me, reader, that Latin is none of my own, I swear by Priscian's[167] pericranium, an oath which I have ignorantly broken many times!) At last I resolved that the next gentleman that I met withal, should be acquaintance whether he would or no: and presently fixing mine eyes upon a gentleman-like object, I looked on him as if I would survey something through him, and make him my perspective. And he much musing at my gazing, and I much gazing at his musing, at last he crossed the way and made toward me, and then I made down the street from him, leaving him to encounter with my man, who came after me, leading my horse; whom he thus accosted: 'My friend,' quoth he, 'doth yonder gentleman' (meaning me) 'know me, that he looks so wistly on me?' 'Truly Sir,' said my man, 'I think not: but my master is a stranger come from London, and would gladly meet some acquaintance to direct him where he may have lodging, and horse-meat.' Presently the gentleman (being of a generous disposition) over-took me, with unexpected and undeserved courtesy, brought me to a lodging, and caused my horse to be put into his own stable: whilst we, discoursing over a pint of Spanish,[168] I related so much English to him, as made him lend me ten shillings: (his name was Master John Maxwell,)[169] which money, I am sure, was the first that I handled after I came from out the walls of London.'

The gentleman who with so much good-nature allowed this acquaintanceship to be thus forced on him, walked about the city with him. Taylor had seen many fortresses in Germany, the Netherlands, Spain, and England, but all, he thought, must give place to Edinburgh Castle, both for strength and situation, and the High Street was 'the fairest and goodliest' that ever his eyes beheld, as well as the largest that he had ever heard of; 'the buildings being all of squared stone, five, six, and seven stories high, and many bye-lanes and closes on each side of the way, wherein are gentlemen's houses, much fairer than the buildings in the High Street; for in the High Street the merchants and tradesmen do dwell; but the gentlemen's mansions and goodliest houses are obscurely founded in the aforesaid lanes; the walls are eight or ten feet thick, exceeding strong, not built for a day, a week, or a month, or a year, but from antiquity to posterity, for many ages.' Here he soon found, or made, so many acquaintances, and those so liberal of their wine and ale, that he says, if any man had asked him a civil question every night be fore he went to bed, all the wit in his head could not have made him a sober answer.

At length he met with Master Bernard Lindsay, one of the grooms of his Majesty's bedchamber: 'he knew my estate was not guilty, because I brought no guilt with me, more than my sins, (and they would not pass current there): he therefore did replenish the vastity of my empty purse, and discharged a piece at me with two bullets of gold, each being in value worth eleven shillings, white money.'[170] He was now in the way of old court acquaintance, and here he gives us an anecdote of his life which well illustrates the utility and capacity of the article of dress known in those days by the appellation of trunk-hose.

'I went two miles from Leith, to a town called Burnt-Island,[171] where I found many of my especial good friends, as Master Robert Hay, one of the grooms of his Majesty's bedchamber;[172] Master David Drummond, one of his gentlemen-pensioners;[173] Master James Acmooty, one of the grooms of the privy-chamber;[174] Captain Murray;[175] Sir Henry Witherington, knight;[176] Captain Tyrie,[177] and divers others: and there Master Hay, Master Drummond, and the good old Captain Murray, did very bountifully furnish me with gold for my expenses; but I being at dinner with these aforesaid gentlemen, as we were discoursing, there befell a strange accident, which I think worth the relating.

'I know not upon what occasion they began to talk of being at sea in former times, and I (amongst the rest) said, I was at the taking of Cales:[178] whereto an English gentleman replied, that he was the next good voyage after at the Islands.[179] I answered him that I was there also. He demanded in what ship I was? I told him in the Rainbow of the Queen's: why (quoth he) do you not know me? I was in the same ship, and my name is Witherington. Sir, said I, I do remember the name well; but by reason that it is near two-and-twenty years since I saw you, I may well forget the knowledge of you. Well, said he, if you were in that ship, pray you

127

tell me some remarkable token that happened in the voyage; whereupon I told him two or three tokens, which he did know to be true. Nay, then, said I, I will tell you another, which (perhaps) you have not forgotten. As our ship and the rest of the fleet did ride at anchor at the Isle of Flores, (one of the isles of the Azores,) there were some fourteen men and boys of our ship that for novelty would go ashore, and see what fruit the island did bear, and what entertainment it would yield us: so being landed, we went up and down and could find nothing but stones, heath, and moss, and we expected oranges, lemons, figs, musk-millions, and potatoes: in the mean space the wind did blow so stiff, and the sea was so extreme rough, that our ship-boat could not come to the land to fetch us, for fear she should be beaten in pieces against the rocks; this continued five days, so that we were almost famished for want of food; but at the last, (I, squandering up and down,) by the providence of God, I happened into a cave or poor habitation, where I found fifteen loaves of bread, each of the quantity of a penny loaf in England; I, having a valiant stomach of the age of almost a hundred and twenty hours breeding, fell to, and ate two loaves and never said grace; and as I was about to make a horse-loaf of the third loaf, I did put twelve of them into my breeches, and my sleeves, and so went mumbling out of the cave, leaning my back against a tree, when upon the sudden a gentleman came to me, and said, friend, what are you eating? Bread (quoth I). For God's sake, said he, give me some! With that I put my hand into my breech, (being my best pantry,) and I gave him a loaf, which he received with many thanks, and said that if ever he could requite it he would. I had no sooner told this tale, but Sir Henry Witherington did acknowledge himself to be the man that I had given the loaf unto two-and-twenty years before; where I found the proverb true, that men have more priviledge than mountains in meeting.'

Taylor now departed from Edinburgh, meaning to see Stirling Castle, visit his 'honourable friends' the Earl of Marr[180] and Sir William Murray, Lord of Abercarney,[181] and return in two days. But when he came to Stirling he found that these friends were gone to the great hunting in the Brea of Marr,[182] and he was told, that if he made haste, he might perhaps overtake them at Brechin. When he reached Brechin, they had been gone four days. So taking another guide, after them he went, by 'strange ways, over mountains and rocks, putting up the first night in the Laird of Eggel's land,[183] at a house where the people could scarcely speak any English,' and where, for the only time in Scotland, he was annoyed by the most unclean of six-legged insects, which he calls Irish musquitoes. Next day he travelled over Mount Skeene; it was warm in the valley, 'but when I came to the top,' he says, 'my teeth began to dance in my head with cold, like virginals' jacks, and withal, a most familiar mist embraced me round, that I could not see through my length any way; withal, it yielded so friendly a dew, that it did moisten through all my clothes.' Up and down he estimated this hill at six miles, 'the way so uneven, stoney, and full of bogs, quagmires, and long heath, that a dog with three legs would there outrun a horse with four.' At night, 'with extreme travail,' he came to the place where he could see the Brae of Marr, 'which is a large country, all composed of such mountains, that Shooter's Hill, Gad's Hill, Highgate Hill,

SOUTHEY'S INTRODUCTION TO *ATTEMPTS IN VERSE*

Hampstead Hill, Birdtop Hill, or Malvern Hills, are but mole-hills in comparison, or like a liver or gizzard under a capon's wing, in respect of the altitude of their tops, or perpendicularity of their bottoms.'

Here he found his friends, with lords and ladies, and hundreds of knights, esquires, and followers, all in one habit, 'as if Lycurgus[184] had been there, and made laws of equality; for at this annual hunting, every one conformed to the habit of the highlandmen, who for the most part speak nothing but Irish, and in former times were those people which were called the Red-Shanks. Their habit is shoes with but one sole a-piece, stockings which they call short-hose, made of a warm stuff of divers colours, which they call tartane; as for breeches, many of them nor their forefathers, never wore any, but a jerkin of the same stuff that their hose is of, their garters being bands or wreathes of hay or straw, with a plaid about their shoulders, which is a mantle of divers colours, much finer and lighter stuff than their hose, with blue flat caps on their heads, a handkerchief knit with two knots about their necks, and thus were they attired. Now their weapons are long bows and forked arrows, swords and targets, harquebusses, muskets, dirks, and Loquhabor-axes;[185] with these arms I found many of them armed for the hunting. As for their attire, any man of what degree soever, that comes amongst them, must not disdain to wear it; for if they do, then they will disdain to hunt, or willingly to bring on their dogs: but if men be kind unto them and be in their habit, then are they conquered with kindness, and the sport will be plentiful.' The Earl of Marr put the Water-Poet 'into this shape,' and after leaving his house he was twelve days 'before he saw either house, corn-field, or habitation for any creature but deer, wild horses, wolves, and such like.' There were, however, 'small cottages built on purpose to lodge in, which they call Lonquhards.'

Taylor fared plentifully at this noble hunting, and entered heartily into the sport. 'I thank my good Lord Erskin,[186] he commanded that I should always be lodged in his lodging, the kitchen being always on the side of a bank, many kettles and pots boiling, and many spits turning and winding, with great variety of cheer: as venison baked, sodden, roast and stewed; beef, mutton, goats, kid, hares, fresh salmon, pidgeons, hens, capons, chickens, partridges, moorecoots, heathcocks, caperkellies, and termagants; good ale, sack, white, and claret, tent,[187] (or alle-gant,)[188] with most potent aquavitæ. All these, and more than these we had contin-ually, in superfluous abundance, caught by falconers, fowlers, fishers, and brought by my lord's tenants and purveyors to victual our camp, which consisteth of four-teen or fifteen hundred men and horses. The manner of the hunting is this: five or six hundred men do rise early in the morning, and they do disperse themselves divers ways, and seven, eight, or ten miles compass, they do bring or chase in the deer in many herds, (two, three, or four hundred in a herd,) to such and such a place, as the noblemen shall appoint them; then when day is come, the lords and gentlemen of their companies do ride or go to the said places, sometimes wad-ing up to the middle through bournes and rivers: and then they being come to the place, do lie down on the ground till those foresaid scouts, which are called the Tinckhell,[189] do bring down the deer. But as the proverb says of a bad cook, so

129

SOUTHEY'S INTRODUCTION TO *ATTEMPTS IN VERSE*

these Tinckhell men do like their own fingers; for besides their bows and arrows, which they carry with them, we can hear now and then an arquebuss or a musket go off, which they do seldom discharge in vain: then after we had stayed there three hours or thereabouts, we might perceive the deer appear on the hills round about us, (their heads making a show like a wood,) which being followed close by the Tinckhell, are chased down into the valley where we lay; then all the valley on each side being waylaid with a hundred couple of strong Irish greyhounds, they are let loose as occasion serves upon the herd of deer, that with dogs, guns, arrows, dirks, and daggers, in the space of two hours, fourscore fat deer were slain; which after are disposed of, some one way and some another, twenty and thirty miles, and more than enough left for us to make merry withal at our rendezvous. I liked the sport so well, that I made these two sonnets following.

> Why should I waste invention, to endite
> *Ovidian* fictions, or Olympian games?
> My misty muse enlightened with more light,
> To a more noble pitch her aim she frames.
> I must relate to my great master, James,
> The Caledonian annual peaceful war;
> How noble minds do eternize their fames,
> By martial meeting in the Brae of Marr:
> How thousand gallant spirits came near and far,
> With swords and targets, arrows, bows, and guns,
> That all the troop, to men of judgement, are
> The God of War's great never conquered sons.
> The sport is manly, yet none bleed but beasts,
> And last the victor on the vanquished feasts.

> If sport like this can on the mountains be,
> Where Phoebus' flames can never melt the snow,
> Then let who list delight in vales below;
> Sky-kissing mountains pleasure are for me:
> What braver object can man's eye-sight see,
> Than noble, worshipful, and worthy wights,
> As if they were prepared for sundry fights,
> Yet all in sweet society agree?
> Through heather, moss, 'mongst frogs and bogs and fogs,
> 'Mongst craggy cliffs and thunder-battered hills,
> Hares, hinds, bucks, roes, are chased by men and dogs,
> Where two hours' hunting fourscore fat deer kills.
> Lowland, your sports are low as is your seat!
> The highland games and minds are high and great.

SOUTHEY'S INTRODUCTION TO *ATTEMPTS IN VERSE*

'Being come to our lodgings, there was such baking, boiling, roasting, and stewing, as if Cook Ruffian had been there to have scalded the devil in his feathers and after supper a fire of fir-wood as high as an indifferent may-pole; for I assure you, that the Earl of Marr will give any man that is his friend, for thanks, as many fir-trees (that are as good as any ship's masts in England) as are worth (if they were in any place near the Thames, or any other portable river) the best earldom in England or Scotland either; for I dare affirm, he hath as many growing there, as would serve for masts (from this time to the end of the world) for all the ships, caracks, hoyes, galleys, boats, drumlers, barks, and water-crafts, that are now or can be in the world these forty years.'

After the hunt broke up he was entertained at Ruthen[190] by the Lord of Engie, at Ballo Castle[191] by the Laird of Graunt,[192] at Tarnaway by the Earl of Murray,[193] at Spinaye by the Bishop of Murray;[194] and by the Marquis of Huntley,[195] at a sumptuous house of his, named the Bog of Geethe.[196] And after five and thirty days' hunting and travelling, he returned to Edinburgh, those lords giving him gold to defray his charges on the journey. He stayed at Edinburgh eight days, to recover 'from falls and bruises received in the highland mountainous hunting.' Many worthy gentlemen there suffered him neither to want wine nor good cheer. 'At Leith,' he says, 'I found my long approved and assured good friend, Master Benjamin Johnson, at one Master John Stuart's house.[197] I thank him for his great kindness towards me, for at my taking leave of him, he gave me a piece of gold of two-and-twenty shillings to drink his health in England, and, withal, willed me to remember his kind commendation to all his friends. So with a friendly farewell I left him, as well as I hope never to see him in a worse estate; for he is amongst noblemen and gentlemen, that know his true worth and their honour, where with much respect and love he is worthily entertained.'

Being now to commence his journey home, according to the bond, he discharged his pockets of all the money he had at the port or gate called the Netherbows, and as he came pennyless within the walls, went moneyless out of them. But he had no meagre days, nor bivouacking at nights, on his homeward road; for Master James Acmooty, with whom he presently fell in, was going to London, and for the sake of his company undertook that neither he nor his horse should want upon the way; an undeserved courtesy, of which Taylor says, his want persuaded his manners to accept; not that he availed himself of it on the whole journey, for he overtook other friends at Newcastle, where Sir Henry Witherington gave him a bay mare, (because he would accept no money,) in requital for the loaf; he tried his own fortune from Topcliffe to York, and obtained letters for the rest of the way, or found acquaintance. His friends came to meet him at Islington, at the sign of the Maidenhead, when with all love he was entertained with much good cheer, and after supper they had a play of the Life and Death of Guy of Warwick,[198]

131

played by the Earl of Derby's men, and on the next morning, Oct. 15, he came to his house at London.

> Thus did I neither spend, or beg, or ask,
> By any course, direct or indirectly;
> But in each tittle I performed my task
> According to my bill most circumspectly.

His next journey, which was also undertaken as a wagering adventure, was to Prague, in the year 1620. He published an account of it, *more suo*,[199] in prose and verse. 'The truth,' he says, 'is, that I did chiefly write it, because I am of much acquaintance, and cannot pass the streets but I am continually stayed by one or other, to know what news; so that sometimes I am four hours before I can go the length of two pair of buts, where such nonsense or senseless questions are propounded to me, that calls many seeming wise men's wisdom in question, drawing aside the curtains of their understandings, and laying their ignorance wide open. First, John Easy takes me, and holds me fast by the fist half an hour; and will needs torture some news out of me from Spinola, whom I was never near by five hundred miles, for he is in the Palatinate country and I was in Bohemia. I am no sooner eased of him, but Gregory Gandergoose, an alderman of Gotham,[200] catches me by the goll, demanding if Bohemia be a great town, and whether there be any meat in it, and whether the last fleet of ships be arrived there.'[201] (You know, reader, that Prague might have been a sea-port, according to Corporal Trim.)[202] 'His mouth being stopt, a third examines me boldly what news from Vienna? where the Emperor's army is, and what the Duke of Bavaria doth? what is become of Count Buquoy? how fare all the Englishmen? where lies the King of Bohemia's forces? what Bethlem Gabor doth? what tidings of Dampeier? and such a tempest of inquisitions that almost shakes my patience in pieces. To ease myself of all which, I was enforced to set pen to paper and let this poor pamphlet (my herald, or nuntius,) travel and talk, while I take my ease with silence.'[203]

The Queen of Bohemia, who was then such in possession, and not in title alone, made him a partaker of her bounty at Prague; and he had her youngest son, Prince Rupert,[204] in his arms, and brought away, to keep as a memorial of this honour, the infant's shoes.

> Lambskin they were, as white as innocence,
> (True patterns for the footsteps of a Prince,)
> And time will come, as I do hope in God,
> He that in childhood with these shoes was shod,
> Shall with his manly feet once trample down
> All Antichristian foes to his renown.

Poor Taylor lived to see the prince employed in a very different war from what these lines anticipated![205]

SOUTHEY'S INTRODUCTION TO *ATTEMPTS IN VERSE*

Two years after this journey he made 'a very merry wherry-ferry voyage from London to York.' Being forced by stress of weather to land at Cromer, the whole town was alarmed, he and his four men were supposed to be pirates, the constables took them into custody, and guards were set upon their wherry.

> They did examine me, I answered then,
> I was John Taylor, and a waterman,
> And that my honest fellow Job, and I,
> Were servants to King James's Majesty;
> How we to York upon a mart were bound,
> And that we landed fearing to be drown'd.
> When all this would not satisfy the crew,
> I freely ope'd my trunks, and bade them view.
> I showed them Books of Chronicles and Kings,
> Some prose, some verse, some idle sonnetings;
> I showed them all my letters to the full.
> Some to York's Archbishop, and some to Hull.

Nothing, however, would satisfy the people, till two magistrates, (Sir Austin Palgrave[206] and Mr. Robert Kempe,)[207] had examined these invaders. These gentlemen knew the Water-Poet by name, and had read some of his books; they administered the oath of allegiance to him and his men, to content the people, and gave him 'corn and wine and lodging too;' and he met then with as much assistance from the sailors there, as he had found incivility at first. He crossed the Wash with some danger, not knowing the place and having no pilot, and being caught in the Hyger.[208] When he reached Boston he was glad to learn that the remainder of his way might be performed by an inland navigation. Accordingly, he went up the Witham, fifty miles, to Lincoln, performing the distance in one day.

> From thence we passed a ditch of weeds and mud,
> Which they do (falsely) there call Forcedike Flood,
> For I'll be sworn no flood I could find there,
> But dirt and filth which scarce my boat would bear:
> 'Tis eight miles long, and there our pains was such,
> As all our travel did not seem so much.
> My men did wade, and draw the boat like horses,
> And scarce could tug her on with all our forces:
> Moil'd, toil'd, mired, tired, still labouring, ever doing,
> Yet were we nine long hours that eight miles going.
> At last when as the day was well nigh spent,
> We got from Forcedike's floodless flood to Trent.

Down the Trent then they proceeded to Gainsborough, which they reached just 'as the windows of the day did shut;' and the next day entered the Humber, but instead of bending their course directly for York, they went out of it to touch at Hull, and had nearly been swamped on the way, an east wind raising such waves against a swift ebb tide, that he had never seen any thing like it before in the course of his waterman's life.

He had letters to the mayor and other members of the corporation, as well as to private individuals, who were requested to make him welcome, and give him Hull cheese, which he says, 'is much like a loaf out of a brewer's basket; for it is composed of two simples, malt and water, in one compound, and is cousin-german to the mightiest ale in England.' Hops not being mentioned in this compound, it seems that the distinction between ale and beer continued to be known in his time. Here he was received not merely like a man whose company was acceptable to every one who could obtain it, but as a person, also, whose visit did honour to the town. Mayor and Aldermen entertained him, and he was pleased, as well he might, with the prosperity and good order of a place, where relief was provided for all the helpless poor and work for all the rest.

> Thanks, Mr. Mayor, for my bacon-gammon!
> Thanks, Roger Parker, for my small fresh salmon!
> 'Twas excellent good; and more the truth to tell ye,
> Boil'd with a fine plum-pudding in the belly.
> The sixth of August, well accompanied
> With best of townsmen to the water-side,
> There did I take my leave, and to my ship
> I with my drum and colours quickly skip:
> The one did dub-a-dub, and rumble brave,
> The ensign in the air did play and wave;
> I launch'd, supposing all things had been done;
> Bounce, from the Blockhouse, quoth a roaring gun;
> And waving hats on both sides, with content,
> I cried adieu! adieu! and thence we went.

That night he got to Cawood, and called the next day on the good old archbishop, Tobias Matthew,[209] who gave him gold and made him dine at his own table, while his men made good cheer in the hall. After dinner they proceeded to York, so finishing their adventure. He offered the boat, as in duty bound, he says, to the Lord Mayor,[210] who after some deliberation declined the present. Taylor, therefore, found a purchaser for it. From the Mayor he got nothing but a cup of claret and some beer. He says,

> I gave his lordship, in red gilded leather,
> A well-bound book of all my works together,
> Which he did take. –

SOUTHEY'S INTRODUCTION TO *ATTEMPTS IN VERSE*

'Here I make a full point, for I received not a point in exchange.' He then returned to London by land, and his Epilogue says,

> Thus have I brought to end a work of pain,
> I wish it may requite me with some gain;
> For well I wot the dangers where I ventured,
> No full-bagg'd man would ever durst have entered.

In the ensuing year (1623) he made a similar voyage from London to Christ Church, in Hampshire, and so up the Avon to Salisbury, and this was 'for toyle, travail, and danger,' the worst and most difficult passage he had yet made. These desperate adventures did not answer the purpose for which they were undertaken, and he complains of this in what he calls (*Tayloricé*) the Scourge of Baseness, a Kicksey Winsey, or a Lerry-Come-Twang.

> I made my journey for no other ends
> But to get money and to try my friends. –
> They took a book worth twelve pence, and were bound
> To give a crown, an angel, or a pound,
> A noble, piece, or half-piece, – what they list:
> They past their words, or freely set their fist.
> Thus got I sixteen hundred hands and fifty,
> Which sum I did suppose was somewhat thrifty;
> And now my youths with shifts and tricks and cavils,
> Above seven hundred, play the sharking javils.

Four thousand and five hundred books he had given out, he says, upon these implied or expressed conditions; they had cost him more than seven-score pounds, and his Scotch walk had been sport to the trouble of vainly tramping about in seeking what was his due. He had given out money as well as books. The censures which were past upon him, and others, who like him went dangerous voyages by sea in small wherries, for 'tempting God by undertaking such perilous courses,' he acknowledges were not undeserved, and said that in this way he had done his last. Yet, it appears, that after this he engaged in a more desperate adventure than any of the former, that of going from London to Queenborough in a paper boat, with two stock-fish tied to two canes for oars! Roger Bird, a vintner, was the principal in this mad enterprize. They took with them eight large and well-blown bladders, which were found necessary in the course of half an hour; for before they had got three miles, the paper bottom fell to pieces, and they had only the skeleton of the boat to trust to, and their bladders, four on each side. There they sat, 'within six inches of the brim.'

> Thousands of people all the shores did hide,
> And thousands more did meet us on the tide,

SOUTHEY'S INTRODUCTION TO *ATTEMPTS IN VERSE*

> With scullers, oars, with ship-boats and with barges,
> To gaze on us they put themselves to charges.
> Thus did we drive, and drive the time away,
> Till pitchy night had driven away the day.
> The sun unto the under world was fled,
> The moon was loth to rise, and kept her bed;
> The stars did twinkle, but the ebon clouds
> Their light, our sight, obscures and overshrouds.
> The tossing billows made our boat to caper,
> Our paper form scarce being form of paper;
> The water four miles broad, no oars to row;
> Night dark, and where we were we did not know:
> And thus 'twixt doubt and fear, hope and despair,
> I fell to work, and Roger Bird to prayer;
> And as the surges up and down did heave us,
> He cried most fervently, good Lord, receive us!

Taylor tells us, honestly, that he prayed as much, but he worked at the same time, which the poor wineman was not waterman enough to do: and having been on the water from Saturday, 'at evening tide,' till Monday morning, they reached Queenborough; and he says, being

> aland,
> I took my fellow Roger by the hand,
> And both of us, ere we two steps did go,
> Gave thanks to God that had preserved us so;
> Confessing that his mercy us protected,
> When as we least deserved, and less expected.

They arrived on the fair day, when the mayor entertained all comers with bread, beer, and oysters. They presented him with the skeleton of their boat, which

> to glorify that town of Kent,
> He meant to hang up for a monument;

but while he was feasting them, the country people tore it piecemeal, every man wishing to carry away a scrap as a memorial of this mad adventure.

Taylor was engaged in a flyting with Fennor,[211] who seems to have been a rival of his own rank: the fashion of such contests in ribaldry prevailed a little before his time in France and in Scotland; our literature has luckily escaped it, at least, I know not of any other example than the present. The circumstances which gave rise to it are related by the Water Poet, 'to any that can read,' in a short epistle prefixed to 'Taylor's Revenge, or the Rhymer, William Fennor, firkt, ferreted, and finely fetcht over the coals.' 'Be it,' he says, 'known unto all men, that I, John

SOUTHEY'S INTRODUCTION TO *ATTEMPTS IN VERSE*

Taylor, waterman, did agree with William Fennor, (who arrogantly and falsely entitles himself the King's Majesty's Rhyming Poet,) to answer me at a trial of wit, on the seventh of October last, (1614,) on the Hope stage, on the Bankside; and the said Fennor received of me ten shillings in earnest of his coming to meet me; whereupon I caused a thousand bills to be printed, and divulged my name a thousand ways and more, giving my friends and divers of my acquaintance notice of this Bear-Garden banquet of dainty conceits; and when the day came that the play should have been performed, the house being filled with a great audience, who had all spent their monies extraordinarily, then this companion for an ass ran away, and left me for a fool, amongst thousands of critical conjurors, where I was ill thought of by my friends, scorned by my foes; and in conclusion, in a greater puzzle than the blind bear in the midst of all her whipbroth. Besides the sum of twenty pounds in money, I lost my reputation amongst many, and gained disgrace instead of my better expectations. In revenge of which wrongs done unto me by the said rhyming rascal, I have written this invective against him; chiefly because the ill-looking hound doth not confess he hath injured me; nor hath not so much honesty as to bring or send me my money that he took for earnest of me, but on the contrary part, he rails and abuses me with his calumnious tongue, and scandalizes me in all companies where he hears me nominated.'

The price of admission had been raised upon this occasion, and when the audience had exhausted their patience in waiting for Fennor, they vented their indignation upon Taylor, pelting as well as abusing him, with that cowardly brutality of which all mobs seem capable. The Water Poet in return sent out a volley of vituperative verse both against them and the defaulter; and in the collected volume of his works, he was just enough to insert Fennor's defence, 'wherein the Waterman, John Taylor, is dasht, sowst, and finally fallen into the Thames, with his slanderous taxation, base imputations, scandalous accusations, and foul abominations, against his Majesty's Rhyming Poet.' From this answer it appears that Fennor, who had obtained reputation enough as an improvisatore to exhibit before James I., had assented to Taylor's project, which was that they should perform a sort of drama between them, Taylor having 'studied several humours in prose,' and Fennor being to play his part extemporaneously in verse; for which he required either 'half the commodity thereof; or security for five pounds; or else twenty shillings in hand, and the rest as the day afforded.' He excused himself for his non-appearance by a lame story, and poured out a volley of recriminative ribaldry, which the Water Poet answered in the same strain. The common estimate of Taylor's writings seems to have been taken from these pieces, which are the worst, and from his Rhymed Chronicles, which are the most worthless of his productions.

He was a married man, and the ensuing lines may show that he 'never accounted his marriage among his infelicities':

I have a wife which I was wont to praise,
But that was in my younger wooing days:

And though she's neither shrew, nor sheep, I vow,
With justice I cannot dispraise her now.
She hath an instrument that's ever strung
To exercise my patience on – her tongue:
But past all question, and beyond all doubt,
She'll ne'er infect my forehead with the gout.
A married man, some say, hath two days gladness,
And all his life else is a lingering sadness;
The one day's mirth is, when he first is married,
The other's when his wife's to burying carried:
One I have had, should I the t'other see,
It could not be a day of mirth to me,
For I, (as many have,) when I did woo,
Myself in tying fast did not undo;
But I have by my long experience found
I had been undone, had I not been bound.
I have my bonds of marriage long enjoyed,
And do not wish my obligation void.

When the troubles came on, the Water Poet, who had often tasted of the royal bounty, was too honest and too brave a man to turn with the tide; he left London, therefore, and retired to Oxford. He had formerly found shelter there during a plague, an account of which he published and dated from Oriel College.[212] In one of his tracts he acknowledges that the very air of the colleges and schools, the books he had read there, and the dictionaries he had pored upon, had much 'illustrated, elevated, and illuminated his intellect;' for he had 'picked out here and there etymologies, expressions, explanations, and significations of hard words out of divers tongues.'[213] He now opened a victualling house there, and employed his pen against the Roundheads, and made himself, it is said, 'much esteemed for his facetious company.' Upon the surrender of Oxford and the ruin of the royal cause, he returned to Westminster, and kept a public house in Phoenix Alley, near Long Acre, where, after the King's death, he set up a Mourning Crown for his sign. This, however, he found it necessary to remove, and then he hung up his own portrait in its stead. His health and spirits he retained to a good old age, and when more than seventy made a journey through Wales, in the year 1652, and published an account of it. Two years afterwards he died, at the age of seventy-four, and was buried in the church-yard of St. Paul's, Covent Garden.

An epitaph was composed upon him somewhat in his own style:

Here lies the Water Poet, honest John,
Who rowed in the streams of Helicon;
Where having many rocks and dangers past,
He at the haven of Heaven arrived at last.

There is a portrait of him bearing date 1655, by his nephew, who was a painter at Oxford, and presented it to the Bodleian, where it was thought not unworthy of a place.[214] He is represented in a black scull-cap, and black gown or rather cloak. The countenance is described to me as one of 'well-fed rotundity; the eyes small, with an expression of cunning, into which their natural shrewdness had probably been deteriorated by the painter; their colour seems to have been hazel: there is scarcely any appearance of eye-brows; the lips have a slight cast of playfulness or satire. The brow is wrinkled, and he is in the fashion of mustachios with a tuft of beard under the lip. The portrait now is, like the building in which it has thus long been preserved, in a state of rapid decay:' 'I hope,' says the friend to whom I am obliged for this account of it, 'his verse is of a more durable quality: – for *ut pictura poësis* would annihilate him altogether.'

> All making, marring, never-turning Time,
> To all that is, is period and is prime;
> Time wears out Fortune, Love, and Death, and Fame.

So sung the Water Poet; – it wore out him, and is now wearing out his picture and his works; and he is not one of those writers for whom a palingenesia can be expected from their dust. Yet we have lately seen the whole of Herrick's poems republished,[215] a coarse-minded and beastly writer, whose dunghill, when the few flowers that grew therein had been transplanted, ought never to have been disturbed. Those flowers indeed are beautiful and perennial; but they should have been removed from the filth and ordure in which they are embedded. There is nothing of John Taylor's which deserves preservation for its intrinsic merit alone, but in the collection of his pieces which I have perused there is a great deal to illustrate the manners of his age; and as he lived more than twenty years after this collection was printed, and continued publishing till the last, there is probably much in his uncollected works also which for the same reason ought to be preserved. A curious and useful volume of selections might be formed from them.[216] There are many perishing writers from whose otherwise worthless works it is much to be desired that excerpts of this kind should be made: a series of such would be not less valuable than the Harleian Miscellany or the Somers Tracts.

If the Water Poet had been in a higher grade of society, and bred to some regular profession, he would probably have been a much less distinguished person in his generation. No spoon could have suited his mouth so well as the wooden one to which he was born. His way of life was best suited to his character, nor could any regular education so fully have brought out the sort of talent which he possessed. Fortunately, also, he came into the world at the right time, and lived in an age when Kings and Queens condescended to notice him, nobles and archbishops admitted him to their table, and mayors and corporations received him with civic honours. The next of our uneducated poets was composed of very different clay, – and did not moisten it so well.

SOUTHEY'S INTRODUCTION TO *ATTEMPTS IN VERSE*

Stephen Duck

Stephen Duck was born at Great Charlton, a little village in Wiltshire, in the beginning of the last century. His parents were in the lowest rank of life; and as it was his hard hap to be complained of by the village schoolmaster for 'taking his learning too fast, even faster than it could be bestowed upon him,'[217] his poor mother took him from school and set him to the plough, 'lest he should become too fine a gentleman for the family that produced him.'[218] He was a boy who, in old times, would have been noticed by the monks of the nearest monastery – would then have made his way to Oxford, or perhaps to Paris, as a begging scholar – have risen to be a bishop or mitred abbot – have done honour to his station, and have left behind him good works and a good name. In his own days, if he had met with timely patronage enough to have placed him at an endowed grammar school, as fair a career might have been opened to him in our Established Church; for he would have deserved its honours, and some of its honours have always been awarded to desert, even in the worst times.

Being from his fourteenth year wholly engaged in the lowest and hardest employments of a country life, Stephen forgot almost all the little arithmetic he had learnt at school, and this made him uneasy, for 'he had a certain longing after knowledge.'[219] That uneasiness, however, was suspended by his longing for a wife also: it returned upon him, after an early marriage, when he had no time to spare, no books, and no money wherewith to purchase any. But in this case also love will find a way; he worked extra hours, and so obtained extra payment, which having so earned he might fairly appropriate to the meritorious object of improving himself. So he bought first a book of vulgar arithmetic, then one of decimals, and a third upon mensuration; and these he studied in those hours which could be spared from sleep, after the labours of the day.

It appears that he met with little encouragement for his intellectual ambition from his wife, nor was it likely that he should. But by good fortune one of his acquaintance, who had been two or three years in service at London, came to reside at Charlton, and brought with him a few books, which, being fond of reading, he had purchased in the great city. With him Stephen became intimate, and they used to read together, and talk over the points which they were thus led to think on. This was the greatest happiness of his life. 'Their minds,' says Spence, were their own, neither improved nor spoiled by laying in a stock of learning. They were, perhaps, equally well inclined to learn; both struggling for a little knowledge; and like a couple of rowers on the same bottom, while they were only striving perhaps which should outdo his companion, they were really each helping the other, and driving the boat on the faster.[220]

'Perhaps you would be willing to know what books their little library consisted of. Milton, the Spectator,[221] and Seneca, were his first favourites; Telemachus,[222] with another piece by the same hand, (the Demonstration of the Being of a God,)[223] and Addison's Defence of Christianity,[224] his next. They had an English Dictionary, and a sort of English Grammar; an Ovid, of long standing with them,

140

SOUTHEY'S INTRODUCTION TO *ATTEMPTS IN VERSE*

and a Bysshe's Art of Poetry,[225] of later acquisition; Seneca's Morals made the name of L'Estrange[226] dear to them; and, as I imagine, might occasion their getting his Josephus,[227] in folio, which was the largest purchase in their collection. They had one volume of Shakespeare with seven of his plays in it. Besides these, Stephen had read three or four other plays; some of Epictetus,[228] Waller,[229] Dryden's Virgil,[230] Prior,[231] Hudibras,[232] Tom Brown,[233] and the London Spy.[234] With these helps,' continues Spence, 'Stephen is grown something of a poet and something of a philosopher. I find by him, that from his infancy he has had a cast in his mind towards poetry. He has delighted, as far back as he can remember, in verses and in singing. He speaks of strange emotions that he has felt on the top-performances of the little choir of songsters in a country chancel; and mentions his first hearing of an organ as a remarkable epocha of his life. He seems to be a pretty good judge too of a musical line; but I imagine that he does not hear verses in his mind as he repeats them. I don't know whether you understand me, I mean that his ideas of notes in a verse, and his manner of repeating the same verse, are often different. For he points out an harmonious line well enough, and yet he generally spoils its harmony by his way of speaking it.'[235]

Paradise Lost carried with it no doubt a strong recommendation in its subject, but it perplexed him, and he read it twice or thrice with a Dictionary, studying it, as a studious youth goes through a Greek or Latin author. The Spectator, too, which he said improved his understanding more than any thing, taught him to appreciate some of the merits of that poem, and Spence says he could point out particular beauties which it required 'a good keen eye to discover.'[236] He frequently took a volume of the Spectator with him to his work, and laboured harder than any one else, like a man engaged to work by the piece, that he might honestly get half an hour for reading one of the numbers; but by sitting down at such times incautiously in the sweat of his brow, he injured his health. The poems which he now and then met with in the Spectator 'helped on his natural bent that way, and made him willing to try whether he could not do something in the same kind himself. This he could do while he was at work; and he pleased himself so well that at last he began to venture these thoughts on paper. What he did of this kind was very inconsiderable; only scattered thoughts, and generally not above four or five lines on the same subject; which, as there was nobody thereabouts that cared for verses, nor any body that could tell him whether they were good or bad, he generally flung into the fire as soon as he had pleased himself enough in reading them.'[237]

But though Stephen was too conscientious to neglect his work at any time for his studies, and consequently never gave his master cause for complaint, he was not so fortunate at home, where he had a person less considerate, if not less reasonable, to deal with. It was his lot at this time to be duck-peck'd by his lawful wife, who held herself to be lawful mistress also, and told all the neighbourhood that her husband dealt with the devil, or was going mad, for he did nothing but talk to himself and tell his fingers. Probably she acquitted the devil of any share in her husband's aberrations, and became reconciled to his conduct when she found that he began to be favourably noticed by persons in a higher station. The

SOUTHEY'S INTRODUCTION TO *ATTEMPTS IN VERSE*

country people, who had long talked of him as a scholar, began now to report that he could make verses, which was yet more surprising, according to their notions: a young Oxonian, Stanley[238] by name, hearing this, sent for Stephen, and was so well satisfied with his conversation, as to desire that he would write him a letter in verse. He had never written what Spence calls a whole copy of verses before; but he now produced about fifty lines, of which the beginning is a fair specimen.

Sir,
I have, before the time prescribed by you,
Exposed my weak production to your view;
Which may, I hope, have pardon at your hand,
Because produced to light by your command.
Perhaps you might expect some finished ode,
Or sacred song to sound the praise of God;
A glorious thought, and laudable! But then,
Think what illiterate poet guides the pen.
Ill suit such tasks with one who holds the plough;
Such lofty subjects with a fate so low.

These verses were shown to some of the neighbouring clergymen, and they, having inquired into his character and talked with him, encouraged him to go on, 'and gave him some presents, which, as things stood then, were a great help to him.'[239] He then put together and completed some verses which he had commenced on Poverty. To Poverty, as his acquaintance and familiar guest, he says,

Thou art no formidable foe,
Except to little souls who think thee so:

and after comparing the good and evil of affluent circumstances and of narrow ones, he concludes thus: –

Since wealth can never make the vicious blest,
Nor poverty subdue the virtuous breast:
Since both from Heaven's unerring hand are sent,
LORD! give me either, give me but content.

Stephen's had been a wholesome course of reading; though he had taken some pleasure in Tom Brown's Letters from the Dead, and the London Spy, he 'did not much care to look into them,' he said, after he became acquainted with the Spectator: he liked what little he had read of Epictetus, 'but 'twas Seneca that had made him happy in his own mind.'[240] The gentlemen of the country began to notice him now, and the little presents he received from them 'made him quite easy as to his circumstances.'[241] The only thing that he was then solicitous about, was how he might succeed as to the poetry he should be employed in; this was his chief

SOUTHEY'S INTRODUCTION TO *ATTEMPTS IN VERSE*

concern. But even this seemed to proceed not so much from any desire of fame as from a principle of gratitude; or, as he expressed it, his longing to please those friends that had been so generous to him.

Mr. Stanley, who was now in holy orders, gave him for a subject of his next poem, his own way of life, and showed his own judgment in so doing. Stephen, accordingly, composed the 'Thresher's Labour,' which, in the collection of his pieces, is inscribed to his first patron. The picture of rural occupations, here drawn from the life, is very different from what we find in pastorals; but the truth of the description is not its only merit, for there are passages in it which would have done no discredit to more celebrated names.

> Soon as the golden harvest quits the plain,
> And Ceres' gifts reward the farmer's pain,
> What corn each sheaf will yield, intent to hear,
> And guess from thence the profits of the year,
> He calls his reapers forth: around we stand
> With deep attention, waiting his command.
> To each our task he readily divides,
> And pointing to our different stations guides;
> As he directs, to distant barns we go,
> Here two for wheat, and there for barley two.
> But first to show what he expects to find,
> These words, or words like these, disclose his mind:
> 'So dry the corn was carried from the field,
> So easily 'twill thresh, so well 'twill yield,
> Sure large day's-works I well may hope for now.
> Come, strip and try; let's see what you can do!'
> Divested of our cloaths, with flail in hand,
> At proper distance, front to front we stand.
> And first the threshal's gently swung, to prove
> Whether with just exactness it will move:
> That once secure, we swiftly whirl them round,
> From the strong planks our crab-tree staves re-bound,
> And echoing barns return the rattling sound.
> Now in the air our knotty weapons fly,
> And now with equal force descend from high;
> Down one, one up, so well they keep the time,
> The Cyclops' hammers could not truer chime;
> Nor with more heavy strokes could Etna groan,
> When Vulcan forged the arms for Thetis' son.
> In briny streams our sweat descends apace,
> Drops from our locks, or trickles down our face.
> No intermission in our work we know;
> The noisy threshal must for ever go.

143

SOUTHEY'S INTRODUCTION TO *ATTEMPTS IN VERSE*

Their master absent, others safely play,
The sleeping threshal does itself betray.

*****

Our eye beholds no pleasing object here,
No chearful sound diverts our listening ear.
The shepherd well may tune his voice to sing,
Inspired with all the beauties of the spring.
No fountains murmur here, no lambkins play,
No linnets warble, and no fields look gay;
'Tis all a gloomy, melancholy scene,
Fit only to provoke the Muse's spleen.
When sooty pease we thresh, you scarce can know
Our native colour, as from work we go:
The sweat, the dust, and suffocating smoke,
Make us so much like Ethiopians look,
We scare our wives, when evening brings us home,
And frighted infants think the bugbear come.
Week after week we this dull task pursue,
Unless when winnowing days produce a new:
A new, indeed, but frequently a worse!
The threshal yields but to the master's curse.
He counts the bushels, counts how much a-day,
Then swears we've idled half our time away;
'Why look ye, rogues, d'ye think that this will do?
Your neighbours thresh as much again as you.'

From this winter and spring work Stephen passes to his summer occupations.

Before the door our welcome master stands,
Tells us the ripen'd grass requires our hands.
The grateful tiding presently imparts
Life to our looks, and spirits to our hearts.
We wish the happy season may be fair;
And, joyful, long to breathe in opener air.
This change of labour seems to give such ease,
With thoughts of happiness ourselves we please.
But, ah! how rarely's happiness complete!
There's always bitter mingled with the sweet.
When first the lark sings prologue to the day,
We rise, admonish'd by his early lay;
This new employ with eager haste to prove,
This new employ, becomes so much our love.

144

SOUTHEY'S INTRODUCTION TO *ATTEMPTS IN VERSE*

Alas! that human joys shou'd change so soon!
Our morning pleasure turns to pain at noon.
The birds salute us as to work we go,
And with new life our bosoms seem to glow.
On our right shoulder hangs the crooked blade,
The weapon destined to uncloath the mead:
Our left supports the whetstone, scrip, and beer,
This for our scythes, and these ourselves to cheer.
And now the field designed to try our might
At length appears and meets our longing sight.
The grass and ground we view with careful eyes,
To see which way the best advantage lies;
And, hero-like, each claims the foremost place.
At first our labour seems a sportive race:
With rapid force our sharpen'd blades we drive,
Strain every nerve, and blow for blow we give.
All strive to vanquish, tho' the victor gains
No other glory but the greatest pains.
But when the scorching sun is mounted high,
And no kind barns with friendly shade are nigh,
Our weary scythes entangle in the grass,
While streams of sweat run trickling down apace;
Our sportive labour we too late lament,
And wish that strength again we vainly spent.

*****

With heat and labour tir'd, our scythes we quit,
Search out a shady tree, and down we sit:
From scrip and bottle hope new strength to gain;
But scrip and bottle too are tried in vain.
Down our parch'd throats we scarce the bread can get,
And, quite o'erspent with toil, but faintly eat;
Nor can the bottle only answer all;
The bottle and the beer are both too small.
Time flows: again we rise from off the grass;
Again each mower takes his proper place;
Not eager now, as late, our strength to prove,
But all contented regular to move.
We often whet, and often view the sun;
As often wish his tedious race was run.
At length he veils his purple face from sight,
And bids the weary labourer good night.
Homewards we move, but spent so much with toil,

145

SOUTHEY'S INTRODUCTION TO *ATTEMPTS IN VERSE*

We slowly walk and rest at every stile.
Our good expecting wives, who think we stay,
Got to the door, soon eye us in the way.
Then from the pot the dumplin's catch'd in haste,
And homely by its side the bacon placed;
Supper and sleep by morn new strength supply,
And out we set again, our work to try;
But not so early quite, nor quite so fast,
As to our cost we did the morning past.
Soon as the rising sun has drank the dew,
Another scene is open to our view:
Our master comes, and at his heels a throng
Of prattling females, arm'd with rake and prong;
Prepar'd, whilst he is here, to make his hay,
Or, if he turns his back, prepared to play;
But here, or gone, sure of this comfort still;
Here's company, so they may chat their fill.
Ah! were their hands so active as their tongues,
How nimbly then would move the rakes and prongs!

The grass again is spread upon the ground,
Till not a vacant place is to be found;
And while the parching sun-beams on it shine,
The haymakers have time allowed to dine;
That soon dispatched, they still sit on the ground,
And the brisk chat, renew'd, afresh goes round.
All talk at once; but seeming all to fear,
That what they speak the rest will hardly hear;
Till by degrees so high their notes they strain,
A stander-by can nought distinguish plain.
So loud's their speech, and so confused their noise,
Scarce puzzled Echo can return the voice.
Yet spite of this, they bravely all go on;
Each scorns to be, or seem to be, outdone.
Meanwhile the changing sky begins to lour,
And hollow winds proclaim a sudden shower;
The tattling crowd can scarce their garments gain,
Before descends the thick impetuous rain;
Their noisy prattle all at once is done,
And to the hedge they soon for shelter run.

Thus have I seen, on a bright summer's day,
On some green brake, a flock of sparrows play;
From twig to twig, from bush to bush they fly,

SOUTHEY'S INTRODUCTION TO *ATTEMPTS IN VERSE*

And with continued chirping fill the sky;
But on a sudden, if a storm appears,
Their chirping noise no longer dins our ears;
They fly for shelter to the thickest bush;
There silent sit, and all at once is hush.

But better fate succeeds this rainy day,
And little labour serves to make the hay.
Fast as 'tis cut, so kindly shines the sun,
Turn'd once or twice, the pleasing work is done.
Next day the cocks appear in equal rows,
Which the glad master in safe ricks bestows.
The spacious fields we now no longer range;
And yet, hard fate! still work for work we change.
Back to the barns we hastily are sent,
Where lately so much time we pensive spent;
Not pensive now, we bless the friendly shade;
And to avoid the parching sun are glad.
Yet little time we in the shade remain,
Before our master calls us forth again;
And says 'for harvest now yourselves prepare;
The ripen'd harvest now demands your care.
Get all things ready, and be quickly drest:
Early next morn I shall disturb your rest.'
Strict to his word, for scarce the dawn appears,
Before his hasty summons fills our ears.
His hasty summons we obey, and rise,
While yet the stars are glimmering in the skies.
With him our guide, we to the wheat-field go,
He to appoint, and we the work to do.

Ye reapers, cast your eyes around the field,
And view the various scenes its beauties yield;
Then look again with a more tender eye,
To think how soon it must in ruin lie!
For, once set in, where'er our blows we deal,
There's no resisting of the well-whet steel:
But here or there, where'er our course we bend,
Sure desolation does our steps attend.

The morning past, we sweat beneath the sun,
And but uneasily our work goes on.
Before us we perplexing thistles find,
And corn blown adverse with the ruffling wind.

SOUTHEY'S INTRODUCTION TO *ATTEMPTS IN VERSE*

Behind, our master waits: and if he spies
One charitable ear, he grudging cries,
'Ye scatter half your wages o'er the land:'
Then scrapes the stubble with his greedy hand.

Let those who feast at ease on dainty fare
Pity the reapers, who their feasts prepare:
For toils scarce ever ceasing press us now;
Rest never does but on the sabbath show;
And barely that our masters will allow.
Think what a painful life we daily lead;
Each morning early rise, go late to bed:
Nor when asleep are we secure from pain,
We then perform our labours o'er again:
Our mimic fancy ever restless seems,
And what we act awake she acts in dreams.
Hard fate! our labours even in sleep don't cease;
Scarce Hercules e'er felt such toils as these!

But soon we rise the bearded crop again,
Soon Phoebus' rays well dry the golden grain.
Pleas'd with the scene, our master glows with joy,
Bids us for carrying all our force employ;
When straight, confusion o'er the field appears,
And stunning clamours fill the workmen's ears;
The bells and clashing whips alternate sound,
And rattling waggons thunder o'er the ground.
The wheat, when carry'd, pease, and other grain,
We soon secure, and leave a fruitless plain;
In noisy triumph the last load moves on,
And loud huzzas proclaim the harvest done.
Our master, joyful at the pleasing sight,
Invites us all to feast with him at night.
A table plentifully spread we find,
And jugs of humming ale to cheer the mind;
Which he, too generous, pushes round so fast,
We think no toil's to come, nor mind the past.
But the next morning soon reveals the cheat,
When the same toils we must again repeat;
To the same barns must back again return,
To labour there for room for next year's corn.

Thus, as the year's revolving course goes round,
No respite from our labour can be found:

148

Like Sisyphus, our work is never done:
Continually rolls back the heavy stone.
New growing labours still succeed the past;
And growing always new, must always last.[242]

This is the best specimen of Stephen Duck's productions in verse, and certainly the command of language and the skill in versification which it displays, manifest perseverance and ability which very well deserved the encouragement he met with. Mr. Stanley proposed to him, as a subject for his next attempt, the story of the Shunamite woman and her child, and this poem was thought by his patrons to be the best of his performances.[243] He first wrote it in blank verse, but upon reading it over he found that the language was not sublime enough to sustain the metre, and therefore he recast it in rhyme; and though Milton was his favourite poet, he never again attempted what he had good sense enough to perceive he was incapable of performing as it ought to be done. 'To know how much he deserves,' says Spence, 'one should converse with him, and hear on what reasons he omitted such a part; why he shortens his stile in this place, and enlarges in that; whence he has such a word, and whence such an idea.'[244] For Stephen made great use of his little reading, enriched his vocabulary by it, and imitated, yet not servilely, what might be adapted to his subject. He also planned his compositions, and 'thought over all the parts, as he intended to arrange them, before he made the verses. For a poem of any length,' the good poetry-professor[245] remarks, 'no doubt, 'tis as necessary to do this as it is to have a draft of a house before you go to building it; and yet, I believe, the common run of our poets have generally thought themselves above it, or never thought of it at all.'[246]

The Thresher now began to be so much talked of, that some knavish bookseller got together a collection of his verses, and published them for his own advantage, with what Stephen calls a very false account of the author, and a fictitious portrait of him, wherein he is represented with Milton in one hand and a flail in the other, coming from the barn towards a table, on which pen, ink, and paper are lying; pigs, poultry, and reapers, making up the rural accompaniments.[247] But the Thresher's Labour had found its way to the Honourable Mrs. Clayton,[248] a lady who was about the Queen's person; she showed it to the Queen, and Queen Caroline,[249] with characteristic goodness, patronized the humble poet. He was invited to Windsor by her desire,[250] that he might be introduced to her; she settled thirty pounds a year upon him, which was then no poor provision, made him one of the yeomen of the guards, and soon afterwards gave him the more fitting appointment of keeper of her select library at Richmond, called Merlin's Cave, where he had apartments assigned him, and was encouraged to pursue his studies so as to qualify himself for ordination in the Established Church. A volume of his verses was now published by subscription, and the names upon the list show with what zeal his friends had exerted themselves in the upper classes of society.[251] Mr. Spence's account of the author was prefixed, and the volume was dedicated to the Queen, 'as a humble tribute of duty, offered from a thankful heart to a

SOUTHEY'S INTRODUCTION TO *ATTEMPTS IN VERSE*

gracious benefactress.'[252] He wrote a modest Preface, 'to bespeak the reader's good nature, and to say something which might incline him to pardon what he could not commend. I have, indeed,' said he, 'but a poor defence to make for the things I have wrote: I do not think them good, and better judges will doubtless think worse of them than I do. Only this I may say of them, that if they have nothing to delight those who may chance to read them, they have nothing to give modesty a blush; if nothing to entertain and improve the mind, they have nothing to debauch and corrupt it. Another motive that I hope may induce the reader to overlook the defects in this volume is, that the oldest poem in it is little more than six years of age; and a considerable part of the time since that was writ, has been spent in endeavouring to learn a language of which I was then entirely ignorant.'[253]

He then apologized for his presumption in having attempted some translations from Horace, saying, that when only endeavouring to understand, he found it difficult to conquer the temptation of imitating some of the thoughts, which 'mightily pleased' him. 'I have not myself,' he says, 'been so fond of writing as might be imagined from seeing so many things of mine as are got together in this book. Several of these are on subjects which were given me by persons to whom I have such great obligations, that I always thought their desires commands. My want of education will be too evident from them for me to mention it here. And I hope when the reader weighs my performances, he will put that and other disadvantages into the scale. I would willingly here make known my obligations to those worthy persons who took notice of me in the midst of poverty and labour, were I not afraid my gratitude, thus publicly expressed, would offend them more than my silence. However, I must beg leave to return my thanks to a Reverend Gentleman of Wiltshire, and to another of Winchester: the former made my life more comfortable as soon as he knew me; the latter, after giving me several testimonies of his bounty and goodness, presented my first essays to a lady of quality attending the Queen, who made my low circumstances known to her Majesty. I hope, too, that all those honourable persons, whose names do me so much credit at the beginning of my book, will accept my acknowledgments and thanks for so liberal a subscription. And as this volume, I feel, will tell them they have not encouraged a poet, I will endeavour to let them see they have been generous to an honest man.'[254]

Swift, to his own discredit, wrote an ill-natured epigram upon him at this time:

> The thresher, Duck, could o'er the Queen prevail;
> The proverb says, no fence against a flail.
> From *threshing* corn, he turns to *thresh* his brains,
> For which her Majesty allows him *grains*;
> Tho' 'tis confest, that those who ever saw
> His poems, think them all not worth a *straw*.
> Thrice happy Duck, employed in threshing *stubble*!
> Thy toil is lessen'd, and thy profits double.[255]

150

SOUTHEY'S INTRODUCTION TO *ATTEMPTS IN VERSE*

The ill-will that called forth these lines was probably towards the Queen; and Swift cared not what pain the expression of it might give to the modest and meritorious man against whom it was directed. But Stephen had now obtained efficient patrons as well as steady friends; and he was in such reputation that Lord Palmerston[256] appropriated the rent of an acre of land, for ever, to provide a dinner and strong beer for the threshers of Charlton at a public-house in that valley, in honour of their former comrade. The dinner is given on the 30th of June.[257] The poet himself was present at one of these anniversaries, probably the first, and speaks thus of it in a pleasing poem addressed to that nobleman.

> Oft as this day returns shall Threshers claim
> Some hours of rest, sacred to Temple's name;
> Oft as this day returns shall Temple cheer
> The Threshers' hearts with mutton, beef, and beer.
> Hence, when their children's children shall admire
> This holiday, and whence derived inquire,
> Some grateful father, partial to my fame,
> Shall thus describe from whence and how it came: –
> 'Here, child, a Thresher liv'd in ancient days;
> Quaint songs he sung and pleasing roundelays.
> A gracious Queen his sonnets did commend,
> And some great Lord, one Temple, was his friend.
> That Lord was pleased this holiday to make,
> And feast the Threshers for that Thresher's sake.'
> Thus shall tradition keep my fame alive;
> The bard may die – the Thresher still survive.[258]

Having obtained orders, he was preferred to the living of Byfleet in Surrey. It has been said that this was 'a singular and absurd transition, and that his small knowledge of Latin was surely not enough to justify such an abuse of church patronage.'[259] There can, however, be no doubt but that his attainments were such as fairly qualified him for this preferment; nor would Spence, (himself in all respects an exemplary and excellent man,) by whose influence he obtained it, have recommended him, had it been otherwise. His character, his inclination, and his abilities, were alike suited to this way of life; and he is said to have been much followed as a preacher, not only while novelty and his reputation were likely to attract congregations, but as long as he lived.

His end was an unhappy one; he became insane, threw himself into the water, near Reading, in 1756, and was drowned. Till that malady occurred he had been a useful parish priest, and approved himself every way worthy of the patronage which had been bestowed upon him. If the malady had shown itself earlier, it might have been ascribed to the transition from a life of great bodily labour to a sedentary one, and to excess in study; but as about thirty years had elapsed since he was taken from the barn, the cause is more likely to have been accidental, or

SOUTHEY'S INTRODUCTION TO *ATTEMPTS IN VERSE*

constitutional. He had probably been always highly sensitive. Spence speaks of him as trembling when the scene between Hamlet and the Ghost was read to him. And he thus describes the effect produced upon him by the speeches of Antony over Cæsar's body: 'as I was reading to him, I observed that his countenance changed often in the most moving parts. His eye was quick and busy all the time, and I never saw applause, or the shifting of proper passions appear so strongly in any face as in his.'[260] It was a fine, strongly-marked countenance, with regular features; but after his fate, the expression in his portrait which the artist intended for thoughtfulness or inspiration, might easily be interpreted as denoting melancholy, and a tendency to madness.

A catalogue of his books, as for sale, was published with those of two other persons soon after his decease.[261] That they should have been numerous enough for this, implies that his love of reading had continued unabated, and that his circumstances had not been straitened. The kindness of his friends at court did not cease at his death, and his daughter was thus allowed to retain his apartments at Richmond.

Stephen Duck seems never to have entertained an overweening opinion of his own genius. Encouraged as he was, he would have written more if he had not been conscious that his talents for poetry were rather imitative than inventive; that he was incapable of imitating what he clearly saw was best; and that it was not likely he could produce any thing better than his first efforts. This is proof of his good sense. He was, indeed, a modest, diligent, studious, good man; and the patronage which he obtained is far more honourable to the spirit of his age, than the temper, which may censure or ridicule it, can be to ours.

Passing over the respectable name of Dodsley,[262] because his poems and an account of his life are to be found in the General Collection of the British Poets,[263] the next writer of the self-taught class is

James Woodhouse[264]

Of Rowley, near Hales-Oven, about seven miles from Birmingham, and two from the Leasowes.[265] He was a village shoemaker, and though he had been taken from school at seven years old, had so far improved the little which he could possibly have learnt there, as to eke out his scanty means by teaching to read and write. He is first heard of at the age of three-and-twenty, and having then a wife and children. Shenstone had at that time found it necessary to forbid that general access to his grounds which he used to allow, so much mischief had wantonly been done there, – a disgraceful characteristic whereby the English populace are distinguished from those of any other country, and by which they injure themselves even more than they injure others, for they make it necessary to exclude them wherever they can be excluded. Woodhouse, upon this occasion, addressed some verses to him, entreating that he might be exempted from this prohibition, and permitted still to recreate himself and indulge his imagination in that sweet scenery; and Shenstone, who was always benevolent and

SOUTHEY'S INTRODUCTION TO *ATTEMPTS IN VERSE*

generous, when he had inquired into the character of the petitioner, admitted him not only into his grounds, but to the use of his library also. His whole reading till then had been in magazines.

Shenstone found that the poor applicant used to work with a pen and ink at his side, while the last was in his lap; – the head at one employ, the hands at another; and when he had composed a couplet or a stanza, he wrote it on his knee. In one of the pieces thus composed, and entitled Spring, there are these affecting stanzas:

> But now domestic cares employ
> And busy every sense,
> Nor leave one hour of grief or joy
> But's furnish'd out from thence:
>
> Save what my little babes afford,
> Whom I behold with glee,
> When smiling at my humble board,
> Or prattling at my knee.
>
> Not that my Daphne's charms are flown,
> These still new pleasures bring,
> 'Tis these inspire content alone;
> 'Tis all I've left of spring.

> *   *   *   *   *

> I wish not, dear connubial state,
> To break thy silken bands;
> I only blame relentless fate,
> That every hour demands.
>
> Nor mourn I much my task austere,
> Which endless wants impose;
> But oh! it wounds my soul to hear
> My Daphne's melting woes!
>
> For oft she sighs and oft she weeps,
> And hangs her pensive head,
> *While blood her furrowed finger steeps,*
> *And stains the passing thread.*
>
> When orient hills the sun behold,
> Our labours are begun:
> And when he streaks the west with gold,
> The task is still undone.

SOUTHEY'S INTRODUCTION TO *ATTEMPTS IN VERSE*

These verses were pointed out to me, for their feeling and their truth, by the greatest poet of the age.[266]

In 1764, five years after this poor man's fortunate introduction to Shenstone, a collection of his poems was published for his benefit, in quarto, price three shillings.[267] It appears from a piece addressed to Shenstone, upon his 'Rural Elegance,' that the books to which he now had access, and the models to which his patron had directed his attention, had induced him to write in a more ambitious strain, and aim at some of the artifices of versification.

> What! cannot He, who form'd the fount of light,
> And shining orbs that ornament the night;
> Who hangs his silken curtains round the sky,
> And trims their skirts with fringe of every dye;
> In sheets of radiance spreads the solar beams
> With softened lustre o'er the tranquil streams;
> Or o'er the glittering surface softly flings
> The whispering winds with gently waving wings,
> While every kindled curl's resplendent rays.
> Quick dart and drown in bright successive blaze;
> Who dipt in countless greens the lawns and bowers,
> And touch'd with every tint the faultless flowers;
> With beauty clothes each beast that roams the plain,
> And birds' rich plumes with ever-varied stain;
> Each fair-scaled fish in watery regions known,
> And insect's robe that mocks the coloured stone;
> Doth he not form the peasant's visual sphere
> To catch each charm that crowns the chequer'd year;
> Construct his ear to seize the passing sound,
> From wind, or wave, or wing, or whistle round;
> From breathing breeze, or tempest's aweful roar;
> Soft lisping rills, or Ocean's thundering shore;
> Unnumber'd notes that fill the echoing field,
> Or mingled minstrelsy the woodlands yield;
> The melting strains and melodies of song
> That float, impassioned, from the human tongue?
> Or fondly feel each sound that sweetly slips
> Thro' ear to heart, from favourite lover's lips;
> And trace the nicer harmony that springs.
> From puny gnats' shrill-sounding treble wings;
> Light fly's sharp counter; bee's strong tenor tone;
> Huge hornet's bass, and beetle's drowsy drone;
> Grasshopper's open shake, quick twittering all the day,
> Or cricket's broken chirp, that chimes the night away?

SOUTHEY'S INTRODUCTION TO *ATTEMPTS IN VERSE*

These lines are extracted, not from the original edition of his poems, but from a volume which he published after an interval of nearly forty years; it is not unlikely, therefore, that they may have been altered during that interval, and, in the author's opinion, improved by bringing them nearer to the fashion which was then in vogue.[268] A process, indeed, is observable, both in the verses of Woodhouse and Stephen Duck, which might be looked for, as almost inevitable: they began by expressing their own thoughts and feelings, in their own language; all which, owing to their stations in life, had a certain charm of freshness as well as truth; but that attraction passes away when they begin to form their style upon some approved model, and they then produce just such verses as any person, with a metrical ear, may be taught to make by a receipt.

In this his second and last publication,[269] the then forgotten author recalled attention to his name only by a modest motto: Sutor ultra crepidam.[270] One passage may be selected, from many which show that he retained in an advanced age that love and enjoyment of natural beauties which were the means of obtaining for him Shenstone's friendly assistance.

Lovelier far than vernal flowers,
The mushrooms shooting after showers;
That fear no more the fatal scythe,
But proudly spread their bonnets blythe,
With coverings form'd of silk and snow,
And lined with brightening pink below.

*   *   *   *   *

But more the later fungus race,
Begot by Phoebus' warm embrace
In summer months on procreant earth,
By damp September brought to birth;
That, just like Jove, produce their seed
From teeming brain for future breed.
Their forms and hues some solace yield,
In wood, or wild, or humid field,
Whose tapering stems, robust or light,
Like columns catch the searching sight,
To claim remark where'er I roam,
Supporting each a stately dome:
Like fair umbrellas furl'd or spread,
Display their many-colour'd head,
Grey, purple, yellow, white, or brown,
Shap'd like War's shield or Prelate's crown,
Like Freedom's cap, or Friar's cowl,
Or China's bright inverted bowl;

And while their broadening disks unfold
Gay silvery gills, or nets of gold,
Beneath their shady-curtain'd cove,
Perform all offices of love.
In beauty chief, the eye to chain,
'Mong whispering pines, or arid plain,
A glittering group assembled stands,
Like Elf's or Fay's embattled bands,
Where every arm appears to wield
With pigmy strength a giant shield,
And deeply dyed in sanguine gore,
With brazen bosses studded o'er;
While magic Fancy's ear confounds
The whistling winds with hostile sounds.[271]

When this volume was published (1803) the author was living near Norbury Park, where he seems to have found a generous friend in Mr. Locke.[272] He was then above sixty-eight years of age; I do not know when he died.[273] In his case, as in Stephen Duck's, the persons who befriended him had the satisfaction of knowing that their kindness was well bestowed. And if the talents which they brought into notice were not of a kind in either case to produce, under cultivation, extraordinary fruits, in both a deserving man was raised from poverty, and placed in circumstances favourable to his moral and intellectual nature.

John Bennet

A few years after the publication of Woodhouse's first volume, another versifyer of the same calling appeared, whose name was John Bennet, and who worked as a journeyman shoemaker at Woodstock, where his father was parish clerk when Warton obtained the curacy of that town. Warton,[274] who was remembered with affection by all who ever knew him, for his thorough good-nature, and the boyish hilarity which he retained through life, is said to have liked the father for his psalm-singing, and to have given the son some instruction for improving his rhymes. He seems to have rendered him greater service in assisting him to procure a very respectable list of subscribers.

There is nothing in his poems which deserves to be extracted for its own sake: a few lines, which express some of the popular prejudices concerning the alteration of the style, may serve as a fair specimen of their average merit, or rather demerit. An old man, conversing upon the subject on Christmas Eve, says—

He should ne'er with true devotion pray
Upon the morrow, call'd New Christmas Day.
Then tells of Glastonbury's holy thorn,
That buds and blossoms on the blessed morn;

SOUTHEY'S INTRODUCTION TO *ATTEMPTS IN VERSE*

Sets forth at large when pleasing midnight peal
On Christmas Eve the welcom'd season hail,
Before the altered time, the flocks and kine
At sound thereof felt impulse nigh divine;
And on their bended knees did straightway fall,
E'er since the era of the sacred stall.

His dame then tells that her rosemary tree,
Until the old season is from blooming free,
But on that day is with new blossoms crown'd,
And sheds its fragrant odours all around.
Again the old man speaks his doubts and fears,
How since that time he was perplexed with cares;
'Cause in those days, so lost, 'twas plainly seen,
An holy sabbath day must intervene.
Then talks it o'er how dear all sorts of food
Did daily grow; nor can he hold it good,
But finds all things are worse since the altered time,
Therefore condemns it for a heinous crime.[275]

Some things worthy of notice are incidentally mentioned in Bennet's verses: as that during a contested election for Oxfordshire, a zealous tallowchandler made blue candles;[276] and, that at Hampton Gay, a village near the Cherwell, which he calls 'great in yewy fame,' there were the twelve apostles, flourishing in yew, Moses and Aaron, Susanna and the elders, all in evergreen likenesses; and moreover, a coach and horses, with coachman and footmen.[277] Bennet relates, also, and with a proper feeling, that if a traveller arrived at Woodstock on a Sunday, during church time, and expressed an inclination to purchase gloves or cutlery, for both which that town was famous,

Lo! messages are sent,
To those well skill'd, the precious wares to vent;
These, now at worship, clothed in ermined state,
And bending underneath the ponderous weight
Of magistracy, prayer and pomp resign,
To offer sacrifice at Mammon's shrine:
Yea, forthwith shun devotion as a crime,
Like Felix, leaving till another time.[278]

Ann Yearsley[279]

Ann Yearsley's is a melancholy story. She was first heard of in 1784, when some verses were shown to Miss Hannah More[280] as the production of a poor illiterate woman who sold milk from door to door. 'The story,' says

Miss More, 'did not engage my faith, but the verses excited my attention; for, though incorrect, they breathed the genuine spirit of poetry, and were rendered still more interesting by a certain natural and strong expression of misery, which seemed to fill the head and mind of the author. On making diligent inquiry into her history and character, I found that she had been born and bred in her present humble station, and had never received the least education, except that her brother had taught her to write. Her mother,[281] who was also a milk-woman, appears to have had sense and piety, and to have given an early tincture of religion to this poor woman's mind. She is about eight-and-twenty, was married very young to a man who is said to be honest and sober, but of a turn of mind very different from her own.[282] Repeated losses and a numerous family, for they had six children in seven years, reduced them very low; and the rigour of the last severe winter sunk them to the extremity of distress. Her aged mother, her six little infants, and herself (expecting every hour to lie in) were actually on the point of perishing, when the gentleman (Mr. Vaughan,)[283] so gratefully mentioned in her poems, providentially heard of their distress, which I am afraid she had too carefully concealed, and hastened to their relief. The poor woman and her children were preserved; but for the unhappy mother all assistance came too late; she had the joy to see it arrive, but it was a joy she was no longer able to bear, and it was more fatal to her than famine had been.' This 'left a settled impression of sorrow on Mrs. Yearsley's mind.'[284]

'When I went to see her,' Miss More continues, 'I observed a perfect simplicity in her manners, without the least affectation or pretension of any kind, she neither attempted to raise my compassion by her distress, nor my admiration by her parts. But on a more familiar acquaintance, I have had reason to be surprised at the justness of her taste, the faculty I least expected to find in her. In truth, her remarks on the books she had read are so accurate, and so consonant to the opinions of the best critics, that from this very circumstance they would appear trite and commonplace to any one who had been in habits of society; for without having ever conversed with any body above her own level, she seems to possess the general principles of sound taste and just thinking.' She had read Paradise Lost and the Night Thoughts,[285] and was well acquainted with both; Pope's Eloisa,[286] a few of Shakespeare's plays, and a translation of the Georgics, which seems particularly to have delighted her. Some classical allusions in her verses she had taken from prints in a shop window, . . . these gratuitous exhibitions, have, like bookstalls, contributed much to the delight and instruction of those upon whom the advantages of education would have been well bestowed. She had never seen a Dictionary, and knew nothing of grammatical rules. Her vocabulary therefore was that of the books which she had read, her syntax that of the ignorant and vulgar with whom she conversed. Miss More described her poems as like those of all unlettered poets, abounding in imagery, metaphor, and personification, her faults in that respect being rather those of superfluity than of want. 'She thought her ear perfect, and the structure of her blank verse so happy and so varied, as even to appear skilful. You will find her,' she says, 'often diffuse from redundancy, and oftener obscure from brevity; but you will seldom find in her those inexplicable poetic sins, the false thought, the puerile conceit, the distorted image, and the incongruous metaphor, the common resources of bad poets, and the not uncommon blemishes of good ones.'[287]

A small volume of her Poems was now published by subscription, the grosser inaccuracies of language having been corrected. Miss More was a most efficient as well as kind patroness; and the volume in consequence went through a second and a third edition.[288] 'It is not intended,' said that patroness, 'to place her in such a state of independence as might seduce her to devote her time to the idleness of poetry. I hope she is convinced that the making of verses is not the great business of human life; and that as a wife and a mother she has duties to fill, the smallest of which is of more value than the finest verses she can write. But as it has pleased God to give her these talents, may they not be made as instruments to mend her situation? Pressing as her distresses are, if I did not think her heart was rightly turned I should be afraid of proposing such a measure, lest it should unsettle the sobriety of her mind, and, by exciting her vanity, indispose her for the laborious employments of her humble condition; but it would be cruel to imagine that we cannot mend her fortune without impairing her virtue. For my own part I do not feel myself actuated by the idle vanity of a discoverer; for I confess that the ambition of bringing to light a genius buried in obscurity, operates much less powerfully on my mind than the wish to rescue a meritorious woman from misery; for it is not fame, but bread, which I am anxious to secure to her.'[289]

The sum of 350l. arising from the first edition of these poems, and the presents made by some of the subscribers, was placed in the funds in the names of Mrs. Montague[290] and Miss Hannah More, as trustees, for the benefit of Mrs. Yearsley and her children. This occasioned an unfortunate difference between the authoress and her first benefactress. Mrs. Yearsley wished to be admitted as a joint-trustee, and that the money should be equally divided, according to the number of her children, and subject to their demand as each arrived at the age of twenty-one. The latter part of the proposal was improvident, the former seemed to imply a caution which, because it was felt to be unnecessary, was thought to be ungrateful. Some angry altercation ensued, and the acrimonious feelings thus excited were not soothed by the interference of friends on Mrs. Yearsley's behalf. It ended in a resignation of the trust, and in a lasting breach between the parties. The whole transaction was vexatious to Miss More, whose benevolent intentions ought not to have been misunderstood; and it was unfortunate for Mrs. Yearsley, who was now represented as a thankless and unworthy person, and who from that time considered as an enemy one who, but for this misunderstanding, would have continued to be her friend and faithful adviser.

Mrs. Yearsley prefixed a narrative in vindication of herself to the fourth edition of her Poems in 1786,[291] and in the following year published a second collection by subscription.[292] She now opened a Circulating Library at Bristol Hot Wells, but not upon a scale which could prove attractive, nor was the place one where much support was to be expected. In 1791 she produced a tragedy called Earl Goodwin, which was represented with little success at the Bristol and Bath Theatres. And in 1795 she published the Royal Captives, an unfinished novel, founded upon the mysterious story of the Iron Mask. 'One of my motives,' she says, 'for publishing the work unfinished is, that the world may speak of me as I am, while I have power to hear. The clouds that hang over my fortunes intervene between me and the public; I incessantly struggle to dissipate them, and feel those struggles vain, and shall drop in the effort. This consolation I shall however bear with me to the verge of life, that to those who have guided me by the sacred and lambent flame of friendship, my memory will be dear.'

This book was noticed in the Monthly Review, with a better feeling than is usually found in periodical criticisms. The unknown writer remarked the striking contrast between the strength of thought and the weakness of judgement which were apparent in the composition, 'the almost continued inflation of the style, and the frequent power of expression, the crude and disjointed manner in which the story was planned and pursued, and the occasional force discovered in the incidents, the characters, and the philosophy at which the authoress aimed. The incidents are generally improbable, not because events more strange and incredible have not happened, but because in the writer's haste to produce great events she has neglected the minutiae which are necessary for that purpose. From the same mistake there is a want of progression in the story. Having related one striking incident which she has not possessed patience and judgement enough to prepare, she hurries forward to another, and thus robs each of that force which she has been so ardent to impart. – If the reader of these volumes has thought before, they will lead him to think again. Those who buy books will much more frequently buy worse than better; and those who love to encourage an enterprizing and, however abashed and subdued, no vulgar spirit, will not think their money ill bestowed.'

Mrs. Yearsley published one or two occasional poems before this, her last publication. The culture which she received, such as it was, came too late; nor does she appear to have derived any other advantage from it than that it enabled her to write with common grammatical accuracy. With extraordinary talents, strong feelings, and an ardent mind, she never produced a poem which found its way into any popular collection; and very few passages can be extracted from her writings which would have any other value than as indicating powers which the possessor knew not how to employ. But it ought to be observed here, that I have never seen either her novel or her tragedy. The best lines which I have noticed are in her second publication.

> Cruel the hand
> Which tears the veil of time from black dishonour;
> *Or, with the iron pen of Justice, cuts*
> *Her cypher on the scars of early shame.*

There is a like felicity of expression in these lines on the remembrance of her mother: –

> How oft with thee, when life's keen tempest howl'd
> Around our heads, did I contented sit,
> Drinking the wiser accents of thy tongue,
> Listless of threatening ill. *My tender eye*
> *Was fix'd on thine, inquisitively sad.*
> *Whilst thine was dim with sorrow*: yet thy soul
> Betray'd no innate weakness, but resolv'd
> To tread thy sojourn calm and undismay'd.

Flourishing reputations (of the gourd tribe) have been made by writers of much less feeling and less capability than are evident in these lines. Ann Yearsley, though gifted with voice, had no strain of her own whereby to be remembered, but she was no mocking-bird.

She died at Melksham in 1806. Her affairs had not been prosperous, and it has been said that she was deranged for some time before her death. I know not what foundation there may have been for this report, more than the probability that such an effect would be wrought upon a highly sensitive mind by embarrassments, disappointments, the sense of supposed injuries, and the perpetual consciousness that her powers, not having been kindlily developed, had failed to produce, what, under favourable circumstances, they could not have failed to bring forth.

The temporary success of Mrs. Yearsley contributed to bring into notice another illiterate versifyer of the same city: this was

John Frederick Bryant

Who was born in Market Street, St. James's, Westminster, 1753. His father was a native of Bristol, and had been bred a tobacco-pipe-maker, the grandfather and all his family being of that business. Not liking the trade he removed to London, worked as a journeyman house painter, and married a servant maid, whose parents were poor honest hard-working people at Sunbury. When Bryant was about fourteen months old he was taken by these relations, who intended to keep him on while his mother was confined with a second infant; but they grew fond of the child, and he remained with them till he was five years old. He was then removed to London, and after a twelvemonths stay was again taken back to Sunbury in a very ill state of health, which he himself always believed was occasioned by grief at his separation from the old people, who were remarkably fond of him, and whose affection had produced in him a corresponding love. 'My mother,' he says, 'had at that time, besides me, my two sisters to look after, . . . one of them quite an infant; and as she also worked very hard at washing and ironing, it consequently did not lie in her way to give me a great deal of indulgence; but my grandmother unjustly suspected her of using me ill.'[293] There he recovered and remained till the year 1760, when his father, accepting a proposal to settle at Bristol, and there follow his original calling, removed thither with his family, and took with him this his eldest child. The boy was greatly affected at being a second time 'torn from the worthy old people and his beloved Sunbury.' He lost his health again, and it was but slowly that his constitution recovered from the effects of the change. He was put to school to an old woman, who taught him to read, and a year of such schooling was all that fell to his lot; for he was then kept at home and employed in packing up tobacco pipes for exportation. 'I had now at intervals,' he says, 'a great deal of leisure; yet though in the country I had been very fond of play, I retained but little inclination for it at this time. Indeed I was but ill fit to be in company with other boys; for I was grown very deaf, and had besides acquired a kind of timidity and bashfulness, which together made me appear very foolish, and occasioned many people to set me down as little better than an idiot.'[294]

The lessons at school had given him no love of reading. The first thing which he read with pleasure was the History of Joseph and his brethren, in an abridgment of the Book of Genesis, which his mother gave him. Other abridgments of the Scriptures delighted him so much, that at length he read the whole Bible; and could not, he says, help lamenting that he should have been 'born in an age in which prophets, prodigies, and miracles, with the frequent visibility of God and angels, were not to be seen or expected.'[295] He acquired also at this time what he calls an immoderate fondness for the wonderful, 'preferring by far the stories of giants, fairies, magicians, or heroes performing impossibilities, to any history or narrative that wore the face of truth.'[296] Some books of this description, the last of the blackletter race, were 'part of the lumber of a set of dusty shelves' in his father's house.[297] The only one which Bryant mentions is the Destruction of Troy, under which title old Caxton's work (the first book printed in the English language,) slightly modernized, so long ago that the very modernizations have an antiquated cast, entertained his boyhood, as some four-and-twenty years later it did mine.[298] His father bought for him that account of the Heathen Gods, from which magazine poets in former days derived their stock of classical knowledge;[299] there he found quotations from Pope's Homer and Dryden's Virgil, which so pleased his ear and delighted his imagination, that he read them again and again, till he had most of them by heart. And at ten years old, when he was learning to write, he tried to make verses. 'I remember,' he says, 'my mother's once laughing heartily upon finding an Invocation to the Muses, in one of my little attempts, the sublime and interesting subject of which was – the description and character of our turnspit-dog. However, my father seemed to be pleased with my humour for rhyming, and would often read my fragments to his acquaintances. I was also very fond of pictures, particularly of landscapes, which I took great pleasure in attempting to draw, as by taking notice of the diminution of distant, and the foreshortening of oblique objects, in those lively representations of nature, I had obtained a little notion of perspective. Many of my rude productions in this line likewise were, by the partiality of a father, supposed not totally destitute of merit, and were by him often shown as curiosities.'[300]

SOUTHEY'S INTRODUCTION TO *ATTEMPTS IN VERSE*

He had another source of enjoyment in music, which he enjoyed the more, because, on the restoration of his hearing, it came to him like the developement of a new sense. And he had opportunities of enjoying it, for the father had some skill in music, was sometimes employed to play at the Assembly Room, and was acquainted with most of the Bath and Bristol musicians, who sometimes had their rehearsals at his house. Seeing the boy's inclination he thought of giving him some instructions, but ill days came on, which left him no time for any thing but hard and hopeless labour. Among the numerous families which the American war reduced to poverty and want, was that of this poor pipe-maker. Till the troubles which broke out about the Stamp Act commenced, his business had been a good one, and though he had a large family he was in tolerable circumstances, having sufficient for the day and no cause to be anxious for the morrow. He had then employed ten journey-people; the loss of his export trade compelled him to part with them all, and depend upon the labour of his own family, though out of nine children there were but four whose services could be of any use, and his profits soon became inadequate to support them. A trifling salary as one of the city trumpeters, and the office of Exchange Keeper, which the Corporation afterwards gave him, and which added to his means ten pounds a year, enabled him to go on, but with diffi-culty; and it now became matter of complaint against poor Bryant, that he attended too much to his books and too little to his work. The occupation was one which he greatly disliked, for it had been his wish to go to sea: he acknowledges that he neglected his business, and that his parents had cause to be displeased with him on that score. At length they forbade him to read, except on Sundays. 'But my mind,' he says, 'was ever among books. Natural philosophy, and particularly astronomy, began at this time to be the favourite subject of my contemplation; but while my mind was busy, endeavouring to explain the mechanism of terrestrial nature, or soaring among the stars, the labour of my hands turned out to little amount; the less so, as I was extraordinarily slow and awkward at my work, even when I did my best and set my mind most upon it, which I believe was owing to the very great dislike I ever had to the business.'[301]

Sunday was now to him more than a day of rest; it was a day of recreation also; he was generally invited to dine and sup with a blind acquaintance of his father's, who was amused by hearing him read, procured books for that purpose, and gen-erally gave him twopence for this innocent Sabbath day's work. This money was all that he possessed, and he commonly laid it out in prints and colours, with which he amused himself by stealth. He was now above eighteen; and longing once more to see his poor old grand-parents, who had loved him so tenderly in his childhood, seeing no chance of ever obtaining leave to visit them, and fear-ing that death would soon put it finally out of his power, he determined to do so without asking his father's consent. Accordingly he wrote the first letter that he ever penned, informing them of his purpose, desired that they would not acquaint his mother with it, but in their next letter mention something by which he might know they had received his, as he had no friend whom he could trust to receive a letter for him. The poor old people wrote presently according to his wish, and in

163

SOUTHEY'S INTRODUCTION TO *ATTEMPTS IN VERSE*

the month of October he set off with a little bundle of clothes, two or three books, and three-halfpence, being the whole of his worldly wealth.

In another respect Bryant was ill prepared for this pilgrim's progress, which a feeling of natural piety had made him undertake. Having lived in the heart of a great city, and been kept at work in it during six days of the week, he had never in his life walked ten miles at a stretch; and having more than doubled that distance when on the first day's journey he reached Chippenham, he found that he was a very bad traveller. There he sold his Bible for sixpence. The next day (being Sunday) he reached Marlborough, through a heavy rain; and was then rendered so ill by the unusual exertion, that he found it necessary to remain there all Monday, selling his best hat for eighteen pence. On Tuesday evening he got to Thatcham, and paid his last twopence for a night's lodging. The next day he walked from morning till night without any other refreshment than a little water, reached Twyford, and sold another book for sixpence. Another day brought him to Brentford, and there he pawned an article of his apparel for sixpence. Friday he entered London, found out some acquaintance of his mother, and learned from them that he might have reached Sunbury without coming to the metropolis. But he was now better able to walk, he was in good spirits also at being so near his resting place; his friends supplied him with some refreshment and a little money, and he reached the place of his destination that same night, where the good old people received him 'with the most immoderate joy.'[302] Next day his grandmother made him write home in her name, desiring his parents to forgive the step which he had taken on their account, as they should not have died in peace if they had not seen him.

He staid with them nine days, which were nine of the happiest he had ever seen, and then departed with the greatest regret, promising to visit them again during the next summer. A little money was raised for his journey; he walked back much better than he had done when outward bound, and got home in health and spirits after an absence of three weeks. His father received him kindly; but 'I leave any one of common feeling,' he says, 'to judge with what astonishment and horror I heard him, when he abruptly informed me that my poor mother (who was big with child) was dead and buried. The letter which I wrote she never saw, as it was not delivered till about two hours after she had expired. We were all in the greatest affliction, as we had reason to be, on the death of so good a mother; but my grief was beyond measure increased by the unfortunate circumstance of my being in such a manner absent from home at the melancholy crisis, the more so as many people laid her death entirely to that account.'[303]

The loss of an excellent wife left upon Bryant's father a lasting melancholy; increasing difficulties tended to sour his temper, and he had some cause for being displeased with his son, who confesses that all the strength of repeated resolutions could not make him confine his attachment to his business, so that in the performance of his work he generally fell short even of what, unskilful as he was, he ought to have done. Though conscious of this, he thought himself unkindly treated, and finding himself altogether unhappy in his father's house, he left it a second time about sixteen months after his return, 'with as little ceremony as at

164

first.'[304] The old people at Sunbury who had so dearly loved him were both dead. His intention was to go to sea, where he thought his sober disposition might help him to preferment: and he meant at the end of each voyage to employ his wages, as far as they would go, in acquiring some knowledge of mathematics. It would have been useless he thought to look for a ship in Bristol, his father being so well known there, and so much respected, that no merchant or master of a vessel would have willingly received him without his consent. He went to London therefore; but it was at a time when able seamen could hardly obtain employment, so he was glad to get work at his own business. This soon failed, and he then led a precarious life, sometimes in his old employ, then as a labourer at Woolwich, where they were digging foundations for the barracks; there he was disabled by the ground falling in upon him, and consequently discharged. He then got into work sometimes with a tobacco-pipe-maker at Woolwich, who was a Bristol man, sometimes as a jobber in the rope-grounds, and when both occupations failed, he attended on the quays, and now and then got a job at the cranes; but there were at that time so many men of all descriptions out of employ, that if there was a job for four or five men to perform, there were generally twenty to scramble for it; and not being so good a scrambler as many of his competitors, he could not earn a bare subsistence, so that he was obliged to part with every thing he could possibly spare, and was once so hard put to it as to go without a morsel of food from Saturday afternoon till Monday night.

At this time he would have enlisted as a soldier in the East India service, if it had not been for a remaining sense of duty to his father, who had always declared his utter disapprobation of any such step. His health began greatly to fail; but he again obtained employment with the pipemaker, though it hardly enabled him to subsist. Having sent some account of his distress to his father, he was directed to some one in reply, who gave him a few shillings, with an injunction to return to Bristol. He promised and intended to do so, but could not, he says, bear the thoughts of going back in such a state and garb as he was then in. He was now employed for nearly two years at the barracks and other public works, carrying a hod for the bricklayers, under which hard labour it pleased God, he says, to give him an amazing increase of strength, so that after a little use he performed it with surprising alacrity. This improvement in his health and wages enabled him to send some trifling presents to his brother and sisters, and at the same time he told his father that if it was then his pleasure he would return immediately. The answer was that his father had been two months dead; that his sister with a brother's help carried on the little business left, which was barely sufficient to maintain those who were in it, and that most of the younger children were in a fair way of being provided for in the public schools. So he was desired not to return.

Meantime, while a laborious life had strengthened a weak constitution, a precarious one, with its full share of privation and distress, had neither broken a strong spirit, nor damped a cheerful one. His talent of stringing together rhymes made him a favourite with most of his comrades, and held others in some degree of awe, . . . he had commenced a satire upon one of them in consequence of a dispute,

SOUTHEY'S INTRODUCTION TO *ATTEMPTS IN VERSE*

and the fear of being thus berhymed so worked upon the offender, that he stopt the satirist's progress by giving a treat of beef-steaks and porter. An opportunity offered of entering upon his own business on his own account, if he could raise a little money in part of payment for the tools and fixtures of the shop from which his friend the Bristol-man was removing. Some of the foremen under whom he had worked readily lent him a few pounds; but when that difficulty was removed, an old grievance stood in his way. The Bristol-man sometime before had asked him to lampoon the daughter of the person to whom the house and shop belonged. He had done this in no measured terms, and was now properly rewarded for it, for the landlord refused to let him the shop, and the expense of removing the fixtures and erecting a new kiln would have been more than he could venture to engage in. Thus disappointed sorely, and probably little pleased with himself for having given the provocation which brought the disappointment on, he resolved upon going to sea, and entered accordingly on board a privateer.

When he had been a fortnight on board, the captain learnt that he was near-sighted, and discharged him for that defect, paying him for the time he had been on board. Poor Bryant had no sooner been set ashore at Wapping than he found that the character of a seaman is by the law-or custom-of England indelible. He was seized by a press-gang, and dreading the treatment on board a man of war, thought himself fortunate when the landlady of their rendezvous interceded for him, and the alternative was offered him of entering the gang. 'That choice,' he says, 'was soon made, and my hand with horror embraced the lawless bludgeon. But here I was in one thing agreeably surprised: I had looked on all in this employment as persons of the most abandoned principles; but I found those with whom I served to be men of great civility and real good nature; and I must do them the justice to affirm, that for the time I was with them I never saw an instance of unnecessary cruelty or insult. We were commanded by Lieutenant Chubb, of the Princess Royal, a gentleman of the greatest humanity. But I was certainly in a very disagreeable situation, being witness to a variety of distress, which could not otherwise than be the effect of our operations, though conducted with the greatest tenderness.'[305] It was not long before the landlady obtained his discharge; there was little difficulty in doing this as he was no seaman; and she took him into her service during the illness of a person who looked after her business. While he was thus employed he wrote a song, not ill adapted for the purpose, inviting men to enter on board the lieutenant's ship.

As his acquaintance with the press-gang and their officer must have led him to look with less dislike upon the naval service, he might probably have entered therein, if he had not about this time formed an attachment to a young woman, which led to an engagement between them. The effect was what such engagements usually produce upon those whose principles are good: it put an end to his precarious course of life. He went to Bristol, hoping to settle there in his own trade, and fixed a time when he was to return to London to be married, and bring back his wife. When that time came the press was hot, and it would have been dangerous for him to have travelled; he proposed therefore that his betrothed should come to

SOUTHEY'S INTRODUCTION TO *ATTEMPTS IN VERSE*

him; and when they met and weighed all circumstances, she thought it would be imprudent to venture upon marrying till his circumstances were better, and that the best plan was for her to get into service at Bristol, and there wait for better times. This was too reasonable for Bryant to gainsay it, for he had hitherto made no progress toward setting up on his own account, but had worked with his brother and sister, their little profit serving for their common maintenance. He now took to a void workshop on their premises, made use of some old tools and fixtures of his father's which were lying unused, and began making pipes for himself, the same kiln serving both him and his sister. Some years past with little success on his part, but there was something to look on to which sweetened life, and his was a hopeful and a cheerful spirit.

He had begun his first attempt in verse by duly invoking the Muse, for, as he had read in the Pantheon, 'let no person despise the Muses unless he designs to bring destruction upon himself.'[306] It was his good hap, contrary to general experience, to find that theirs is no thankless service; and his first proof of this was that by making songs for some convivial meetings which he frequented, and singing them himself, he procured friends and customers, and occasioned moreover a consumption of his own tobacco-pipes. Fortune seeming then a little to relent, and his affairs beginning to wear rather a more favourable aspect, he married. As this had not been done in haste, it was not repented at leisure. His wife worked very hard in the business, and attended his customers in the city, while he went about the country with a hamper of pipes upon his shoulders, travelling in this manner ten, fifteen, and often twenty miles out. This he generally did twice a week; and sometimes amused himself during these solitary excursions by composing verses as he trudged along. One of those afflictions against which no prudence can provide threw him back in the world. 'My wife,' he says, 'lying-in, we bore the expense tolerably. To be sure our profit had not turned out so much as we could have earned at journey-work; still the hopes of getting into more business kept up our spirits. But my wife catching cold rather before her month was expired, it unfortunately affected one of her breasts in such a manner, that after every other experiment had been tried, she was forced to submit to the operation of the surgeon's knife; and was on the whole near half-a-year under his hands, during which time she was incapable of affording me any assistance.'[307]

Soon after her recovery he was informed that there was a house lying void at Swansea, in which tobacco-pipes had been formerly manufactured, and where all the fixtures, tools, &c. were remaining since the death of the late occupier. Bryant thought it worth while to set out for that place, in hope of taking the house (as he knew it to be a place of considerable trade), or if that failed, of getting a few orders; so he departed on a Saturday afternoon, taking with him a few shillings-worth of his goods by the sale of which to bear his expenses. This little cargo he was lucky enough to dispose of before he reached the New Passage. 'Arriving there a good while before bed time, I sat in the kitchen of the inn,' he says, contemplating my schemes, and enjoying by anticipation the advantages I should probably derive by having the monopoly of a capital sea-port town, till from this

167

SOUTHEY'S INTRODUCTION TO *ATTEMPTS IN VERSE*

pleasing reverie I was awakened by a farmer attempting to sing, which, through intoxication, finding himself incapable of doing, after several efforts, he gave it over, to the regret of some of the company who had asked him for a song. Upon which, from a natural desire to please, I seized the opportunity to offer them one myself; which being accepted and sung, so well pleased them, that from one song to another, they kept me at it till almost midnight; in the mean time I partook of the good cheer of the company scot-free.'[308]

Trifling as this incident seemed at the time, it speedily in its consequences turned the tide of his fortune. Arriving at Swansea after two days delightful walk, on the Monday, he found that the house for which he came to treat had been for more than a twelvemonth occupied, and by one in a different branch of business. Thus ended his hopes; the next day he obtained orders for as large a quantity of pipes as he could get ready within a certain time, set off on his return towards evening, and slept at Neath. On the following morning his stock of money was reduced to a few halfpence, which in the course of the day was so far reduced by other calls, that there did not remain enough to pay for a night's lodging, and after walking till night had closed, he took shelter in a barn near Cardiff. His condition had never been more forlorn, for he had not enough to pay for his fare across the Severn; however he trudged on, trusting to Providence, which had better things in store for him than he had dreamt of, even in his warmest hopes, and reached the Passage House between three and four on the following afternoon, some three hours before the tide served for crossing. The good nature and the social talents, of which he had given proof there a few nights before, were remembered by some of the boatmen who had been then his boon companions; they recognised him at the door, shook hands with him heartily, and insisted on his favouring them with a few songs while they waited for the tide. Bryant told them in reply, that he had travelled so far with an empty pocket and an empty stomach as to be incapable of singing, and he informed them of his additional distress in not having wherewithal to pay his passage. The good-natured fellows soon set both his stomach and his heart at rest; they promised him that he should not be left behind, called for bread and cheese, and regaled him with drink. So being thus put in tune he sung several songs, and the kitchen rung once more with his voice and the applause of his delighted auditors.

At this time a gentleman arrived, and being too much in haste to wait for the passage-boat, ordered the small one to be got ready. While this was doing and the stranger was taking some refreshment, Bryant continued to amuse the company in the kitchen. He was standing at the door when the gentleman went down to the beach, and perceiving that the person who attended him could not conveniently carry the luggage to the water side, he lent a hand. The gentleman then asked if he was going to pass; offered him a seat in the boat, and said, 'you shall sing me one or two of your songs on the way, and when we get on the other side I will give you something to wet your whistle.'[309] When they were fairly under sail Bryant began, and having ended the song, asked leave to sing one of his own making, for he was a poet himself. This he said, expecting only to occasion a laugh. But the gentleman listened attentively, made him repeat other of his verses, pointed out some mis-pronunciations, and drew from him the particulars of his situation. When they were on shore he made Bryant a present, gave him his address, desired him to send him copies of one or two of the pieces which he particularly admired, and told him he might expect to hear from him ere long.

Bryant has not mentioned the name of his benefactor, nor left any clue by which it might be discovered; that stranger, therefore, must have been one of those who like not to have their good deeds known.[310] A most effectual benefactor he proved; he moved in high life, and introduced Bryant to so many persons who liked to do good, and were wealthy enough to gratify their bountiful inclinations, that the poor rhymer was enabled by their liberality to give up a miserable occupation, in which his eyes suffered from exposure to the fire, and to set up as a stationer, bookbinder, and printseller in London. There, in 1787, he published a collection of his verses, chiefly for the purpose of presenting it to those who had assisted in relieving him from a state of extreme indigence. A brief advertisement was prefixed by some friendly and judicious person, saying, that it had been thought respectful by some of his encouragers, to prefix a few lines concerning the author and the verses which were now made public. He had been found, upon the fullest inquiry, to be a man of strict probity, and to have supported the character of an industrious and honest man when struggling with a degree of poverty more than sufficient to have repressed the indulging of a poetical inclination. The verses were intended for the perusal of those who might be desirous of seeing the gradual progress of natural poetical genius, unassisted by education, and therefore it had been thought proper to print progressive specimens of them, from the first essay down to the work on which he was at that time engaged. Peculiar merit was not to be looked for in the earlier poems, separately considered; but such readers as might find no amusement in observing the growth of a poetical spirit, might possibly find their time not misspent in reading some of the later compositions. A long list of benefactors followed the advertisement; and an account of his life, written by himself, and exactly as he wrote it, except as to the spelling, was prefixed to the verses.[311]

From this small collection, for it fills only four octavo sheets, a few specimens will exemplify the writer's capabilities. The first is from one of his convivial pieces.

> Now some folks like your hunting song,
>   Some sing about the wars,
> For some men of the chase are fond,
>   And a few of the field of Mars.
> While some affect your toping songs,
>   (The votaries of wine,)
> The lover swears your love-sick
>   Are the only songs divine.

SOUTHEY'S INTRODUCTION TO *ATTEMPTS IN VERSE*

The sailor likes your sea-songs best,
   In which he'll take some pride,
And wonder if he lets you rest
   Till he has sung you a full broadside.
The miller sings his mill-clack song;
   Your party songs for some;
The husbandman holds fast the can,
   Loud roaring harvest home?[312]

The theme then changes, and he proceeds to extol the glories of a convivial meeting at the Sun in Christmas Street.[313] Reader, I am a Bristol-man myself by birth, and remember the sign; and remember poor Bryant's workshop in the same street, which for several years I passed morning and evening, with a satchel in my hand, or across my shoulder, on my way to and from school. I remember the shop at the distance of five-and-forty years, by its wretched appearance; and Bryant himself I must often have seen there, smeared with pipe-clay, and his eyes bleared by the furnace. Even then, however, these lines will show that there were hours when he was 'o'er all the ills of life victorious,' though he did not pursue his victory so far as Tam o'Shanter.[314]

Our lips the circling tankard greeting,
   Our pipes with fragrance charge the air;
Success we drink, and every draught repeating,
   Or damn the churl, or toast the fair.

While thus the social joys are flowing,
   In every eye while pleasures beam,
While with celestial flame each breast is glowing,
   The sky-born sons of Jove we seem.

Meanwhile the song in strains harmonious,
   With Fancy's flights enchants our ears,
Now hear the thundering chorus roar symphonious,
   And stun the world and drown the spheres, –
   And stun the world and drown the spheres.[315]

In a very different strain are these lines, addressed to a piece of unwrought pipe-clay; the author probably intended them for a sonnet, a species of poem for which at that time he was not likely to have had any other models than Milton and Charlotte Smith.[316]

Rude mass of earth, from which with moiled hands
   (Compulsive taught) the brittle tubes I form,
   Oft listless, while my vagrant fancy warm

170

SOUTHEY'S INTRODUCTION TO *ATTEMPTS IN VERSE*

Roves, heedless of necessity's demands,
Amid Parnassian bowers, or wishful eyes
   The flight of genius, while sublime she soars,
   Of moral truth in search, or earth explores,
Or sails with science through the starry skies:
Yet must I own, unsightly clod! thy claim
   To my attention, for thou art my stead.
   When grows importunate the voice of need,
   And in the furnace thy last change I speed,
Ah! then how eager do I urge the flame,
How anxious watch thee, 'mid that glowing fire
That threats my eye-balls with extinction dire.[317]

The last specimen which I shall produce is a prayer: it is the best of his productions.

Amid the ceaseless din of human strife,
The groans of entering and departing life;
Amid the songs of joy, the wails of woe,
That living nature utters here below;
Amid the harmony of all the spheres:
In concert, unenjoy'd by mortal ears;
Amid Heaven's trumpets loud, by angels blown,
And lyres of seraphim, around thy throne,
O great Supreme! and while their voices join,
Proclaiming praise and glory only thine,
Presuming more, perhaps, than angels dare,
A trembling worm of earth intrudes his prayer.
   Thou great, eternal, awful, gracious cause
Of Nature's being, motion, form, and laws!
That gav'st me tastes of pleasure and of pain;
That gav'st me passions, which alternate reign,
And reason, passion's riot to restrain:
By whom I first inspir'd this mortal breath;
In whom I trust for being after death;
Should I enjoy thy first great blessing, health;
And should thy providence bestow me wealth,
And crown me parent of a numerous race,
Whose virtues should my name and fortune grace;
To love, to duty should my fair adhere;
Should ev'ry friend approve himself sincere;
Shouldst Thou my life reserve to ripest age,
And give me all the wisdom of the sage;
O! let no cursed avarice my store.
Withhold from friend distress'd, or from the poor!

SOUTHEY'S INTRODUCTION TO *ATTEMPTS IN VERSE*

In love, or friendship, or paternal care,
In each enjoyment with the world I share,
Through life, O! give this feeling heart to be,
For ever warm with gratitude to Thee!
  But should thy wisdom the reverse ordain,
And send me pale disease, and life-consuming pain;
Should pinching poverty still keep me down,
To pine beneath my fellow-mortals' frown;
Did I paternal feelings never know,
Or should my fruitful loins bring future woe;
Should an unfaithful wife dishonour bring;
Should slight of fancied friends my bosom wring;
Should my weak mind endure the scoff of fame,
And Dulness be my substituted name;
Should nature early find herself outworn,
And that her earth to earth must soon return,
Without a friend to comfort or to mourn –
Amidst this gloomy complicated throng
Of sharp afflictions, while I press along,
Through each, or real pain or seeming ill,
O give me resignation to thy will![318]

From a pencil note in Mr. Park's[319] copy of Bryant's verses, I learn that he was patronized by the Chief Baron Macdonald[320] . . . that he removed from Long Acre to the Strand . . . which seems to imply that he was prosperous in his new trade . . . and that he died there of consumption in 1791.

I do not introduce Robert Bloomfield here, because his poems are worthy of preservation separately, and in general collections; and because it is my intention one day to manifest at more length my respect for one whose talents were of no common standard, and whose character was in all respects exemplary. It is little to the credit of the age, that the latter days of a man whose name was at one time so deservedly popular, should have been past in poverty, and perhaps shortened by distress, that distress having been brought on by no misconduct or imprudence of his own.[321]

A newspaper paragraph, which has been inserted in one of the volumes before me, quotes from Sheridan the elder, an ill-natured passage in allusion to the writers who have here been noticed. 'Wonder,' he says, 'usually accompanied by a bad taste, looks only for what is uncommon; and if a work comes out under the name of a thresher, a bricklayer, a milkwoman, or – a lord, it is sure to be eagerly sought after by the million.'[322]

'Persons of quality' require no defence when they appear as authors in these days: and, indeed, as mean a spirit may be shown in traducing a book because it is written by a lord, as in extolling it beyond its deserts for the same reason. But when we are told that the thresher, the milkwoman, and the tobacco-pipe-maker did not deserve the patronage they found, – when it is laid down as a maxim of philosophical criticism that poetry ought never to be encouraged unless it is excellent in its kind, that it is an art in which inferior execution is not to be tolerated, – a luxury, and must therefore be rejected unless it is of the very best, – such reasoning may be addressed with success to cockered and sickly intellects, but it will never impose upon a healthy understanding, a generous spirit, or a good heart.

Bad poetry – (if it be harmless in its intent and tendency) can do no harm, unless it passes for good, becomes fashionable, and so tends to deprave still further a vitiated public taste, and still further to debase a corrupted language. Bad criticism is a much worse thing, because a much more injurious one, both to the self-satisfied writer and the assentient reader; not to mention that without the assistance of bad criticism, bad poetry would but seldom make its way.

The mediocres have long been a numerous and an increasing race, and they must necessarily multiply with the progress of civilization. But it would be difficult to say wherefore it should be treated as an offence against the public, to publish verses which no one is obliged either to purchase or to read. Booksellers are not likely to speculate at their own cost in such wares; there is a direct gain to other branches of trade; employment is given where it is wanted; and if pecuniary loss be a matter of indifference to the author, there is then no injury to himself, and he could not have indulged himself in a more innocent folly, if folly it should deserve to be called. But if he is a good and amiable man, he will be both the better and the happier for writing verses. 'Poetry,' says Landor, 'opens many sources of tenderness, that lie for ever in the rock without it.'[323]

If, indeed, a poet feels in himself a constant craving for reputation, and a desire of depreciating those who have been more successful than himself, – if he looks upon them as his competitors and rivals, not as his brethren in the art, – then verily it is unfortunate for such a man that he possesses the talent of versifying. And in that case he will soon betake himself to criticism, as a more congenial calling; for bad poets become malevolent critics, just as weak wine turns to vinegar.

The benevolent persons who patronized Stephen Duck, did it, not with the hope of rearing a great poet, but for the sake of placing a worthy man in a station more suited to his intellectual endowments, than that in which he was born. Bryant, was befriended in a manner not dissimilar, for the same reason. In the cases of Woodhouse and Ann Yearsley, the intention was to better their condition in their own way of life. The Woodstock shoemaker was chiefly indebted for the patronage which he received, to Thomas Warton's good-nature, for my predecessor Warton[324] was the best natured man that ever wore a great wig. My motives for bringing forward the present attempts in verse have already been explained.

It will be seen, from Mr. Jones's account of himself, that his opportunities of self-instruction have been even less than were possessed by any of the uneducated aspirants who preceded him. Had it been his fortune to have enjoyed those advantages, of which the great majority of educated persons make no use whatever after they become their own masters, he might in all probability have held more than a respectable place among the poets of his age; and the whole tenor of his conduct

173

shows that he would have done his duty in any station of life to which he might have been called. But except during the time when he had access to Shakespeare's plays, he seems to have read little other poetry than what is occasionally to be found in provincial newspapers. From them he has sometimes copied a pattern, or a tune, – nothing more: he has expressed his own observations, his own fancies, his own feelings, and they are such, though often rudely, unskilfully, and sometimes obscurely expressed, as to show that he has been gifted with the eye, and the ear, and the feeling of a poet: the art is wanting, and it is now too late for him to acquire it.

No other alterations have been made in his pieces than by occasional omissions, sometimes altering a word in such cases for the sake of connection, – and by correcting a very few grammatical errors.

I would have said something here concerning the March of Intellect, and the beneficial direction which might be given it by those who are not for beating it to the tune of *Ça ira.*[325] But I shall have other opportunity for this, and it is now time that Mr. Jones should speak for himself.

Before I conclude, I must, however, in my own behalf, give notice to all whom it may concern, that I, Robert Southey, Poet Laureate, somewhat advanced in years, and having business enough of my own fully to occupy as much time as can be devoted to it, consistently with a due regard to health, do hereby decline perusing or inspecting any manuscript from any person whatsoever, and desire that no application on that score may be made to me from this time forth; this resolution, which for most just cause is taken and here notified, being, like the laws of the Medes and the Persians, not to be changed.

Also, I give notice, that I have entered into a society for the discouragement of autograph collectors; which society will not be dissolved till the legislature in its wisdom shall take measures for suppressing that troublesome and increasing sect.

Lastly, I shall be obliged to those journals which will have the kindness to make these notices more widely known. And if my county member, Sir James Graham,[326] would be pleased to mention them in the House of Commons, – which he may do with as much propriety as when he spoke of the same person there on a former occasion,[327] – they would then have the advantage of being taken down by the reporters, inserted in all the daily newspapers, copied into the weekly and provincial ones, and finally recorded in the Parliamentary Debates.

An Account of John Jones's Life Written by Himself

TO ROBERT SOUTHEY ESQ.

The place of my birth, Sir, which happened in January, 1774, was the village of Clearwell, in Newland, in that part of Gloucestershire called the Forest of Dean. My father, Sir, from the period to which my memory extends until the time of his death, was employed in the gardens of Charles Edwin, Esq.,[328] father of the late

Thomas Wyndham, Esq., many years M.P. for Glamorganshire; my mother kept a small shop in the village, in which I was useful to her, at a very early age, in going to and fro to Monmouth, about six miles distance, for the necessaries required in her little way of business. This I must have commenced doing when little more than seven years of age, up to which period I had been a short time at school, to an old woman, with whom I learnt my letters and spelling, but I believe I made but little progress in reading. The only person in the village who taught writing at that time was an old man, by trade a stone-cutter, and he only on winter evenings – after his return from his daily labour; to him I went the best part of two winters, and that, Sir, was the finishing of my education. At the age of ten I was engaged to drive plough at the 'squire's, and at different places, and continued that kind of employment for four years; and up to this period, Sir, I do not recollect to have read in any book but the Psalter and Testament, and sometimes a chapter in the Bible, by reading verses alternately with other boys: but with the little money that came into my possession I purchased songs – the Mournful Lady's Garland,[329] and such stories as are generally hawked about in a pedlar's basket, and which I was very fond of reading, and was often affected to tears by them. At the age of fourteen, Sir, I went to a friend of my father's, who kept a small inn, in Chepstow, where I remained about three years, during which time I was very actively employed, and do not remember to have made any advance in reading or writing; but at the end of that time, having had many small sums given me, I was in possession of four guineas, and with that, Sir, I set off for Bath, where I had a cousin who had been many years a servant there, and who was very kind to me, and soon procured me a place as foot-boy; and Mrs. Edwin[330] being at that time in Bath, was so good as to say what she knew of me, which proved to be satisfactory in point of character. The family consisted of two ladies only, and I had an old Frenchman over me as butler; and it being about the time that the French Revolution commenced, he was very interested in the politics of the day, and frequently went out soon after breakfast and returned but a short time before dinner; therefore, Sir, I had to lay the cloth and to place every thing in readiness by the time he came home; this I used to do an hour or two before the necessary time, for there was a book-case in the dining-room which was left open, and by this means I was enabled to spend many a delightful hour at it; and as plays were what mostly engaged my attention at that time, and Shakespeare's being in the collection, I read the whole of them, and some of them twice over; and when I could not be in the dining-room I read in the Bible below stairs, and, I believe, went regularly through it; but the history of Joseph, Ruth, and some other parts, pleasing me most, I read those passages many times over. At the end of two years I engaged myself with a lady who only kept myself and two female servants, but here, Sir, I had nothing to read; but as I found I had improved myself in reading, it occurred to me, Sir, that I ought to do something in writing, and nothing less than an attempt to write a play could content me; and big with the idea of such an undertaking, I hurried away to the stationer's, and expended almost all my money in the purchase of a dictionary, paper, pens, &c., but having no place to myself, and being desirous that no person should be made acquainted with my intention, and having only my bed-room in the garret to retire to, and that being out of the reach of the sound of the bell, I could do but little at it; but I finished it before I left my situation, in which I staid two years. I then went to see my friends, Sir, and took it with me; and I paid my old schoolmaster, the stone-cutter, for writing it out for me, reading it out to him as he proceeded, for my writing no person could read but myself, and when done, Sir, he thought it such a marvellous thing for a boy who had only been a few winter evenings to school to him, and praised it so much, that I was induced to send it off by the coach to London, directing it to the manager of the Haymarket Theatre; and after a long time, Sir, I received a letter, and I wonder now at the forbearance with which it was written, giving me the information that it would not do for representation, and advising me not to spend my time in such difficult undertakings; but I could hardly bring myself to believe that they had not copied it off, or stole the plot, or played me some dirty trick in it. In those proceedings, Sir, which I have kept a profound secret from that time until the present moment, I spent all my money, and then set off for Bath in search of another situation, and that I might avoid ridicule I destroyed my play, and the only part of it that remains on my memory is the following song or glee, which I had put into the mouths of some soldiers just before entering on the field of battle.

> Come, come, my boys, let's prepare to meet the foe,
> Come, come, my boys, let's drink before we go;
>   When in battle, cannons rattle, we can't do so.
> Here, good, good, good, may the bottle go,
> There, pop, and off our noddles go.
> And when we're there, we shall not fare,
> As we do here, taking good cheer
> Through the sweet brown lips of a bottle-O;
> Then come, come, come, let's drink, drink, drink,
> And take good cheer awhile we're here,
> Lest, pop, and off our noddles go.

I soon engaged myself again, Sir, with an old gentleman and his three nieces, whose names were Alexander, uncle and sisters of the present Lord Chief Baron,[331] and I had not been in the family many months before, young as I was, I was made upper servant, and as I received a little card money[332] at times, I soon was enabled to procure me some books, which I did by subscribing two or three quarters to the library, and the ladies were very kind to me, and often lent me others, and about this time, Sir, I bought the first and almost the only book of poems I was ever master of, which was called Jane's Beauties,[333] and this I read over several times; but my chief reading now was history, and I made some poetical attempts, but I kept copies of none of them excepting the epitaph on Molly Mutton, an old woman very well known about the streets of Bath at that time; but on some of my verses falling into the hands of the ladies, they were much amused with them, and,

I believe, expressed regret that I had not been better educated. The housekeeper, Sir, was very kind to me, and on my expressing sorrow at her departure once when she was going to see her friends, she desired me to write something extempore in which my regret might be more strongly expressed, when in a few minutes I remember putting the following lines into her hand:

> There something is, my Martha dear,
>   So amiable about thee,
> The house is Heaven, when thou art here,
>   But Hell to me without thee.

After living with this family five years, Sir, I left them in consequence of their going to reside in Scotland, and unto this hour I remember them with gratitude and respect. This brings me to the year 1800, when I engaged myself with a gentleman of the name of Wynch, who likewise treated me very kindly, and in whose service I attempted to compose a few pieces in verse, chiefly songs, two of which only I put in my book, and one of those you have marked for transcription; I have two or three others in my memory, which, perhaps, Sir, I may send for your opinion. From Mr. Wynch, I went to Mr. Lynch, with whom I went to Ireland; but not liking that country I left him, Sir, in about a year and three or four months, but he was a kind and indulgent master and was unwilling to part with me; and in a letter of recommendation which he gave me, he was pleased to say that my conduct had not in a single instance been otherwise than he could have wished it to have been; and with that character, Sir, I entered into the family which I am now serving, in January, 1804, and have continued in it first with the father, and then with the son,[334] only during an interval of eighteen months, up to the present hour; and during which period most of my trifles have been composed, and some of my former attempts brought (perhaps) a little nearer perfection; but I have seldom sat down to study any thing, for in many instances when I have done so a ring at the bell, or a knock at the door, or something or other, would disturb me, and not wishing to be seen, I frequently used to either crumple my paper up in my pocket, or take the trouble to lock it up, and before I could arrange it again, I was often, Sir, again disturbed; from this, Sir, I got into the habit of trusting entirely to my memory, and most of my little pieces have been completed and borne in mind for weeks before I have committed them to paper; from this I am led to believe that there are but few situations in life in which attempts of the kind may not be made under less discouraging circumstances. Having a wife and three children to sup-port, Sir, I have had some little difficulties to contend with, but, thank God, I have encountered them pretty well; I have received many little helps from the family, for which I hope, Sir, I may be allowed to say, that I have shown my gratitude by a faithful discharge of my duty; but within the last year my children have all gone to service. Having been rather busy this last week, Sir, I have taken up but little time in the preparation of this, and I am fearful you will think it comes before you in a discreditable shape, but I hope you will be able to collect from it all that may

SOUTHEY'S INTRODUCTION TO *ATTEMPTS IN VERSE*

be required for your benevolent purpose; but should you wish to be empowered to speak with greater confidence of my character, by having the testimony of others in support of my own, I believe, Sir, I should not find much difficulty in obtaining it; for it affords me some little gratification, Sir, to think that in the few families I have served, I have lived respected, for in none do I remember of ever being accused of an immoral action, nor with all my propensity to rhyme, have I been charged with a neglect of duty. I therefore hope, Sir, that if some of the fruits of humble muse my be destined to see the light, and should not be thought worthy of commendation, no person of a beneficent disposition will regret any little encouragement given to an old servant under such circumstances; but above all, Sir, I hope there will be found no person so ill-natured as to upbraid you for the part you have taken in their introduction, when it is done from motives the most kind and disinterested. I will endeavour, Sir, to let you have the verses by the time you wish, and will do my best to improve them; but as yet I have said but little to any person respecting them, and I believe, Sir, I must not address my friends on the subject, until I again trespass on your kindness for instructions how to proceed, for which Sir, there can be no hurry.

Believe me, Sir,

Your most obliged
and most grateful servant,

JOHN JONES.
KIRKBY HALL,

August 15th, 1827.

5

SOUTHEY'S REVIEW OF ELIZA BRAY[335]

Fables, and other Pieces in Verse, by Mary Maria Colling, with some Account of the Author. In Letters to Robert Southey, Esq., P. L. By Mrs. Bray, author of 'Fitz of Fitzford,' 'The Talba,' &c. &c, London, 1831,

The Quarterly Review, 47 (1832), 81–103

═══════

This very pleasing volume contains a tale which may be presented here both as a contrast and companion to the melancholy story of Lucretia Davidson.

Mrs. Bray (who is well, and deserves to be yet better, known for her historical novels),[336] observed some four or five years ago, among several poor women who used to sit immediately under the reading-desk, in Tavistock Church, a young woman very neatly dressed, and remarkable for a countenance as intelligent as it was pleasing. Upon inquiring who she was, it appeared that she was a servant in the family of a gentleman of the place; and that she had the character of being a clever girl, and fond of poetry. Some time after, she took her seat in the pew, near Mrs. Bray, belonging to the family in which she lived. That lady inquired no further concerning her, though she never failed to look on her with peculiar interest, for her expressive features and her decorous behaviour; but in the spring of 1831 she received, through the hands of one of her own servants, a small parcel from her, containing a few of her poems, with a request, very modestly proffered, that she would be kind enough to look them over at her leisure, and say what she thought of them.

The circumstances which encouraged her to do this are not less interesting than characteristic. The country immediately about Tavistock is the scene of Mrs. Bray's last novel, 'Fitz of Fitzford, a Legend of Devon,'[337] and Marys master perceiving that she wished to read it, lent it her, with his wonted kindness. After reading some chapters in the house, instead of hurrying through the story for the mere desire of gratifying curiosity by getting at its events, a refinement occurred to her, and she determined to go on with it in her own way. So, on summer evenings, in company with her sister Anne, she used to take the book to Whitchurch Down; and then they took their seats upon a certain rock, from whence they commanded a full view of

DOI: 10.4324/9781003431343-6

the principal places in which the incidents of the tale were carried on. They could see the old ruined gateway of Fitz-Ford; Holwell, where Lady Howard set-on the blood-hound to track Standwich, is just by; Dartmoor, the resort of his wild people, was before them; Brent Tor, where the boy fires the beacon, in the distance; and in the valley below, the vicarage house, in which the authoress lived.[338] To read it there, she said, was the way to enjoy it most; and as she looked at the valley and read on, she thought that if the authoress knew her she would be kind to her; for there were many kind feelings in the book, and they seemed to be written as if they came from the heart; and after some time, and being encouraged by one of the servants at the vicarage so to do, she ventured upon what, in its results, has given as much pleasure to Mrs. Bray as it has produced benefit to herself.

After she had been emboldened to take this adventurous step, – 'I heard,' says Mrs. Bray, 'a good deal about her from various quarters; but these accounts not always agreeing together, I determined to learn what I could from the poor girl herself. The first time I saw her, she was so agitated that I gained little intelligence; but the second, taking her into my own room, I did all I could to conciliate her feelings, and having in a great degree overcome her timidity, I obtained from her a regular account of herself, given in the most artless manner. I shall here repeat the substance of it, with every attention to fidelity. My information respecting her singular worth, her early talents, and the excellence of her character, I derive from a lady who has known her from childhood, and from the worthy gentleman in whose family she has lived for so many years.'[339]

Mary Maria Colling was born at Tavistock, in 1805, of poor but honest parents. The father was a husbandman,[340] and the child, when very young, was sent to school to an old woman, that she might be out of the way. It seems not to have been expected that she should be taught anything more there than sewing and knitting; and in these she made little progress; but hearing others taught to read she wished to learn also; the good old woman then found her a willing and apt pupil, and soon outrunning her tasks, with supererogatory diligence she stored up in her memory the whole of Watts's Hymns,[341] and of a sixpenny book, which, with some little stories, contained also a few pieces in verse. This was done for the delight which an active mind finds when employing itself according to its own inclination; but it turned to good account, for when the schoolmistress, as a punishment for neglecting her needle, would sometimes keep her in after school hours, Mary often managed to soften her displeasure, and procure her own enlargement, by repeating something out of the sixpenny book, with perfect exactness. This poor woman was one of a class upon which the machinery of modern education has borne as cruelly as machinery of a different kind upon 'the spinners and the knitters in the sun.'[342] The modern school, with all its advantages, furnishes no such characters for painting, and for poetry, which paints in words, as Shenstone and Kirke White drew, in this class, from the life.[343]

At ten years she was entered at the free-school to learn needle-work; but then some kind ladies, who visited the school, were induced to notice her by the amiable character which she bore at home; and they taught her to read perfectly well. She could write a little before, but scarcely can tell how she learnt to do so. Here

SOUTHEY'S REVIEW OF *MARY COLLING*

she wrote from copies; but she rarely went on writing-days, the object in placing her there having only been that she might learn needle-work; and as her mother was repeatedly ill, and had a young family, Mary was obliged, for weeks together, to stay at home, and nurse her brothers and sisters: thus her schooling amounted to very little. Here, as at her former school, 'she received small praise for sewing;' but 'she was considered the spelling-wonder among the children, and her memory was so remarkably good, that she could repeat anything by heart with little more trouble than that of reading it over.'[344] When she was about thirteen she left the school, and shortly afterwards was placed at a loom, to learn the business of weaving. Some neighbour, who saw her thus employed, said, whether hopefully or in sadness, 'that Providence had designed that child for better things!'[345] So, indeed, it proved. She was soon delivered from the house of bondage; and she had already shown herself to be worthy of the better fortune that awaited her; for, at this time, what may truly be called 'a beautiful incident in her life' occurred; – I wish, says Mrs. Bray, in repeating it, 'I could convey to you any idea of the feeling manner with which she related it to me. It grieved her heart, she said, to see that her father could neither write nor read; for his Bible could not *speak* to him; and so she taught him both herself, before she went to place.'[346] –

"'At fourteen years old," she said, "it pleased God to give her a good service;" for Mrs. General Hughes[347] being in want of a young person to assist in the family, directed one of her servants to inquire after some little girl, who could fill such an easy station, till one, more competent, could be engaged. The servant, in returning home, after a fruitless search, chanced to meet our Mary, who, on hearing the circumstance, most gladly offered her services. The next day she presented herself before Mrs. Hughes, who was so much interested by the artless manners, and the intelligence of the child, that she immediately engaged her; and Mary remained with her kind protectress as long as she lived. "The dear old lady," she said, "was very good to her, and grew as fond of her as if she had been her own child. She died in her arms; and, when upon her death-bed, she charged her son to be a kind friend to poor Mary, and to take care of her; which he has done from that hour to the present: there could not be a better master," she said, "nor a better man in the world."'[348]

Thus fortunately placed, Mary has continued to eat 'well-earned, the bread of service,'[349] happy in her humble station, and, though with a 'mounting spirit,'[350] seeming to have no wish beyond it. Kinder or more considerate treatment, indeed, than in this benevolent family she could nowhere have possibly found, and they have not been more sensible of her worth, than she has been of their goodness. Her love of reading has not made her less active, less diligent, less faithful, as a servant. Some envy it has excited among the ill-minded in her own station, and this might be expected; for if the inequalities of rank and fortune were trampled down, the inequality of intellect and of mental culture would be more invidious, and speedily be deemed more intolerable than any which vulgar violence had abolished. But though ill-natured people had not been wanting in their endeavours to 'set her master against her,' they were disappointed in their object; Mr. Hughes was so far from discouraging her, that he 'bought her several good books for her benefit, and some sermons as a Christmas present.'[351] For this excellent master, Mrs. Bray says, she seems to feel that sort of grateful respect and regard which Louisa had for Oberlin.[352] A few books had been lent her by her first benefactress, Miss C. Bedford,[353] who has continued to be her kind friend; and a few she has purchased from her wages, expending as little as she possibly could upon her clothes, that she might have to spare for other purposes; and from her small means she has been very dutiful and generous to her own family. The amount of her reading has, however, been very little, 'excepting that she has made herself perfectly well acquainted with that one true book, which, independent of its sacred character, is, perhaps, of all books the most calculated to elevate the mind, and to form a pure, just, and simple taste – the Bible. Here she is quite at home, and knows whole chapters of it by heart.'[354] The crafty politicians of the Romish Church act with the wisdom of the serpent, when they proscribe the Bible, for they well know, that if the Ark be introduced into the temple of their idolatry, Dagon[355] must fall. But even those Roman Catholics, whose religion is their religion indeed, and not their faction, seem to have been rendered incapable of conceiving the effect which the Bible produces upon those who have been trained up in the way they should go – the delight and the reverence with which it is perused – how it expands and elevates the mind, while, at the same time, it consoles the heart, and satisfies and strengthens it.

'Finding, excepting in her Bible, that she had really read very little poetry, I asked her how she came to understand such words as zephyra, Aurora, &c., and that Flora was the goddess of flowers, as I observed allusions to such persons and things continually in her poems. I also asked how she had formed her way of writing, and learnt such bold and forcible expressions? To the former question she replied, "That she had a dictionary; at the end of it there was an explanation about the gods and goddesses, and there she had learnt it: that if she met with a word in reading which she did not understand, she never passed it over, but looked it out in her dictionary, and seldom forgot how a word was spelt if she once saw it in print; and as to her language, she had gained that from hearing Mr. Bray preach. To listen to him was her greatest delight, and she thought she owed much to his sermons. "As a proof of it," she said, "he had inspired her to attempt poetry." It was on the following occasion: about six years ago, he preached a sermon on the power of God manifested in the creation of the world; she was struck with it, and, on her return home, composed her first essay in verse, the lines on "CREATION."'[356]

Mary's attainments, as they provoked envy in some excited admiration in others, and the wonder as usual was magnified. Mrs. Bray heard that she was fond of astronomy, and asked her if this were true. Her answer was, 'she had once read a book that came in her way on the subject, and she liked to learn any thing she could, but she knew very little about it; only she could never look at the beautiful moon and the stars without wishing to understand their courses.'[357]

Some time after she had discovered that she could make verses, she began to compose her fables, though she had then never read any except a few prose ones in the little six penny book, which she had learnt by heart in early childhood.

SOUTHEY'S REVIEW OF *MARY COLLING*

'I was anxious,' says Mrs. Bray, 'to learn what could have induced her to think of writing fables, not having been, from her own account, at all prompted to do so by reading them. She blushed like crimson when I asked her, smiled, and at last I drew out the confession. She said, "that her master, seeing she did not go out much, or run about like other girls, from kindness to her gave her a slip of garden to amuse herself with cultivating it in her leisure hours; till, at length, all the flower garden came under her care. The river Tavy flowed at the foot of it; and here she found the greatest delight. She would tell me truth, though she was afraid to speak it, lest I should think her mazed; but when of an evening she was amongst the flower-beds, and saw them all so lively and so beautiful, *she used to fancy the flowers talked to her.* Thus, a peony growing near her laurel tree, she fancied the one reproaching the other for not being so fine as itself, and so composed her little fable of the 'Peony and the Laurel.' And these kind of thoughts used to come into her head in a moment, and then she turned them into verses and fables."' – pp. 11, 12.[358]

'When I mentioned to Mr. Bray, that she said she used to fancy the flowers talked to her, and that she had composed fables before she had read any, he remarked, that this poor girl, like Æsop, was in a state of servitude; and possibly that persons of their stamp of mind so situated, feeling themselves so far beyond the ordinary society of their own sphere, might be led to seek it in a world they created for themselves by the vivacity of their own imaginations, and thus hold discourse, as it were, with flowers, and trees, and animals.' – pp. 14, 15.[359]

One extract more may complete Mrs. Bray's lively account of this remarkable young woman: 'She is very modest, and seems imbued with a deep sense of religious feeling, the surest safeguard against vanity; since such a fault is seldom found in a mind accustomed to serious thoughts on sacred subjects. It is more frequently the vice of those who think too much about themselves, and too little about their God. She has the Devonshire accent, but not coarsely; and, though a perfect country girl in every thing, – in her smile, her cap, her little straw bonnet, and her curtsy, – yet there is nothing vulgar about her. The elevated feelings of her character have given to her manners that indescribable mark of mind, which shows itself amidst the greatest simplicity, and is never to be mistaken.

As, in noticing those who are at all distinguished for talent or worth, it is customary to say something of their persons, I may be allowed, perhaps, to state, that nature has been liberal to her in this particular. Her features are regularly handsome, especially the forehead, eyebrows, and eyes; the latter peculiarly so when animated in conversation. And I may here observe, that Mary Colling the servant, and Mary Colling talking about poetry and flowers, scarcely appears to be one and the same person. If I had not seated her for a couple of hours by my side, and won upon her to open her heart, I should never even have guessed the animated, interesting being she could become in conversation. I do assure you, when I looked on the beautiful expression of her countenance, so tempered with modesty, and listened to the feeling modulation of her voice, "soft and low," for she has that "excellent thing in woman,"[360] as she repeated to me her own admirable lines on

Creation, I could not help entertaining for her a degree of admiration that was not unmixed with reverence and regard.' – pp. 17, 18.[361]

The portrait of Mary Colling, which is prefixed to the volume, accords well with this description of her countenance. It was not till after this account of her had been written, and Mrs. Bray, with the warmth of true benevolence, had taken upon herself the task of bringing her verses before the public, that that lady was made acquainted by Mr. Hughes with some circumstances concerning her family, more remarkable than are often met with in the romance of real life. They cannot be better related than in Mrs. Bray's own words:

'Mary's maternal grandfather, George Philp, was a native of Tavistock, respectably born, though, by various mischances, his friends were so reduced in the world, that they caused George to follow the business of a tailor. Mr. Hughes was assured by a lady of this place, now dead, a Mrs. Murray, who knew him well, that Philp was one of the handsomest young men she had ever beheld. His education had been better than his fortunes; he had a high spirit, and longed for manly enterprize. His business of a tailor, therefore, became a subject of discontent to him, and the good town of Plymouth (only fourteen miles off), with its port and its fine shipping, was for ever in his mind, and he, like Robinson Crusoe, would be satisfied with nothing but going to sea; though, also, like the hero of De Foe, he was not wanting in friends who assured him that, if he did so, "God would not bless him."[362] But youth, ardour, and ambition have each a voice more powerful than that of prudence; so away went George Philp, and leaving his shears and his thimble, and Tavistock, and all care behind him, he became as gay and as gallant a sailor as ever ploughed the wild ocean in the service of the king.

For some few years nothing was heard of him; till at length, to the wonder of all Tavistock, George Philp suddenly appeared in his native town, bringing with him a young and beautiful bride, whose manners, appearance, and the possession of several rings, &c., all proclaimed her to be of a rank much above that of the handsome sailor to whom she was wedded.

Philp and his bride were universally admitted to be the finest couple that had ever been seen in Tavistock; and on the Sunday after his return, it was with evident delight and pride that George carried her to church to attend divine service. Every body admired her, and every body inquired who she might be, and nobody could answer, since nothing was known to satisfy such inquiries; the bride and bridegroom maintaining the utmost reserve on all that related to the subject of their marriage. Whatever might have been the family of the bride, or the worth of her jewels, it appeared she had no money; for George Philp, whose spirit of enterprize had yielded, perhaps, to one of a tenderer nature, in order to maintain himself and his wife, instead of mounting the deck, was once more obliged to mount the shop-board at his old business in Tavistock. For awhile curiosity and rumour busied themselves to the full in endeavouring to "pluck out the heart of his mystery;"[363] but these, unsatisfied, gradually died away, and the people were content to say, that "Mrs. Philp was for certain a gentlewoman born, but a very wisht sort of a body."

Her character and her manners, from all I can learn at this distance of time, were marked and peculiar. She did not seem happy, but she never complained. She had a high, independent spirit, but refused no employment, however mean, to earn bread for her children. She was ardently fond of her husband, but kept aloof from his connexions. She was well-bred to all persons, but associated with no one; and though in her way of life, in her dress and her industry, she entirely suited herself to her condition (and that was truly a poor one), yet she never parted from her few jewels till, long after, absolute want compelled her to do so. To all inquiries relative to her own family, for many years she remained totally silent. However, after her severe misfortunes – which I shall presently have occasion to relate – something of her history became known, though, even to her own children, and to the day of her death, she was never very communicative upon the subject. The following particulars will not be read without interest.

'It appears that Mrs. Philp's maiden name was Domville, and that she had been left an orphan at an early age, both her parents dying of the small-pox. Her maternal uncle, whose name was White, lived near Arundel in Sussex; and after the death of her parents he took her home, treated her with every kindness, and gave her, when she was old enough to know their use, valuable clothes, and some jewels that had belonged to her mother. Mary Domville grew up a beautiful girl, and though a favourite, was nevertheless so high-spirited, that, not wishing to be obliged to her relative for support, she left the comfortable asylum his house had afforded her, and fled to the Isle of Wight. If she took offence at anything in her uncle's conduct towards her, it does not appear. To whom she fled, or by what means, is likewise unknown. She acknowledged having there entered into the service of two sisters, as a sort of attendant or upper servant; but these ladies, seeing how much she was above her condition, treated her as a friend and companion, and became exceedingly attached to her. The uncle traced her out; and, at various times, endeavoured to prevail with her to return to his protection: but all his solicitations proved vain; she would never live with him again. Whilst in the Isle of Wight she first saw George Philp, the young and handsome sailor. A mutual attachment followed, and the same rash spirit that had tempted her, perhaps, to quit the asylum of her uncle's roof, might now have induced her to enter upon a hasty and unadvised marriage. Be this as it may, married she was; and whatever had been the rashness of her former conduct, her wedded life was without reproach. She bore her change of fortune with resignation; made a tender mother, and an industrious, affectionate wife.

For some years George Philp continued his business; but it is most likely he still entertained a lingering regard for his late profession, and would much rather have plied the oar on the broad ocean, than the needle and shears on the shop-board of a country town. However, he had made a resolution to abandon the seafaring life for ever. But his resolution, may be, was something like Benedict's, who, when he determined to die single, thought he should never live to be married;[364] for, on the first temptation, it melted away like ice before the sun. A fine frigate, the Vestal, was launched at Plymouth,[365] and fitted out for a particular service in the formation of a settlement in some far-distant and foreign land. The crew were all picked men, and the gallantry and spirit of George Philp being well known to the late Admiral Vincent,[366] he was recommended by this gentleman to the officer in command, and speedily nominated to a confidential appointment, with an offer of support, likewise, for his youthful son, would he join his father in the enterprize. George Philp, full of golden dreams of success and ambition, in the same buoyancy of spirit with which he had first gone to sea so many years before, now accepted this new offer of service; and his son, a fine lad of fourteen years old, gladly consented to join his father in the voyage.

All was arranged, and the morning came on which George was to bid adieu to his wife and to his native town, once more to seek an uncertain fortune amidst the dangers and the toils of the sea. Mrs. Philp, whose affection for her husband and her son was well known, supported this trial with that peculiar and marked restraint she had, in so many instances since her marriage, placed as a curb upon her strong and high feelings. It was a scene never to be forgotten by those who witnessed it. George wept; but she shed no tear whilst he was in her sight, and continued to hold her babe, of four months old, at her bosom, whilst another child, a girl nine years of age, hung about her father, and, crying, asked him, "When he would come back again, and why he went away to sea from herself and her mother?" The boy, whose nature was exceedingly affectionate, kissed his mother a thousand times, and, as he did so, gave her a parting gift, the model of a little pair of andirons, as a chimney-ornament, that he had bought as a remembrance for her at Plymouth; and promised her "that he would bring her a token from every foreign land on which he set his foot." The last kiss was given; the mother's last blessing was bestowed; and that last look, which turns again and again, till it is blinded with tears, was fixed on the sorrowing mother and bereaved wife. George departed, leading by the hand his youthful son, to follow his dreams of ambition; and his deserted partner was left with God for her hope and her infants for her care, to maintain them as she best could till her husband's return.' – pp. 22–29.[367]

The sad sequel may be foreboded. No tidings arrived either from husband or son, or of the ship in which they sailed. The poor wife and mother passed laborious days and sleepless nights in miserable hope; her health was affected; and when at last it was known that a vessel, which from all circumstances there was reason to conclude was the Vestal, had been lost, with all on board, in a tempest off Newfoundland,[368] the certainty of the calamity which had befallen her was more tolerable than the apprehension she had so long endured. It called forth the strength of her strong character. Before this she had perfectly subdued her mind to her fortunes; and, under this last and irremediable affliction, she recovered that external composure, which, till anxiety for her husband and son disturbed it, she had maintained from the time of her first appearance in Tavistock. The secret of her youth died with her; and if she had anything more than the rashness of her marriage to reproach herself with, no doubt she derived some support from the thought, bitter as it was, that her punishment had been allotted to her in this world, and to the full measure of her offence. But it is equally possible that she had been more sinned against than sinning; and this conclusion may with most probability be inferred from her whole demeanour in adversity.

'She had now two fatherless children and herself to support by her own and sole exertions; since, such were the peculiar feelings of her mind, she would accept of no assistance from any one; and, though kindly advised to attempt it, refused to hold any communication with her own family to procure relief for her children in this day of distress. The motive for such refusal she would never divulge to the hour of her death; and, though so proud in independence, she was most humble in toiling for her daily bread, laboured incessantly, and declined not the meanest employment by which she could maintain herself and her little ones. She would often (so Mary tells me) toil all day, come home in the evening to give food to her children, place them in bed, cry over them, and look upon the last little present given her by her lost son, and go out again to her work, and labour sometimes till twelve o'clock at night ere she took the least rest. Her few jewels were now sold, one by one, not according to their value, but for what she could most readily get for them to help her necessities.

She had one ring, I think it was diamond, that she had reserved for the last. Some dear remembrance was, in all probability, connected with it; for, like Isabella, she had preserved it through all her misery; and now, like her also, parted with it to "stop the cries of hunger for a time."[369] It was sold for three guineas, being nothing in comparison with its actual value. Possibly this was the last relic of her better fortunes; for after the ring was gone, she was scarcely ever heard to allude to her former life or to her family, even in the presence of her own daughters. One of them married Edmund Colling, the father of our poet. The child was named Mary *Maria* (being, in fact, a repetition of the first name), at the express desire of her maternal grandmother Philp, for such had been the favourite names in her own family.

Mary Colling, who was only five years old when this beloved grandmother died, tells me she has the most distinct remembrance of her; and that "she did not talk like Devonshire people." There was something high-spirited and reserved about her to most persons, but to little Mary she was gentleness and affection itself. She has never yet talked to me about her grandmother without shedding tears, and speaks of her with a warmth of gratitude that it is delightful to witness. She has, indeed, those strong and genuine emotions that frequently show themselves in an honest burst of feeling.

When the widow of George Philp grew old, though in extreme poverty, and no longer capable of work, she would willingly have starved rather than have sought relief from the parish; but she was at length prevailed with by her neighbours to accept it. To the last, her reserve, her calm but high spirit, her ardent affection for her grandchild Mary, who was her chief care even on her death-bed, never deserted her; and she expired as she lived, firm, collected, and resigned. Mary Colling perfectly well remembers attending her grandmother on her death-bed; and that not long before she died, she embraced her, and as she bestowed her last blessing, wished "that she was in Abraham's bosom, and could carry that dear little lamb thither in her own."

The child Mary loved her most affectionately; and, after her eyes were closed in death, for some time she thought her sleeping. She shed many bitter tears, and when she saw her grandmother did not wake up again, she stole to the bed and kissed her. To this hour she remembers her funeral, as the saddest day of her own life. And she told me, when I noticed having first seen her in the aisle of Tavistock church, under the reading-desk, that she used to sit there from a melancholy recollection, not, however, unmixed with pleasing feelings, that it was *there*, when a child of four or five years old, whilst seated by the knees of her beloved grandmother, she had first listened to the word of God, and learnt to call upon his name that he would bless her.'[370]

In this part of her narrative Mrs. Bray has inserted Mary's lines

ON THE DEATH OF MY MATERNAL GRANDMOTHER

Affection loves the sad employ.
The grief which steals a secret joy;
That softly strikes, but sweetly heals,
The tender smart that nature feels.

This from experience well I know,
Conscious what gratitude I owe
To one who hath resign'd her breath.
And sleeps within the arms of Death.

Blest shade! accept my humble lay;
'Tis all that tenderness can pay.
For all thy toils and all thy cares.
Bestowed upon mine infant years.

Anxious to guard, intent to please,
'Twas thine to give my bosom ease;
And oft, while pillow'd on thy breast,
A kiss upon my cheek was prest.

What joy was in my bosom raised,
When by thy kindness I was praised;
Or ran to thee and sought relief
For every little infant grief!

What was my joy, what was my pride,
I mind when prattling by thy side;
When oft thy feeble arms would stretch

To pick the flowers above my reach.

No wants from thee did I conceal;
I sought thine house at every meal;
Though e'er so little thine might be,
A bit was always sav'd for me.

When stretch'd upon the bed of death,
I heard thee speak with falt'ring breath;
Though thy departure was so near,
I was the object of thy care.

And when the vital spark was fled,
I fondly climb'd beside thy bed;
Not knowing then what death could mean,
I kiss'd thee o'er and o'er again:

But seem'd affronted in my mind.
Thinking that thou wert grown unkind.
And wonder'd what the cause could be
That thou no kiss return'd to me.

I mind when, on thy burial day.
With grief I saw thee borne away;
I then was told I should not mourn.
For by and by thou would'st return.

These hopes awhile did I maintain,
That I should see thy face again;
And often thought how long 'twould be
Before thou would'st return to me.

High were my expectations grown,
Till reason's light began to dawn:
The fond mistake she soon remov'd,
And chas'd the hopes I long had lov'd.

These thoughts renew'd create a sigh.
And I with nature will comply;
The tears which now fast fall can prove.
That I remember still thy love.

Oh, yes! perhaps to thee 'tis known.
How oft I've sat and wept alone;

When there the artless tear might be
Unseen by all save heaven and thee.

Each word by thy fond lips express'd.
Is still the treasure of my breast;
When thy remembrance, oft renew'd.
Is by affection's tear bedew'd.[371]

Here we may add, that when Mary, after the publication of this volume was advised to put the money which she had received for it into the Savings Bank, she replied, that the first thing she intended to do with any part of it, was to place a stone on the grave of her grandmother; 'she had carefully attended to the grave for many years, and did not like that it should lie without anything to mark it.'[372] This alone would show, if proof were wanting, that the kindness which Mary Colling has met with from the benevolent editor of this volume, and from her other friends, has been most worthily bestowed. Indeed, the success which this interesting little volume has already obtained, great as it is for one in her station, has produced no other feelings in her well-regulated mind than those of thankfulness and the warmest gratitude. More than once she has said to Mrs. Bray, 'that having been so long accustomed to domestic labour, she is quite sure that she should not be happy without it; and that this very labour gives her a greater relish for the pursuits which she delights to follow in her evening hours of leisure.'

Montesinos[373] supposes it will be one consequence of general education and the diffusion of cheap books, that more poems will be written, and fewer published, for that both in poetry and the kindred art of painting, imitative power will be so commonly called forth, that it will no longer be mistaken for an indication of genius. The exertion of such talents is now, in most cases, stimulated by emulation, and most frequently ends in disappointment; emulation then, which is the endemic fever of the times, takes a worse type and degenerates into envy. But let them be cultivated for their own sake, not with a view to popular applause, – for the pleasure which they impart within their own circle, – for the moral and intellectual improvement which is obtained in the pursuit, – and they contribute then, in no slight degree, to adorn society, and to increase the sum of its innocent and beneficial enjoyments. 'Poetry,' says Mackenzie, in one of his youthful letters,[1] 'let the prudence of the world say what it will, is, at least, one of the noblest amusements. Our philanthropy is almost always increased by it. There is a certain poetic ground on which we cannot tread without feelings that mend the heart; and many who are not able to reach the Parnassian heights, may yet advance so near as to be bettered by the air of the climate.'

---

1 Elphinston's Forty Years' Correspondence, vol. i. p. 169. [Henry Mackenzie, writing to Elphinston on 16 December 1768, in *Forty Years' Correspondence Between Geniusses Ov Boath Sexes and James Elphinston,* 6 vols (London, 1791), I, 169.]

Cultivation destroys wild flowers as civilization destroys wild animals. The greater number of those who are called uneducated poets in the present age, have actually received more education in their favourite art than those upon whom the utmost pains of regular culture were bestowed fifty years ago.

We shall not instance in proof of this the author of the 'Corn Law Rhymes,' whose poetry cannot be commended too highly for the genius which is displayed in it, nor condemned too severely for the spirit of ferocious jacobinism which it breathes: this writer is not to be instanced, because it must be evident to any person who understands the art of poetry, that he has both studied and practised it as an art, and, probably, belongs quite as much to the operatives of literature as of any other class; few of its operatives are gifted with such ability; but *as he tenders his own soul, let him keep his thoughts from blood!*[374] Neither shall we instance Mr. Struthers of Glasgow – whose 'Sabbath' exhibits many of the best *graces* of composition and versification, in company with the more precious graces of natural genius, and a deeply devotional spirit: he also, though practising a humble trade, has obviously made poetry, as an art, the subject of elaborate study.[375] But we may instance Charles Crocker,[376] the humble Chichester shoemaker, and Robert Millhouse,[377] the weaver of Nottingham, as men, who having the poetic feeling, have acquired its utterance, and made themselves acquainted with the forms and diction of poetry by sedulously availing themselves of those means of instruction, which, living as they have done in large towns, were within their reach. Mr. Crocker tells us that he carefully studied an English grammar; and that he attended a lecture of Mr. Thelwall's on Milton and Shakspeare, and learned from it far more of the art of versification than he could possibly have acquired by reading; for the lecturer examined the structure of Milton's verses, and entered minutely into the nature of the feet of which they are composed.[378]

He tells us also, that he hired books from a circulating library; and purchased the poems of Milton, Cowper, Goldsmith, Collins,[379] and others; committed much of them to memory, and used to repeat them when at work. A good foundation had been laid for this at the Grey-Coat School, in Chichester, where he was happily placed from the age of seven till between eleven and twelve, when he was apprenticed to his trade; for there, in his own words, 'were sown the seeds of those religious principles, which, springing up, have, through life, rendered his condition more than commonly blest; supplying comfort and consolation amid trials and difficulties, and crowning the hours of health and industry with the highest and purest enjoyments.'[380]

Mr. Millhouse had, in like manner, eagerly read many of our best poets, whose works had been placed, by cheap editions, within his reach. It is not wonderful, therefore, though the greater part of his poetry was composed at the loom, and written down at such brief intervals as the close application required at his employment would allow, that the structure and the diction would do no discredit to one who had received all the advantages of modern education. So too with the Chichester poet: both have taken great and successful pains in educating themselves for their favourite pursuit. And both are also deserving of especial notice, as exemplifying that such pursuits, under the guidance of good principles, may be indulged in by persons of their station, not only without injury to themselves in any way, but to their great advantage. They have neglected no calling 'for this idle trade;'[381] have left no duty unperformed; it has elevated them as moral and intellectual beings, without taking them from the last and the loom; it has been the solace of their patient industry, and given them gratifications of a higher kind than wealth can purchase.

The same means of self-education were not within Mary Colling's reach; and a woman in her station can have none of that assistance which a man derives from society. Newspapers are not so accessible to her; and in this sort of education newspapers bear no inconsiderable part. Many of these, while they feed the discontented with sedition, and communicate to the wicked the newest and most approved modes by which murder or arson may be committed with the least probability of detection, allow now and then a column or a corner for the notice of new books, and for extracts of criticism or poetry. The little poetry which Mr. Jones had read seems to have reached him through these channels. If we compare such current poetry as is thus circulated with that which was published in the magazines forty or fifty years ago, we shall see how little assistance was attainable by persons of this description then, and what facilities are afforded to them now. The march of intellect here has been proceeding at quick time.

There are, however, and probably always will be, a few choice 'sons of song,' who deserve to be called uneducated *par excellence*, because they bravely choose to remain so, and, despising all adventitious aid, trust to their native genius. Two of this description have recently been introduced to our notice, and we take the opportunity of introducing them to the public. One, who is a weaver, by name, we believe, James Barnfield of Cam in Gloucestershire, (for this is written on the back of the copy with which we have been favoured,) has – we must not say strung his lyre – but wetted his whistle, in honour of the late elevation of Colonel Berkeley to the peerage,[382] – one of the first creations under the peer-mongering administration. Thus he begins his lyric strain –

> Come all you men of honour,
>   And raise a joyful cheer;
> The worthy brave Lord Segrave
>   Is raised to a peer.
> Great exaltation now resound,
> And in this 'lustrous family found,
> Their character spread the country round,
>   Now cheer, brave cheer!

And thus he concludes it –

> So now for the conclusion
>   And finish this my song,
> Sing praises to Lord Segrave
>   With a melodious tongue.
> May brighter lustre deck his brow,
> That we may praise him through and through,

And mighty blessings on him flow,
Now cheer, brave cheer!

Neither Cam nor Isis,[383] in the days of their *Gaudia* and *Luctus*,[384] ever produced a poet who understood the principle of encomiastic poetry better than this bard of Cam in Gloucestershire; when some *Dignus laude vir*,[385] or rather, if we may use a maccaronic[386] verb, *dignus lordari*,[387] some personage whom a prime-minister hath delighted to honour, is to be celebrated in song, the best way is certainly to praise him through and through, especially if his 'character spread the country round.'[388] This choice composition was forwarded to us as 'another specimen of the uneducated.' If the communication were meant as a civility, the obliging unknown is hereby thanked for it; and if it were intended to be sarcastic, still he is thanked for what has been made useful. Cardinal d'Ossat spoke like a wise man as he was when he said, '*Ce que la Fortune sembloit me présenter de la main gauche, je le pris de la droite.*'[389]

The other of these no-school poets favoured us with some samples of his poetry, and an introductory letter, and we cannot favour him better than by transcribing that letter for insertion here. He need not 'blush to find it fame,' famous as he describes himself to be; and by so contributing to his celebrity we shall atone for the sin of our ignorance in not having known any thing either of him or his productions, (for such ignorance we must confess, though 'not to know him' might 'argue ourselves unknown,') till he made himself thus known to us:

Trowbridge, 26th April, 1831.

I doubt not but you have seen in most of the London papers various extracts from the numerous poetical works which I have written; nor will you, I am persuaded, accuse me of arrogance if I enumerate some of the Royal and illustreates individuals with whom I have lately corresponded. On the death of his late Majesty,[390] I felt myself called upon, in my capacity of poet, to write some very elegant and pathetic lines on the occasion, which I transmitted to the King, with a congratulation of his Majesty's accession to the throne.[391] I also addressed his Grace the Duke of Wellington[392] on the state and condition of the nation, pointing out the cause of the general and universal distress. I have also written to Sir Robert Peel,[393] and sent him two copies of poetry which I composed on his Majesty's proclamation.[394] I have likewise received the title of Poet Laureate to the Town of Trowbridge, from the editor of Bell's Life in London,[395] in return for some of my sublime productions. And, moreover, I not only caused the king to be proclaimed here, but actually proclaimed him myself. And to convince you that I am no impostor, I will name a few, amongst the many of my admirers is John Bennet[396] and J. D. Astley,[397] Esqrs., two members for the county; the Rev. George Crabbe,[398] a brother poet; W. E. Waldron[399] and E. K. Mortimer,[400] Esqrs., and magistrates.

I have sent you a few copies which I have composed to his Majesty's honour for your perusal, and, if you do approve of it, I should like for his Majesty to have a sight of them, and an answer what his Majesty thinks of them.

I remain your most humble servant in all respects,

John Alford, P.L.T.

'A few outlines' must furnish our first extract, as having the interest which auto-biography always possesses, whether it be in prose or verse: –

> Out of obscurity I rise,
> And men of knowledge do surprise;
> But they can't see, nor neither know
> The spring from whence my verses flow.
> I am a man of humble name,
> My father a shearman of the same;
> My occupation lost, I tried
> For other work then to provide,
> For eight small children and a wife,
> With whom I lived with scarce a strife;
> Of late I've trod the path of rhyme,
> And work'd it into verse and time.
> See from my works what progress made!
> Peruse! compare! extract from shade!
> They'll bear the test, and will defy
> The scoffer's and the critic's eye.
> Though rage and madness may infame,
> Yet still I bear the Laureat's name:
> Little, nor White, can't be admir'd, –
> John Alford is the man inspir'd.

The other specimens have the higher claim of national interest, – being from a poem

ON STATE REFORM

> Behold now with joy and wonder we see,
> Reform in the House it surely must be;
> No longer for boroughmongers to have a place
> To send their bad members, or dare show their face.
>
> Reform in the land has been all the cry;
> And we loyal Britons, we cannot see why
> We should not have power to send members too,
> Especially now there's so much to do.

SOUTHEY'S REVIEW OF *MARY COLLING*

Earl Grey[401] he proposed to have a reform,
To save old Britannia from a threatening storm.
We all shall be glad; – we'll drink and we'll toast;
Our royal Britannia shall never be lost.

But let us not boast till the battle is won;
For we see and we know reform's not begun;
For certain great snakes still lies in the grass,
That use all their power for the Bill not to pass.

Those boroughmonger men in the House they have got,
They all are so crafty – a very bad lot;
But William the Fourth has brought it about;
Since they are turn'd mad, he turn'd them all out.

King William the Fourth he rose up in haste,
And chas'd those bad members all out of their place.
O may there be wise men now choos'd for to stand
To plead for the poor and the good of the land!

Two motives (besides the hope of gratifying our readers) have induced us to present these specimens to the public. The first is, that, not holding the seals of the home department, we could not, in compliance with the author's desire, lay the poems themselves before the King; and, considering the business of that department in these times, we think they will be more likely to meet his Majesty's eye, or reach his ear, through this channel, than if we had transmitted them to Lord Melbourne.[402] Secondly, seeing that this journal has, with all sincerity, in the discharge of what we believe to be our duty, opposed the ministerial plans of reform, we have felt ourselves bound in fairness not to withhold from Earl Grey and his administration the advantage of the Trowbridge laureate's declaration in their favour. John Alford's approbation should be worth something to those by whom the *Vox Populi* has been courted at such cost!

The Curiosities of Illiterature might furnish materials for an entertaining, and not uninstructive, volume.

Persons of such genius as these admirers of my Lords Grey and Segrave are manifestly independent of all culture; but in Mary Colling's case much might have been expected from a little of that education which is 'on thousands misbestowed,' or rather which thousands find utterly unprofitable. Her language is not like that of Mr. Crocker and Mr. Millhouse – the current language of poetry. Their compositions are, in this respect, as well as in all others, quite as presentable as those of the noble and honourable contributors to Mr. Heath's 'Keepsake;'[403] whereas, in hers, provincialisms sometimes occur, and, more frequently, the expletive verb, which, having crept into our language imperceptibly (no one has yet traced how), disfigured it grievously under the three latter Stuarts, and now occurs only in the

195

colloquial language of humble life.[404] In England, that language has not escaped the imputation of ignorance and vulgarity, because nothing has been done to consecrate it: the attempt would be too late now, even if it were otherwise possible, – which it is not, for this reason, that the common speech differs in almost every county, and therefore cannot be generalized. It would have been a great advantage for Mary Colling if we had had a Doric dialect, like the Scotch.[405]

Imitation will not make genius, (which, indeed, cannot be made,) but neither will it mar it. In poetry, as well as in painting and in architecture, the better the models which the student has before him, the more he is likely to profit by his studies, if there be no deficiency either of power or judgment on his part. This uninstructed poetess hitherto has had very few, but she has evinced a remarkable aptitude for deriving from them all that could be obtained. In two of her pieces she has caught Cunningham's[406] manner; and a picture of Envy, which she had seen in some little book when a child, lay in her mind for years, and at last gave birth to these spirited stanzas: –

> 'Twas midnight – and the whirlwind's yell
> Had started Horror from her cell;
> The beasts, appall'd, mid nature moan'd,
> The ocean raved, the forest groan'd.
> The heavens put on their blackest frown;
> Each star a direful ray shot down;
> When Etna, with a thund'ring yell,
> Foam'd out on earth the hag of hell.
> As through the world she swiftly glided,
> The winds her snaky locks divided;
> Ten thousand hisses rent the air;
> Her eagle talons wrought despair.
> Fair flowers were blasted by her breath,
> And she was arm'd with more than death;
> For youth and age, and virtue's self,
> Fell victims to the green-eyed elf.
> In sulph'rous glooms she rode along,
> Flames play'd around her forky tongue;
> Her canker'd breast hove with despair-
> Hell's blackest curse held empire there. – pp. 44, 45.[407]

One characteristic specimen more must conclude our extracts from this pleasing volume:

A LETTER TO MY SISTER ANNE

> Dear Anne, I'm to my promise true,
> I now sit down to write to you:

SOUTHEY'S REVIEW OF *MARY COLLING*

But as for news, I've none to tell,
It may suffice to say I'm well;
But then, I think, it is not meet
To send an almost empty sheet,
To save my credit, I will try
To write of years that are gone by;
When you and I did often stray,
On many a sunny summer's day.
What feast did we with farthings make!
How proud we were to give and take!
And in the meadows with what pride
We've gather'd flowers from Tavy's side;
When I did range through brier and brake
That I the prettiest bunch might make!
And oft, in many a rugged thorn,
Our hands and aprons have we torn;
And then what projects did we try,
To hide the same from mother's eye!
Sometimes beneath the trees we've sat,
Reading of Whittington's famed cat;
Or talk'd till tears our eyes bedew'd
About the children in the wood.
The schemes we form'd proved fancy bold:
How often in our walks we've told
What great things we should surely do,
If we were like Fanny Drew!
And don't you recollect at night
Our neighbour John would, with delight,
Sit by the fire, when 'twas our glory
To hear him tell some goblin story;
Of rogues who lived at Roborough rock;
Of ghosts that walk'd at twelve o'clock;
How oft was seen on such a lawn,
A coach with headless horses drawn;
Of hounds on Heathfield seen to rise,[408]
With horned heads and flaming eyes;
What wonders some old witch could do?
Nor did we doubt but all was true.
And though these years are long gone by
As firm as e'er affection's tie
For as to that I've little fear,
Nor time nor change can it impair.
My service, with respects, record
To master and to mistress Ford;

And pray do mind my dear canary,
And then you'll please your sister Mary. –

'This canary,' says Mrs. Bray, was a curiosity in natural history; as not only Mary Colling, but other persons who heard it, assure me it could talk. The talking canary is since dead; and I am much inclined to believe Mary killed it with kindness, by giving it pieces of cake and sweet things whenever it would call out to her, as it often did, "Give us a bit," or "Pretty bird," &c.' – pp. 73–75.[409]

Marivaux[410] says, speaking of '*l'humeur grossiere qu'on contracte dans les viles occupations,*' – '*il semble que l'esprit se laisse abattre, par la misère et qu'il ne soit capable d'aucun sentiment elevé.*'[411] Some occupations undoubtedly there are which brutalize those who follow them, and render the heart as callous as the hands; but happily there are not, and cannot be many of these, not more than will always be filled by persons who have no repugnance for them, and seldom take to them till they have rendered themselves unfit for anything better. And few as these occupations are, they will be fewer when that improvement in society shall have been effected, – that radical – that only real reform, which must be made in this country, unless, as the plain consequence and just punishment of our sins, both of commission and omission, England is to be utterly rebarbarised. During more than twenty years, it has been the constant doctrine of this journal, that the condition of our working classes must be physically and morally improved, if we would avert the horrors of *a bellum servile,*[412] – if we would prevent such convulsions as those by which France and the Low Countries were shaken in the days of the Artevalds[413] and of the Jacquerie,[414] – and Germany, during the peasants' war.[415] There would be no danger of such a catastrophe if our rulers had directed their attention to the moral economy of nations, instead of giving ear to the professors of that pseudo-science by which political economy has been mystified, to the ruin of thousands and tens of thousands. This kingdom can never again be safe till the great body of the community are contented in their stations. God alone knows how long it may be before any set of ministers will even dream of safety; but whoever, in his sphere, endeavours to improve the condition of those who are around him and below him, performs his part of that moral and religious statute labour which duty requires, and prepares the way for safety and for happier times.

One characteristic of the English populace, – perhaps we ought to say people, for it extends to the middle classes, – is their propensity to mischief. The people of most other countries may safely be admitted into parks, gardens, public buildings, and galleries of pictures and of statues; but in England it is necessary to exclude them, as much as possible, from all such places, not only because the proportion of rogues and ruffians is far greater here, to our shame be it spoken, than in any other Christian country, but because there is no security against the wanton mischief and gross offences which are committed in mere sport. This disgraceful part of the English character (for such it is, and as such all foreigners regard it) can neither be soon nor easily corrected; but anything tends to correct it that contributes to give the people a taste for intellectual pleasures, – anything that contributes to their innocent enjoyment, – anything that excites them to wholesome and pleasurable activity of body and of mind; and the faster the march of intellect can be made to proceed in this direction, and the farther it goes, the better.

It is necessary for the general weal that the goods of fortune should be unequally distributed, – that there should be high and low, rich and poor, – that there should be great riches, but not that there should be miserable poverty, – that there should be masters and servants, but not slaves; but it is not necessary that there should be that mental and moral inequality which at present exists beyond what is natural and inevitable. A little of that levelling influence which is allowed on the race-course and on the cricket-ground, might, with excellent effect, be introduced by better things. Modern refinement has widened the interval between masters and mistresses, and their domestics, much to the injury of the latter: farther refinement should tend to bring them again into the relation in which they formerly stood to each other.

Every one who has read 'Boswell's Life of Johnson' (and who that reads anything has not read that delightful miscellany?) must have admired the single stanza which Johnson preserved in his memory from a forgotten poem by a clergyman named Gifford, whose name, but for that beautiful stanza, would have been forgotten also:

Verse sweetens toil, however rude the sound.
All at her work the village maiden sings;
Nor while she turns the giddy wheel around,
Revolves the sad vicissitude of things.[416]

What singing is to the spinners and the knitters in the sun, or rather what it used to be, (for machinery has silenced their songs!) what it still is to the boatmen of the south and the herdsmen of the Alps, verse, in another sense of the word, has been to Mary Colling, and her fellow-poets in humble life; and knowledge, in any of its numerous branches, might be, if facilities for it were afforded to all who are desirous of obtaining it. The good is very great which might be done by parochial libraries, if they were judiciously extended, and by servants' libraries in the houses of the wealthy. But of such libraries, books of direct moral and religious instruction should form the smallest part; for to put such books into the hands of those who are in no degree prepared for them by their feelings and the course of time, is administering as physic that which can never be wholesome, unless it is taken as food.

'Sunday,' said Dr. Johnson, 'was a heavy day to me when I was a boy. My mother confined me on that day, and made me read "The Whole Duty of Man," from a great part of which I could derive no instruction. When, for instance, I had read the chapter on theft, which, from my infancy, I had been taught was wrong, I was no more convinced that theft was wrong than before; so there was no accession of knowledge. A boy should be introduced to such books by having his attention directed to the arrangement, to the style, and other excellences of composition; so that the mind, being thus engaged by an amusing variety of objects, may not grow weary.'[417]

But when it is desired that persons should instruct themselves, and with no stronger motive than the desire of knowledge, and the pleasure which they find in the pursuit, the books which are provided for them must carry their own attraction. The more they can inform and gratify an inquisitive mind, the better; but any are useful if they amuse minds which would otherwise be idle, any, in truth, that are not mischievous. History is attractive to most readers; biography, travels, natural history, fiction, and poetry, to almost all. The populace in Italy are not unacquainted with Ariosto and Tasso,[418] though the Italians are not a more intellectual people than the English. It has lately been stated, that in a subscription library at Glasgow, to which the operatives have access, the books most in request are the 'Newgate Calendar,'[419] and Sir Walter Scott's novels.

Perhaps station in life has never been so signally disregarded in this country, in deference to literary merit, as it was some forty or fifty years ago in Portugal, when the two poets, Domingo dos Reis Quita, and Francisco Dias Gomez,[420] were members of the Royal Academy at Lisbon: the first of these writers was a barber; the second a poor tradesman, who kept one of those humble shops in which every thing belonging to common household use is sold; and the first prince of the blood was at that time President of the Academy. Britton, the small-coal man, indeed, was admitted into high company for his musical talents; for as misfortune makes men acquainted with strange bed-fellows, so music, as well as dogs, horses, and cricket, bring them into strange society. The pursuits of agriculture, while they were in fashion, had the same harmonizing effect. In our own country, however, genius in humble life has seldom or never been neglected after it has once found means of making itself known; and to this both Scotland and England may at this day proudly bear testimony. But it is not the number of authors in humble life (nor, indeed, in any station) that we are desirous to have increased; it is the number of readers; we would have the intellectual pleasures of the higher and educated classes extended, as far as possible, to all; and greatly extended they may be, for the benefit of all.

There is, at this time, a weaver in the city of Norwich, who takes his place at the loom, during the summer months, at five in the morning, and yet rises two hours earlier for the pleasure of cultivating a flower-garden. That pleasure most persons in the country and in the smaller towns may enjoy; and none of those who enjoy it will frequent the public-house, or that new seminary of mischief, sedition, and sin of every kind, the beer-shop. The country also affords facilities for all the interesting pursuits connected with natural history; and, except London, none of our cities are so large as to preclude their inhabitants from those enjoyments which the country affords. In towns there are advantages for scientific pursuits; and some of the highest enjoyments which art can afford are open for all who have eyes to see and ears to hear, – those enjoyments which are derived from music and from architecture. When we say that these are to be found in our cathedrals, let us not be accused of inviting people thither, as to a theatre, for the sake of entertainment;

though no ill would be done even if that undisguised motive took them within reach of sound instruction and the words of life; and some of those who entered the church with no better impulse might haply remain to pray. But we speak of music as a pleasure common to all, and which is capable of being improved as a highly intellectual gratification. In many countries it contributes greatly to the happiness of the people; indeed, it would not be a mere refinement to affirm that the Spanish guitar has no inconsiderable effect in making the peasantry of that delightful country contented with their lot; they are held by the ear, and will not be led by the nose to their own destruction; the revolutionary drum will not draw them into the dance of death!

Would you then, says the objector, have the lower classes instructed in literature and in the arts and sciences? – We would encourage them as far as possible to instruct themselves, being perfectly convinced that it would be for the benefit of all. The enemy scatters his tares among the good seed, in fields where the sower has been before him; but that enemy has the wastes to himself in full occupancy, and it is the unweeded garden which is possessed by 'things rank and gross in nature.'[421] Give the people such moral and intellectual pleasures as can be given them, and you will in the same degree withdraw them from such as are injurious to themselves and others. No wise man would wish to see High Life below Stairs[422] in reality; for this, which, upon the stage, is an excellent farce, leads to tragedy whenever it is no fiction. But the wise and the good, who see what men are, and rightly consider what they were created to be, must, as they love their country and their kind, wish to see intellectual life, moral life, spiritual life everywhere.

APPENDIX I

Correspondence Concerning the *Lives*

Southey to Mary Anne Hughes[423] (Warter, IV, 61–62)

Keswick, Sept. 21. 1827

My Dear Mrs. Hughes,

[. . .]

I have undertaken to introduce some verses written by an old servant, whose unpoetical name is John Jones. Perhaps I may come to you for help in soliciting subscriptions; but this is not yet determined: it will, however, be but a trifling matter for one little volume, from 7s. 6d. to 10s. at the utmost. You will be pleased with the simplicity and modesty of his letters, amused with the account of himself, and pleased also to see how much intellectual enjoyment may be attained, under the most unfavourable circumstances, by those who know how to look for it. This is a theme on which I hope to preach a useful discourse in the preface; so that I have two objects in this undertaking: – to raise a little money which may help this poor man in his old age, and to dwell upon certain truths which are at present mixed up with a great deal of mischief, but which in themselves are most salutary and important.

Southey to Mary Anne Hughes (Warter, IV, 66–67)

Keswick, Oct. 19. 1827

My Dear Mrs. Hughes,

The particulars respecting my poor poet, are simply these, – That he is in the service of Mr. Bruere, of Kirby Hall, near Catterick. – That he is between 50 and 60, and bears the best of characters: that he is not brought forward as another 'Bloomfield,' or 'Pet Pig'[424] of the muses, (like the 'Ettrick Shepherd,)[425] but as showing how much intellectual enjoyment, and moral improvement connected with it, is within the reach of the humblest condition, and may be cultivated without interfering with the performance of the humblest duties.

202

APPENDIX I

My intention is to get as good a list of subscribers as I can (the price of the volume will be from 7s. 6d. to half-a-guinea) – and then offer the book to Murray;[426] if he will give as much for it as he would give me for the introductory matter in another shape, it will be a great windfall for John Jones; – and if we get a good list, he will give more. You will be amused with the poor man's introduction to me, who, as being P. L.,[427] am looked upon to be a sort of Lord Chancellor in poetry, having preferment to bestow; you will be pleased with his rare simplicity (though it falls short of the Welshman who came to look for his son in Cadogan summut, the day that I dined in Amen Corner),[428] and you will be entertained with the story of his early studies. His rhymes show that nature had done her part for making him a poet, but everything else has been wanting. Had it been his fortune to have fallen in with me some years ago, I might, as he sensibly and modestly says, have made something of him. However what he has made of himself will suffice for the moral lesson that I shall draw from it. There is in his verses that sort of eye, ear, and love for natural objects which characterizes Cunningham's poems, and the better poems of Izaac Walton's friend, Charles Cotton.

Southey to Grosvenor C. Bedford,[429] Esq. (*Life and Correspondence*, V, 315)

Keswick, Oct. 31, 1827

My dear Grosvenor,

Thank you for the interest you take in my scheme for serving honest John Jones. There is no one point, Grosvenor, in which you and I accord more entirely, than in our feelings concerning servants, and our behaviour towards them. The savings' banks may do for this class all, or almost all that you desire, if there be but religious education to give them an early sense of duty, which I think it will be more easy to give than to bring about the desired amendment in the behaviour of their superiors. To amend that, there must be a thorough reform in our schools, public and private, which should cut up the tyranny of the boys over their juniors by the roots.

You have seen exactly in the true light what my views and motives are with regard to Jones. I want to read a wholesome lecture in this age of Mechanics' Institutes, and of University College.[430] I want to show how much moral and intellectual improvement is within the reach of those who are made more our inferiors, than there is any necessity that they should be, to show that they have minds to be enlarged, and feelings to be gratified, as well as souls to be saved, which is the only admission that some persons are willing to make, and that grudgingly enough; and if I can by so doing, put a hundred pounds into Jones's pocket (which, if a few persons will bestir themselves for me, there is every likelihood of doing), I shall have the satisfaction of giving him a great deal of happiness for a time, and of rendering him some substantial benefit also.

203

APPENDIX I

Southey to Margaret Holford Hodson[431] (*Life and Correspondence*, V, 317–18)

Keswick, Nov. 16. 1827

My dear Madam,

Mr. Charles Hodson[432] may, perhaps, have told you that I was likely to bring forward the rhymes of an old servant for publication by subscription, and that, in that case, it was my intention to solicit your assistance in procuring names for my list.

The man's name is John Jones, – it could not be a more unpoetical one, but he could not help it, the Muses have forgiven him for it, and so I hope will you. He lives with Mr. Bruere of Kirkby Hall near Catterick, and has served the family faithfully for twenty years. Mr. Otter (the biographer of Dr. Clarke)[433] assures me of this. Jones is just of my age, in his fifty-fourth year. If I can get a tolerably good list of subscribers, I will offer the list and the book to Murray, and get what I can for it. The price may be from 7s. 6d. to 10s. If we have any good success, something may be obtained which would assist him in the decline of life.

Do not suppose that I present him to notice as a heaven-born genius, and that I have found another Bloomfield. There is enough to show that Nature had given him the eye, and the ear, and the heart of a poet; and this is sufficient for my purpose; quite so to render any reader satisfied that he has bestowed his bounty well in subscribing to the volume. The good sense and good feeling of the man are worth more than his genius; and my intention is to take the opportunity for showing how much intellectual enjoyment, and moral improvement in consequence, is within the reach of persons in the very humblest ways of life; and this moral cultivation, instead of unfitting them for their station, tends to make them perform their duties more diligently and more cheerfully; and this I mean to oppose to the modern march of intellect, directed as that is with the worst intentions and to the worst ends. This will be the subject of my introduction, with some remarks upon the poetry of uneducated men. Jones tells his own story, and I am sure you will be pleased with it and his manner of telling it, and with the simplicity and good sense of his letters.

Southey to the Right Hon. C. W. W. Wynn,[434] M.P. (Warter, IV, 70–71)

Keswick, Nov. 16. 1827

My Dear Wynn,

[...]

I am going to print a little volume of rhymes by an old servant, in the hope of getting a little money for him, which may help toward his subsistence in the decline of life. The verses show a degree of natural talent which, under favourable culture, would have produced good fruit. But what is of more consequence, that talent, having taken a good direction, has contributed greatly to his moral

APPENDIX I

improvement, and consequently to his happiness; and this it is which has induced me to try what can be done for him. For it may be useful to show, as it is certainly very gratifying to see, how much intellectual enjoyment is within the reach of persons in the very humblest walks of life. The man's name is John Jones, for which I hope you will like him the better, though unluckily for himself he was born in Monmouthshire, a little on the wrong side the border.[435] However, he certainly is Welsh by blood as well as by name. I pray you for his name-sake, and still more for his worth-sake (for I am assured that he is an excellent man, and has faithfully served one family more than twenty years), let me put your name in my list; and if your daughters will interest themselves for him, they will render me a great kindness in helping me to render him a great service at little cost. I have enlisted Mrs. Hughes in the cause, who, as I told her, is the person whose interest I should first endeavour to secure if I were to offer myself a candidate upon any vacancy whatever, even of the kingdom of Poland or of the Popedom itself.

The verses will be introduced by the letters in which he introduced himself to me, his own account of himself, and some remarks upon poets of that class, mechanic's institutes, and the march of intellect. That march I am very desirous of expediting, no man more so; but I do not like the tune to which it goes.

Southey to Mary Anne Hughes (Warter, IV, 80)

Keswick, Dec. 31. 1827

My Dear Mrs. Hughes,

Thank you once more for such good service to 'John Jones,' as no one except yourself would have rendered. The Bishop of Durham[436] wrote to me, in very obliging terms, repeating the invitation which you had communicated when he was first removed to Durham. If he be in town about the latter end of May, I shall feel bound to call at his door as soon as may be after my arrival. In the North there is little likelihood of my being able to visit him; for though the distance is but a summer day's journey, the zigzaging which it would be necessary to make in stagecoaches would treble the time. I could get from this place to London with more expedition. Heaven prosper the steam carriages! that I may set up one of my own, and move at pleasure in any direction.

Southey to Margaret Holford Hodson (*Life and Correspondence*, V, 327–30)

Keswick, Aug. 14. 1828

My dear Madam,

[. . .]

I have made an arrangement with Murray concerning John Jones's rhymes. He will publish them, and give Jones the whole of his subscription copies; they

APPENDIX I

amount to little more than 200 at present, but the list may be increased as much as we can. The verses will go to press as soon as Murray enables me to prepare the introduction by procuring for me the works of certain low and untaught rhymers of whom I wish to speak – Taylor the Water Poet, Stephen Duck, &c.

Southey to the Rev. Neville White[437] (Warter, IV, 164)

Keswick, January 10. 1830

My Dear Neville,

The next book which I shall have to send you will be the concluding volume of the 'Peninsular War,'[438] which will soon be – not ready – but half printed. I am closely employed upon it, and shall rejoice to reach the end of so great an undertaking, though far from weary of my work. Indeed I never feel weary of anything which I have in hand, and this is a great blessing. What I am most desirous of now is, to get a fortnight's interval for the introduction to my poor John Jones's verses, which have been too long delayed. He is a good creature, and never breathes a thought of impatience; nor would he feel one, if he knew my way of life and the demands upon my time, and the necessity of keeping the ways and means right, wherein the greater part of it is, and must be, employed. Yours most affectionately,

Southey to Eliza Bray (Warter, IV, 211–13)

Keswick, March 14. 1831

My Dear Madam,

[...]

Your Mary Colling is an extraordinary person. I meant to have said something, in the introduction to John Jones's verses, upon the good effects which might arise from encouraging any intellectual habits and pursuits, and more especially the love of poetry, in persons of humble life, when these things are not connected with ambition and the desire of advancing themselves in life, but pursued for their own sake. But in the desire of giving to the subscribers of that volume something which might prevent those who had little feeling, from grumbling at having subscribed for verses in which they saw nothing to their liking, I was led on so far that no room was left for this.

Murray, without consulting me, has advertised what is intended as a mere Introduction, and, indeed, appears as such, as if it were a deliberate work to which the poor man's verses are merely appended. On two accounts I am sorry for this; first (which is of little consequence), because at first it should seem to make me, who have only written an Introduction, responsible for a separate work, and liable to be censured for having done it incompletely, instead of being thanked for what was supererogatory, as well as gratuitous; and secondly (which vexes me), because poor

206

APPENDIX I

Jones may possibly feel hurt himself at being thus put behind my chair, which, on this occasion, certainly is not his proper place. Murray gives him his subscribers' copies, for which I gave my labour; and if there be any eventual profit upon the book, Murray promises him a share of it. Without looking to the contingency, I hope he will get about £100 by his copies: and this will be some help in declining life. If you find reason to think that something might be secured by printing a little volume of this poor girl's, I will very willingly subscribe, and endeavour to obtain a few names, though there are but few that I can look for. [. . .]

Southey to Eliza Bray (Warter, IV, 215–17)

Keswick, April 26. 1831

My Dear Mrs. Bray,

I ought to have made time for answering your last very interesting communication sooner. But I was called from home to take, as Poet Laureate, the declaration which has been substituted for the test, and that brought on a visit, and then came more business, and some of those unexpected interruptions from which I am never at any season secure.

Your Mary Colling is so remarkable a person herself, and in everything relating to her, that there can be no doubt of attracting sufficient notice to a volume of her verses. I will take care (but this must not be spoken of) that her story shall be told in the 'Quarterly Review' as soon as the book is published, and, meantime, will get as many names as I can for the subscription-list. As a matter of mere curiosity, I will also endeavour to find out whether anything of her grandmother's early history can be discovered in the part of the country from whence she came. There is a channel through which I think I can make the inquiry with some possibility of success.

[. . .]

Believe me, dear Mrs. Bray, Yours with sincere regard,

Robert Southey

P.S. I must not forget to request that you will thank Mary Colling for the lines which she has addressed to me.[439] On the whole it is better that her portrait should not be published till she is known.[440] Her advantage will be best consulted by giving the first notice of her in the 'Quarterly Review' just as the book is ready.

Southey to Eliza Bray (Warter, IV, 228–30)

Keswick, July 14. 1831

My Dear Mrs. Bray,

[. . .]

I am the last person from whom anything like captious or minute criticism is to be apprehended.[441] The only part of your letter which seems unfitting is, where you speak of my kindness to Mary Colling, because, in plain truth, I have not shown her any that deserves such an acknowledgment. Some real service, I hope, it may be in my power to do by reviewing the book as soon as it is ready, and I shall have the more pleasure in doing it, because it will give me an opportunity, which could not otherwise have been found, of showing a proper sense of respect and good will toward Mary Colling's benefactress.

One caution I am led to give by what you say of Mary's health. Nervous as she is, and easily made ill, it will be most desirable to avoid anything that might be likely to excite a nervous disposition; and there is great danger of doing this, if an expectation is held out in your letters, of her becoming a proficient in the art of poetry. That sweet American girl, Lucretia Davidson, was, beyond all doubt, killed by excitement of this kind. If she can be provided with books and a wholesome portion of leisure, there is no fear of her failing to make good use of both. But I earnestly hope that she will continue to exercise her gifts for the pure pleasure which she has hitherto taken in exercising them, and not with any view of obtaining celebrity. If that comes, be it welcome! but to seek it would be to make herself a prey to hopes, and fears, and anxieties, which, if they did not injure her constitution, would destroy her health of mind. You will not misunderstand me. To possess our souls in peace, is the greatest blessing we can attain in this world; and we lose that, if we render ourselves dependent for happiness upon the opinion of the public. I believe that nothing is so wholesome for the heart as to express its feelings in verse (the only way in which we dare express its best feelings), if this be done from its own free and pure impulse, but when the desire of applause becomes the prime motive, few things tend more surely to injure the moral character. That result, indeed, is not to be apprehended in her case; but I am afraid of the physical effects which over-excitement and too much intellectual exercitation may produce, especially if accompanied by any anxious desire of manifesting improvement.

I write this in consequence of what I have observed in others, not of anything experienced in myself, who am the least sensitive, as to praise or censure, of all writers. You will say that this is, because I have been so much used to both, and in some degree, no doubt, it is, but in a much greater to a very comfortable temper, and a thorough conviction that they who seek anxiously the applause of their own age, must be contented with it, for they will never have that of any succeeding one.

Your account of Mr. Hughes[442] is exceedingly lively and amusing. I shall very much like to see him. If your weather is like ours, I trust you are daily enjoying it, and profiting by it. [. . .]

Thank Mary for her verses.

Southey to Eliza Bray (Warter, IV, 266)

Keswick, March 14. 1832

My Dear Mrs. Bray,

I had inserted more specimens of Mary's poetry than are found in the 'Review,'[443] but in these things you know an editor uses his own discretion. I miss also a more

APPENDIX I

ludicrous specimen of doggrel verses than either of those which are there presented. Every one from whom I hear of it is delighted with the book, and with you, and with Mary Colling, and with Mary Colling's sweet face, which I can assure you has been greatly admired at Copenhagen.

[. . .]

My reason for not giving more direct praise to Mary Colling was, that direct praise would not have been likely to serve her book so well, and would have had more the appearance of coming from one whose immediate object was to serve her. It was better therefore to let the story recommend itself, and the extracts speak in their own praise, and to show (against a very prevalent opinion) that intellectual pursuits by persons in humble life ought to be encouraged for the general good. Upon this subject I have more to say in due time.

Southey to the Rev. William Lisle Bowles[444] (*Life and Correspondence* VI, 193–94)

Keswick, July 30. 1832

My dear Sir,

[. . .]

After having reviewed in the Quarterly Review Grahame's Georgics, Montgomery's Poems, and his World before the Flood, and Landor's Count Julian, I found it necessary to resolve that I would not review the work of any living poet.[445] Applications to me from strangers, and from others in all degrees of acquaintanceship, were so frequent, that it became expedient to be provided with a general reason for refusing, which could offend no one; there was no other means of avoiding offence. Many would otherwise have resented the refusal, and more would have been more deeply displeased if they had not been extolled according to their own estimate of their own merits. From this resolution I did not consider myself as departing when I drew up the account of Mary Colling; her story and her character interested me greatly, and would, I thought, interest most readers. I wished to render her some service, and have the satisfaction of knowing that this has been in some measure effected. It was a case wherein a little praise, through that channel, might be the means of producing some permanent benefit to one who has gentle blood in her veins, and whose sweet countenance, if you look at her portrait, will say more in her favour than any words of mine could do.

I have no wish to encourage the growth of humble authors, still less of adventurers in literature, God knows. But I earnestly wish, especially in an age when all persons can read, to encourage in all who have any love of reading that sort of disposition which would lead them to take pleasure in your poems, and in mine, and in any which are addressed, as ours always have been, to the better feelings of our nature. The tendency of our social system has long been to brutalise the lower classes, and this it is that renders the prospect before us so fearful. I wish to see their moral and intellectual condition as much as possible improved; it seems

APPENDIX I

to me that great improvement is possible, and that in bettering their condition the general good is promoted.

Southey to Katharine Southey[446] (*Life and Correspondence* **VI, 321–22**)

Stockleigh Pomeroy, Jan. 1. 1837

My dear Daughter,

[...]

[re Mary Colling:] Verily I never saw any person in, and about whom, every thing was more entirely what you could wish, and what it ought to be. She is the pattern of neatness and propriety, simplicity and good sense. Her old master, Mr. Hughes, is as proud of her as if she was his daughter. They live in a small house, the garden of which extends to the river Tavy, a beautiful stream; and her kitchen is such a kitchen for neatness and comfort, that you would say at once no person who could not be happy there deserved to be happy anywhere else. Strangers (and there are many whom Mrs. Bray's book draws to Tavistock and Dartmoor)[447] generally inquire for her, and find means to see her, and she has already a little library of books which have been presented to her by such persons.

Mr. Bray's[448] is the only house in which I have eaten upon pewter since I was a child; he has a complete service of it, with his crest engraved upon it, and bright as silver. The house (built for him by the Duck, as the Duke of Bedford[449] is called in Tavistock,) is a very good one, the garden large and pleasantly laid out; it includes some of the ruins, and a door from it opens upon a delightful walk on the Tavy. In spite of the weather we had two pleasant walks, one of about ten miles, the other about six; but of Dartmoor we could see nothing. Our time passed pleasantly, Mary paying us a visit every day; some more Fables in her own handwriting will be among the most interesting autographs that I have to dispose of.

APPENDIX II

Reviews of and Comments on the *Lives*

'Attempts in Verse, by John Jones, an old Servant; with some Account of the Writer, written by himself; and an Introductory Essay on the Lives and Works of Uneducated Poets. By Robert Southey, Esq., Poet Laureate. 8vo. London: 1831,' *The Edinburgh Review,* **54 (1831), 69–84.**

In editing the poems of Mr John Jones, which are, with modest propriety, entitled his 'Attempts in Verse,' Mr Southey has probably been actuated by the same amiable feelings which induced him, many years ago, to throw the shelter of his eminent name over works of far higher excellence, and to introduce to the world the previously neglected poems of Henry Kirke White.

In that instance, the public promptly ratified the opinion of the editor; and considered the production of the poems, and the accompanying memoir, to be creditable alike to the judgment and to the feelings of Mr Southey. It is to be feared that only a part of this praise can be awarded to this second act of his editorial patronage. We give him credit for having been solely impelled by the desire to do a good-natured action; and think, moreover, that he deserves praise for not having been withheld from such a purpose by the dread of ridicule and unfair censure. It could be no advantage to Mr Southey to appear as the Maecenas of so humble a poetaster as Mr John Jones; and there have probably been many men of his literary celebrity who would have feared to incur a compromise of their dignity by such a step. But after giving due praise to the motives of Mr Southey, we must take the liberty of demurring when we come to consider the advisableness of the publication before us, and some of the opinions which it is found to maintain. To the poems of John Jones we shall very briefly advert; for they owe our notice of them rather to their editor than any importance of their own. Their author is a servant in a Yorkshire family, who, hearing that Mr Southey is in the vicinity of his master's residence, writes to him, requesting that he may be allowed to send his poems for Mr Southey's perusal, to which that gentleman good-naturedly consents. The poems are sent, accompanied by a very creditable letter, in which the writer, after speaking with becoming modesty of his performance, asks if it would be too contemptible to 'solicit a subscription,' for, since, if it were not so considered, he would naturally be 'glad to improve his humble circumstances by such means.'

APPENDIX II

'This letter,' says Mr Southey, 'did not diminish the favourable opinion which I had formed of the writer from his first communication. Upon perusing the poems, I wished they had been either better or worse. Had I consulted my own convenience, or been fearful of exposing myself to misrepresentation and censure, I should have told my humble applicant that although his verses contained abundant proof of a talent for poetry, which, if it had been cultivated, might have produced good fruit, they would not be deemed worthy of publication in these times. But on the other hand, there were in them such indications of a kind and happy disposition, so much observation of natural objects, such a relish of the innocent pleasures offered by nature to the eye, and ear, and heart, which are not closed against them, and so pleasing an example of the moral benefit derived from those pleasures, when they are received by a thankful and thoughtful mind, that I persuaded myself there were many persons who would partake, in perusing them, the same kind of gratification which I had felt. There were many, I thought, who would be pleased at seeing how much intellectual enjoyment had been attained in humble life, and in very unfavourable circumstances; and that this exercise of the mind, instead of rendering the individual discontented with his station, had conduced greatly to his happiness, and if it had not made him a good man, had contributed to keep him so. This pleasure should in itself, methought, be sufficient to content those subscribers who might kindly patronise a little volume of his verses. Moreover, I considered that as the Age of Reason had commenced, and we were advancing with quick step in the March of Intellect, Mr Jones would in all likelihood be the last versifier of his class; something might properly be said of his predecessors, the poets in low life, who with more or less good fortune had obtained notice in their day; and here would be matter for an introductory essay, not uninteresting in itself, and contributing something towards our literary history. And if I could thus render some little service to a man of more than ordinary worth (for such upon the best testimony Mr Jones appeared to be), it would be something not to be repented of, even though I should fail in the hope (which failure, however, I did not apprehend) of affording some gratification to "gentle readers:" for readers there still are, who, having escaped the epidemic disease of criticism, are willing to be pleased, and grateful to those from whose writings they derive amusement or instruction.'

Prefixed to the poems of John Jones is a short memoir by himself, in the form of a letter to Mr Southey, in which he describes, simply and naturally, his progress in life, the situations in which he had been placed, and the difficulties which he had experienced in acquiring knowledge, and in composing his poetical effusions. He says 'I entered into the family which I am now serving, in January, 1804, and have continued in it, first with the father, and then with the son, only during an interval of eighteen months, up to the present hour; and during which period most of my trifles have been composed, and some of my former attempts brought (perhaps) a little nearer perfection; but I have seldom sat down to study any thing, for in many instances when I have done so, a ring at the bell, or a knock at the door, or something or other, would disturb me, and not wishing to be seen, I frequently used to either crumple my paper up in my pocket, or take the trouble to lock it up, and

APPENDIX II

before I could arrange it again, I was often, sir, again disturbed; from this, sir, I got into the habit of trusting entirely to my memory, and most of my little pieces have been completed and borne in mind for weeks before I have committed them to paper: from this I am led to believe that there are but few situations in life in which attempts of the kind may not be made under less discouraging circumstances.'

The circumstances were indeed discouraging, and it would be illiberal to visit with severity of criticism poems which have been so produced. Mr Southey says of them, that though containing 'abundant proofs of a talent for poetry, which, if it had been cultivated, might have produced good fruit, they would not be deemed worthy of publication in these times.' This is measured praise; and leads us to conclude that the Laureate has not discovered in Mr Jones any indications of genius of a high order. That a man of defective education, and living in a menial capacity, should write any thing that can be dignified with the name of poetry, is a strong presumption of the existence of poetical talent. But there are many degrees of this talent, from the mere aptitude for rhyming, to the loftiest rank of imaginative power; and Mr Jones assuredly has not exhibited any even uncultivated germs of that 'mens divinior,'[450] which alone can lead to the attainment of the highest poetical excellence. Education might have rendered him a pleasing poet; but we are not warranted in imagining that, under any circumstances, he would have been a great one. His poems bear the stamp of mediocrity. We see no signs of a vigorous fancy struggling through defects of expression and of taste, sparkling amidst the dross with which it is encumbered. His verses seem written for the most part with very respectable correctness and care. They have perhaps more polish than might have been expected; but they want originality and force. Among them are some which it would be easy to ridicule; but we abstain from the ungenerous task. Defects of taste should be lightly visited in one to whom it is highly creditable to have exhibited so much. As a specimen, the following may suffice: it is the commencement of a poem entitled 'Reflections on Visiting a Spring at different Seasons of the Year.'

'Twas early in summer, and mild was the ray
Which beam'd from the sun on the waning of day;
And the air was serene, and the leaves on the trees
Were hardly emotion'd, so soft was the breeze;
The birds were in song in the wood on the hill,
And softly a murmur arose from the rill
Which ran through the mead, where its channel was seen,
By herbage more rude, and more tufted and green;
The teams, clinking home, had the fallow resign'd,
And whistling the ploughmen their cares to the wind,
When, pensive and slow, up the hamlet I bent,
And meeting the stream on its margin I went;
I stray'd to the spot whence it sprang from the earth,
Most pure in its nature and silent its birth;

APPENDIX II

It ran from a mound with green moss o'erspread,
Its birth-place was shaded by shrubs at its head;
'Twas onward impell'd by its kindred more strong,
And driven from home it went murmuring along.
In indolent ease on the bank I reclined,
And gazed on the stream, till awoke in my mind
A thought of the joys in its windings 'twould yield,
To the birds of the air and the beasts of the field,
To the web-footed tribe on its surface that ride,
And the bright-speckled trout in its bosom that glide,
To the poor thirsty beggar who drinks in his palms,
And softens the crusts he obtains for his alms;
To the thrifty old dame, who, with low-bowing head,
Shall search it for cresses, to barter for bread;
To the youth, who, in groups, on its borders shall play,
And launch their frail barks to be wreck'd in a day;
To the low in their need, and the high in their pride,
Who tenant the domes which are rear'd by its side,
And I mentally said, as in beauty it ran,
'Flow on, thou bright stream, thou'rt a blessing to man.'

But it is not so much to the poems of John Jones, as to the remarks of Mr Southey, and his Introductory Essay on the Lives and Works of our Uneducated Poets, that it is our intention to advert.

This introductory essay is ushered in with the singular observation, that 'As the age of Reason had commenced, and we were advancing with quick step in the March of Intellect, Mr Jones would in all likelihood be the last versifier of his class; and something might properly be said of his predecessors, the poets in low life, who, with more or less good fortune, had obtained notice in their day.' By 'the March of Intellect' in the above sentence, is meant, we presume, not merely the progress of scientific improvement, but the more general diffusion of knowledge among the poorer classes. To find this diffusion of knowledge spoken of in distasteful terms by Mr Southey, can surprise no one who is acquainted with the writings of that gentleman. Yet even to these it must seem extraordinary to discover such reproachful expressions in a work, the tendency of which is to encourage, among the working classes, a pursuit which demands a very high degree of mental cultivation. The prediction above quoted, that such a diffusion of knowledge is likely to prevent the future appearance of versifiers in humble life, is one which we should hardly have thought necessary to notice seriously, if it had come from a pen of less influence than Mr Southey's. His proposition, translated into plain unfigurative language, is, that the more the poor are educated, the less are they likely to write poetry. In the first place, we disbelieve the predicted result; and secondly, we say, that if true, it is not a subject for regret, as it is evidently considered by Mr Southey. It seems almost a waste of words to confute so untenable

APPENDIX II

a theory as that education is unfavourable to the developement of poetical talent. The rare occurrence of uneducated poets, and the wonder excited by their appearance, – the indispensableness of something more than the mere rudiments of education to afford to the incipient poet a competent store of the materials with which he works, the fact, that our most distinguished poets have almost uniformly been men of studious habits, and of various and extensive reading – of which we have an example in the Laureate himself – these are circumstances on which it is needless to enlarge – which, when heard, must be acknowledged, and when acknowledged, must convince; and we gladly close this part of an argument, in which the humblest disputant could gain no honour by confuting even the editor of the work before us. Indeed, it can scarcely be imagined that Mr Southey could seriously maintain such an opinion; and that he must mean rather, that the poor who receive the advantages of education will, at the same time, learn to apply their acquirements to more useful purposes than writing verses. But there is this difficulty in such a supposition, that a reproach would thereby be cast upon the practice of versifying, which Mr Southey is very far from intending; and it is evident, from the tone of his book, that he does not contemplate with the pleasure which it ought to afford to a benevolent mind like his, the prospect of the poorer classes being inclined to apply the fruits of their extended education to works of practical utility. We must therefore conclude, that he does not believe that the condition of the poor will be improved by such an education as will induce them to apply their acquired knowledge to purposes which are commonly called useful; but that it is better either to keep them ignorant, or to give them just so much information as will encourage a developement of the imaginative or poetical part of their nature, without awakening them, more than can be helped, to any exercise of their reasoning powers. If this is not what is intended, then the praise bestowed upon uneducated poets, the encouraging complacency with which their efforts are regarded, and the sarcastic allusions to the Age of Reason and the March of Intellect, which is to arrest the progress of such commendable efforts, are utterly without a meaning.

But a writer who feels so strongly as Mr Southey, can never, even when he is least logical, be accused of writing without a meaning. Mr Southey, both in this, and in other writings in which his ideas are more distinctly expressed, teaches us that poetry softens and humanizes the heart of man, while it is the tendency of science to harden and corrupt it. It would be useless to plead that Mr Southey may never have expressed this sentiment in these precise words, while he has written much from which no other inference can be drawn.

According to this theory, the poor man who has a turn for versifying is likely to be more moral than one who discovers a bent for calculation or mechanics; a cultivation of the former talent will tend to constitute a pious man and a good subject, the latter, if encouraged, may too probably lead to republicanism and irreligion. A labourer may write lines on a linnet, and be praised for this amiable exercise of his humble talent; but if he reads any of the cheap works on science with which the press now teems, if he presumes to learn the scientific name of his

215

favourite bird, – to consider its relation to other birds, – to know that it belongs to the genus Fringilla, and to ascertain the marks by which he might distinguish the name of any wandering stranger of the same tribe that happened to fall within his notice, – if he does this, then he becomes a naturalist, a scientific enquirer – and, as such, must fall under the ban of Mr Southey. Let him apostrophize a flower in rhyme, but let him not learn its botanical name, or more of its properties than can be extracted from the Galenical lore of the oldest woman in the parish: He finds a fossil bone – let him pen a sonnet about it if he pleases; but let him beware of consulting a geologist, lest he become a hardy sceptic; – doubt if there ever was a deluge, and question the Mosaic account of the creation. Utterly do we reprobate and disavow the doctrine, that it is otherwise than beneficial for minds of every degree to be rendered intimate with the mysteries of nature, that the study of nature can be injurious to the morality and religious faith of any man whose morality and faith would have been safe without it, that the faith of the rustic who believes that the sun moves round the earth, and that the stars are small lamps, is more devout and pure than that of the same man would be when informed of the real sublimity of the scene around him. It is a doctrine of which any illustration is equivalent to a reductio ad absurdum. It is very natural that the Poet Laureate should think well of poetry. Some persons may smile at such an illustration of a propensity which they may have thought peculiar to humbler callings – namely, that of attributing to a production or pursuit many more excellent qualities and advantages than can be discovered in it by the rest of the world; and they may have expected that a very cultivated mind would have soared above a prejudice of this description. Mr Southey recommends poetry as eminently favourable to morality, and considers that amiable man will be both the better and the 'happier for writing verses.' Mr Southey is a celebrated poet, and is, we believe, at the same time a very pious and amiable man. It is therefore not unnatural that a talent for poetry should be associated in his mind with piety and morality; but if he thinks that they are necessarily connected, and that poetry is naturally conducive to those other more important qualities, he must attend rather to his own feelings than to the examples which experience would furnish. It would be an invidious, but easy task, to form a long list of men richly endowed with the gift of poetry, in whom pure morality and religious faith had been too notoriously deficient. It is unnecessary to mention names, for many – and enough – must occur to every reader; but we must remind Mr Southey that the brightest name among the 'uneducated poets' of this empire is that of one whose imagination and passions were unfortunately often too strong for the control of his judgment, and to whom the inborn gift of poetry, which he so exuberantly possessed, far from leading him into the paths of morality and peace, seem rather to have been false lights that lured him from them.[451] It is the province of poetry to appeal to the passions rather than to the judgment; and the passions are the most erring part of human nature. Mr Southey does not seem to reckon among possible contingencies the immoral direction of poetical talent. It is true, the verse-making rustic may celebrate the simple virtues which poets associate with rural life, and draw moral lessons from the

APPENDIX II

contemplation of nature, but he may equally dedicate his muse to the unhallowed task of lending a baneful interest to violence and crime. A reverence for antiquity, for social distinctions, and for the established order of things, are not necessary concomitants of an aptitude for verse. Liberty, the watchword under which rebellion always marches, has a spirit-stirring sound, especially to young and ardent minds, in which imagination prevails over judgment; and the lyre of the poet will echo as readily to its call as to images of pastoral peace. Mr Southey must remember that even he once celebrated Wat Tyler.[452] Anarchy has its laureate as well as monarchy, and the strains of the former are commonly most popular. A reference to his notice of the uneducated poets whom he has selected for celebration, will show that their versifying powers were not always exercised in a commendable manner. Taylor's contests in ribaldry with Fennor,[453] another rhymer of humble life, were not creditable to either; and Bryant[454] seems to have hung his satirical talent *in terrorem* over his associates, and to have allowed himself to be employed by one of them to lampoon the daughter of a respectable tradesman. We should be glad if it could have been proved that poetry is peculiarly conducive to morality; but we fear it cannot be shown that either the possession of the poetical faculty, or the perusal of works of that description, is calculated to ensure this desirable effect. To recommend poetry to the poorer classes, because there are in existence sundry moral poems which they would probably find among the least attractive, has little more sense in it, than to say that religious admonition is the peculiar attribute of prose, because sermons are written in that form. It matters not even though it could be shown that the *essentials* of poetry are akin to all that is most moral; for when we talk of poetry to the uneducated classes, they will think not of the essence, but only of the form. If the pursuit of poetry cannot be shown to be necessarily productive of moral benefit to persons in humble life, still less, we fear, can it be proved that it is calculated to ameliorate their worldly condition. We know no instance of any poor uneducated person whose prosperity and happiness has been essentially promoted by the developement of this talent. Six persons of this class are commemorated in the volume before us. Taylor the Water-Poet, Stephen Duck, James Woodhouse, John Bennet, Ann Yearsley, and John Frederick Bryant – of whom two died mad; and all appear to have undergone severe trials, and to have been very little raised, by the possession of this talent, above the lowly sphere in which they were born. It is also observable, that all of them seem to have owed even the precarious prosperity which they occasionally enjoyed to fortunate accidents, and the charitable notice of their superiors in wealth. Bryant owed his advancement to a song of his own making, which he sang in an inn-kitchen – Ann Yearsley to the casual notice of Mrs Hannah More, with whom she afterwards quarreled – Woodhouse to the patronage of Shenstone – Bennet to that of Warton – Duck was patronised by various persons, and at last by Queen Caroline, who settled a pension upon him – Taylor was a supple, ready-witted humorist, well skilled in the art of living at other men's cost. Such was his proficiency in this art, that he undertook to travel on foot from London to Edinburgh, not carrying any money to or fro; neither begging, borrowing, or asking 'meat, drink, or lodging.'

217

APPENDIX II

This journey, he says, was undertaken 'to make trial of his friends;' and we are informed by Mr Southey that it was not an arduous one, 'for he was at that time a well-known person; and he carried in his tongue a gift which, wherever he might be entertained, would be accepted as current payment for his entertainment.' To this important and praiseworthy excursion, of which Taylor published an account in quaint prose, and quainter doggrel, entitled, 'The Pennyless Pilgrimage, or the Moneyless Perambulations of John Taylor, alias the King's Majesty's Water-Poet,' Mr Southey devotes twenty-three pages of a small volume.

Our readers will naturally desire to see some specimens of a work which has attracted so much of the Laureate's attention. Of the following verses, we will merely say, that their excellence is quite of a piece with the importance of the information they convey. They describe Taylor's reception at Manchester.

> Their loves they on the tenter-hooks did rack,
> Roast, boil'd, baked, too-too-much, white, claret, sack;
> Nothing they thought too heavy, or too hot,
> Cann followed cann, and pot succeeded pot.
> Thus what they could do, all they thought too little,
> Striving in love the traveller to whittle.
> We went into the house of one John Pinners,
> (A man that lives amongst a crew of sinners,)
> And there eight several sorts of ale we had,
> All able to make one stark drunk, or mad.
> But I with courage bravely flinched not,
> And gave the town leave to discharge the shot.
> We had at one time set upon the table,
> Good ale of Hyssop ('twas no Esop-fable);
> Then had we ale of Sage, and ale of Malt,
> And ale of Wormwood that could make one halt;
> With ale of Rosemary, and of Bettony,
> And two ales more, or else I needs must lie.
> But to conclude this drinking aley tale,
> We had a sort of ale called Scurvy ale.
> Thus all these men at their own charge and cost
> Did strive whose love should be expressed most;
> And farther to declare their boundless loves,
> They saw I wanted, and they gave me, gloves.

'Taylor makes another excursion "from London to Christ Church, in Hampshire, and so up the Avon to Salisbury," and this was "for toyle, travail, and danger," the worst and most difficult passage he had yet made. These desperate adventures did not answer the purpose for which they were undertaken, and he complains of this in what he calls (Tayloricé) the Scourge of Baseness, a Kicksey Winsey, or a Lerry-Come-Twang.'

APPENDIX II

I made my journey for no other ends
But to get money and to try my friends.
They took a book worth twelve pence, and were bound
To give a crown, an angel, or a pound,
A noble, piece, or half-piece, – what they list:
They past their words, or freely set their fist.
Thus got I sixteen hundred hands and fifty,
Which sum I did suppose was somewhat thrifty;
And now my youths with shifts and tricks and cavils,
Above seven hundred, play the sharking javils.

'The manner,' says Mr Southey, 'in which he [Taylor] published his books, which were separately of little bulk, was to print them at his own cost, make presents of them, and then hope for "sweet remuneration" from the persons whom he had "thus delighted to honour."' The following passage is quoted from a dedication to Charles I., in which Taylor says, 'My gracious sovereign, your majesty's poor undeserved servant, having formerly oftentimes presented to your highness many such pamphlets, the best fruits of my lean and steril invention, always your princely affability and bounty did express and manifest your royal and generous disposition; and your gracious father, of ever-blessed and famous memory, did not only like and encourage, but also more than reward the barren gleanings of my poetical inventions.'

There is nothing extraordinary in this, when we consider that even much later, men of acknowledged talent were not ashamed to write fulsome dedications; but it is a circumstance degrading to literature, and that part of its history which we would most gladly forget – and it is pitiable in this instance, to see a man of no slight cleverness begging in such abject terms. The fact is, that all the uneducated poets whom Mr Southey has noticed were, in a more or less degree, literary mendicants. They obtained from private charity that assistance which the public would not grant. Their productions were not of sufficient value to obtain remuneration on the score of intrinsic merit, and their rewards were wrung either from the pity of their benefactors, or from their wondering curiosity at the occurrence of so rare a monster as an uneducated poet. None of them really enjoyed the blessings of independence – the proud and happy feeling that their own exertions were sufficient for their support. Mr Southey seems to contemplate this state of dependence with peculiar complacency. We are not very sure that he does not consider the spirit of the present age too independent, and that it might be improved by a gentle encouragement of that spirit of humble servility, which once prompted poor authors to ply rich patrons with begging dedications, and to look up with trembling hope for the casual bounty of those who possessed in abundance the good things of this life. The best and happiest times, it would seem, were those in which the poor begged for sustenance at the doors of a convent. Those which we call erroneously 'the dark ages,' were, it seems, the best times for the advancement of humble talent. Then a clever boy like Stephen Duck 'would have been noticed by the monks of

APPENDIX II

the nearest monastery, would then have made his way to Oxford, or perhaps to Paris, as a begging scholar – have risen to be a bishop or mitred abbot – have done honour to his station, and have left behind him good works and a good name.' Those were golden days! But then came a period which we benighted Protestants still call that of the Reformation, and Duck, who lived long after it, fell on harder times – but still not utterly cruel – for there were yet patrons in the land, and Duck found a royal one; and 'the patronage which he obtained,' says Mr Southey, 'is far more honourable to the spirit of his age, than the temper which may censure or ridicule it can be to ours.' Whatever it may please Mr Southey to consider the temper of our age, we, albeit reckoned among the infected, are not disposed to censure or ridicule the benevolent feelings which may prompt any one to become the patron of humble merit; but we do censure that maudlin spirit of short-sighted humanity, that fritters its beneficence in temporary and misplaced relief, and would thoughtlessly aggravate misfortune for the sake of indulging sensibility in its subsequent removal. It is the best charity to prevent the necessity of charitable assistance. Doubtless there is in the charitable alleviation of distress much that is gratifying to the heart of the benefactor, and much the contemplation of which is delightful to an amiable mind. But shall we therefore encourage mendicancy, that the world may teem with moving pictures of picturesque poverty and theatrical generosity to interest the sensibilities of the man of feeling? True rational humanity would not willingly see any one dependent upon the capricious bounty of another. Unable to reverse that general law, which prescribes labour as the lot of man, it endeavours to direct the labour of the poor into a channel where they may claim a recompense from the exigencies of others, and not from their compassion. It would endow them with a right to receive assistance, instead of teaching them to supplicate for alms. Mr Southey would doubtless be unwilling to encourage idleness and mendicancy; but there is in reality little difference between encouraging men not to labour at all, but to depend for their support on the charity of others, and encouraging them to pursue a species of labour for which there is no real demand, and from which the only returns which they obtain are in reality alms, considerately cloaked under the fictitious name of a reward. We do not deny, that the public, though in general the best patron, sometimes awards a too tardy and insufficient recompense to the literary benefactors of mankind; and in such instances we deem it right that the powerful and discerning few should be enabled to direct the stream of national bounty to the encouragement and reward of labours which the acquirements and comprehension of the generality of mankind do not enable them to appreciate. But widely different from this truly praiseworthy patronage, is the disposition to encourage works which are neither beautiful nor useful, and whose only claim (if claim it can be called) is the temporary interest they may offer to the curious, and the compassionate consideration that they are wonderfully good, for writings that were produced under such disadvantages.

Experience does not authorize us to regard it as probable, that the world will be favoured with any poetry of very exalted merit from persons in humble life and of defective education. There have appeared among uneducated persons, many

APPENDIX II

instances of extraordinary capacity for various sciences and pursuits. The science of numbers, of mechanics, of language, of music, painting, sculpture, architecture, have all had followers in humble life, who have discovered a strong native genius for each of these separate branches of art and learning, and have risen to eminence in their peculiar line. But poetry is not equally rich in examples of successful votaries from the ranks of the poor. Not one of the six writers recorded by Mr Southey, can be regarded as a successful example; for nothing but the scarcity of such instances could have preserved them, like other valueless rarities, from the oblivion into which, notwithstanding even the embalming power of Mr Southey's pen, they are fated at no very distant period to fall. It would appear, either that habits of manual labour are unfavourable to poetry, or that a talent for it is less inborn than acquired, or that it is much affected by external circumstances, or that a considerable degree of education is essential to its full developement. To which of these causes we attribute the dearth of distinguished poets from the humbler walks of life, it is not at present necessary to enquire. The fact of such a paucity is sufficient for our purpose; and it is an additional argument against encouraging the poor and defectively educated to lend their minds to a pursuit in which the presumption of success is so considerably against them. Unless they happen to possess such powerful native talent, as it is needless to encourage and impossible to suppress, they are not likely to produce such writings as will obtain them advancement and success – real, unforced, unpatronised success; – the success which arises from the delight and admiration of thousands, and not from the casual benevolence of individual patronage.

It might have been supposed, that of all things in the world which are not immoral, one of the least deserving encouragement was indifferent poetry. Mr Southey nevertheless protests indignantly against this opinion. 'When,' says he, 'it is laid down as a maxim of philosophical criticism, that poetry ought never to be encouraged unless it is excellent in its kind – that it is an art in which inferior execution is not to be tolerated – a luxury, and must therefore be rejected unless it is of the very best; such reasoning may be addressed with success to cockered and sickly intellects, but it will never impose upon a healthy understanding, a generous spirit, or a good heart.' Mr Southey, with that poetical tendency to metaphor which sometimes possesses him when he appears to reason, seems to have written the above passage under the influence of rather a forced analogy between the digestive powers of the human frame, and the operations of the mind. If in the above remarks we substitute 'food' for 'poetry,' 'appetite' for 'intellect,' and 'the 'stomach' for 'the understanding,' much of what Mr Southey has predicated will undoubtedly be true; since it is certain that a perfectly healthy person can eat with impunity many kinds of food that cannot be taken by one who is sickly. It is a sign of bodily health to be able to digest coarse food which cannot be eaten by the invalid; and in like manner, according to Mr Southey, it is the sign of a healthy understanding' to be able to tolerate bad verses, which would be rejected by a 'sickly 'intellect.' Mr Southey may very probably have accustomed himself to talk of poetry as 'food for the mind,' till he has learned to confound the immaterial

221

APPENDIX II

with the substantial; but we must remind him of one great failure in the parallel on which he appears to lean. It will not, we suppose, be denied, that the mind, and especially that faculty which enables us to judge of the excellence of poetry, requires cultivation, without which it cannot exercise its functions effectively; but we have never yet heard of any such cultivation of the digestive powers. If man were born as decidedly a criticising and poetry-reading, as he is an eating and drinking animal, and were likely to possess these faculties in most perfection in an unsophisticated state of nature, we should then allow that there would be much force in the observations of Mr Southey. But the reverse of this is notoriously the case. Our power of estimating poetry is in a great degree acquired. The boy with an innate taste for poetry, who first finds a copy of bellman's verses,[455] is pleased with the jingle, and thinks the wretched doggrel excellent. He soon finds better verses, and becomes ashamed of the objects of his earliest admiration. In course of time a volume of Pope or Milton falls in his way, and he becomes sensible of what is really excellent in poetry, and learns to distinguish it from that which, although not positively bad, is commonplace and of subordinate merit. Is this boy's mind, we ask, in a less healthy state at this advanced period of his critical discernment, than when he thought the bellman's verses excellent? or has his intellect 'been rendered sickly' by the dainty fare with which his mental tastes have latterly been pampered?

But the encouragement of inferior poetry is, according to Mr Southey, a sign not only of a 'healthy understanding' but of 'a 'generous spirit,' and 'a good heart.' If Mr Southey means that indulgence towards the failings of others, and a disposition to look leniently upon their imperfect productions, are the results of generosity and goodness of heart, we thoroughly agree with him; but it is not merely indulgence for which he contends, it is encouragement. Now, though it is impossible to prove a negative, and it is very possible that the encourager of bad verses may be at the same time very generous and good hearted, yet there is no necessary connexion between that practice and those moral qualities; any more than it is necessarily a sign of generosity and a good heart to deal only with inferior tradesmen, and buy nothing but the worst commodities. A person who should be thus amiably content to buy bad things when he might have better, would, we fear, be considered a fool for his pains, even by those whom he permitted to supply him; and we cannot think that the encourager of bad poetry would remain long exempted from a similar censure. It is useless, we might almost say mischievous, to maintain that any thing ought to be 'encouraged' that is not excellent in its kind. Let those who have not arrived at excellence be encouraged to proceed, and to exert themselves, in order that they may attain it. This is good and praiseworthy encouragement; but let it be remembered, that this good purpose cannot be effected but by mingling with the exhortation to future exertions, an unqualified censure of present imperfections. This, the only sound and rational encouragement, is directly opposed to that lenient tolerance of 'inferior execution,' which appears to receive the commendation of Mr Southey. Men are encouraged to do really well, not by making them satisfied with their present mediocrity, but by exhibiting it to them in the true light, and stimulating them to higher excellence. Whatever may be speciously said about the virtues of charity and contentment, we may be assured that he is no benefactor of the human race who would teach us to be satisfied with inferior excellence in any thing, while higher excellence is attainable.

Among the statements which we are told can be addressed with success only 'to *cockered* and sickly intellects,' is this, that poetry is a luxury, and must therefore be rejected unless it is 'of the very best.' It is needless to discuss this question at much length. It may be natural for the lover of poetry to contend that it is something much better and more important than a luxury, but it is nevertheless treated as such by the world at large, and we fear that nothing that can be said will induce the public to regard poetry in any other light. All the most important business of life is transacted in prose – all the most important lessons of religion and morality are inculcated in prose – we reason in prose – we argue in prose – we harangue in prose. There were times when laws were chanted, and Orpheus and Amphion were, it is believed, poetical legislators, as were almost all legislators among barbarous people, whose reason must be addressed through the medium of their imagination. But these times are past recall; and we fear, whatever it may be contended poetry ought to be, Mr Southey must be contented with the place which it actually occupies. That place is both honourable and popular; and it will not conduce to its success to claim for it more than is its due.

In conclusion, we must say, that much as we have differed from Mr Southey, we have been glad to see that he is inclined to look with favour upon the mental labours of the poorer classes. We trust that his agreeable pen will be hereafter exercised in their behalf; but with this material difference, that instead of luring them into the flowery region of poetry, he will rather teach them to cultivate pursuits which are more in harmony with their daily habits, and to prefer the useful to the ornamental.

'Attempts in Verse. By John Jones, an Old Servant. With some Account of the Writer, written by Himself; and an Introductory Essay on the Lives and Works of our Uneducated Poets. By Robert Southey, Esq. London. 1830,' *The Quarterly Review*, 44 (1831), 52–82

In the autumn of 1827, Mr Southey was spending a few weeks with his family at Harrowgate, when a letter reached him from John Jones, butler to a country gentleman in that district of Yorkshire, who, hearing that the poet laureate was so near him, had plucked up courage to submit to his notice some of his own 'attempts in verse.' He was touched by the modest address of this humble aspirant; and the inclosed specimen of his rhymes, however rude and imperfect, exhibited such simplicity of thought and kindliness of disposition, such minute and intelligent observation of Nature, such lively sensibility – and, withal, such occasional felicities of diction, that he was induced to make further inquiries into the history of the man. It turned out that Jones had maintained through a long life the character of a most faithful and exemplary domestic, having been no fewer than twenty-four

APPENDIX II

years with the family, who, still retaining him in their service, had long since learned to regard and value him as a friend. The poet laureate encouraged him, therefore, to transmit more of his verses, and the result is the volume before us – not more than a third of which, however, is occupied with the 'Attempts' of the good old butler of Kirby Hall, the rest being given to a chapter of our literary history from his editor's own pen, which, we venture to say, will be not less generally attractive than the 'Life of John Bunyan,' reviewed in our last Number.

'There were many,' says Mr Southey, 'I thought, who would be pleased at seeing how much intellectual enjoyment had been attained in humble life, and in very unfavourable circumstances; and that this exercise of the mind, instead of rendering the individual discontented with his station, had conduced greatly to his happiness, and if it had not made him a good man, had contributed to keep him so. This pleasure should in itself, methought, be sufficient to content those subscribers who might kindly patronize a little volume of his verses.'

John Jones's own account of the circumstances under which his 'Attempts' have been produced, cannot fail to impress every mind with the moral lesson thus briefly pointed to by the editor. After a simple chronicle of his earlier life, he thus concludes:

I entered into the family which I am now serving in January, 1804, and have continued in it, first with the father, and then with the son, only during an interval of eighteen months, up to the present hour; and during which period most of my trifles have been composed, and some of my former attempts brought (perhaps) a little nearer perfection: but I have seldom sat down to study anything; for in many instances when I have done so, a ring at the bell, or a knock at the door, or something or other, would disturb me; and not wishing to be seen, I frequently used to either crumple my paper up in my pocket, or take the trouble to lock it up, and before I could arrange it again, I was often, Sir, again disturbed; from this, Sir, I got into the habit of trusting entirely to my memory, and most of my little pieces have been completed and borne in mind for weeks before I have committed them to paper. From this I am led to believe that there are but few situations in life in which attempts of the kind may not be made under less discouraging circumstances. Having a wife and three children to support, Sir, I have had some little difficulties to contend with; but, thank God, I have encountered them pretty well. I have received many little helps from the family, for which I hope, Sir, I may be allowed to say that I have shown my gratitude, by a faithful discharge of my duty; but, within the last year, my children have all gone to service. Having been rather busy this last week, Sir, I have taken up but little time in the preparation of this, and I am fearful you will think it comes before you in a discreditable shape; but I hope you will be able to collect from it all that may be required for your benevolent purpose: but should you wish to be empowered to speak with greater confidence of my character, by having the testimony of others in support of my own, I believe, Sir, I should not find much difficulty in obtaining it; for it affords me some little gratification, Sir, to think that in the few families I have served, I have lived respected, for in none do I remember of ever being accused of

APPENDIX II

an immoral action, nor with all my propensity to rhyme have I been charged with a neglect of duty. I therefore hope, Sir, that if some of the fruits of my humble muse be destined to see the light, and should not be thought worthy of commendation, no person of a beneficent disposition will regret any little encouragement given to an old servant under such circumstances.' pp. 179, 180.

The tranquil, affectionate, and contented spirit that shines out in the 'Attempts' is in keeping with the tone of this letter; and if Burns was right when he told Dugald Stewart that no man could understand the pleasure he felt in seeing the smoke curling up from a cottage chimney, who had not been born and bred, like himself, in such abodes, and therefore knew how much worth and happiness they contain;[456] and if the works of that great poet have, in spite of many licentious passages, been found, on the whole, productive of a wholesome effect in society, through their aim and power to awaken sympathy and respect between classes whom fortune has placed asunder, surely this old man's verses ought to meet with no cold reception among those who appreciate the value of kindly relations between masters and dependants. In them they will trace the natural influence of that old system of manners which was once general throughout England; under which the young domestic was looked after, by his master and mistress, with a sort of parental solicitude – admonished kindly for petty faults, commended for good conduct, advised, and encouraged and which held out to him who should spend a series of years honestly and dutifully in one household, the sure hope of being considered and treated in old age as a humble friend. Persons who breathe habitually the air of a crowded city, where the habits of life are such that the man often knows little more of his master than that master does of his next-door neighbour, will gather instruction as well as pleasure from the glimpses which John Jones's history and lucubrations afford of the interior machinery of life in a yet unsophisticated region of the country. His little complimentary stanzas on the birth-days, and such other festivals of the family – his inscriptions to their neighbour Mrs Laurence of Studley Park, and the like, are equally honourable to himself and his benevolent superiors; and the simple purity of his verses of love or gallantry, inspired by village beauties of his own station, may kindle a blush on the cheeks of most of those whose effusions are now warbled over fashionable piano-fortes.

The stanzas which first claimed and won the favourable consideration of the Poet Laureate were these 'To a Robin Red-Breast:'

[for the excerpted poem see p. 102]

We now return to Mr Southey's preface – which, after the sentences already quoted from it, thus proceeds:

Moreover, I considered that as the age of reason had commenced, and we were advancing with quick step in the March of Intellect, Mr Jones would in all likelihood be the last versifier of his class – something might properly be said of his predecessors, the poets in low life, who with more or less good fortune had obtained notice in their day; here would be matter for an introductory essay, not

225

APPENDIX II

uninteresting in itself, and contributing something towards our literary history; and if I could thus render some little service to a man of more than ordinary worth, (for such, upon the best testimony, Mr Jones appeared to be,) it would be something not to be repented of. – p. 12.

Every one will rejoice that Mr Southey has been led to write the essay thus introduced; but we, at least, cannot agree with him in thinking it likely that John Jones will be the last versifier of his class. It will take, we suspect, a long while before the march of intellect can be productive of such sweeping effects – and we are quite sure, neither Mr Southey nor we shall live to see the day. In spite of the diligence with which the self-elected schoolmasters are now scattering abroad their dry husks, we do not consider it as at all probable that, among those in the humbler classes of society who acquire the power of reading, the great majority will ever be satisfied with such fare. Their shamefully crude and wofully dull compendiums of the *omne scibile*,[457] however gravely and even pompously lauded by authorities which ought to have been far above such condescensions, will soon run out their little hour and sleep with the trunkmaker. The solid wholesome literature of England will resume its rights; and, as the circle of cultivation widens, extend its influence, at once expanding the intellectual, and concentrating and purifying the moral energies of unborn readers. The great body of mankind must at all times continue, in the words of John Jones,

To earn, before they eat, their bread.

Say the diffusers of Useful Knowledge[458] what they choose, the literature most serviceable, and most acceptable too, to hardworking men, will ever be that which tends to elevate and humanize the heart, through its appeals to the imagination; and the great poets who have ennobled our language will hardly possess more readers than they have hitherto done, without having their imitators increased in at least an equal proportion. The truth is, that several humble poets have very recently published volumes, which would have attracted more notice than Mr Jones's – but that '*carent vate sacro*'[459] – they have not been so fortunate as to come before the world with prefaces from pens such as Mr Southey's. We allude in particular to the poor cobbler of Chichester, Charles Crocker, and John Wright,[460] who describes himself as 'illiterate in the largest sense, never having had but six months' schooling in very early life,' and who has contrived, amidst the severest toils of a cotton manufactory at Glasgow, to embody images of rural scenery and trains of moral reflection, in stanzas, some of which would have done no discredit to more distinguished names.

In the 'Introductory Essay on the lives and works of our uneducated Poets,' which will float John Jones to posterity, the Editor has by no means exhausted his subject, but he has selected an interesting and multifarious bead-roll of specimens; for example, a Thames waterman – a farm-servant from Wiltshire – a village cobbler from the neighbourhood of Birmingham – a journeyman shoemaker of Woodstock – a milk-woman, and a maker of tobacco-pipes, both from his own native city of Bristol. The names of Duck, Woodhouse, Bennet, and even the more recent ones of Ann Yearsley and John Frederic Bryant, have probably never met the eye of many who will read Mr Southey's account of them; but the name, at least, of John Taylor, must be sufficiently familiar to them all. 'The water poet' enjoyed in his day greater celebrity than the whole of the rest put together; his talents were of a higher order than any of theirs – his life more picturesque, his experience and information much wider; his writings out of sight more numerous, various, and vigorous; and he occupies a proportionate space in the Essay of the Poet Laureate, who thus introduces him:

The distinction between the language of high and low life could not be broadly marked, till our language was fully formed, in the Elizabethan age: then the mother tongue of the lower classes ceased to be the language of composition; that of the peasantry was antiquated, that of the inferior citizens had become vulgar. It was not necessary that a poet should be learned in Greek and Latin, but it was that he should speak the language of polished society.

Another change also, in like manner widening the intellectual distinctions of society, had by that time taken place. In barbarous ages the lord had as little advantage over his vassal in refinement of mind as of diction. War was his only business; and war, even in the brightest days of chivalry, tended as surely to brutalize the feelings of the chiefs, and render their hearts callous, as the occupations of husbandry did to case-harden and coarsen the hind and the herdsman; but when arts and luxuries (of that allowable kind for which a less equivocal term is to be desired) had found their way from cloisters into courts and castles, an improvement, as well of intellect as of manners, rapidly ensued. Then, also, the relations of states became more complicated, and courts in consequence more politic: the minds of the great grew at the same time more excursive and more reflecting; and in the relaxation which they sought in poetry, something more was required than the minstrels afforded in their lays, whether of ribaldry or romance. Learning being scarce, they who possessed a little were proud of exhibiting in their writings the extent of that small stock; and the patrons whom they courted, and who themselves were in the same stage of intellectual culture, were flattered at being addressed in a strain which must have been unintelligible to the multitude. When literature revived, the same kind of pleasure which had just before been given by a pedantic vocabulary, was produced by classical allusions, and imitations of ancient, or of Italian writers. The language then improved so suddenly, that it changed more in the course of one generation than it had done in the two preceding centuries; Elizabeth, who grew up while it was comparatively barbarous, lived to see it made capable of giving adequate expression to the loftiest conceptions of human imagination. Poets were then, perhaps, more abundant than they have been in any subsequent age until the present: and, as a necessary consequence of that abundance, all tricks of style were tried, and all fantasticalities of conceit abounded; they who were poets by imitative desire or endeavour, putting forth their strength in artificial and ambitious

APPENDIX II

efforts, while the true poets held the true course, though the best of them did not always escape from what had thus been made the vice of their age.

[the review continues with long extracts from and summaries of Southey's discussion of John Taylor, the Water-Poet]

We have dwelt so long on the Water-poet, that we must hurry over his successors; of whom, however, it is pleasing to find, notwithstanding the reflection with which Mr Southey concludes the life of Taylor, that hardly one failed to receive, in his day, a tolerable share of notice and assistance from his superiors in station.

Stephen Duck (now hardly remembered but by Swift's malicious epigram) attracted by his verses, while a poor hardworking farm-servant, the notice of a young Oxonian, by name Stanley, who gave him such encouragement, and such advice, that he at last deserved and obtained the patronage of Queen Caroline. Her Majesty settled £30 a-year on him (which was then no poor provision), made him a yeoman of the guard, and soon afterwards keeper of her private library at Richmond, where he had apartments given him, and was encouraged to pursue his studies with a view to holy orders. His poems being published by subscription, under the care of Mr Spence, met with very considerable success; and he himself was at length preferred to the living of Byfleet in Surrey, where he maintained the character of an exemplary parish priest; and long after his first celebrity had worn itself out, was much followed as a preacher. Stephen united keen susceptibility of temperament with patience, modesty, and all those household virtues, which it has been the cant to proclaim hardly reconcileable with the impulses of the '*mens divinior*.'[461] But his end was unhappy: the sensibilities which originally drew him from obscurity, and for which, when his mind had been opened by instruction, he discovered himself to be gifted with no such powers of expression as could hold out the prospect of lasting distinction in literature, seem to have turned inwards with fatal violence. Placed in a situation of external comfort and respectability far beyond the warmest dreams of his youth surrounded with honourable duties, which he discharged not only blamelessly, but with general applause the one darling hope, on which his boyish heart had fastened its ambition, had withered, exactly as his reading and intercourse with the upper world had extended – he went mad, and drowned himself, near Reading, in 1756. The best of his verses are among the earliest of them; and no one can read some of the descriptions of rural life, so unlike the effusions of the pastoral-mongers, which they contain, without admitting that his original patrons had some reason to expect from his maturer pen 'things that the world would not willingly let die.' A small specimen must suffice here:

[excerpts Duck's description of reaping]

'At one time,' says Mr Southey, 'he was in such reputation, that Lord Palmerston appropriated the rent of an acre of land, for ever, to provide a dinner and

APPENDIX II

strong beer for the threshers of Charlton at a public-house in that valley, in honour of their former comrade. The dinner is given on the 30th of June. The poet himself was present at one of these anniversaries, probably the first, and speaks thus of it in a pleasing poem addressed to that nobleman.

[excerpt]

[. . .] Mr Southey proceeds to the cobbler of Rowley, James Woodhouse, who had the good fortune to have the benevolent Shenstone for his neighbour, and therefore wanted neither advice nor assistance, so soon as his turn for ballad-inditing had made him known beyond his stall. This too was a good, honest, sober, humble-minded man; and, being judiciously patronized in his own calling, so as to improve his condition, but not subjected to the hazardous experiment of a forcible elevation out of his natural sphere and method of life, his days were passed and ended in more comfort than has fallen to the lot of most of the masters in the art. The sedentary occupation which he followed leaves abundant opportunity for meditation; and if, as has been alleged, more than their just proportion of the murders recorded in our Newgate Calendars belongs to this brooding fraternity, it may serve to balance the account, that it has also produced more rhymers than any other of the handicrafts.

> Crispin's sons
> Have, from uncounted time, with ale and buns,
> Cherish'd the gift of song, which sorrow quells;
> And, working single in their low-built cells,
> Oft cheat the tedium of a winter's night
> With anthems.
> (Charles Lamb – Album Verses (1830), p. 57)[462]

Two of these ultra-crepidarians are included in Mr Southey's present chapter of chronicles; we have already incidentally alluded to another, now flourishing at Chichester – a man who is described to us as not less estimable in character than his predecessor of Woodstock; – and there remains a name (we hope still a living one), worth all these put together – that of Mr John Struthers, of Glasgow, author of 'The Sabbath;' a poem of which unaffected piety is not the only inspiration; and which, but for its unfortunate coincidence of subject with the nearly contemporary one of the late amiable James Grahame,[463] would probably have attracted a considerable share of favour, even in these hypercritical days.

'Shenstone found that the poor applicant (Woodhouse) used to work with a pen and ink at his side, while the last was in his lap; – the head at one employ, the hands at another; and when he had composed a couplet or a stanza, he wrote it on his knee. In one of the pieces thus composed, and entitled 'Spring,' there are these affecting stanzas:

229

APPENDIX II

[excerpts Woodhouse's stanzas on domestic labour and poverty; the excerpts and summarises Southey's narratives about James Bennet and Ann Yearsley]

The proud name of Robert Burns does not occur in this Essay; Mr Southey estimates him too justly to class him, on any pretext, with uneducated poets. That extraordinary man, before he produced any of the pieces on which his fame is built, had educated himself abundantly; and when he died, at the age of thirty-seven, knew more of books, as well as of men, than fifty out of a hundred in any of the learned professions in any country of the world are ever likely to do. We might speak in nearly the same way of Burns' two popular successors in Scottish minstrelsy. When the Ettrick Shepherd was first heard of, he had indeed but just learned to write by copying the letters of a printed ballad, as he lay watching his flock on the mountains; but thirty years or more have passed since then, and his acquirements are now such, that the Royal Society of Literature, in patronizing him, might be justly said to honour a laborious and successful student, as well as a masculine and fertile genius. We may take the liberty of adding, in this place, what may not perhaps be known to the excellent managers of that excellent institution, that a more worthy, modest, sober and loyal man does not exist in his Majesty's dominions than this distinguished poet, whom some of his waggish friends have taken up the absurd fancy of exhibiting in print as a sort of boozing buffoon; and who is now, instead of revelling in the licence of tavern-suppers and party politics, bearing up, as he may, against severe and unmerited misfortunes, in as dreary a solitude as ever nursed the melancholy of a poetical temperament.[464] Mr Allan Cunningham needs no testimony either to his intellectual accomplishments or his moral worth; nor, thanks to his own virtuous diligence, does he need any patronage. He has been fortunate enough to secure a respectable establishment in the studio of a great artist, who is not less good than great, and would thus be sufficiently in the eye of the world, even were his literary talents less industriously exercised than they have hitherto been. His recent Lives of the British Painters and Sculptors[465] form one of the most agreeable books in the language; and it will always remain one of the most remarkable and delightful facts in the history of letters, that such a work – one conveying so much valuable knowledge in a style so unaffectedly attractive – so imbued throughout, not only with lively sensibility, amiable feelings, honesty and candour, but mature and liberal taste, was produced by a man who, some twenty years before, earned his daily bread as a common stone-mason in the wilds of Nithsdale. Examples like these will plead the cause of struggling genius, wherever it may be found, more powerfully than all the arguments in the world.*

*We hope to be pardoned for taking this opportunity of bearing witness to the wise and generous method in which the Managers of the London Literary Fund conduct that admirable charity. It may not be known in many parts of the empire that such an institution exists at all; and even this casual notice may be serviceable

APPENDIX II

to its revenues. We have had occasion to observe the equal promptitude and delicacy with which its Committee are ever ready to administer to the necessities of the unfortunate scholar, who can satisfy them that his misery is not the just punishment of immoral habits. Some of the brightest names in contemporary literature have been beholden to the bounty of this Institution; and in numerous instances its interference has shielded friendless merit from utter ruin.

APPENDIX III

The Poems of John Jones

The Author to His Book

Poor rugged offspring of my humble Muse,
The world may spurn thee, and thy faults abuse;
For in thy progress not a peaceful hour
Had I to form thee, and no classic power;
Plain simple Nature, in her homely way,
With sudden impulse sung each artless lay,
To state her feelings, or express a thought
Of what her knowledge or her fancy caught;
No state of ease the hapless Muse enjoyed,
The hands were busy, and the ears annoyed
By those quick sounds with which the tongues are rife,
Of mortals bustling in domestic life.
For far from sounds of strife and noisy mirth
Doth Fancy love to give her musings birth.
Nursed in a soil which felt no cheering rays,
And laughter fearing, without hope of praise,
Nor on thee having leisure to bestow,
Thou wert uncherished, and thy growth was slow;
But when through time some incident arose
That called the heart to pleasure or to woes,
Which Nature kindly asked the Muse to paint,
Her willing fervor broke through all restraint,
And soon depicted what the bosom felt,
And then to thee some little substance dealt.
Loved child of fancy! not endeared for worth,
But as a toy to him who gave thee birth,
Not oft intruded on another's view,
Few of thy nature or existence knew,
And when beheld, opinions, coldly given,
Still chilled the source by which thou might'st have thriven.

APPENDIX III

But on thee chance beamed a more genial ray,
Which lit and led thee into Southey's way;
And he saw even in thy small share of skill,
That there was in thee something pleasing still,
Where those who met thee with a nature kind
Might some congenial charm, amusing find;
And at the risk of every critic's strife,
He lends his hand to lead thee into life,
For which I'll nurse, whate'er my fate may be,
A grateful thought to life's extremity.

To help thee forward, when thou first could'st run,
Some promised stoutly, but have little done;
Others, whose strains came in a softer swell,
Found kindred spirits, and have served thee well;
For every kindness, be it great or small,
I feel most grateful, and, I thank them all.

The Journey of Life

The Journey of Life
There are none can presage;
From all we can learn
'Tis an uncertain stage;
If short or extended,
No mortal can say,
What up-hills or down-hills
There are in the way;
Yet were all we travellers
Social inclined,
And true honest hearted,
And loving and kind;
Nor man to man scornful,
Nor man to man wrong,
How happily we might
All travel along!
But Pow'r will oppress thee,
And Pride pass thee by,
And Folly will laugh
At a tear in thine eye;
And, should dark misfortune
Thy prospects o'ercast,
E'en Friendship will leave thee
Exposed to the blast;

APPENDIX III

And Envy and Malice
Augment thy distress;
And Cunning and Avarice
Thy little make less.
But, strengthen'd by Virtue,
Still bravely contend,
And Hope will uphold thee,
And God be thy friend.

The Snowball

I heard the wint'ry north winds blow,
   One dreary, cold, and cheerless night,
And thickly fell large flakes of snow,
   Which clothed the world in spotless white.

When morn awoke, it seem'd to say,
   'I'm dawning forth a day of woe,
The birds shall know nor vacant spray,
   Nor what to do, nor where to go.'

I slowly beat my trackless way,
   The walk, the garden's summit sought,
Contemplating the scene to-day
   The last unconscious night had wrought.

The fallow brown, the verdant mead,
   And rugged heath within my view,
Had lost their charms; o'er all was spread
   A robe of one unvaried hue.

'Here look,' I said, 'ye proud, and know,
   As these are now, in semblance seen
And undistinguish'd in the snow,
   You'll be beneath a turf of green.

The snow shall yield to milder skies,
   The fields their genial hue shall wear;
But when from earth your spirits rise,
   The poor as comely forms shall bear.'

With musings thus my mind was fraught,
   When faintly gleam'd the rising sun,
An airy wish my fancy caught,
   A ball of snow it fixt upon.

APPENDIX III

Elated by a childish pride
　I wound a snowball round and high,
And more than once I turn'd aside
　To shun the gaze of passers by.

How oft what men alone enjoy,
　Their public precepts seem to chide;
How prone was I to play the boy,
　But wish'd, proud world, from thee to hide.

Dost thou man's guileless foibles see?
　Those, in thine ire, thou'lt magnify,
Attach them to some obloquy,
　And damn them in the public eye.

Sweet virtue's sober, chaste career,
　Dost thou in wanton sport molest,
Nor pity's tender, balmy tear,
　Falls uninsulted by thy jest!

When ponderous grown, I view'd with care
　My fancy's child, so fondly rear'd,
And found, tho' erst it shone so fair,
　'Twas now impure, and unendear'd.

Its progress tracing from its birth
　In every turn it made to power,
It bore oppressive on the earth,
　And crush'd the root of many a flower.

Does man not more oppression show
　In every turn from low degree?
Yes, yes, my pompous ball of snow,
　Strong semblance of the world's in thee!

This flow'ry tribe, to thee a prey,
　Alas! to these, with longing eyes,
Some mind congenial oft may stray,
　In hope to view their offspring rise;

But, maim'd and bare, in vain the spring
　Shall come their verdure to restore;
In vain each shower refreshment bring,
　They'll rear on earth their heads no more.

235

APPENDIX III

Bedeck'd no more in lovely hue,
    The breath no more their sweets inhale,
The longing eye no flower shall view,
    And on their charms no bee regale.

But why, cold lump, to thee declaim,
    Or why, ye flowers, your fate deplore,
When suff'ring souls my pity claim,
    And real woes deserve it more?

Of those who range yon heights sublime,
    Where splendour Fortune's idols show,
Are some, man marvels how they climb,
    Emerg'd from indigence below.

Could he their tracks, as thine, behold,
    Congenial crimes his eye might meet,
And many a flower of mortal mould
    Untimely crush'd beneath his feet.

Ambition rears the buoyant head,
    And pride, in power, is slow to spare;
On those they pass, in scorn, they tread
    With all the mighty pomp they bear.

As thine, the Miser's heart is cold,
    Destructive each of Nature's plan;
Thou, earth, and he, imprisons gold,
    The food of flowers and staff of man.

Increase of gold adds might to power,
    And vice more strong augmenteth woe,
He'll catch the drops of every shower
    And stagnate streams Heav'n meant should flow.

Oh! could but these his channels shun,
    And branch in streamlets unconfined,
Some would in generous courses run,
    And draughts of comfort yield mankind.

Tho' pity leaves no plaint unsung,
    Though misery bleeds at every pore,
He'll mock the tale of either tongue,
    And turn them weeping from the door.

APPENDIX III

Soon he, like thee, shall disappear,
    Attended by no child of woe;
Where Virtue's children shed a tear,
    His children's tears shall cease to flow.

And, torn from life, what tongue shall say,
    Or how he fares, or where may dwell?
None e'er from hence the scene survey,
    And none that see will ever tell.

But thank thee well, for what I know;
    My bosom's yearning with desire
Of what thou'st taught me in the snow,
    My friend, to tell beside the fire.

Near stream'd the Mole, close at its brink
    Arose a cot of neat degree;
I heard, methought, the wicket clink,
    And, led by fancy, went to see.

Its humble tenant met my sight,
    (How chance, sometimes, strange things will do!)
The hair that crown'd his head was white –
    The name he bore – was Snowball, too.

His cheeks the bloom of health had on,
    His form the prime of life array'd;
A smile, which on his features shone,
    Of death no tardy thoughts betray'd.

Sweet sprightly souls, all flaxen-brow'd,
    Around their sire young antics wrought;
To each a willing head he bow'd,
    Whose lips a parting kiss besought.

From man to snow my fancy sped,
    And still what sage, methought, can say –
(Though hope with years the mortal fed,)
    Which first shall pass, of these, away?

The leaves, but on the spray, we see,
    Our knowledge o'er their course extends;
And man in life to-day may be,
    But there of him our knowledge ends.

APPENDIX III

By passions strong, when reason's blind,
    He's led until the blow be given;
When lo! his passport's left unsigned,
    And closed he'll find the gates of Heaven.

What stores the ant and bee provide,
    When leaves and blossoms clothe the boughs;
Oh! Man, with all thy sense and pride,
    How much outdone art thou by those!

Now fast the snow was seen to shrink,
    And Nature's face more gay to beam,
And what the earth refused to drink,
    Wound slowly on and join'd the stream.

But lingering there, my snowball stood,
    Till many suns stole down the sky;
A remnant yet escaped the flood,
    When pass'd the sexton, mournful, by.

'Ho! man,' said I, 'why bow thine head?
    That step so slow, and brow of care,
Says thou, a meddler with the dead,
    Of woes must no light burthen bear.

With unconcern, by sorrow's side,
    Aye, with the sod just drench'd with tears,
Thou'rt seen, from love's fond eye to hide
    Of life the pride, and joy of years.'

'In vain,' said he, 'those tears are shed;
    'Tis meet on death the sod should close,
And grief 'twould be to spirits fled,
    Could love recall them from repose.

Since, weary of the world's caprice,
    Man here in murmurs dire complains,
Why mourn, when he shall pass where bliss
    In every sweet perfection reigns?

Tho' in thy path Fate's webs be spun
    Which catch thy every hope that flies,

APPENDIX III

If well thy earthly task be done,
   Thou yet a blissful soul shalt rise.

But haste, for time speeds fast on wings,
   Whilst man is reckless, slow, or gay,
Tho' oft some kind alarum rings,
   To warn him of the coming day,

Heaven oft a shaft abruptly sends,
   Its power a wayward world to show;
E'en now, from whence yon smoke ascends,
   Is mourn'd an unexpected blow.

And closed are eyes the morn awoke;
   To other realms a spirit's fled;
This hour hath dealt the fatal stroke,
   And Snowball's stretch'd on death's cold bed.

But, rest our plaintive converse here,
   To toll his mournful knell I'm bound,
Soon, on the breeze, thy pensive ear
   Will note its deep and solemn sound.'

My trembling heart beat in my breast
   To think, when pondering o'er death's hour,
That he, who did the thought suggest,
   Should bow so soon beneath its power.

Those tender souls, who skipp'd with pride,
   To share his smile around the door,
Nor saw that death lurk'd by his side,
   Nor thought that soon he'd smile no more.

Man, think, what e'er thy state reveals
   Youth, health, or strength, these all had he;
Yet, then was Death close at his heels,
   And now as close to thine may be.

On this reflection prone to dwell,
   I, to and fro, the walk paced on,
Oft murmuring, as I heard the knell,
   'Yes! ere the snow, poor Snowball's gone!'

APPENDIX III

Why That Sigh, &c.

Why that sigh art thou suppressing,
   Did it take its flight from grief?
Yes, that rising tear's confessing
   Thou art pain'd, and need'st relief.

To my mental vision show it,
   Fear thee not to trouble me;
'Twill less painful be to know it,
   Than what dumb suspense will be.

If some pregnant cloud appals thee,
   Love may shield thee from the shower;
If perplexing cares inthral thee,
   Counsel may dispel their power.

If reflection doth remind thee
   Of the fleeting state of breath,
And of one thou'st left behind thee
   In the darksome shades of death,

Once the idol of affection,
   Once the joy of youthful years,
One to whom sweet recollection
   Pays those tributary tears,

Pure's the grateful spring that fed them,
   Down their channels let them steal,
'Tis a pensive bliss to shed them,
   Which the virtuous, only, feel.

If thou'st view'd some scene before thee,
   Which in fancy's overcast,
And thou fear'st the kind beam o'er thee
   Will not light thee to the last,

Let such prospects ne'er deject thee,
   Be they dark, or be they clear;
That a guide will e'er direct thee,
   Never doubt, and never fear.

APPENDIX III

Lines
Addressed
To Mrs. Lawrence,[466] *Studley Park, Yorkshire.*
On New Year's Day, 1824

Oh! Lady of Studley, resplendent in worth
   Is the Star which on thee its mild influence beams,
Attracted by virtue, when bright'ning on earth,
   It play'd on thy breast and dissolved it in streams.
And ceaseless and pure, from the heart-springs they flow,
   The channels of pity they love to explore,
And many a comfort they yield as they go,
   To the aged, the weary, the care-worn and poor.

Oh! Lady, 'tis sweet in the bye-path to tread
   Which leadeth to penury's door,
To succour the ailing, and pillow the head
   Which had not a pillow before;
To cherish the widow; the orphan protect,
   Whom death of its guides has despoiled,
And train it to knowledge, and teach it respect,
   And rear it a virtuous child.

And, Lady, 'tis sweet to the bounteous soul,
   Which prides in the good it can do,
To have such resources within its controul,
   As Heaven hath measured to you.
And may they increase, still empowering the will
   To solace affliction in tears,
Whilst He who discerns how your trusts you fulfil,
   Awards you health, honour, and years.

This day to a bantling hath Time given birth,
   Which bears the Omnipotent's plan,
As well as the various changes of earth,
   The yearly allotment of man.
That its portion for you may be tempered as sweet
   As a sensible hope can desire,
Is the wish of a soul to whom hope is a cheat,
   The poor humble bard you inspire.

APPENDIX III

A Voice From Ripon
January 1, 1825

Full fast came the herald, from Studley's bowers,
   Of our Lady's[467] danger informing,
And fear made sad our evening hours,
   Tho' gay had we been in the morning.

A night's repose, in suspense, we sought,
   But none took we for sorrow,
Our sleep was chased by the restless thought
   Of what might be on the morrow.

When the morning beam'd and in the west
   Inquiring looks we were casting,
How oft our mental tongues express'd,
   'May the life of our Lady be lasting!'

But from the west we no tidings gain'd
   But what despair indited,
Not a thought had we that was not pain'd,
   Not a hope that was not blighted.

'Till, sweet as the morning ray appears
   To the night-bewildered stranger,
A sound broke forth on our pensive ears,
   That lessen'd our Lady's danger.

And now, as reviving nature glows
   In spring, when the sun grows stronger,
We joy in the love our Ruler shows
   In the meed of our Lady longer.

Tho' bridal'd not, and children none,
   To many has she been a mother,
And when to the regions of bliss she's gone,
   We shall see not such another.

Like her, ye more reckless, whom fortune befriends,
   Have an eye to the prospect before ye;
She dispenses the blessings which Heaven sends,
   In paving her way to its glory.

The gloom of sorrow that sate on each brow
   Declared with what grief we should mourn her;
And the pleasure that brightens each countenance now,
   Is light to the love which is borne her.

APPENDIX III

Deep in the Dell

Deep in the dell, when pensive straying,
    Far from every noisy sound,
I saw a spring in beauty playing
    From a rock with foliage crowned;
And as its airy bound 'twas taking,
    And its form a radiance shed,
A crag beneath, the torrent breaking,
    Around in parting streams it spread.

And each a channel lonely winding,
    Dull and slowly seem'd to run,
And turn'd, methought, in hope of finding
    That with which its course begun;
From either side to each inclining,
    One by one, the current fed;
Fast it flowed, when all combining,
    Praises murmuring as it sped.

'Twas like, methought, two souls existing,
    Young in years and light in care,
When in social bands enlisting,
    Life is sweet, and hope is fair.
Joys, which mutual love provides them,
    Cheer their course, and on they go
Till some turn of fate divides them,
    Strange and dreary ways to know.

In lonely hours, anticipation
    Paints the scene of joys to come;
And when 'tis view'd, how inclination
    Woos the path which leads to home,
And when those souls, in memory chaptered,
    The seat of love's attraction swell,
Congenial spirits flow enraptured,
    Like the waters down the dell.

An Address to a Dead Cat,
which had fallen from the ivy-tree that runs up
the tower of Kirkby Fleetham church, Yorkshire;
up which it is supposed it had climbed after birds

Wert thou by mad ambition fired,
Or wert by sensual hopes inspired? –
But, by whatever thou on wert led
It matters not, life's spark is fled.

APPENDIX III

I ween the fluttering tribe above
In airy tumult won thy love,
And, branch by branch, their height to gain,
Thou climb'dst, unconsciously and vain.

When creeping on, thro' foliage green,
In hope by art to rise unseen,
The nearing sounds thy fancy charm'd,
Nor look below thy fears alarm'd.
With cautious step and eye intent,
Surprise thy aim, and ruthless bent,
The height was gained, the birds had fled,
And thou a victim in their stead.

When danger met thy wond'ring eyes,
Most loud and piteous were thy cries,
And pity heard, and breathed a sigh,
And grieved she could not climb so high.

On faithless boughs, unyielding rest,
When weary morn and hunger prest,
A blast most rude the branches tost,
Thy hold exhausted nature lost,
And down to earth impetuous sent:
In cries and groans thy life was spent.

Had to thy wants no heed been shown,
And thou the pangs of hunger known,
And urged on by a sense so keen,
More piteous would thy fate have been;
For life will waste on stinted fare,
And life is first in nature's care.

But ever wont wert thou to find,
Of food thy fill, a welcome kind,
And daily in thy peaceful dome
Wert petted, stroked, and call'd poor Tom!
To please thee, too, 'twas the resort
Of cats, for play, – and mice for sport.

With comforts thus, strewn in thy way,
Less prone thou should'st have been to stray,
And not indulgence sought in strife,
And led a wild advent'rous life;

APPENDIX III

But life hath for thy errors paid,
And low thy daring spirit's laid.

Did passions, Tom, to thine a-kin,
But prompt alone thy race to sin,
How many hearts, with woe oppress'd,
How many sighs, which pain the breast,
How many bitter tears that flow,
Had mortals ne'er been doom'd to know,
Whom none can cheer, and nought console, –
For forms, who risk, with life, a soul!

There are (a wanton course to run,)
Those who a home and bliss will shun;
But gone, alas! within the door
The sweets of bliss are felt no more,
But to the threshhold may be traced
From every scene the wanderer's paced,
Where Riot sung, or Folly played, –
A path by evil tidings made, –
And on 'tis trode, without a turn,
Till deep for woe a channel's worn.
It fills! it streams! a flood appears!
And all the dome's deluged with tears.

At worth's expense their passions fed,
They're soon to vice from folly led,
Desires, increasing every hour,
As streams augment by every shower,
And pamper'd till they're tyrants grown, –
Subdue each power, and wield their own;
They seek their food by stealth or strife,
Offend the laws, and forfeit life.

Too gay in sober life to move,
And envious of the show above,
And vainly will'd to rise like thee,
Will others climb ambition's tree,
And wind, in specious guise, their way,
Thro' branches clothed in bright array,
Ascend its height, by force or guile,
And glare, in glorious pomp, awhile.

But wasting strength will soon betray
Their want of power their hold to stay,

APPENDIX III

When, with reluctance to depart,
A union's form'd with pride and art,
Who form a tale of pleasing sounds,
And some demure pretext propounds,
And if the snare fresh succours bring,
They yet a little longer cling.

But patient time will truth disclose,
And every art by which they rose,
And suffering dupes, with vengeful frown,
A storm will raise, and shake them down,
And shame, the second wife of pride,
Will lead them off, in shades to hide.

Would those who climb, and those who stray,
Above their height, and from their way,
A moment pause – to calm the breath,
And ponder o'er thy fall and death,
And let the truths by thee defined
Restrain the wanderings of the mind,
And mould them to a just degree, –
How well, for Men, and Cats, 'twould be!

Lines,
Occasioned by Walking over
Some Fallen Leaves

Fallen leaves, your rustlings waken
    Fancy from a gentle sleep;
Note will of ye now be taken,
    O'er ye as I slowly creep.

Yes, her eyes are backward wending,
    And in early life you're seen
Where kind spring, your race befriending,
    Led ye forth in buds of green.

Now she sees you far advancing,
    To the mild beam opening wide,
Now in gentle zephyrs dancing,
    In your full expanded pride.

In the glory of existence,
    Now you're ey'd from hill and glade,

246

APPENDIX III

To the sun ye show resistance,
    And ye yield a cooling shade.

Now a change in life o'ertakes ye,
    And ye wear a golden cast;
Now your charms and strength forsake ye,
    And ye sicken in the blast.

Now from every tree you're spreading,
    Borne away on wind and stream;
On ye now I'm rudely treading, –
    Get ye down to whence ye came.

'Hush!' methinks I hear ye saying,
    'Thine no better doom will be;
Life's tree, on which thou art staying,
    Is a frail unstable tree.

Many souls now on it number'd,
    In some near approaching squall,
Down shall come, with crime encumber'd,
    And more deep than us may fall.

Be not with thyself elated;
    Be thou not so proud of birth;
Thou to us art near related,
    Children all of mother Earth.

Let our frail existence tell thee,
    Thine is but a breath of air,
Soon a puff to earth shall fell thee,
    And with us thou'lt mingle there.'

Yes! from earth, we are descended,
    And a-kin, I'll not deny,
Nor that, when my course is ended,
    With you there my frame may lie.

I've a spirit which must leave it
    For eternal pain or ease,
Help me, oh my God, to save it,
    Lest I fall more low than these!

APPENDIX III

The Butterfly to His Love

Extend thy wings, my dear,
And we will round the bowers go;
The sun is warm and clear,
And inviting is the day;
The dews have left the blade,
And fragrant now the flowers blow,
And, as they blow to fade,
Let's enjoy them while we may!
We're not of mortal mould
To die, and then unfold
Our eyes in still a brighter world,
Its glories to explore;
Our life is but a summer long;
Then let us rove its sweets among,
For when the blast blows bleak and strong,
We sleep, to wake no more.

To A Wild Heath Flower

Sweet flow'ret! from Nature's indulgence thou'rt cast,
Thy home's on the cold heath, thy nurse is the blast,
No shrub spreads its branches to shelter thy form,
Thou'rt shook by the winds, and thou'rt beat by the storm;
But the bird of the moor on thy substance is fed,
And thou giv'st to the hare of the mountain a bed;
In youth, from the cold winds thou'lt grant them a space,
And in age, when the fowler's at war with their race.
The winds may assail thee, the tempest may rage,
Thy nature is proof to the war which they wage;
Thou'lt smile in the conflict, and blossoms unfold,
Where the nurslings of favour would shrink from the cold;
Though rugged and sterile the seat of thy birth,
Simplicity formed thee of beauty and worth.

Remain then, sweet blossom, the pride of the moor,
In loneliness flourish, unpampered and pure, –
Expand in the tempest, and bloom on the brow.
An emblem of sweet independence art thou;
And the soul who beholds thee unhurt in the strife
Shall learn to contend with the troubles of life;
And when the cold wind of adversity's felt,
And the shafts of affliction are ruthfully dealt,
His spirit, unbroken, shall rise to the last,

APPENDIX III

And his virtues shall open and bloom in the blast,
And his joys shall be sweet when the storm is at rest,
And the sun beams of glory shall play on his breast.

Old Mawley to His Ass.

*The Following Account of Whom Appeared
in the Sun Newspaper of April, 1828*

'An old man died last week at Langport, near Lewes, upwards of eighty years old. He had resided on the family estate of the Tourles[468] nearly fifty years, one of whom bequeathed him an annual income, which he has regularly enjoyed; and from the present head of the family he has received very beneficent attention; on his death-bed he desired that his old donkey, which he had daily strode for forty-five years, should be killed and buried by his side. His general avocation was to look after the rabbits, and the youngsters of several generations have been awed by the call of "here comes old Mawley," when they were employed in birds' nesting on the race hill.'

Together we have borne the blast,
For five-and forty winters past,
But we are now both waning fast,
  My poor old Ass.

Our sun is sinking in the west,
By night's dark shades we're closely prest,
And soon shall reach our home of rest,
  My faithful Ass.

A faithful friend thou'st been to me
As ever beast to man could be,
And grateful is my heart to thee,
  My good old Ass.

In many a long and daily round
O'er rugged ways and miry ground,
On thee I've ease and comfort found,
  My steady Ass.

We've met the storm's tremendous ire,
The thunder's crash and lightnings fire,
And never would'st thou fear or tire,
  My patient Ass.

APPENDIX III

Through rain and hail, and drifting snow,
And winds as keen as Heaven could blow,
Thy willing nature bade thee go,
        My gentle Ass.

O'er every rough and slippery road,
With patient care thou'st firmly strode,
And sav'd, more than thyself, thy load,
        My worthy Ass.

And in thy long-spent youthful day,
The sprightly pranks thou'st wont to play,
Drew from love's sun a tender ray,
        My merry Ass.

More strong it grew from year to year,
Till time and worth hath made thee dear;
Oft o'er thee now I shed a tear,
        My poor old Ass.

And can I go, when life shall end,
And leave so good and kind a friend,
In cold neglect thy days to end,
        My hapless Ass?

Unhoused by night, by day unfed,
In lonely lanes in mire to tread,
With not to shelter thee a shed,
        My suffering Ass?

How would the ruthless youngsters stride
Thy bare back bones and goad thy side,
And chequer with long stripes thy hide,
        Unhappy Ass!

And thou would'st then a visit pay
To where thou'dst known a better day,
And thence be rudely chased away,
        My injured Ass.

And to be chastened like a thief
Whence hope had led thee for relief,
Would break thy poor old heart with grief,
        My honest Ass.

APPENDIX III

And from the door should'st slowly creep,
And in some quagmire dank and deep
Thou'dst sink, and take thy long night's sleep,
   My weary Ass.

And must thy doom be so severe?
Oh! no, the thought awakes a tear,
I cannot go and leave thee here,
   My faithful Ass.

The reckless may the thought deride,
The wise, perchance, may gently chide;
But we will moulder side by side,
   My loving Ass.

I'll will, that, at my latest sigh,
Thou, too, some easy death shalt die,
And in one grave we both will lie,
   My own old Ass.

We, in thy youth, associates were,
We've lived an undivided pair,
And so to earth we'll go, and there,
   My kind old Ass,

One stone shall cover thou and me;
And where we lie the world may see,
For this our epitaph shall be,
   My friend and Ass.

Epitaph

Oh! stay, a moment here expend,
For here, where thou shalt soon extend,
Lie I, old Mawley, and my friend,
My faithful Ass.
Hast thou a friend as good as mine,
And gratitude was never thine?
Oh! blush thou then, before its shrine,
For shame, and pass.

To The Tongue

Thou herald both of love and ire,
Thou chord of truth – thou arrant liar,

251

APPENDIX III

Thou calmer and thou cause of strife,
Thou blessing and thou curse of life,
How doth the power to thee consigned,
In adverse ways affect mankind!

Tuned are thy softest strains to move
Some fair, whose ear's awake to love;
In which such sweets thy art instils,
That every nerve with transport thrills;
And hushed is every thought to sleep
Which o'er the heart should sentry keep;
And every scene's illumed with rays
That beam from hope on future days,
And on love's stream most sweetly goes,
And thou'rt the fount from whence it flows.

And when from sources pure it springs,
A balm for many a wound it brings,
And many draughts, when woes are rife,
'Twill yield, to cool the thirsts of life;
And ne'er its pleasing powers deny
Till nature sinks and leaves it dry.

But oft it flows from art, and tries
To tempt the taste, and lead the eyes,
And lures some object to the brink,
And fondly urges it to drink,
And, hopeful that its balmy powers
May solace yield in future hours,
The draught is quaft, the error's known,
Repentance comes, and peace is flown,
And in the victim's plaints is sung, –
'Oh! woe betide a guileful tongue.'

Thy sounds break forth in anger loud,
Like thunder from a stormy cloud,
And many souls from sweet repose
Provoke to strife or wake to woes.
When passions strong subdue the sense,
Charged with some vain or vile pretence,
Thou deal'st thy harsh invective round,
And every softer voice is drown'd:
The gentle fear, the wise retreat,

APPENDIX III

And poor dependents mourn their state
So hard, when laden low, to be
Beneath their load reviled by thee.

As on life's rugged road they tread,
To earn, before they eat, their bread;
When hard they toil and keen their pains,
Their comforts few, and small their gains;
Oh! wouldst thou, with thy kindest powers,
Direct them in their arduous hours,
And rule the weak with mild control,
And ease the heavy burthen'd soul,
And tell them that they're task'd on earth
To try their patience and their worth,
And they who best its trouble bear
Will merit most kind Heaven's care.

Oh! then, illumed with hope's mild ray,
Through life's hard, toilsome, gloomy day,
They'd journey on with hearts more light,
And peaceful lay them down at night.

If thus, what tears would cease to flow,
What pangs their hearts would cease to know,
How many troubled thoughts would rest,
What murmurs would be unexpressed!
When in the cause of truth thou'rt heard,
Thy sounds are sweet in every word,
On virtue's ear they kindly swell,
And where they rise she loves to dwell.
Through life's gay scenes, where folly tries
To win the gaze of youthful eyes,
Where art might lure and vice betray,
They guide her on her lovely way,
To that high eminence of years,
Which rises o'er the vale of fears,
From whence the mind, when backward cast,
Grows pleased to view the dangers past.

When falsehood's tales thou'rt prone to tell,
In loathsome shades thou'rt doom'd to dwell,
And shunn'd thy haunts, thy counsels spurn'd,
Nor ear of worth is to thee turn'd;
And aught of good, or aught of ill,

APPENDIX III

To lure or shun, as suits thy will,
Thou'lt spread with art what vice may plot,
And those deceive who know thee not;
And should mistrust proclaim thy shame,
Thou'lt shift, with dexterous skill, the blame,
And some poor guileless soul revile,
And from it turn love's stream awhile.
But when the misty scene grows clear
And truth's discern'd, dost thou appear
A thing clad in the world's disgust,
Whom none can love and none will trust.

And when, in penury or pain,
Woe bids thee sound her plaintive strain,
And thou and an assisting tear
Meet, that the eye and thou, the ear
Of pity, thy pathetic lay
Through her soft nature pleads its way,
And gains her heart, where deep distress
Finds consolation and redress.

And should the aid to suffering dealt
Be in some needful moment felt,
Reflection comes, to soothe the mind
With charms of every pleasing kind.

When wrath seems kindling in the breast,
By murmurs only yet expressed,
Would'st thou in patient stillness bide,
And let the ruffled thought subside,
Or with, if thou must needs be heard
In thy defence, a soothing word
With reason tempered, stay the strife
That might, if dared, endanger life,
Oh! haply, in a moment's gleam,
Where scowl'd a frown, a smile might beam,
Perchance outheld, for pity's sake,
A hand that 'twould be joy to shake.

Should'st thou with daring meet the shower,
And to a storm provoke its power,
That storm might to a tempest grow,
And reason, the mind's rudder, go,
And passions high, like billows run;

APPENDIX III

And ere the dreadful strife was done,
Life's bark might on a rock be tost,
And in the wreck a soul be lost;
And many, suffering by the strife,
Would brand thee as the curse of life.
Methinks I hear thee mercy crave,
For thou art but the passions' slave.
Then go, but with respect, from me,
And tell them what I've told to thee.

To Lydia,
with a Coloured Egg, on Easter Monday

In Scotia so fair, 'tis a custom they say,
   Old Time hath brought down with his stream,
Each friend to present with an egg on this day,
   As a token of love or esteem.

But why or wherefore, is a matter, I wot,
   Tradition withholds from my view,
And since the original cause I have not,
   I'll brood over this for one new.

It bears, my dear Lyd, when minutely defined,
   A fanciful semblance of thee,
Thy heart is its centre, its white is thy mind,
   Its shell and thine honour agree.

If once, from neglect, an egg falls to the ground,
   No art can its virtue restore;
If once at its post honour's not to be found,
   We look there for honour no more.

Since honour's defection will virtue expose,
   And bliss with its purity dwells,
The treasure within thy fair bosom enclose,
   As eggs are enclosed in their shells.

Hark! Hark! &c.

Hark! hark! sweetly the nightingale
Sings, as the moon's peeping over the mountain;
Hark! hark! through the soft evening gale,
How her notes swell from the tree by the fountain;

APPENDIX III

Her coming is cheering,
The summer is nearing,
Sweet nature is smiling, and spring warmly glowing,
And early to greet them,
My love and I'll meet them
Adown in the vale where the primrose is blowing.

Hark! hark! still hear the nightingale
Sing, on the lake as the moon's brightly beaming;
Hark! hark! now her notes on the gale
Come from the dell where the water is streaming;
The verdure is springing,
The airy choir singing,
The flowers will bloom and their fragrance be shedding,
Arise, nor be loathful,
Ye sleepy and slothful,
And view, when the morn beams, the sweets that are spreading.

Hark! hark! still sings the nightingale,
Whilst a dark cloud is the moon's rays confining;
Hark! hark! now her voice on the gale
Comes from the brake where the woodbine's entwining;
The summer is coming,
The insects are humming,
All nature's expanding in beauty and order;
My love and I'll wander
Where streamlets meander,
And where the blue violets bloom on their border.

To Eliza, with a Little Gold Key

Eliza, this ring I'll entrust to thy care,
If thou wilt of the charge but approve,
The worth it encloses thou only shalt share,
'Tis the key of my heart and its love.

If fortune should from thee its blessings withstay,
Oh! come in the sorrowful hour,
'Twill open a bosom sincere as the day,
That will solace thee all in its power.

A few chosen souls have the means of access,
And friendship and kindness may free,

APPENDIX III

But I have enclosed in a private recess
What shall only be opened to thee.

The Friend of My Heart

When my heart droops under worldly displeasure,
And restless emotions its comforts destroy,
In friendship is found a resource beyond measure,
For chasing the cares which the bosom annoy.
Sweet counsel addressing, each moral impressing,
Bestowing each blessing the mind can impart –
Oh! fate, let thy dictates be e'er so distressing,
Preserve for me ever the friend of my heart.

So when the wild storm has disturbed the main ocean,
And peril and toil have the seaman oppressed,
A calm soon, like friendship, shall still its emotion,
And lull, in soft slumbers, his bosom to rest.
Tho' dangers surrounding, and troubles confounding,
If friendship's abounding, 'twill solace impart.
Oh! fate, let thy arrows be ever so wounding,
Preserve for me ever the friend of my heart.

The mortal advancing his own pleasures only,
From whose frigid bosom no sympathy flows,
Shall pass thro', unpitied, unsheltered, and lonely,
The wild and bleak storms, when adversity blows;
No love shall caress him, no friend shall address him,
Tho' care may oppress him and wound like a dart.
Oh! fate, let my prospects be e'er so depressing,
Preserve to me ever the friend of my heart.

Mary Killcrow

In the hamlet, where time introduced me to light,
A poor little pitiful stranger on earth,
Till nurs'd with affection, and kiss'd with delight,
And cherish'd by her whom I pain'd at my birth,
Rose sounds which now often resound in mine ears,
And objects which fancy attached to the mind,
And memory hath borne through the tempests of years,
Whilst things of more import fell listless behind;

And out of its relics it loveth to show
A dapper old woman named Mary Killcrow.

Two asses had Mary, with saddles and sacks,
And cheerfully with them she trudged through the mire,
And twice in the day, with these full on their backs,
They bore from the coalpit our fuel for fire.
Her body was wrapp'd in a mantle of grey,
By a kerchief of blue was her bonnet confined,
And a staff in her hand, if her asses should stray,
With a point in the end, to reprove them behind:

But seldom they felt or a prick or a blow,
So mild was the nature of Mary Killcrow.
The features of Mary were ruffled with age,
And faded her beauties, whatever they were;
The sun in its strength, and the storm in its rage,
Had rendered her brown, had she ever been fair.
Her figure was round, and her stature was low,
And sturdy her limbs, but to quickness inclin'd;
And Mary oft trode the first track in the snow,
With a rude band of hay round each ancle entwin'd.
If wont some defects thy exterior to show,
Rare virtues embellish'd thee, Mary Killcrow.

The male ass was Ned, and the female was Bess;
She oft for their sustenance clipp'd the wild blade,
And ere her own supper she cull'd them a mess,
And ere her own breakfast their hunger was staid:
Their saddles were stuff'd with the softest of hair,
Their beds were composed of the driest of fern;
And many an orphan might wish to lie there,
And there the obdurate might sympathy learn.
There are mothers to children such love never show,
As thou didst thine asses, good Mary Killcrow.

The course of her journey wound where, in the dean,
Britannia's best bulwarks in olden time grew,[469]
And ran o'er a common where often was seen
The vilest disturber her peace ever knew.
An ass unrestrain'd there a wanton life led,
And Turk was the name which the libertine bore;
He'd bray after Bess in defiance of Ned,
When woful the fray and appalling the roar;

APPENDIX III

They'd list not to reason, nor reverence show
To the tongue nor the staff of old Mary Killcrow.

If laden, Ned's burthen soon fell to the ground;
If lighten'd, Ned from her more speedily ran;
To what chance might offer poor Bess would be bound:
Whene'er the bold rivals the conflict began,
The onset was hail'd by the sound of each trump;
Teeth, tongue, heels and nostrils, alike unconfin'd,
The might of the jaws and the strength of the rump
Were rudely enforc'd, or before or behind;
Bess oft gave a leer, and oft with it would go
The sad lamentations of Mary Killcrow.

Disadvantaged was Ned, was each circumstance weigh'd,
For toil and accoutrements straighten'd each joint;
But Mary was kind, and oft sent to his aid
A stroke with her staff or a thrust with her point.
The vanquished would run and the victor would bray,
Whilst Mary from Turk stood the guardian of Bess;
And there must she stand, from the end of the fray,
Till mortal came by to relieve her distress:
No neighbour around thee thy troubles would know,
And haste not to succour thee, Mary Killcrow.

Assistance derived and disasters redress'd,
Poor Mary, departing, would brandish her goad;
But lest her disturber again should molest,
'Twas needful to chase him afar from the road.
He stopp'd with the form, which declin'd to pursue,
And kick'd at the stones which were after him flung;
And when she had dwindled away from his view,
The smart of his wounds would he balm with his tongue.
How oft after crime, when his passions are low,
Man smarts like the ass behind Mary Killcrow.

Poor Mary had journey'd divested of fear,
Had not her vile enemy come by surprize;
But nature had deaden'd the pass to her ear,
Her bonnet contracted the scope of her eyes;
The foe to evade she would often unclose
Her kerchief, when near where the mischief might lurk,
And with her old spectacles striding her nose,
Would take a long look for the dissolute Turk.

259

APPENDIX III

There are those who have felt a more dissolute foe,
Than thou and thine asses, good Mary Killcrow.

Thy heart was sincere and thy nature profuse;
Thou would'st brave the rude blast if our fuel should fail,
Nor in the storm's enmity would'st thou refuse
If want chill'd the hearth of one cot in the vale.
Round the hills which enclose it in childhood I wound,
Through the woods which adorn it when older I ranged,
On the hills in its season the primrose I found,
And sloes in the woods when the season was changed;
When winter had whiten'd the summits with snow,
I woo'd the bright coals of old Mary Killcrow.

Heaven sent for thee, Mary, whose wisdom enacts,
That flesh is but dust, and but dust it shall be;
Thine asses are moulder'd, but saddles and sacks
Will long hang in mournful remembrance of thee.
Tho' in the earth's bosom thy wasting form lies,
When angels shall sound the ascension of souls,
Tho' dark was thy calling, thy spirit shall rise
More bright than the flame which arose from thy coals.
Ye pious and good, when to Heaven ye go,
You'll see in her glory old Mary Killcrow.

Home

I've climb'd the Alpine mountains,
    I've stray'd where Jordan streams,
I've drank of cooling fountains
    In Thibet's sultry beams.
Tho' enterprize impels me
    In distant climes to roam,
Sweet fancy fondly tells me
    The seat of bliss is home.

Each thought's enwrapt in wonder
    When riding on the deep;
The scene enchants me under,
    When standing on the steep.
Some charm in art or nature
    I find where'er I roam,
But none in form or feature
    The heart endears like home.

APPENDIX III

To rivals I compare thee,
    And, priding in thy worth,
Most sweet's the love I bear thee,
    Thou Isle that gav'st me birth.
Whate'er my cares may chasten
    When far from thee I roam,
I woo the gales to hasten
    The bark that bears me home.

And sweet's the heart's emotion,
    When through the mist appears
The land within the ocean,
    The nurse of early years.
When friends await the greeting,
    The blissful moment's come,
Enraptured is the meeting,
    And sweet the welcome home.

An Address to a Violet,
Occasioned by Reading the
Following Lines in an Address to
the Same Flower

'Oh! stay awhile, till warmer showers
And brighter suns shall on thee play.'[470]

———

That thou should'st not thy charms unfold,
And shed thy sweets when winds are cold,
Some reckless mortal bids thee stay
Till milder beams shall on thee play,
To chase the cheerless blast, and warm
Thy lovely, gentle, fragrant form.

Oh! heed thee not the changeful thing;
But come the earliest pride of spring,
And when her robes thy features bear,
Fond love shall come and meet thee there.

And when in lonely glens thou'rt found,
And youth shall tread the fairy ground,
Of soft emotions thou shalt tell
With which their gentle bosoms swell,
When hope is weak, and love is young
And dreads to venture on the tongue.

APPENDIX III

A meed thou'lt be, when cull'd with care,
To some sweet, blooming, guileless fair;
And as from hand to hand thou'rt past,
The pressure soft – the eye downcast –
The crimson'd blush, and trembling frame,
Will speak of what they dare not name.

And thou shalt in her bosom lie
And move to many a gentle sigh,
And charm the thought and please the breath,
Till thou by love art nurs'd to death.

Should'st thou await a warmer hour
Thou'lt rivals meet in every bower,
Whose pompous forms will shade from view
Thy lowly simple head of blue,
And in the breeze around thee play
In flow'ry pride and colours gay,
And soon the eye allure from thee,
And win the love which thine should be.
But 'tis in specious charms they shine,
That yield no sweets in worth like thine,
But such too oft to favour rise,
Whilst worth, neglected, fades and dies.

Then let thy favour'd form appear
As erst, and when no rival's near;
And still youth's happy emblem prove,
And show the sweets of early love;
And still in glens remote and wild
Be nature's first and sweetest child.

Jane Barnaby

Jane Barnaby, my dear Jane,
   I'm wearing wan, and old.
As herds at close of eve, Jane,
   Are summon'd to the fold,
I soon to mine shall be, Jane,
   My close of life is near,
And much I need our Shepherd's care,
   Jane Barnaby, my dear.

Jane Barnaby, my dear Jane,
   I'm wearisome on earth,
Nor less in want of aid, Jane,

APPENDIX III

Than when I had my birth;
Then with a mother's love, Jane,
  I strengthen'd with the year,
But now I'm fast upon the wane,
  Jane Barnaby, my dear.

Jane Barnaby, my dear Jane,
  Death, terrorless, I see,
My only source of woe, Jane,
  Is lonely leaving thee;
But purity of life, Jane,
  Hath won thee hearts sincere,
And love will yield thee fellowship,
  Jane Barnaby, my dear.

Jane Barnaby, my dear Jane,
  Thy tenderness is sweet,
And grateful is this heart
  That soon will cease to beat.
Thou wert its earliest love, Jane,
  Thou art its solace here,
Thou'lt be its last remembrance,
  Jane Barnaby, my dear.

Jane Barnaby, my dear Jane,
  There's bliss divine in store,
And soft will be the calm, Jane,
  When troubled life is o'er;
Then in my weal rejoice, Jane,
  When I shall disappear,
Nor bathe thy pillow with thy tears,
  Jane Barnaby, my dear.

Jane Barnaby, my dear Jane,
  I go where thou shalt come,
And that shall be our last, Jane,
  Our undivided home.
The painful there shall rest, Jane,
  The weary shall have cheer,
'Tis virtue's sweet Elysium,'
  Jane Barnaby, my dear.

Jane Barnaby, my dear Jane,
  Life's flood is ebbing fast,

A few more soft'ning sighs, Jane,
  The shoals will all be past.
To bear my spirit hence, Jane,
  Death's bark is hov'ring near;
Adieu, adieu, a short adieu,
  Jane Barnaby, my dear.

Sally Roy

Thou art gentle in thy nature,
  Sally Roy, Sally Roy,
Thou art comely in each feature,
  Sally Roy, Sally Roy,
Thou art sweet, and thou'rt endearing,
Thou art kind, and thou art cheering,
E'er in loveliness appearing,
  Sally Roy, Sally Roy.

As the sun the morning brightens,
  Sally Roy, Sally Roy,
As the moon the evening lightens,
  Sally Roy, Sally Roy,
To the world a light thou'rt lending,
Worth and beauty in it blending,
Oh! thou'rt one of Heaven's sending,
  Sally Roy, Sally Roy.

For the love of thy assistance,
  Sally Roy, Sally Roy,
May'st thou beam thro' my existence,
  Sally Roy, Sally Roy.
Should the cares of life distress me,
With sweet comfort thou'lt address me,
Like an angel sent to bless me,
  Sally Roy, Sally Roy.

Should the frown of fate hang o'er me,
  Sally Roy, Sally Roy,
Should'st thou fade and die before me,
  Sally Roy, Sally Roy,
Oh! the tears of grief will blind me,
In a dark world left behind thee,
Not a ray of hope will find me,
  Sally Roy, Sally Roy.

APPENDIX III

By Love We Were Led, Jane

By love we were led, Jane,
　To woo and to wed, Jane,
To promise, in consort, life's journey to go;
　In ailment, in health, Jane,
　In want, and in wealth, Jane,
To mingle our portions of pleasure and woe.

　As onwards we steal, Jane,
　Each turn may reveal, Jane,
Some pleasing allurement to tempt us to stray;
　And envy and strife, Jane,
　Annoyants of life, Jane,
May ruffle our bosoms, and trouble our way.

　And hence 'twill be meet, Jane,
　If life shall be sweet, Jane,
With caution and love undivided to steer;
　To tread in the road, Jane,
　Where prudence hath trode, Jane,
And take at the dwelling of reason our cheer.

　To shun in the crowd, Jane,
　The pert and the proud, Jane,
The vile, and the profligate, mean, and the vain;
　To truth to adhere, Jane,
　And virtue revere, Jane,
That worth may be pleas'd to be seen in our train.

　There are some who may tire, Jane,
　And aidance require, Jane,
And many a bosom affliction may pain;
　O'er those we should bend, Jane,
　And pity extend, Jane,
The sorrowful cheer, and the needy sustain.

　We daily should call, Jane,
　On Him who rules all, Jane,
And render him thanks for the help he hath given;
　Repent, if we have stray'd, Jane,
　And sue for His aid, Jane,
To guide us thro' all the world's mazes to Heav'n.

　If thus we conform, Jane,
　In every rude storm, Jane,

A charm o'er the mind will in stillness console;
  And turning at last, Jane,
  To gaze on the past, Jane,
How sweetly the scene will give cheer to the soul.

A Fanciful Description of a Passage Down
Part of the River Wye, of a Cottage
and its Inhabitants, &c.

A Fragment

Mid scenes where nature, robed in sweet attire,
Yields charms to please, and grandeur to inspire,
Where fancy grows enraptured as she views,
The Wye her lovely winding course pursues,
Whose airy turns, quick as in sport, delight,
For every turn pours transport on the sight.

High shelving hills in daring forms surprise,
And shade o'er shade in proud progression rise,
Dividing those with gentle slopes between
Vale vale succeeding variegates the scene
Of clustered fields, which teem with waving grain;
Meandering streams fast murmuring for the main,
And lawns and herds, the passing eye admires;
And village churches crown'd with humble spires,
And peeping cots with, pliant to the breeze,
The curling smoke ascending thro' the trees;
And orchards, ranged in uniform array,
In various tints their various fruits display,
And shallows oft admitting thirsty cows,
And staring cow-boys jerking awkward bows.

Oft thro' some space a wild-heath hill is seen,
And lesser hills progressive rise between;
Those groups of herds, in fleecy concourse line,
And blooming whins in yellow spangles shine.
Round some a pass, beguileful of their steeps,
In length'ning windings to the summit creeps;
The traveller there who for his palfry feels,
Dismounting, trails him patient at his heels,
And onward climbs, with palpitating breast,
Whilst fancy dwells on some lov'd spot to rest.

APPENDIX III

There he is seen, where sweet expansions show
Enchantment spread in nature's lap below.

Of various mansions which those scenes disclose,
Some display industry, and some repose,
The drying net at some low dwelling tells
Where, of the finny race, a scourger dwells;
The farmers shine with neat thatch'd stacks of corn,
Some ancient piles, two sober yews adorn.
Some smile with shrubs, and woven wood-bine bowers,
Where oft the fair are seen midst beds of flowers,
Some humble domes – for show, nor power, nor place,
Display a useful cultivated space.

Thro' lovely changes thus the eyes are led
To where old Tintern rears its ancient head,
Whose lingering beauties time still leaves behind,
To awe with grandeur and instruct mankind;
In ivy's arms the proud reserve is held,
Whose strong attachment time hath not repell'd.
And still, with zeal the like ne'er man inspired,
'Tis sought in ruin, and in age admired.
Leaving those gems of ancient art behind,
Nature awaits to chase them from the mind,
With all her powers arranged on either shore,
In all the charms of her romantic store.

Stupendous hills the current's course divide,
With trees o'erspread, and branching out in pride,
More bold and grand, some prominently reign,
The sovereigns, and the nobles, in their train,
Some rock breaks forth, and on each winding beams,
As left and right by turns the current streams.
Each side, as each now in arrangement swell,
In soft luxuriance slopes into a dell,
Till winding where, between the opening glades,
The lawns of Piercefield teem with lovely shades;
High on the brow is seen each verdant gleam,
Thence, waving foliage, skirting to the stream,
From trees in seeming strife, all up the steep,
To view their charms reflected in the deep.

Athwart the stream, worn bare by winter storms,
Here cliffs arise in more gigantic forms;

APPENDIX III

Those tufts of trees in various shades surround,
And minor rocks in many forms abound;
Some from their beds in rugged shape emerge,
And some with foliage crowding on the verge;
Round others torn with elemental strife
Some old trees' roots are creeping after life,
Which still they find, tho' mortal marvels how,
And shed a few gay branches o'er the brow.

The eye to ease, and give the ear its spells,
Sweet Echo here with various handmaids dwells;
Arranged are those for intercourse of sound,
Within communing distances around;
Weary nor listless, ready as they rise,
No sound conveyed her unresounded dies,
But quick, the like, her matchless art returns,
The passing theme the next progressive learns,
So on to each the airy charm is tost,
Until escaping, 'tis in silence lost.

As misers love where vast returns abound,
Here rustics come for interest of sound;
Fond swains are prone to hail their idols whence
The name endeared reverberates on the sense.
Here truant school-boys, ling'ring by the hour,
Sustain reproof, to raise the mimic power;
In sportive mood, respondence to invoke
The sober woodman magnifies his stroke;
The milk-maid's song, the lowing of her cow,
The herdsman's halloo, loit'ring on the brow,
The neighing colts, which o'er their fences peep,
The bleating flocks that browse along the steep,
The sheep-dog's bark, restrictive of their bounds,
The huntsman's horn, the concert of the hounds,
The ploughman's shout when reynard breaks in view,
The cracking whips of numbers who pursue,
The crash of fences steeds unmanaged cause,
The bursting laugh each luckless rider draws,
The farmer's ire, whom beasts nor burthens spare,
Affrighted rooks tumultuous in the air,
Are heard and echo'd and re-echo'd here,
Till sweet confusion crowds upon the ear.

There lies between where those high rocks extend,
And whence below expanding groves ascend,
An open space of sweet enchanting ground,

268

APPENDIX III

Lovely itself, and charm'd by all around,
Where nature strews beneath the wand'rer's feet
Luxuriant verdure and wild flowers sweet;
Where cluster'd shrubs in wild divisions spread,
Sweet in the breeze their fragrant essence shed;
And trees dispers'd, whose form their nature show,
Less prone to rise than branch in peace below:
So distant those, they seem, to fancy's eye,
To shun the spot that rears a fellow nigh;
Or, loathing crowds, had from the woods retir'd,
Or, proud of bulk, came forth to be admired.
A winding walk through this enchantment steals,
Where the deep dell a chaste abode reveals.
A shelving hill, of rock and heath, behind,
Conceals the dome and shields it from the wind;
A space before a holly hedge defends,
A tinkling gate communication lends,
Which past, the eye's enraptured with a view
Of fragrant flowers, adorn'd in every hue,
In mounds arranged with taste and neatly drest,
Which verdant bounds of well-shorn box invest;
Round these you're led by paths of golden dye
To where the low-built mansion meets the eye;
A neat thatch'd roof o'erspreads its whiten'd walls,
A vine's fond tendrils round its bosom crawls;
For light and air on either side is seen
A vitreous bow, which wears a face of green;
Distanced alike, a door the two divides,
With tutor'd woodbines climbing up its sides;
Uniting o'er, a flowery arch is made,
Which odour yields to all who seek its shade.
Its state internal no neglect betrays;
In modest neatness, taste the whole displays;
No want it feels, no luxury it shares,
Objects for use, but none for show it wears,
Save a few emblems on the mantel's height,
And a few landscapes which engage the sight,
And those, embellish'd with no common powers,
The sweet beguilings of an inmate's hours,
Who traced with fervor, or with fondness rear'd
Some child of fancy, or some scene endear'd.

The sober matron of the household store
The serious weight of threescore winters bore,
But, prone to action and by temperance fed,

269

APPENDIX III

Health's roseate bloom still o'er her features spread.
Cast on, in youth, that intermediate state
That lies between the lowly and the great,
To pass enabled life on either side,
As fate or chance her destiny might guide;
Assiduous bent, and flexible to bow,
Should fortune fall and mix her with the low;
Of sense possess'd, accomplishments and ease
That would, in scenes more elevated, please;
And, – what defects proud prejudice might find,
Bright gems enrich'd of every moral kind.

Full sixteen springs to this delightful glade
Her tuneful tribute Philomel had paid,
Since here she came in solitude to dwell,
But who, none knew, and none from whence could tell.
The curious sifted, others showed surprize,
And rumour spread what falsehood could surmise;
But truth and virtue from her dwelling stole,
And shed some ray still fatal to the whole;
Each baneful drop some beam of merit dried,
Conjecture sunk, and defamation died.

Mov'd in her train, and much her care engross'd,
A child, whose years four summers' suns had cross'd,
Whose opening gems, and charms of mental kind,
Which pleas'd the eye, and charm'd to love the mind,
Led fancy forward fondly to presume,
When one should ripen and the other bloom,
Of nature's gifts she would a store unfold,
Sweet to the sense and lovely to behold.

Attention watch'd, as comprehension grew,
And spread fresh stores of knowledge to her view,
And taught her fancy that its useful powers
Would soften nature and delight the hours,
And lead the mind by its enlightening beams
To that pure fount whence flow life's hopeful streams.

With life's best fruits was thus her reason charged,
Her mind delighted and her sense enlarged;
Truth o'er the treasure ruled with conscious sway,
And virtue awed each passion that would stray;
Mild temperance taught her where her confines went,

APPENDIX III

Nor farther prudence e'er her wishes sent.
Chaste her ideas, dignified her mind,
With love, she felt compassion for mankind;
Serene in sorrow and in pleasure mild,
And prone to solace every suffering child;
She gave to friendship sympathy in grief,
A tear to pity, and to want relief;
With mercy, error had instruction given,
Which show'd the way repentance went to Heaven;
And was, though bless'd with moral gifts so rare,
In every movement graceful, sweet, and fair.

The name of Gertrude bore the elder dame,
Who call'd Ianthe, and the younger came.
But by what power her rule the fair obey'd,
Was yet a secret time had not betray'd:
None, save her ruler, knew the mystic clue,
And ceaseless caution guarded all she knew.

Quick at each call, in meek obedience ran
A sober, simple, civil, serving man,
Mild in his nature, but his will was strong;
His heart well-meaning but his judgment wrong;
His bosom guileless and his aim direct,
No arts he practised and would none suspect;
By objects lured of every specious kind,
He sped, nor caution e'er his way defined,
When shown the charm, with heedless haste he'd run,
And oft became the dupe of fraud or fun.

If small his wisdom, Nature's gifts were large,
And many callings would his thrift discharge:
The fruitful garden own'd his skilful powers,
His care the herbage and his taste the flowers;
The hedge he trimm'd, the neat box borders shore,
And made the lawn the nice green coat it wore;
He put the walk's fine mellow surface on,
The knives he polish'd and the shoes he shone;
The beer he brew'd, the cows he milk'd and fed,
And in its chaise a patient donkey led;
And wound each mistress round the summits nigh,
Or launch'd the boat and trailed them on the Wye;
And woo'd the maid, it may be meet to tell,
And Job his name, and her's was Dollabelle.

APPENDIX III

Thus, from the shouts mirth's wanton votaries raise,
Gay pleasure's lurements and mad folly's praise,
Here, pure in soul, sweet scenes in peace they trod,
And shunn'd a troubled for a calm abode,
And rural bliss in all its charms enjoy'd,
By cares unwearied, nor by crimes annoy'd;
And with the needy shar'd the comforts given,
And show'd the wealthy a sure way to Heaven.

So have I seen, where potent springs abound,
The water play in foaming eddies round,
But shun the tumult as its whirls subside,
And peaceful down its smooth-worn channel glide,
Where long its pure unsullied course it held,
By storm nor ruffled, nor by flood impell'd,
And gave to Nature solace as it went,
And to the world a placid mirror lent.

*   *   *   *   *

Written in Alnwick Castle, November, 1823

Oh! splendid old Alnwick, how glorious to trace
    In the lines which thy records contain,
The daring exploits which ennobled the race
    Of the Lords of thy ancient domain.
In the old feudal times, when the foe dared thy might,
    And thy vassals were zealous and brave,
Thy valorous chiefs, ever first in the fight,
    Or courted renown or a grave.

And many and bold were the bands that assail'd
    The peace of thy sumptuous halls;
And daring intruders, more distant, prevail'd,
    Which called for redress from thy walls;
But the rude hand of time hath now swept them away,
    And levell'd their domes to his will;
Whilst thou art seen tow'ring more proudly to day,
    And a Percy the lord of thee still.[471]

But the mild rays of reason which beam on the earth,
    Have left those dark customs behind,
And man, who ferocity learnt from his birth,
    Is become in his nature refined;
Good fellowship reigns, and benevolence sheds
    Her solace in every degree,

APPENDIX III

And bright is the stream, and benignly it spreads,
　Of her fount which arises in thee.

The loud northern blast o'er thy turrets may blow,
　When winter thy portals invests,
Such excellence dwells in thy bosom below,
　Such welcome and cheer for thy guests,
That the season's unfelt, whilst the needy around,
　O'er whom thy indulgence prevails,
In the strains of eulogium mingle their sound,
　And send forth thy praise on the gales.

By the pillars of time may thy head be upheld,
　And ages yet pride in thy name,
As the emblems are traced of thy sons who excell'd
　In the proud emulations of fame.
May the currents of wealth which now flow in thy way,
　Ne'er cease in their ardour to run;
Nor the name, nor the race of thy chieftain decay,
　'Till the last thread of time shall be spun.

The World's Like a Tyrant, &c.

The world's like a tyrant and ruthless to me,
No solace it yields, and none beaming I see,
Tho' rugged my way, and I'm laden with care,
No rest can I find with the burthen I bear.

I have borne it till weary; yet time, as I go,
Progressively adds to my measure of woe;
Oh! would it were full, and more heavily prest,
And that to earth's bosom it sunk me to rest.

That my sleep will be sweet in the cradle of death,
And my spirit rejoice in the stillness of breath,
Is a comfort, by hope, thus in whisperings given,
'There! there! thou shalt rest,' and it pointeth to Heaven.

Laver's Banks[472]

To woo the morning air
　On Laver's banks I stray'd,
And who should wander there
　But a lovely lonely maid.
Who stood and on the streamlet gazed,

APPENDIX III

Till tears fell from her eye.
And mingled with the waters clear
   That slowly murmured by.

To learn her source of woe
   I asked in accents mild,
And if I could not comfort
   Afford to sorrow's child?
She said she wept for forms most dear,
   For ever from her gone,
And whom from early childhood
   She had lov'd to look upon.

Affection's tender eye
   A mother sought in vain,
They had laid her in the grave
   Where her father long had lain.
It touch'd the secret chord of love,
   And woke the heart to mourn,
When thinking, like the passing stream,
   They never would return.

I said, thou lovely maiden,
   Thy tears of sorrow stay;
The source still feeds the stream
   As the waters pass away;
And from the heavenly fount of life
   The current still flows on,
Affording blessings on its way
   For those for ever gone.

With those who sleep in death
   Be all thy cares resign'd,
And turn on life a cheerful eye,
   And thou shalt comfort find.
Oh! would'st thou crown a wish but now
   Become my bosom's guest,
I'd make thee mine and love thee dear,
   And lull thy cares to rest.

As leaves in autumn die
   Unsuccour'd on the spray,
Her woes uncherish'd in the mind

APPENDIX III

Stole silently away.
And soon her tender heart grew charm'd
    In love's soft glowing beam,
And now we bless the happy morn
    We met by Laver's stream.

My Mary Is No More!

The airy choir the morning greets
    With harmony divine,
The verdant spring with flow'ry sweets
    Strews every path but mine.
My hopeful scenes of life are past,
    My dreams of bliss are o'er,
My love's sweet rose its bloom hath cast,
    My Mary is no more!

Her voice surpass'd in tuneful powers
    The sweetest birds that sing,
Her charms excell'd the fairest flowers
    That scent the breath of spring;
A soul more pure, a heart more kind,
    So fair a form ne'er bore,
And oh! what rays illumed her mind!
    But Mary is no more!

This blooming flower, so sweet and fair,
    On me its fragrance shed,
I gave it all my love and care,
    And hope my wishes fed;
But e'er I cull'd the lovely gem
    The spoiler stept before,
And pluck'd it rudely from its stem,
    And Mary is no more!

Celestial maid! she's call'd to share
    The sweetest joys of heaven;
Her form was deem'd a bliss too rare
    To mortal to be given.
Yet fancy still pourtrays her near,
    And views her o'er and o'er,
Whilst beaming in each eye, a tear
    Says, Mary is no more!

APPENDIX III

Reflections
on Visiting a Spring at Different Seasons of the Year

'Twas early in summer, and mild was the ray
Which beam'd from the sun on the waning of day;
And the air was serene, and the leaves on the trees
Were hardly emotion'd, so soft was the breeze;
The birds were in song in the wood on the hill,
And softly a murmur arose from the rill
Which ran thro' the mead, where its channel was seen,
By herbage more rude, and more tufted and green;
The teams, clinking home, had the fallow resign'd,
And whistling the ploughmen their cares to the wind,
When, pensive and slow, up the hamlet I bent,
And meeting the stream on its margin I went;
I stray'd to the spot whence it sprang from the earth,
Most pure in its nature and silent its birth;
It ran from a mound with green moss o'erspread,
Its birth-place was shaded by shrubs at its head;
'Twas onward impell'd by its kindred more strong,
And driven from home it went murmuring along.

In indolent ease on the bank I reclin'd,
And gazed on the stream, till awoke in my mind
A thought of the joys in its windings 'twould yield,
To the birds of the air and the beasts of the field,
To the web-footed tribe on its surface that ride,
And the bright-speckled trout in its bosom that glide,
To the poor thirsty beggar who drinks in his palms,
And softens the crusts he obtains for his alms;
To the thrifty old dame who, with low-bowing head,
Shall search it for cresses, to barter for bread;
To the youth who, in groups, on its borders shall play,
And launch their frail barks to be wreck'd in a day;
To the low in their need, and the high in their pride,
Who tenant the domes which are rear'd by its side,
And I mentally said, as in beauty it ran,
'Flow on thou bright stream, thou'rt a blessing to man.'

A hill rose before, which a clump of beech crown'd,
Beguiling its steeps, to its summit I wound,
And saw the smoke rise thro' the trees on the plain,
From a mansion which stood in a stately domain,
And my mind running in a contemplative stream,
The worthy possessor it took for its theme.

APPENDIX III

By wisdom admir'd, and by virtue belov'd,
In the sphere of the great, like a magnet, he mov'd;
His honour was firm, and his friendship esteem'd,
Its warmth rose a charm where its influence beam'd;
With nature serene, and with manners refin'd,
He heighten'd the glory and joy of mankind.

A stream of benevolence flow'd from his soul,
And o'er its endowments had pity control,
For succour, in need, from his hand to have dealt,
No roof was too low, if there honesty dwelt;
And thus to the dwellings of want he was led,
And the naked he cloth'd, and the hungry he fed,
Instructed the young, and supported the old,
In summer thro' heat, and in winter thro' cold.

The midways of life, with a laudable zeal
He trode, and was hail'd a promoter of weal;
And many a soul would, in gratitude, tell,
In an intricate case he had counsell'd him well.
And o'er the expanse, as my vision I spread,
I thought of the joys which his bounty had shed,
And I said, tho' on earth few thy equals may be,
To the spring at the mound, there's a likeness in thee.

The summer was gone, and the autumn was past,
And winter's stern mandates were borne on the blast,
So ruthless it reign'd in its scourge of distress,
The sun lost its strength, and sweet nature her dress.
The birds in sad silence their grievances bore,
The red-breast alone sang for crumbs at my door;
All barren the plains, and the herds, by the cold,
Were chas'd from the pastures, and fed in the fold.
I listen'd, but heard not a sound from the stream,
My eye on the fallow discern'd not a team;
The ploughman's shrill notes, too, had ceas'd to be rife,
His hands begg'd his breath at the threshold of life.
To the streamlet, when wrapt in my mantle, I sped,
But its motion was still'd, and its visitants fled;
No float on its surface was gliding its way,
No object was seen on its bosom to play,
No draught it afforded, no charm it display'd,
Its beauty was lost when its bounty was staid;
Those souls, in whose need, 'twas not wont to deny,

APPENDIX III

Now wound from earth's bosom, by toil, a supply;
And yet, by its source, 'twas in amplitude fed,
But, chill'd at its birth, it lay useless and dead;
And I thought of the tribe, that its state would deplore,
And I said, what a change since I saw thee before.
The hill I surmounted, 'twas bleak on the brow,
And dreary the view it afforded me now,
Their late golden plumes, from the trees had been torn,
Nor a hawberry left for a bird on a thorn;
The dome, on the plain, I was wont to admire,
Now show'd by its smoke a reduction of fire,
For death, like the season, a change had wrought there,
Man's comforter gone, and a miser his heir –
So deep in whose nature was avarice grown,
Tho' large his possessions, no bounty was shown.
Distress o'er the hamlet soon mournfully spread,
The poor unemployed, and their children unfed;
The sick on their pallets in wretchedness pined,
Their solace was gone, and its sources confined;
The dome was in sorrow's dark heraldry drest,
Its cheer was expended, and mirth was suppress'd;
The stalls were all vacant, the timber had bow'd,
No herds rang'd the meadows, the pastures were plough'd;
The old neighing favourites that stray'd o'er the ground,
Were led to the kennels, and slain for the hounds.
The cellars were emptied, the servants discharged,
Expenditure lessen'd, and income enlarged,
And I said, in thy soul there's a semblance reveal'd,
To the spring at the mound now 'tis cold and congeal'd.
To the cold cell of death soon the miser was borne,
And great was his grief from his hoards to be torn:
'Twas thought he would pass from his objects of love
Unregretted below, and unwelcom'd above.
Howe'er his disposal, his God may arrange,
The mortals were few who rejoic'd at the change;
For the currents of wealth which he damm'd, in his haste,
A prodigal turn'd into riot and waste;
Down courses voluptuous it stream'd to the brink,
And dry was each space where the thirsty would drink;
For sensual pleasures 'twas destined to flow,
Lured virtue from peace, and then sank her in woe.

And when a strong winter was loosing its hold,
To see what the scene might to fancy unfold,
I thought, to the spring as I wandered once more,

APPENDIX III

A resemblance it now to the prodigal bore.
As the air lost its sting, and the water its chains,
In wanton confusion it ran o'er the plains;
As the mass at its head was expent by the sun,
Its virtues were lost in the courses it run;
Its heart yet unsoften'd, a passage denied
To all whom its bounty once amply supplied;
Down easy descents it was sportively led,
And o'er surfaces fair devastation it spread.
Yet time, I thought, soon would its wand'rings arrest,
And objects again with its uses be blest;
But the wasture of wealth, the world long might lament,
For reckless is Man till his substance be spent.

Mary St. Clair

How my heart yearns for thee, Mary St. Clair,
Fondly it turns to thee, Mary St. Clair;
   Tho' pangs of hopeless care,
   Thou doom'st my breast to bear,
Still thou art cherish'd there, Mary St. Clair!

Till my heart cease to glow, Mary St. Clair,
Till my blood cease to flow, Mary St. Clair,
   Thy lovely form shall be
   Dearest on earth to me,
Tho' no kind word from thee soothes my despair.

Should I despairing die, Mary St. Clair,
Life, love, without thee, I never can bear;
   Follow my mournful bier,
   Let fall a grateful tear
O'er him who lov'd thee dear Mary St. Clair!

Orran and Bertha

'Come, Bertha, the Spring is its influence shedding,
O'er hill and o'er dale the gay verdure is spreading,
The leaves clothe the branches, the birds are all wedding,
   The world looks around us both lovely and rare;
Since bountiful Nature's such beauties exposing,
Let's stray o'er the hills ere the day shall be closing;
The dews will be falling, the birds will be dozing,
   Come! haste, my love, haste!' said the youth to the fair.

APPENDIX III

Her nature inclin'd to her lover's inviting,
The beauties of Spring to her heart were delighting,
Love's purest emotions her thoughts were exciting
    To scenes most congenial, its pleasures to share.
With Nature and Love every sentiment warming,
With smiles sweet and tender, in dress most adorning,
She look'd like the Spring in the freshness of morning,
    When Orran in his link'd the arm of his fair.

The scenes which the Winter had robb'd of their treasure
Were shunn'd, like to man under Fortune's displeasure,
But in their new vestments were greeted with pleasure
    By every tun'd bird which enlivens the air;
Their clothing was sweet and the music transporting,
The flowers on the breeze were their fragrance exporting,
The doves were heard cooing – the lambs were seen sporting,
    All yielding delight to the youth and his fair.

Here, through a green tuft, the pale primrose was peeping;
There, round a wild shrub, the sweet woodbine was creeping;
Each scene, in advance, had some joy in its keeping
    Congenial to love and beguileful of care;
Thus, charm'd in their progress, still charm'd they proceeded;
Now Nature, now Love, in engaging succeeded,
No thought was left vacant for Time, who, unheeded,
    Stole by, and was closing day's scene on the pair.

They stray'd o'er the hills every feature admiring,
Till day, for the loss of the sun, was expiring;
The clouds look'd as tho' they were something conspiring
    To check in their glory the fond loving pair.
The birds in succession their harmony slighted,
Till nature grew dim and no longer delighted,
'A wild storm's approaching, we shall be benighted,
    Come, haste, my love, haste,' said the youth to the fair.

Their steps they retraced with what speed they could master;
The storm was revengeful, and hurried on faster,
Soon darkness o'erspread them, oh! luckless disaster,
    What troubles some mortals are destin'd to bear!
The hollow blast blew, and the rain began streaming,
And foam'd down the hills whilst the lightning was beaming,
The thunder roll'd loud, and the fair one was screaming,
    'Take comfort, my love!' said the youth to the fair.

APPENDIX III

'Oh! where is there comfort? alas! do but say, love
Nor comfort nor hope will be found but with day, love,
Shall not we be wandering the long night astray, love?
    Oh! tell me, my Orran, and ease my despair.'
'Hush! no, my love, no, all our cares are dispelling,
I now hear the stream that flows near to thy dwelling,
From each growing source 'twill with anger be swelling,
    Come, haste, that in safety we pass it, my fair.'

But through the dark night they were long in exploring
Their way to the stream, which was traced by its roaring,
When, wild, down the hills the rough torrents came pouring;
    'Twas swell'd – that to pass it few mortals would dare.
'Oh! stay, my lov'd Bertha, oh! stay, e'er you venture,
I'll ford the rude waters; perchance in the centre
Too deep 'twill be found for love's treasure to enter;
    Oh! stay, my love, stay,' said the youth to the fair.

He plunged in the stream with a fond lover's pleasure,
He stemm'd the rough torrent its deep bed to measure,
No space was propitious to bear o'er his treasure,
    His strength was exhausting, his heart worn with care;
He still persever'd, still love's ardour expos'd him,
Rude objects, borne down with the current, oppos'd him;
He struggled, 'twas vain, the deep waters enclos'd him,
    And down with the flood he was forced from his fair.

She heard the last effort with which he contended,
She heard the last cry which his bosom expended,
She lists yet again, – but the conflict was ended,
    No effort, no voice, and no Orran was there.
Bereft and forlorn, with such woes to confound her,
The loud clashing elements beating around her,
The day dawned, when frantic the villagers found her,
    Crying 'Orran, why stay you so long from your fair?'

When loud beats the storm, to her woes it awakes her,
And o'er them she'll ponder till reason forsakes her,
And, carelessly robed, from her home will betake her,
    And lonely and sad to the waters repair:
And gaze on the stream, and bewail her adorer,
And fondly beseech it her love to restore her,
And say to each object that fleeteth before her,
    'Oh! tell him to haste with love's speed to his fair.'

281

APPENDIX III

The Children's Dirge
at the Interment of a Gold Fish

Little fish, whose lovely dye
Nature gave to charm the eye,
Magnified in water clear,
Gliding in thy glassy sphere
To and fro, in gold attir'd,
Proud and pleased to be admired;
We have seen thee in thy day,
Beaming bright and frisking gay,
Deeming not that death so true
Soon might come and change thy hue,
And that eyes which felt delight
Soon would wish thee out of sight;
But 'tis done, and life's no more,
All thy pride and glitter's o'er;
All thy charms have felt decay,
Admiration steals away.
Thou'st but play'd a pageant part,
Won the eyes without the heart;
What alone the eyes revere,
Goes like thee without a tear.

Little fish, thy life was spent
Not as life for us is meant;
We, however fair, must be
More adorn'd internally;
Not applause to wish to gain
By a course so light and vain;
Not by specious means excite
Love that vanishes with sight;
Not to trifle time away;
We have mental dues to pay.
We must store within the mind
All that sense and worth can find;
Twill create affection strong,
Rooting deep and lasting long;
Twill adorn us when in breath,
'Twill exalt us after death.

Here thy long night's bed is made,
Deep beneath the verdant blade;
Thou therein must lie and rot,

APPENDIX III

Turn to earth and be forgot;
But in this, thou simple thing,
Honour treats thee like a king.
Get thee in and hide from view,
Little golden fish, adieu!

*An Excuse to
a Young Lady,
For Not Writing Some Verses
on Her Birth-Day*

You ask on the day
  Of your birth for a lay,
And like other themes of the kind,
  It must run in a strain
  (For young ladies are vain)
Of praise, both of person and mind.

But I'll wait, if you please,
  For my own love of ease,
Your merits as well to requite;
  They'll be better pourtray'd
  When, by time and your aid,
They are brought more conspicuous to life.

*Written for
a Young Lady
to Present to Her Parents
on the First Day of the Year 1825*

The morn's awoke that one year more
Gives Time to number with his score,
And adds, for youth that would aspire,
A step to climb a little higher;
But bears, alas! with less of will,
On burthen'd age more heavy still.

Though mild hath been, in rule the past,
It oft to ire provoked the blast,
And rous'd old Ocean into strife,
Who prodigal hath been of life;
And in its lingering latest hours
Man bent, contracted by its powers;
The air it arm'd, congeal'd the plains,

283

APPENDIX III

And nature left embound in chains.
When not an odour scents the breeze,
When only ice-drops pearl the trees,
And not a bird is heard to sing,
And not an insect on the wing,
And not to run is heard a rill;
In bondage earth, and labour still;
When hoary meads no verdure yield,
And famish'd flocks forsake the field,
And nature in her wide controul
Hath not a charm to soothe the soul; –
When in the dearth of joys to please,
You slumber in domestic ease,
Oh! have an hour of gloom beguil'd,
And hear the wish that moves your child.

Oh! may the stranger, newly told,
To you congenial scenes unfold;
And may no season, in its reign,
A rugged, evil hour contain,
But all be calm and all be kind,
To please the eye and soothe the mind;
The spring, refreshing, soft, and rare,
The summer blooming, sweet, and fair,
And autumn, in its bounty great,
And winter in its mildest state,
And may, in neither, ruthless storms
Defeat the hopes which reason forms.
May I, in mental powers, disclose
In every change, such worth as those;
Enticed along to sense and thought,
With care, and fond affection, taught;
May I fair buds of promise show,
And shed endearments as I go;
And may the blossoms of the mind
Diffuse the fragrance of its kind,
Until, matured by time, it bears
The fruits that bless a parent's cares.

Lines on
Parting from Miss H.[473]
When Two Years Old

Thou lovely, sweet engaging dear!
Thy artless prattling tongue to hear,

APPENDIX III

Thy ways to trace, thy smiles to view,
Thy dimpled cheeks of rosy hue,
Make every heart enraptur'd move
With admiration, and with love.

Can I, who've borne thee in my arms
So oft, – thou dawning bud of charms!
Can I each tender thought repel,
And take a listless, cold farewell?
No, no, sweet child! from thee to part,
Creates emotions in my heart,
Which ne'er will be by aught repress'd,
Till time one thought shall lull to rest;
A thought that this fond look may be
The last I e'er may have of thee.

Where'er my wandering steps may stray,
Howe'er my thoughts may fade away,
Most dear will one for thee remain,
Till I nor stray nor think again.

May thine and every mortal's friend
His care to thee, and love, extend,
And shield thee thro' this vale of life,
In every scene of woe and strife!

But if, for thy eternal weal,
Tis meet thou should'st of sorrow feel,
To calm desire, or change the will,
To call some wandering thoughts from ill,
To train them in the track allow'd,
To curb the vain and bend the proud;
May but to thee enough be given
To show how sweet's the path to Heaven!

Thou Tell'st Me, My Love, &c.

Thou tell'st me, my love with thy bloom will be fleeting,
Or cool, like the eve, when the sun wears away;
But in thy fair bosom such virtues are meeting,
As love will ensure when thy beauties decay.
Then grieve not, if time throws a shade o'er each feature;
No loss of thy charms shall my favour controul,
Nor toil to secure them, but leave them to nature,
I love thee for those far more dear to the soul.

285

APPENDIX III

The Ivy so green, yon old structure entwining,
Withstands the rude shock of each tempest that blows,
And seems to its object more proudly inclining,
As, year after year, fast to ruin it goes;
And so on in years will I solace and bless thee,
Tho' time may be ruthless and prey on thy charms;
As Ivy – the ruin, I'll fondly caress thee,
Until the last relic shall fall from my arms.

But ere from the branches the pile may be shaken,
Some hand to the root may a weapon apply,
And from its attraction averse to be taken,
'Twill cling on its bosom repining, and die.
And thus, if by Fate, life's career to be ending,
A bow should be bent, and the shaft should be mine,
Reluctant to leave thee, my fond arms extending
More firmly around thee, I'd wither on thine.

Louisa to Julia,[474]
with a Bunch of Flowers, on
Her Birth-Day in November

Tho' dreary the season, and gloomy the hour,
The day hath a charm, and revered it shall be,
One thought it awakens, most sweet in its power,
It gave, in its kindness, a sister to me.

Then Julia, this bouquet accept on the day,
And give me a smile of regard in exchange;
In us, as in Winter, these show not decay,
The sweets of affection no season shall change.

To Maria[475]
on Her Birthday

The pensive soul, with joys imprest,
Will trace the source from which they flow;
The grateful heart will know no rest,
Till it its fond emotions show;
Man's mind – research, his fear and love
Are led by this to realms above.

Whate'er in nature charms his eyes,
Whate'er mild form his heart holds dear,
His health, the bliss his friend supplies,

APPENDIX III

His night's repose, his daily cheer, –
Howe'er, on earth, to him they're given,
They flow from the pure fount of Heaven.

Yon tree, now waving in the wind,
Comes yearly bending with its fruit,
Shall it awake remembrance kind,
And not the power which gave it root?
Love wanting thought's too weak to rise,
Reflection bears it to the skies.

Now in the soft'nings of my care,
I feel, my friend, I'm largely bless'd,
By those sweet fruits of virtues rare
By Heaven implanted in thy breast;
Their bed my tenderest care shall be,
And He my praise who made it thee.

Yes! thou shalt be, beneath mine eye,
With friendship's mildest nurture fed,
And no vile weed shall come thee nigh,
And no rude foot shall on thee tread,
Nor in each season's keenest hour
Shall e'er my will repress my power.

May He, who with those fruits and flowers
Thy mind enrich'd, and graced thy form,
Refresh thee with congenial showers,
And shield thee from each ruthless storm!
That long each rising fair may find
A form by which to shape her mind.

To a Friend of Early Life, on Her Birthday

Does not the man of soul sincere,
Who holds his country's welfare dear,
Rejoice when noble deeds are done,
And battles fought, and victories won,
When Justice makes Oppression yield,
And Honour triumphs in the field?

Does not within his bosom bound
His heart, when time, revolving round,

APPENDIX III

A day unfolds, on which the Sun
Of Glory o'er his country shone,
And when his sires, with dauntless zeal,
Preferr'd to life, its fame and weal?

And such a soul shall comprehend
As sweet sensations for a friend,
Who, in domestic life, is great
As any pillar to the state;
Who treads the mazy scenes of youth
With honour, chastity, and truth;

Whose gentle heart's by nature kind,
Whose moral precepts charm the mind,
Who shuns the baneful haunts of strife,
And woos the tranquil scenes of life,
In whose whole course a charm's unfurl'd,
Which binds our natures to the world.

Now passing on from youth to age,
Where cares oppress in every stage,
Where lurking ills poor life annoy,
And aim a shaft at every joy;
Mild, from thy way, those virtues beam,
Illume my paths, and wake my theme;
Nor could I, conscious of thy worth,
Deny the day which gave thee birth,
To let my muse my thoughts rehearse,
In humble, but in grateful verse.

We, from the strange promiscuous throng,
Which crowd life's devious course along,
Were by our guide design'd to steer
Our way awhile, unsever'd here;
And many a rugged day, and rude,
When ills would frown, and cares obtrude,
We social aid each other lent,
To chase the gloom of discontent.

May long, my friend, our progress be
Through scenes remote from enmity;
But ne'er, to man, will fate disclose,
Or how it lies, or where it goes;
But tho' bedimm'd we thus advance,

APPENDIX III

Thro' turnings various, left to chance,
We still may trace where prudence sped,
And on with hope and cheerful tread;
Nor go shall prudence, cautious fair,
Through scenes that know no troubles there,
But those, my friend, tho' keenly felt,
Are Heaven's decrees, and kindly dealt.

Or if, from hence, our progress leads
Through dreary ways or flow'ry meads,
Or vales of bliss, or hills of care,
Or barren heaths of shelter bare,
How soon we each our road may change,
For fate will worldly schemes derange,
Our journey long, or period near,
He only knows who sent us here.

And He, alone, possesses power,
To shorten or prolong the hour;
He kens where tends man's restless will,
Unerring Judge of good and ill;
O'er weal and woe, control He wields,
And to the soul its portion deals;
Then should not man due reverence show
To Him, from whom his blessings flow,
By yielding thanks for those in store,
And humbly hoping still for more.

When, mingling on in life's advance,
Thou'lt meet at some strange turn of chance,
A soul of whom fate may approve
To lead thee down the paths of love,
Win sweet consent, become allied,
And bear thee hence a hopeful bride:
Whate'er new paths thy feet shall press,
Whate'er new friends thy form shall bless,
Whate'er new charms to thee reveal,
Oft o'er the past thy thoughts will steal;
And as on youthful scenes they dwell,
Of souls endear'd will memory tell,
When thus thy pensive mind shall stray,
And at this period pause and say,
In calms, in storms, in suns, and showers,
Here friendship cheer'd the passing hours.

APPENDIX III

Lines Written for Miss L. S. Bruere[476]
to Present to her Mother[477] *on her Birthday*

Yon orb, my Mamma, the luminary of earth,
Beams bright on the morn of the day of my birth,
And fondly I come, ere it fades to the view,
To tender my heart's young emotions to you;
Emotions, Mamma, which instinctively rise,
With each thought of the form that gave light to mine eyes.

I bring, my Mamma, for affection and care,
As much as a bosom so tender can bear;
And am rearing a hope, that, as reason appears,
My love and my duty will strengthen with years;
And am nursing a thought, that, with you for my guide,
To solace your love, I may merit your pride.

To render, Mamma, as life's summit I gain,
Each step, as I rise, uncreative of pain, –
I'll aim, in advancing, with diligence kind,
To shape by your precepts the frame of my mind;
And its form will be pure, and its nature be mild,
Should your image, Mamma, be discern'd in your child.

Lines
Addressed to the
Misses L. and T.[478] *Sadlier Bruere.*
on the First Day of the Year 1824

Time's last son on record, the year that is dead,
Which left you in charge of the one in its stead,
In safety hath borne you, on land and by sea,
In sickness and sorrow, and left you in glee:
And may its successor, as well as the past,
In safety enshroud you in every rude blast!
For in worth, and in charms, ye are early and rife,
Two sweet little flowers in the garden of life,
As fresh as the rose, and as fair as the day,
And as mild and as sweet as the mornings in May.
Tho' tender in stalk, ye are lovely in hue,
Few flowers in the gardens more hopeful to view,
And long may ye bloom, and give joy to the eye,
Refresh'd by the dews which are shed from on high;
And still may the sense by your fragrance be charm'd,
As still by the rays of affection you're warm'd;

290

Expanding in thought, as you're cultur'd with care,
Till time shall have form'd you as perfect as fair!
May venomous weeds ne'er anigh you be found,
To poison your sweets, or unhallow the ground.
But still in the garden, two favourites, stay,
Till leaf after leaf of your bloom falls away;
And hence when remov'd, for the loss they sustain,
They who mourn you be bless'd with a hope of your gain,
A hope that, tho' lost to the world and its love,
To flourish more fair you're transplanted above!

Lines
Written for
Miss L. S. B.[479] *to Present to Her Mother,*[480]
on Her Birth-Day,
with Some Primroses and Violets

With primroses pale, and with violets blue,
The Spring hath the first robe of nature array'd,
I cull'd these with care, and I bring them to you,
From a sense that your love should with sweets be repaid.
They well will denote, to your vigilant eye,
The expansion of scenes more endear'd to the sight,
As the great orb of day shall ascend in the sky,
Sweet Nature will beam in her glory more bright.
On earth introduced with those sweetest of flowers,
May I, as with joy they the senses renew,
Inhaling their fragrance, inherit their powers,
And shed, in each season, a sweetness on you!
And if the advancement of charms they disclose,
In which the endowments of Nature combine,
May the sweets that I breathe have the virtue of those,
And gladden your heart with the progress of mine!

Written for A. S. B.[481]
On His Birth-Day,
when Eight Years Old,
December 17th, 1828

Yes! I'm advanced another year,
    Another's sunk behind me;
But who, when this shall disappear,
    Knows where the next may find me?
For, as the sun one day beams clear,
    And may the next be clouded,

APPENDIX III

I may to-day in life appear,
    And be to-morrow shrouded.

Since life is but a dubious state,
    And over its existence
Presides a Being good as great,
    I'll ask His kind assistance.
In climbing on from youth to age,
    And every year I heighten,
Let such pursuits my mind engage,
    As may in honour brighten.

Contending with my tasks of life,
    Some mazes may perplex me,
Which should be met with noble strife,
    Not irritate, nor vex me.
Such combats will exalt the soul,
    As still my journey lengthens,
And give the mind still more controul,
    As year by year it strengthens.

Sweet love and care were, day by day,
    Throughout the last, my portion,
And shall it from me pass away
    Without one fond emotion?
Oh no! a thought's most kindly felt
    For all the joys I'm knowing,
I love those souls by whom they're dealt,
    And Him from whom they're flowing.

May still such hopes beam from my mind
    As stimulate affection,
And still my guardian Angel find
    Me worthy of protection!
If, cheer'd by love and led by care,
    I gain life's highest station,
Oh, may my grateful spirit there
    Promote its own salvation!

On the Death of Lord Byron

Thy destiny's cast and before thee;
    And sever'd thy body and breath,
Thou'rt left, and the Muses deplore thee,
    On the dark and cold desert of death.

APPENDIX III

The strains of thy lyre were enchanting,
  And bore over nature controul,
But yet was another chord wanting,
  To attune it more sweet to the soul.

The sound that's to merit inspiring,
  Its sweet introduction to love,
And cheering to worth in aspiring
  To a seat with the blissful above.

Tho' reckless of these was thy story,
  And left to more impotent lays,
The Corsair shall glow in thy glory,
  The Wanton shall bask in thy praise.

The isle of thy birth is the rarest,
  Thy home was the proudest to have,
The fair of her soil are the fairest,
  The bravest, her sons, of the brave.

The land of thy sires was forsaken,
  Its worthies thy genius abused,
No pride in her virgins was taken,
  Its sons were a tribute refused.

In climes now inglorious a ranger,
  With passions unbridled and strong,
Love's current was turn'd on the stranger,
  And the dissolute nurs'd in thy song.

Had thy fame and thy country's together
  In an orbit conjunctively shone,
'Twould have beam'd on illuming each other,
  Till Time had extinguish'd the sun.

On the Battle of Waterloo

In storm and tempest arose the day,
  Which show'd the foe to view,
Who, vain and impatient for the fray,
  Aloud the onset blew;
    And the fight with vengeful ire began,

APPENDIX III

And the fire in ceaseless thunder ran,
    From line to line, and from man to man,
Death's shafts destructive flew.

The hearts were brave, and the bands were strong,
    Which hope led to the field,
The fight was fierce, and the strife was long,
    And neither host would yield:
        When many valorous deeds were done,
        And the day by patient prowess won,
        Then on England's triumph set the sun,
    And the foe could find no shield.

And those who oft for glory fought,
    Were doomed no more to know,
But now, in their speed their safety sought,
    And death kept with the slow;
        For a band unwearied in the fight,
        By wrongs provoked, pursued their flight,
        And many lay, ere the morning's light,
    Down on their gorgets low,

Now pity o'er the brave prevail'd,
    Who trod the field of gore,
And many a bold heart's mansion hail'd,
    To ask if life was o'er:
        'Twas long from some choice spirits fled,
        And the last chill'd drop some just had bled,
        But many maim'd from among the dead,
    And off the field, they bore.

And many sigh'd for a comrade lost,
    Who had cheer'd his arduous hours;
And many a weeping fair was cross'd,
    By love's disastrous powers;
        And yet there beam'd through their grief a pride,
        For the envious deaths their heroes died,
        Which might have been thro' tears descried,
    Just like the sun in showers.

And the scene shall long fond thoughts renew,
    Tho' tears bedim the eye;
And long, with that field of fame in view,
    Shall a Briton's heart beat high,

294

APPENDIX III

Who treads the soil where the valiant fell,
And views the mounds which their ashes swell,
And reads the tombs which their glories tell,
In Belgium where they lie.

Poor Kitty

No joy in early youth denied,
  No thought adverse distress'd me;
My parent's care my wants supplied,
  Who to their bosoms press'd me;
But death, whose power no arm can brave,
  Or plaints arrest of pity,
Hath borne them from me to the grave,
  And friendless left poor Kitty.

No home wherein to hide my head,
  No earthly friend to guide me,
Too young in years to earn my bread,
  Whatever will betide me!
A wandering, houseless child of care,
  A candidate for pity,
If bless'd by Heaven with aught to spare,
  Relieve the wants of Kitty!

By early admonitions taught
  That life's beset with danger,
It fills with dread, and pains with thought,
  An unprotected stranger.
If shelter'd from its snares awhile,
  Beneath some roof of pity,
What fervent prayers with Heaven's smile
  Would bless the friends of Kitty!

Lines
Occasioned by Reading
the Following Printed Bill,
Fixed in the Beak of One
in a Group of Five Stuffed
Owls in the Shop Window
of a Bird Stuffer,
at Richmond, Yorkshire

'We five owls were once alive;
On birds and mice we used to thrive;

295

APPENDIX III

Through barns and towers oft did fly
In search of prey both wet and dry
And on each shining summer's day
In hollow trees we pass'd our time away,
Till the cruel sportsman forc'd us to the field,
Then unto the gun we were obliged to yield;
But now we have undergone dissection,
To add and join this grand collection.
Glass eyes we have got and cannot see,
Spectacles are of use, but not to we;
Now no more birds or mice we pursue,
For we are stuff'd, and it is true,
By Mr. Stevenson, – who stuff'd us five,
And hundreds more, as though they were alive.'

W. STEVENSON,
Stuffer of Birds, Animals, Reptiles, and Fish;
Dealer in Fishing-Tackle,
Richmond, Yorkshire.'

Indeed, ye five,
Were ye alive?
Was wisdom doom'd to suffer?
And did your brains
Reward the pains
Of Stevenson your stuffer?

Why in his lines
Such merit shines,
The wonder now is known;
He, vain pretence,
Purloin'd your sense,
And pass'd it for his own!

The fraud forgive;
Your fame will live,
And pass to future times,
And long the sight
And sense delight,
In feathers and in rhymes.

May, to the six,
From chance and tricks,
Be kind protection given!
The owls are worth

APPENDIX III

The charge of earth;
The man, the care of Heaven!

On the Death of Gaffer Gun

Poor old Gaffer Gun,
Thy labour is done,
The sod thou shalt sever no more;
Thy doublet and flail
Are hung on a nail,
But the corn's left undress'd on the floor.

The Lord of the soil
Set a time for thy toil,
Tho' thy work should be left in the rough;
And true to the hour,
Invested with power,
Death came, and cried 'Gaffer, enough!'

With insight profound,
As the season came round,
To thy sickle and scythe thou'dst an eye;
But ere the corn's brown
Thou, alas! art cut down,
And now in death's stack-yard must lie.

And when to be tried,
Soul and body divide,
May thy sins be, as chaff, lightly driven;
But as grain, bright and sound,
May thy spirit be found,
And 'twill meet a good market in Heaven.

To a Gentleman
Who Married a Second Wife
Three Days After the Interment
of His First

Says the moral divine,
''Tis a sin to repine
At whatever fate may ordain thee;
Be it mild or severe,
'Tis the best for thee here,
From sorrow 'tis wise to refrain thee.'

APPENDIX III

And wisdom thou'st shown,
In a loss of thine own,
A form once ador'd beyond measure;
Thy grief lost its hold,
As the object grew cold,
And thy heart soon was wean'd of its treasure

And Heaven was kind
To a soul so resign'd,
And favour'd thee more than another;
As Death thro' one door
A faded joy bore,
Love danced with one in at the other.

And give it thy care!
For many's the fair
More slow would have been to endear thee;
But, panting for breath,
And undaunted by death,
She ran to caress and to cheer thee.

Slow wooers impart,
That the springs of the heart
Take patience and time in discerning,
But, quick-sighted dears,
You saw, thro' your tears,
Love's passion was mutually burning.

But, 'twas reckless to pay,
By three days delay,
The useless expense of a carriage;
In that which you rode
To death's dark abode,
You might have return'd from your marriage.

And what tongues would have told,
How you went with a cold –
But soon you return'd with a warm one;
And fame would have ran
With the worth of the man
Possessed of such powers to charm one.

My Nose

What leads me on where'er I go,
In sun and shade, in joy and woe,

APPENDIX III

Thro' fog and tempest, rain and snow?
        My Nose.

In youth's most ardent reckless day,
And when arose disputes at play,
What would be foremost in the fray?
        My Nose.

And should my tongue rude blows provoke,
What would protrude and brave each stroke,
Till coral streams its pains bespoke?
        My Nose.

And falling in an airy bound,
In chase of some new charm or sound,
To save me what came first to ground?
        My Nose.

When some dark pass I would explore,
With neither shut nor open door,
What oft for me hard usage bore?
        My Nose.

And when in want I yearn'd to eat,
And hunger might my judgement cheat,
What prompted me to food most sweet?
        My Nose.

Mid violet banks and woodbine bowers,
And beds where bloom'd the fairest flowers,
What fed me with their fragrant powers?
        My Nose.

Each eye may need in age a guide,
And when young helpmates I provide,
Thy back thou'lt lend for them to stride,
        My Nose.

And can I or in care or glee,
Refuse my aid and love to thee,
Who thus hast felt and bled for me,
        My Nose?

No; when cold winter's winds blow high,
And bite thee hard, and thou shalt cry,

APPENDIX III

Thy tears with sympathy I'll dry,
      My Nose.

And if for snuff thy love shall come,
Thy slaves, my finger and my thumb,
Shall faithful be, and bear thee some,
      My Nose.

Still as I follow thee along,
Oh! may'st thou never lead me wrong,
But thou must hush our sleeping song,
      My Nose!

From a Cobler to B.
On Returning Him an Old Pair of Shoes

Your shoes have I look'd o'er and o'er,
    And tell you as a friend,
The more I look'd, I thought the more
    Their case too bad to mend.

Their seams are rent, and soles abused,
    Beyond my art's redress;
Their upper parts, more rudely used,
    Seem weeping in distress.

Had they not turn'd aside, I ween,
    Thro' your untoward ways,
They might their maker's pride have been,
    And borne you many days.

But keep then steadfast in your mind;
    Expose them on a shelf,
And well they'll serve you to remind
    A sinner of himself.

Oh! think, like these may be your plight,
    As you their state discern,
Should you not mend and walk upright,
    Ere you too old are worn.

And should you mend, and Man shall cry,
    What brought vice to a close?

APPENDIX III

Raise to the shelf a reverend eye,
   And say, ''Twas those old shoes.'

And with your name bequeath them down,
   And earnestly desire,
That every rising race be shown,
   What turn'd from sin its sire.

Verses
Written for a Boy to Learn and Repeat
Who Had Committed a Small Theft

Oh God! whose searching eye doth see
   Mine every deed – ill done or well –
No thought of mine's unknown to thee;
   Unknown is no untruth I tell.

A liar's tongue dost thou disclaim,
   Against a thief denouncest woe;
And all who vilify thy name
   Are punish'd in the gulf below.

An act of theft my name hath stain'd,
   Which I denied with daring vow;
But injur'd truth my guilt proclaim'd,
   And conscious shame o'erwhelms me now.

How much, O God, my crime offends,
   How ruthful its effect appears;
Displeas'd art Thou, and mortal friends;
   And dim a father's eyes with tears.

But with that kind, benignant aid,
   Which Thou canst give and I implore,
I'll seek the path from which I stray'd,
   And swerve from them and Thee no more.

But hope, and aim, in life to be
   What truth and virtue may approve;
And glorify and honour Thee,
   And recompense a parent's love.

APPENDIX III

A Prayer in Affliction

Thou Maker of all things, Thou Lord of all living,
    Thou whom to thy creatures such wonders disclose,
Oh! look down with mercy benign and forgiving,
    And chase from my turbulent bosom its woes.

Or grant, if affliction shall still be thy pleasure,
    That ne'er, to evade it, I wander astray;
But make of those precepts my soul's dearest treasure,
    Thou hast set forth to guide us on life's troubled way,

Then, tho' in my progress rude storms may assail me,
    And in a world selfish no shelter be given,
As darkness enclose me, I'll hope Thou wilt hail me,
    And bid me repose in the mansion of heaven.

An Epitaph
on Philip and Mary Jones

Grim Death conceals beneath these stones,
The mortal part of Philip Jones,
Where erst his wife, poor Sarah, lay,
And fast they now return to clay.

Tho' life exalts thine head on high,
Look pensive down on where they lie;
And know, howe'er with gifts endow'd,
How rich or poor, how meek or proud,
Time levels all to one degree,
And soon what they are thou shalt be.

Be just, like them, that death may deal
The latest pang thou'rt doom'd to feel;
That when to earth thy body's given,
Thy soul may find repose in Heaven.

Lines on the Death of Miss Sadlier Bruere,[482]
Who Died, And Was Interred by the Side
of Miss Burnet, Who Was Buried
but a Few Days Before Her,
at Brighton, September, 1828, Aged 22.
Tours, December 1, 1828

APPENDIX III

Thou wert seen, faded blossom with joy and endear'd
As the first of thy kind on the stem that appear'd;
Thou wert watch'd with affection, and hope with thee grew,
As, with promise, thy form still expanded to view;
Thou wert come to the period when nature displays
The sweets with which time for her culture repays,
And when to the world thou wert opening in bloom,
Thou wert chill'd by the blast, and enclos'd in a tomb.

Thou wert miss'd in the group when the eye look'd around,
And miss'd by the ear was thy voice in the sound,
Thy chamber was darksome, thy bell was unrung,
Thy footstep unheard, and thy lyre unstrung:
A stillness prevail'd at the mournful repast;
In tears was the eye on thy vacant seat cast;
Each scene wearing gloom, and each brow bearing care,
Too plainly denoted that death had been there.

Thou wert laid by the side of thine emblem in years;
Ere dry was her grave thine was moisten'd with tears:
And ye hold to the world a joint lesson of truth,
That life is not safe in the keeping of youth.
Could care avert death, and the heart's treasure save,
Ye had not been doom'd to a premature grave,
Now ye sleep on the hill by the sea-beaten shore,
And the voice of the storm shall awake ye no more.

To earth we consign'd thee, and made an advance,
The thought to beguile, to the vineyards of France.
But 'twould not be cheated; of all that was rare,
Fond nature kept whispering a wish thou could'st share:
No air softly swelling, no chord struck with glee,
But awoke in the bosom remembrance of thee.
Even now, as the cold winds adown the leaves bring,
We sigh that our flow'ret was blighted in spring.

Life's pilgrimage is but a trial of trust,
And bliss, at its period, the meed of the just.
Why then should we mourn thee, with sigh or with tear,
And at thy advancement in trouble appear?
To the home which thou'rt gone to we're destin'd to go,
And the further we journey the greater our woe.
To thee, more deserving, the favour was given,
To pass, whilst we wander, a near road to Heaven.

APPENDIX III

*To Our Worthy Shepherd, Mr. Way,
on Hearing of His Rearing Some
Young Wolves*

Tours, June, 1829

As the sheep of the fold
Whom your Rev'rence has told
   The sinful and vile to be loathing,
And of wolves to beware,
For, without moral care,
   They'll steal on the flock in sheep's clothing;

We, alas! Mr. Way,
Must distrust what you say,
   When next you entreat us to heed them;
When, leaving us then,
You go home to their den
   With fatherly fondness to feed them.

May our Shepherd above
Keep us still in your love,
   Though the wolves may a portion inherit;
If those must prevail
O'er the flesh, which is frail,
   Let us be illumed with the Spirit.

ENDNOTES

Southey's Review of *The Life of Dermody*

1 James Grant Raymond (1771–1817), a Scot, had married in Dublin. He worked in London as an actor and manager of the English Opera at the Drury Lane Theatre. He was a friend of Dermody in London.

2 The young Dermody had recently lost a brother and his mother. In Fielding's *Tom Jones* (1749), the orphan hero sets off for London alone after being turned out of his adoptive father's house.

3 The tune was composed by Henry Purcell. In 1686, it acquired lyrics that played on fears of an Irish Catholic takeover of both Britain and Ireland when King James II brought Irish regiments to England to bolster his power. It remained popular with the supporters of Protestant succession during the 1688–1690 campaigns against James that resulted in William of Orange gaining the crown.

4 Milton, *Comus*, line 118.

5 This was probably Rev. Stewart Lynch (d. 1788), curate of St Werburgh's, Dublin, and bookseller.

6 [Robert?] Houlton (d. 1801) had moved to Dublin from England in 1768. In that year, he published *Indisputable Facts Relative to the Suttonian Art of Inoculation*, advertising himself as a smallpox doctor in Ireland. He also wrote poems, essays, and opera librettos. In 1796, he was in debtor's prison in London.

7 The Irish dramatist, songwriter, comic actor, and theatre manager Andrew Cherry (1762–1812). He made his debut at Drury Lane, London, in 1802.

8 Richard Daly (1758–1813), the Irish actor and theatrical manager who, between 1786 and 1797, held the royal patent for staging productions in Dublin.

9 Philip Astley (1741–1812), proprietor of equestrian theatres ('circuses') in London and, from 1789, in Peter St. Dublin. There, he and others performed feats of trick riding.

10 Kamchatka, the peninsula in the far northeast of Russia.

11 Glue.

12 Robert Owenson (1744–1812), singer, actor, and theatre manager.

13 Owenson, of humble farming lineage, had himself led a varied and itinerant life and knew what it was to depend upon a patron. He had alienated his benefactor, who had fostered his education in London, by having an affair with an opera singer.

14 Matthew Young (1750–1800). Young was an eminent mathematician and natural philosopher and was Erasmus Smith's Professor of natural and experimental philosophy at Trinity College, Dublin, 1786–1799.

15 The treatise on logic by Richard Murray (c. 1726–1799), Provost of Trinity College Dublin, published first in 1759, was a staple textbook used in Ireland for over a century.

ENDNOTES

16 Gilbert Austin (1753–1837), schoolmaster and author of articles on chemistry, of sermons, and of *Chironomia, or a Treatise on Rhetorical Delivery* (1806).

17 *Poems* (Dublin, 1789).

18 Mary née Hickman, Countess Charlemont (d. 1807), wife of James Caulfeild, first Earl of Charlemont.

19 One of the numerous Gore clan, head of which was Arthur Saunders Gore, second Earl of Arran (1734–1809).

20 Anne Crofton, later first Baroness Crofton (1751–1817), wife of Sir Edward Crofton, second Baronet (1748–1797).

21 William Robert FitzGerald, second Duke of Leinster (1749–1804).

22 John Dederick Ayckbourn (1745–1807), a glass seller of German origin. His premises were on Grafton St, Dublin.

23 A Mr Martin.

24 Owenson's wife, Jane, née Hill, died in 1789.

25 (1732–1818), an administrator and politician – a mainstay of government in Ireland.

26 Joseph Atkinson, who was, by 1799, Deputy Judge Advocate General in Dublin.

27 Elizabeth Rawdon, née Hastings (1731–1808), the Dowager Countess of Moira who presided over a literary salon at Moira House. Maria Edgeworth and Charlotte Brooke were encouraged by her.

28 The Revd Henry Boyd (1749?–1832), Vicar of Killeigh. Boyd published a translation of Dante's *Inferno* (1785) and of the whole *Divina commedia* (1802).

29 Robert Burns (1759–1786), the Scottish poet, who had become a byword for alcoholism after the biography included in James D. Currie's four-volume edition of his works (1800) – this went into its eighth edition in 1820.

30 Henry Grattan (1746–1820), the reformist politician.

31 Henry Flood (1732–1791), Grattan's friend and fellow reformist politician.

32 Catherine Macaulay, *The History of England from the Accession of James I to the Revolution* (1763–1783).

33 Thomas Percy (1729–1811), bishop of Dromore, poet, and scholar.

34 William Preston (1750–1807), lawyer, poet, dramatist, and founder of the Royal Irish Academy and the Dublin Literary Society.

35 Joseph Cooper Walker (1762–1810). An antiquarian, Walker was in the literary circle of Grattan and the Dowager Countess Moira. He was a founder of the Royal Irish Academy.

36 Joseph Sterling (1765–1794), an antiquarian and author of *Poems* (Dublin, 1782), which included *Odes from the Icelandic*. Sterling was co-author of *Cambuscan: or the Squire's Tale of Chaucer* (Dublin, 1785).

37 Edward Tighe (1740–1801), lawyer, writer, and politician.

38 Beating him with a stick.

39 In Shakespeare's *Henry V*.

40 This was published in 1793.

41 Arthur Wolfe (1739–1803), first Viscount Kilwarden, politician, and judge.

42 Press-ganged into the navy.

43 Perhaps William Emerson (d. 1821), a Belfast merchant.

44 A waterside area of Dublin.

45 Moira House, Dublin.

46 George Forbes, sixth Earl of Granard (1760–1837), the Dowager Countess of Moira's son-in-law.

47 The Earl of Moira, Francis Edward Rawdon-Hastings, later first Marquess of Hastings (1754–1826), the Dowager Countess's son.

48 Robert Faulder (1747–1815), whose premises were at 42 New Bond St.

49 Charles Allingham (c. 1778–1850), the artist who painted Dermody's portrait in 1802 (it is now held in the National Gallery of Ireland).

ENDNOTES

50 The London booksellers who had published *The Farmer's Boy*, by the 'uneducated' poet Robert Bloomfield, in 1800 – to great popular success. Their edition of Dermody, *Poems, Moral, and Descriptive*, also appeared in 1800.

51 Here meaning Alexander the Great (356–323 BC), the Greek conqueror who was hailed as the son of the god Ammon.

52 From Nathaniel Lee, *The Rival Queens: Or, the Death of Alexander the Great* (1677), act 2, scene 1.

53 Playing upon Alexander Pope's translation of Horace, Satire I, lines 127–28: 'There St John mingles with my friendly bowl / The feast of reason and the flow of soul.'

54 Charles Bragge Bathurst (1754–1831), a politician and administrator, MP for Bristol, and treasurer of the Navy. Bathurst was a friend of the Addington brothers.

55 John Hiley Addington (1759–1818). Addington was MP and Lord of the Treasury, and then Secretary of the Treasury. His brother was Henry Addington.

56 Henry Addington, later first Viscount Sidmouth (1757–1844), was Prime Minister from 1801 to 1804.

57 Sir James Bland Burges (1752–1824), an MP, was the author of *Richard the First: a Poem in Eighteen Books* (1801).

58 Edmund Baker was the secretary of the Royal Literary Fund from 1800 to 1807.

59 Published in *Poems on Various Subjects* (London, 1802).

60 Bayezid I (c. 1360–1403) was the Ottoman Sultan from 1389 to 1402. He was defeated by the Mongol leader Timur (1336–1405) and, according to legend, imprisoned in an iron cage, having said that, if he had been victorious, he would have imprisoned Timur thus. Christopher Marlowe dramatized the story in *Tamburlaine the Great* (1587/88), Part I.

61 Near Gray's Inn, London.

62 *Peace, a Poem* was published by the firm of John Hatchard (1769–1849) in 1801.

63 From 'Free Confession to a Friend' in *Poems on Various Subjects* (pp. 199–201).

64 *Poems on Various Subjects* was published by John Hatchard in 1802.

65 Sir William Cusack Smith (1766–1836). A poet and essayist, Smith was, by profession, a lawyer. He was made a Baron of the Exchequer (a judge in the Court of Common Pleas) in 1801.

66 That is, Chatterton died – or killed himself – before he became generally renowned, although he had in fact already attracted interest from literary men, including Horace Walpole, Samuel Johnson, and John Wilkes. Southey, collaborating with Joseph Cottle, edited Chatterton's works for a posthumous edition of 1803. *The Works of Thomas Chatterton*, eds. Robert Southey and Joseph Cottle (London, 1803).

Southey's Account of the Life of Henry Kirke White

67 *The Works of Thomas Chatterton*, ed. Robert Southey and Joseph Cottle (London, 1803).

68 John White (1747–1822) and his wife, Mary, née Nevill (1756–1833).

69 The Revd John Blanchard (1759–1827) was the master at the Nottingham Academy.

70 Henry Shipley (1763–1808).

71 HKW's eldest sister was Hannah (b. 1779). The school, in which the White family also resided, proved very successful.

72 The partnership of lawyers George Coldham (1766–1815) and Henry Enfield (1775–1845).

73 Charles McCormick (1742–1807) was living quietly in Nottingham so as to avoid arrest after the United Irishman rebellion in Ireland in 1798. HKW recognized him from an engraving in his *The History of England, from the Death of George the Second to the Peace of 1783, Designed as a Continuation to Hume and Smollett's History of England* (London, 1795). McCormick also authored *Memoirs of the Right Honourable Edmund Burke* (London, 1797).

ENDNOTES

74 Quintus Roscius Gallus (d. 62 BC), the Roman actor.

75 *The Monthly Preceptor, or Juvenile Museum of Knowledge and Entertainment* (1800–3). 'Museum' was later changed to 'Library' in its title.

76 Proverbs 30:8.

77 *The Monthly Mirror* (1795–1811) had heavily featured the work of Bloomfield and Dermody. For Kirke White's contributions to it, see *The Collected Poems of Henry Kirke White*, ed. Tim Fulford (Liverpool, 2023).

78 The literary gentleman, poet, and patron Capel Lofft (1751–1824) and the book collector and editor Thomas Hill (1760–1840) had helped bring Bloomfield's manuscript *The Farmer's Boy* into print with Vernor and Hood, the firm that published *The Monthly Mirror*.

79 Elizabeth, Countess of Derby (1759–1829).

80 Elizabeth, Princess Berkeley, Margravine of Brandenburg-Ansbach, previously Elizabeth Craven, Baroness Craven (1750–1828).

81 Georgiana, Duchess of Devonshire (1757–1806).

82 John Neville White (1782–1845), Henry's brother, who worked as a hosier in London and later became a priest.

83 *The Monthly Review*, 43 (1804), 218.

84 Southey was acquainted with Samuel Hamilton, editor of *The Critical Review*.

85 Southey had reviewed *Clifton Grove* favourably in *The Annual Review*, 2 (1803), 552–54.

86 43 (1804), 335–36.

87 William Gifford (1756–1826), the poet and critic, had been apprenticed to a shoemaker. He was assisted in getting an education by a local benefactor, William Cookesley (1741–1781), of Ashburton, Devon. In his translation of *The Satires of Decimus Junius Juvenalis* (London, 1802), pp. xiii-xiv, Gifford thanked Cooksley.

88 Solomon Piggott (1779–1845), a curate of St Mary's Church, Nottingham.

89 Thomas Scott, *The Force of Truth: An Authentic Narrative* (London, 1779).

90 The Revd John Dashwood (c. 1778–1861), a curate at St Mary's, Nottingham.

91 Robert White Almond (1785–1853), Rector of St Peter's, Nottingham, 1814–1853.

92 The Revd Thomas Catton (1758–1838), tutor of St John's College, Cambridge.

93 Charles Simeon (1759–1836), an evangelical fellow of King's College, Cambridge.

94 William Wilberforce (1759–1833), the evangelical MP.

95 Thomas Robinson (1749–1813) was an evangelical minister in Leicester.

96 The Elland Society funded selected evangelical young men to train for the Anglican priesthood.

97 The Revd Lorenzo Grainger (1768–1833).

98 'May grace be granted me to accomplish these things.'

99 Benjamin Maddock (1781–1871), of Nottingham, later Vicar of Tadcaster.

100 The love story of Iñes de Castro (1325–55) was told in the Portuguese epic poem *The Lusíadas* by Luís de Camões.

101 For his edition of the poet.

Southey's Review of *Lucretia Davidson*

102 Samuel Finley Breese Morse (1791–1872), the painter and developer of Morse code and the electromagnetic telegraph.

103 August Friedrich Ferdinand von Kotzebue (1761–1819), the highly popular and prolific German dramatist whose *The Stranger*, the English version of *Menschenhass und Reue*, was a runaway success on the American stage.

104 Oliver Goldsmith (1728–1774), whose plays included *The Good-Natur'd Man* (1768) and *She Stoops to Conquer* (1773).

ENDNOTES

105 Thomas Chatterton and Henry Kirke White. Southey had edited the works of both of these boy poets, in 1803 and 1807, respectively.

106 Thomas Moore (1779–1852). 'Dear harp of my country' ('The Farewell to My Harp') is one of Moore's *Irish Melodies* (1807–1834).

107 Shakespeare, *A Midsummer Night's Dream*, act 5, scene 1.

108 Emma Hart Willard (1787–1870). The school, now known by the name of its founder, still educates girls in Troy.

109 This poem appeared in Southey's *The Remains of Henry Kirke White*, 2 vols (London, 1807), II, 191. The last stanzas are:

> Thus far have I pursued my solemn theme
> With self-rewarding toil, thus far have sung
> Of godlike deeds, far loftier than beseem
> The lyre which I in early days have strung:
> And now my spirit's faint, and I have hung
> The shell, that solaced me in saddest hour,
> On the dark cypress! And the strings which rung
> With Jesus' praise, their harpings now are o'er,
> Or, when the breeze comes by, moan and are heard no more.
>
> And must the harp of Judah sleep again,
> Shall I no more reanimate the lay!
> Oh! thou who visitest the sons of men,
> Thou who dost listen when the humble pray,
> One little space prolong my mournful day!
> One little lapse suspend thy last decree!
> I am a youthful traveller in the way,
> And this slight boon would consecrate to thee,
> Ere I with Death shake hands, and smile that I am free.

110 Southey quotes from his own introductory essay in *The Remains of Henry Kirke White*, 2 vols (London, 1807), I, 58 (see p. 88).

Southey's Introduction to *Attempts in Verse*

111 Banks (1743–1820) was President of the Royal Society, a noted botanist and zoologist and a patron of science and exploration. He had conducted scientific investigations when circumnavigating the world on Captain Cook's first expedition.

112 George Coleman the younger (1762–1836). Author of the successful plays *Inkle and Yarico* and *The Iron Chest*, Coleman was appointed Licenser of Plays – censor – in 1824.

113 The office of Poet Laureate.

114 In 1807. This publication – collecting the works of the labouring-class boy poet Henry Kirke White – was very popular. It went through ten editions while still in copyright; from 1824, numerous pirated versions also appeared.

115 Traditionally, the Poet Laureate had been given an annual allowance of a 'butt' (barrel) of 'sack' – fortified Spanish wine. Although this allowance had been stopped by King James II, it was used by satirists to mock Southey, the former republican radical, for taking the monarch's (and government's) pay. See, for example, Leigh Hunt, 'Dr Southey and Lord Byron,' *The Examiner*, 881 (19 December 1824), 802.

116 John Cunningham (1729–1773), the Newcastle-based poet and actor, author of *Love in a Mist*, and Charles Cotton (1630–1687), author of 'The Retirement' and contributor to *The Compleat Angler.* Cotton's direct and colloquial style was admired by

ENDNOTES

Charles Lamb and Wordsworth as well as by Southey; it was praised by Coleridge in Chapter XIX of *Biographia Literaria*.

117 Probably Sara Hutchinson (1775–1835), Wordsworth's sister-in-law – several of the Wordsworth family having been at Harrogate with the Southeys.

118 For a modern account of Taylor, see Bernard Capp, *The World of John Taylor the Water Poet 1578–1653* (Oxford, 1994).

119 Theobalds House, in Hertfordshire, was the country seat of Lord Burghley, adviser to the monarch. In 1607, King James I acquired it.

120 The town near which the King and courtiers enjoyed watching horseracing.

121 Perhaps to visit the nearby house Audley End, rebuilt between 1605 and 1614 by Thomas Howard (1561–1626), first Earl of Suffolk and Lord Treasurer to King James.

122 Sir Francis Bacon (1561–1626) was Attorney General from 1613 to 1617.

123 Sir Julius Caesar (1557/1558–1636) was made Master of the Rolls in 1614.

124 A marine poem fit for a water poet. Christopher Marlowe's *Hero and Leander* (1598) versified the Greek myth in which Leander swam the Hellespont to meet his beloved, Hero.

125 The Muses.

126 See following notes.

127 Probably John Murray (1601–1640), who became first Earl of Annandale in 1624.

128 In 1616, Ben Jonson (1572–1637) was granted a royal pension of 100 marks a year, giving him both wealth and status. He had once, however, been a bricklayer and a common soldier.

129 John Ramsay, first Earl of Holderness (c. 1580–1626). Ramsay, one of the favourites of King James I, was not made Earl until 1621.

130 Sir William Wade (1546–1623) was Lieutenant of the Tower of London.

131 Various forms of mark used by the illiterate to represent their signature. 'John Thompson' here is a generic name: A. N. Other or John Doe.

132 Niobe was punished by the Greek deities, who killed all her children; she was then turned into a rock, perpetually wet with her tears. Alecto, Tisiphone, and Megæra were the Greek Furies – spirits of wrath and vengeance. 'Lacrymae': in tears.

133 'Known by all men': a term that commenced all legal bonds.

134 Bellman's verses were the doggerel poems by which beadles – local officials responsible for dealing with minor offenders – sought tips from the well-to-do populace at Christmastime.

135 Taylor's verse summaries of the Bible: *Verbum Sempiternum* and *Salvator Mundi*.

136 Joshua Sylvester (1563–1618), whose translation *Du Bartas his divine weekes and works* (1608) Southey admired, writing on 2 March 1815 to Joseph Cottle (*CLRS* 2562): 'You who perhaps are not so tolerant in these matters as I am, would perhaps be disgusted with the conceits of Du Bartas & the quaintnesses of his translator: I can see all their faults & yet admire the powers which both have perverted.'

137 (1588–1667).

138 'And I have; I want; I care.' The poem responded to Wither's satirical poem of 1621 *Wither's Motto: Nec habeo, nec careo, nec curo* ('I have not, I want not, I care not').

139 Southey's enthusiasm for Wither's writing dated back to, at least, 18 October 1798, when Charles Lamb wrote to him having procured him a copy of Wither's *Emblems The Letters of Charles and Mary Lamb*, ed. Edwin J. Marrs, vol. I (Ithaca and London, 1975), 136–37. In 1818, Lamb published an essay, 'On the poetical works of George Wither.'

140 Chaucer's *The Parliament of Fowls*.

141 William Falconer (1732–1769), sailor and author of *The Shipwreck. A Sentimental and Descriptive Poem*. Falconer was 'poor' because he suffered the same fate as the mariners described in his poem: in 1769, he drowned when his ship was lost at sea with all hands. Southey had reviewed an edition of Falconer's *Shipwreck* in *The Annual Review for 1804*, 3 (1805), 577–80.

142 Bowlines.

143 Halyards.

310

ENDNOTES

144 The god of the East Wind.

145 Aeolus: god of the winds.

146 Thomas Coryat (c. 1577–1617), the traveller, who hailed from Odcombe in Somerset.

147 Iambic tetrameter couplets, as in Samuel Butler's mock-heroic poem *Hudibras* (1663–1678).

148 Samuel Rowlands (1570?–1630?), author of epigrammatic poems. *Sculler's Travels* appeared in 1612.

149 In the German lands: today in Baden-Württemberg.

150 Southey's ballad 'Roprecht the Robber,' written by 9 May 1829 and published in *Sharpe's London Magazine. The Three Chapters*, 1 (July 1829), 17–30. See the text and notes in *RSLPW*, I, 322–37.

151 Jonson went on foot from London to Edinburgh in July, August, and September 1618. For an edition of an account of this journey, see James Loxley, Anna Groundwater, and Julie Sanders (eds), *Ben Jonson's Walk to Scotland* (Cambridge, 2015).

152 See *All's Well That Ends Well*, 3.6. A once-proverbial expression meaning a poor, niggardly reception, a brush-off.

153 Philemon Holland (1552–1637) translated *The History of Twelve Caesars*, by the Roman historian Suetonius Tranquillus, for an edition published in 1606. The full quip, playing on Suetonius's name ('the tranquil'): ran 'Phil: Holland with translations doth so fill us, / He will not let Suetonius be Tranquillus.'

154 (1566–1627).

155 (1577–1628).

156 An inn on Cheetham Hill, Manchester.

157 Thomas Banister served as Mayor of Preston in 1610, 1617, and 1625.

158 Thomas Covell (1561–1639) was the keeper of the castle and the adjoining gaol at Lancaster, in which capacity he provided board and lodging to guests willing and unwilling.

159 Edmond Branthwaite, of Carlingill, Westmoreland.

160 John Corney, Vicar of Orton, who died in 1643.

161 Dalston (c. 1556–c. 1633) of Dalston Hall, near Carilsle, was an important figure in the county – Captain of Carlisle castle and several times High Sheriff. Elizabeth, his daughter from his second marriage, married Sir Thomas Braithwaite (c. 1581–c. 1622).

162 Southey refers to *Barnabae Itinerarium or Barnabees Journall* (1638) by Thomas Braithwaite's younger brother, the poet Richard Braithwaite (1588–1673). Like Taylor's poem, this work, originally written in Latin but then translated into English, versifies the poet's pub-crawling travels across the country. Southey's speculation that Braithwaite was related to the Branthwaites of Carlingill has not been verified. 'Barnabee' is the anti–water poet, presumably, not because he travels by land, but because he drinks only alcohol.

163 (1581–1623). Curwen was a JP for Cumberland at the time of Taylor's visit; in 1619, he became High Sheriff. His first wife was Sir John Dalston's daughter Catherine.

164 Adam Robinson was the mayor of Carlisle in 1617.

165 Hero of Thomas Nashe's 1592 satire *Pierce Penilesse. His Supplication to the Devil. Describing the overspreading of vice, and suppression of virtue.*

166 A legal phrase meaning that the persons on whom a writ is to be served are not to be found.

167 Priscianus Caesariensis (fl. AD 500), author of the Latin textbook, *Institutiones Grammaticae* (The Institutes of Grammar).

168 Sack: fortified Spanish wine.

169 Possibly Sir John Maxwell, 13th of Pollok (1595–1647).

170 Lindsay (1560–1628) had been gifted by King James VI of Scotland and I of England the area of Leith known as the King's Wark. Lindsay was entitled to collect a tax of

ENDNOTES

£4 Scots on every tun of wine sold in the taverns in the King's Wark, of which there were never to be more than four.

171 A town and dock on the north shore of the Firth of Forth.

172 Hay (b. 1579) was, in 1618, a gentleman of the King's Chamber and the master of the King's Robes.

173 Drummond, known as 'Glauren Davie,' was the son of George (known as Gavine) Drummond, second Earl of Kildees.

174 James or John Auchmoutie (fl. 1580–1635), a courtier and masque-dancer.

175 Captain George Murray, brother of John Murray, first Earl of Tullibardine, who had accompanied James VI in Denmark in 1590.

176 (c.1567–1623), of Swinburne Castle, Northumberland.

177 Captain Thomas Tyrie, of the Royal Guard.

178 Cadiz. The English fleet took this Spanish port in July 1596.

179 The 1597 expedition to take the Azores and capture the Spanish treasure fleet. It was commanded by the Earl of Essex, Thomas Howard, and Sir Walter Raleigh.

180 John Erskine, Earl of Mar (1558–1634), a powerful friend of the King.

181 Sir William Moray, ninth of Abercairny (1561–1740).

182 Braemar. That is, the highest part of the Marr area, between the Dee and Don Rivers.

183 Ogil, near Forfar. The Laird was James Lyon.

184 The lawgiver of classical Sparta (fl. c. 820 BC), who reputedly introduced common mess halls, so that men of all ranks dined on an equal footing.

185 The Lochaber pole axe.

186 That is, the Earl of Mar, John Erskine.

187 'Tinto': red wine from Spain.

188 A dark, sweet wine from Alicante, Spain.

189 Or 'tinschellis.'

190 Ruthven. After the killing of John Ruthven, third Earl of Gowrie (c. 1577–1600), during an attack on King James, Ruthven Castle became the possession of the Scottish Crown, and the barony of Ruthven was granted to James's supporter David Murray, later first Viscount of Stormont (d. 1631). The nearby lands of Engie were held by Archibald Campbell, seventh Earl of Argyll (c. 1575–1638), and, by 1619, by his son, Archibald Marquess of Argyll (later eighth Earl of Argyll) (1607–1661).

191 Ballachastell, near Inverness.

192 John Grant of Freuchie (c. 1568–1622).

193 Tarnaway (Darnway) Castle, near Forres, in Moray, seat of James Stuart, third Earl of Moray (1581–1638).

194 Spynie Palace, seat of the Bishops of Moray. The current bishop was Alexander Douglas (1561–1623).

195 George Gordon, first Marquess of Huntly (1562–1636).

196 Bog-o-Gight, now Gordon Castle, near Fochabers in Moray.

197 John Stuart, cousin of the King, Water-Bailie, and owner of the ship *The Post of Leith*.

198 By John Day (1574–1640) and Thomas Dekker (1572–1632).

199 'In his usual manner.'

200 The Nottinghamshire village renowned in folklore for the credulity of its inhabitants.

201 Perhaps alluding to Shakespeare's error, noted by Ben Jonson, in *The Winter's Tale*. Bohemia has no coast.

202 In Laurence Sterne's *Tristram Shandy* (1759), Corporal Trim tells Uncle Toby the 'Story of the King of Bohemia and his Seven Castles': 'The King of *Bohemia*, an' please your honour, replied the corporal, was *unfortunate*, as thus – That taking great pleasure and delight in navigation and all sort of sea affairs – and there *happening* throughout the whole kingdom of *Bohemia*, to be no seaport town whatever – How the duce should there – *Trim?* cried my uncle *Toby*; for *Bohemia* being totally inland, it could have happen'd no otherwise – It might, said Trim, if it had pleased God.'

ENDNOTES

203 These questions relate to the political situation that prevailed in Bohemia when Taylor visited. The Holy Roman Emperor Ferdinand II (1578–1637), based in Vienna, had been deposed as King of Bohemia in 1619 in favour of the Protestant Frederick V (1596–1632), whose wife, Elizabeth Stuart (1596–1662), thus became Queen of Bohemia (in November). Elizabeth was the daughter of King James VI of Scotland and I of England (Taylor had been hosted by James's courtiers when visiting Scotland in 1618). Ferdinand's army, combining forces commanded by Charles Bonaventure de Longueval, second Count of Bucquoy (1571–1621), and by Maximilian I, Duke of Bavaria (1573–1651), went to war with Bohemia to win back the lost crown and restore Catholicism in the country. Bethlen Gábor (1580–1629) was Prince of Transylvania. A Protestant ally of Protestant Bohemia, he attacked the emperor's lands in Hungary and Austria in 1619, taking Bratislava in October but failing to take Vienna. A defeat in November 1619 at Humenné forced him to withdraw his army from Austria and Hungary. Henri Duval, Count of Dampierre (1580–1620), was a commander in the emperor's army. In August 1619, his troops were defeated at Wisternitz in Moravia by forces loyal to Frederick. The war continued until the Battle of White Mountain on 8 November 1620, at which the Bohemians were defeated by Ferdinand's army, which then entered Prague. Frederick and Elizabeth were forced to flee the kingdom.

204 Prince Rupert of the Rhine, Duke of Cumberland, was born on 17 December 1619. He died in 1682.

205 Rupert was the commander of the Royalist cavalry during the Civil War in Britain.

206 Sir Austin Palgrave (1567–1639), of North Barningham.

207 Robert Kempe, of Antingham, near Cromer.

208 Taylor described this bore, the 'aegir,' caused by the meeting of tidal and river currents, in his poem:

> Besides the Flood Runs there, with such great force,
> That I imagine it out-runnes a Horse:
> And with a head some 4. foot high, that Rores,
> It on the sodaine swels and beats the Shores.
> It tumbled vs a Ground vpon the Sands,
> And all that wee could doe with wit, or hands,
> Could not resist it, but we were in doubt
> It would haue beaten our Boates bottome out.
> It hath lesse mercy then *Beare, Wolfe,* or *Tyger,*
> And in those Countries it is call'd the *Hyger*.

209 (1546–1628). Matthew had been the archbishop of York since 1606.

210 In 1621–1622, the lord mayor of York was Christopher Dickenson; in 1622–1623, the post was held by William Brearey (1645–1702).

211 William Fennor (fl. 1617), an English poet of Dutch origin, also known as Wilhelmus Vener. The flyting controversy took place in 1614.

212 *The Fearefull Summer, or, Londons Calamity, The Countries Courtesy, and both their Misery* by Iohn Taylor (Oxford, 1625).

213 From *No Mercurius Aulicus: But some merry flashes of Intelligence, with the Pretended Parliaments Forces besiedging of Oxford foure miles off, and the terrible taking in of a Mill, instead of the King and Citie* (Oxford, 1644).

214 This portrait is still held at the Bodleian Library.

215 An edition of Robert Herrick's *Poetical Works* had been published in two volumes in Edinburgh in 1823.

216 The works included in the 1630 folio edition were republished by the Spenser Society in a Manchester edition of 1869. Five volumes of works by Taylor not included in the 1630 folio edition were published by the Spenser Society between 1870 and 1878. A volume of *Early Prose and Poetical Works* was published in London in 1888.

ENDNOTES

217 This quotation concerning the life of Duck is taken from 'Some Account of the Life of Stephen Duck,' prefacing Duck's *Poems on Several Subjects* (London, 1730), p. iii.

218 Ibid., p. iv.

219 From Joseph Spence (1699–1768), *A Full and Authentick Account of Stephen Duck, the Wiltshire Poet* (London, 1731), p. 6. Spence, a friend of Pope, was the literary gentleman who 'discovered' Duck.

220 From *A Full and Authentick Account*, pp. 8–9.

221 The magazine of that name, edited by Joseph Addison and Richard Steele from 1711 to 1714.

222 *The Adventures of Telemachus, the Son of Ulysses*, by François Fénelon, tr. John Ozell (London, 1715).

223 Fenelon's *A Demonstration of the Existence and Attributes of God, Drawn from the Knowledge of Nature* (London, 1720).

224 Joseph Addison, *The Evidences of the Christian Religion* (London, 1730).

225 Edward Bysshe, *The Art of English Poetry* (1708).

226 Sir Roger L'Estrange (1616–1704) translated Seneca: *Seneca's Morals Abstracted in Three Parts* (London, 1679).

227 *The Whole Works of Flavius Josephus, Translated into English by Sir Roger L'Estrange, Knight* (London, 1702).

228 Epictetus (AD 50–135), the Greek Stoic philosopher.

229 Edmund Waller (1606–87), poet.

230 John Dryden's translation of the *Works of Virgil* was first published in 1697.

231 Matthew Prior (1664–1721), poet.

232 Samuel Butler, *Hudibras* (1663–1678).

233 Tom Brown (1663–1704), satirical poet.

234 Edward 'Ned' Ward's periodical *The London Spy*, describing ramblings around the capital, was collected in an edition of 1700.

235 From *A Full and Authentick Account*, pp. 9–10.

236 From *A Full and Authentick Account*, p. 11.

237 From *A Full and Authentick Account*, p. 12.

238 Hoby Stanley (1699–1737), who had taken his MA at Oxford in 1723.

239 From *A Full and Authentick Account*, p. 13.

240 From *A Full and Authentick Account*, p. 25.

241 From *A Full and Authentick Account*, p. 25.

242 Southey's quotations from 'The Thresher's Labour' are from the revised version in Duck's *Poems on Several Occasions* (London, 1736), pp. 11–27. On the original and revised texts, see Peter J. McGonigle, 'Stephen Duck and the text of *The Thresher's Labour*,' *The Library*, 6th ser., 4 (1982), 288–96.

243 'The Shunnamite,' from *Poems on Several Occasions*, pp. 28–46.

244 From *A Full and Authentick Account*, p. 15.

245 Spence was Professor of Poetry at Oxford.

246 From *A Full and Authentick Account*, p. 15.

247 Southey refers to *Poems on Several Subjects*, which featured the image described here as its frontispiece.

248 Charlotte Clayton (1679–1742), later Lady Sundon, was a Lady of the Bedchamber of the Queen.

249 Caroline of Brandenburg-Ansbach (1683–1737) was Queen of Great Britain and Ireland and Electress of Hanover from 1727 until her death as the wife of King George II.

250 In 1730.

251 *Poems on Several Occasions* (London, 1736).

252 *Poems on Several Occasions*, p. iv.

253 *Poems on Several Occasions*, pp. 8–9.

ENDNOTES

254 *Poems on Several Occasions*, pp. ix–x.

255 Jonathan Swift, 'On Stephen Duck the Thresher, and Favourite Poet,' from Swift's *Poems on Several Occasions* (Dublin, 1737), p. 304.

256 Henry Temple, first Viscount Palmerston (c. 1673–1757), of East Sheen, Surrey, and Broadlands, Hampshire.

257 It is still today held every year, at the Cat Inn (formerly the Red Lion), Charlton, Wiltshire.

258 'A Description of a Journey to Marlborough, Bath, Portsmouth, &c. To the Right Honourable the Lord Viscount Palmerston,' *Poems on Several Occasions*, p. 211.

259 A verdict made in Alexander Chalmers, *The General Biographical Dictionary Containing an Historical and Critical Account of the Lives and Writings of the Most Eminent Persons in Every Nation*, vol. XII (London, 1813), p. 391.

260 *Poems on Several Occasions*, p. 24.

261 *A Catalogue of Several Libraries Lately Purchased . . . Risely Risley Brewer Esq., Rev. Stephen Duck, and T. Wallis, M.D. of Stamford . . . Which Will Be Sold . . . Aug. 12, 1756 . . . by J. Whiston and Benj. White* (London, 1756).

262 Robert Dodsley (1703–1764), who came to notice with his 1729 work *Servitude: a Poem written by a Footman* and became one of the most successful booksellers, editors, and publishers of the eighteenth century. Like Duck, Dodsley was encouraged and befriended by Joseph Spence.

263 Volume XI of *The Works of the British Poets, With Prefaces, Biographical and Critical; Containing Wilkie, Dodsley, Smart, Langhorne, Bruce, Chatterton, Graeme, Glover, Shaw, Lovibond, Penrose, Mickle, Jago, Scott, Johnson, Whitehead, W. Jenyns, Logan, Warton, Cotton, and Blacklock* (London and Edinburgh, 1795).

264 (1735–1820).

265 The house and landscape garden of the poet William Shenstone (1714–1763).

266 Southey refers to Wordsworth.

267 *Poems on Sundry Occasions* (London, 1764) was published by the bookselling firm established by the former labouring-class poet Robert Dodsley.

268 Southey refers to Woodhouse's collection *Norbury Park: a Poem; with Several Others, Written on Various Occasions* (London, 1803), in which 'Epistle to Shenstone in the Shades: On Reading His "Rural Elegance"' occupies pp. 96–101. Woodhouse notes that the poem was written in 1784.

269 In fact, Woodhouse had published two collections before *Norbury Park*: *Poems on Sundry Occasions* and *Poems on Several Occasions* (1788). In 1804, he published the verse *Love Letters to my Wife* and, in 1815, anonymously and in abridged form, *The Life and Lucubrations of Crispinus Scriblerus*. The full text of this last work was published in *The Life and Poetical Works of James Woodhouse*, ed. R. R. Woodhouse (London, 1896).

270 'Shoemaker, not beyond the shoe': that is, work only within your area of expertise; cobbler, stick to your last. From Pliny the Elder, *Naturalis Historia*, 35.85·

271 'Autumn and the Redbreast, an Ode. Written from the Country, 1787,' in *Norbury Park*, pp. 112–32.

272 William Locke (1732–1810). Locke was a collector of art and friend of Fanny Burney.

273 Woodhouse died after a road accident in which he was struck by a carriage, in 1820.

274 Thomas Warton (1728–90), poet.

275 From 'Christmas Eve' in *Poems on Several Occasions* (London, 1774), pp. 37–46.

276 'On a Noted Tallow Chandler,' *Poems on Several Occasions*, p. 134.

277 'Hampton Gay,' *Poems on Several Occasions*, pp. 58–66.

278 'Sunday,' *Poems on Several Occasions*, pp. 80–87.

279 (1753–1806).

280 More (1745–1833) was a Bristol author and educationalist.

281 Anne Cromatie (d. 1784).

ENDNOTES

282 John Yearsley (1748–1803).

283 Richard Vaughan (*fl.* 1752–95), a local man who lived in Oldbury House on St Michael's Hill, now part of Bristol University. Vaughan was a financier who, in 1752, helped establish Bristol's second bank at the Old Dutch House. In early 1784, he seems either to have chanced upon the Yearsley family as they sheltered in a barn or sought them out after hearing a rumour of their predicament.

284 Southey quotes Hannah More, Yearsley's 'discoverer,' from More's Prefatory Letter to Yearsley's first volume of poetry: *Poems on Several Occasions*, 4th edn. (1786), pp. vi–viii.

285 Edward Young, *Night Thoughts* (1742–45).

286 Alexander Pope, 'Eloisa to Abelard' (1717).

287 From More's Prefatory Letter to *Poems on Several Occasions*, pp. viii–xi.

288 *Poems on Several Occasions* went through four editions by the end of 1786.

289 From More's Prefatory Letter to *Poems on Several Occasions*, pp. xv–xvi.

290 Elizabeth Montagu (1718–1800), the historian and poet, who was also the patron and employer of James Woodhouse.

291 Yearsley's narrative appears in *Poems on Several Occasions*, pp. xviii–xxxi.

292 *Poems, on Various Subjects* (London, 1787).

293 From the 'Life' of himself that Bryant included in his *Verses* – published from his shop in Long Acre, London, 1787, p. iii.

294 'Life,' pp. iii–iv.

295 'Life,' p. iv.

296 'Life,' p. v.

297 'Life,' p. v.

298 Bryant mentions this book, *The Auncient Historie, of the Destruction of Troy* (London, 1597), on p. v of 'Life.' William Caxton had translated and printed the *Recueil des histoires de Troie* in 1473.

299 *The Pantheon Representing the Fabulous Histories of the Heathen Gods and Most Illustrious Heroes in a Short, Plain and Familiar Method by Way of Dialogue*, trs. Andrew Tooke (London, 1698 and numerous later editions).

300 'Life,' p. vi.

301 'Life,' p. viii.

302 'Life,' p. xii.

303 'Life,' p. xii.

304 'Life,' p. xiii.

305 'Life,' pp. xx–xxi.

306 From Chapter IX, 'The Muses, their Image, Names and Number,' *The Pantheon: Representing the Fabulous Histories of the Heathen Gods and Most Illustrious Heroes*, tr. Andrew Tooke, 11th ed. (London, 1729), p. 192.

307 'Life,' p. xxiii.

308 'Life,' pp. xxiv–v.

309 'Life,' p. xxviii.

310 He is identified in Bryant's brief obituary in *The Times*, 26 March 1791: 'Last week, of a decline, at his apartments in Harvey's Buildings, in the Strand, Mr. John Frederick Bryant, aged 37, well-known as a pipe-maker in Bristol, till his poetic turn was accidentally discovered by Mr. MacDonald, the Solicitor General, who procured him a numerous and respectable subscription, and with other eminent persons, continued his patronage till Mr. Bryant's decease.' This was Archibald Macdonald, later first Baronet (1747–1826).

311 This was the afore-noted *Verses* (London, 1787).

312 *Verses*, pp. 24–25.

313 'Written for a Club of Convivials,' *Verses*, p. 22.

ENDNOTES

314 Line 58 of Robert Burns's 'Tam o' Shanter.'

315 *Verses*, pp. 25–26.

316 Smith (1749–1806) was the author of the popular *Elegiac Sonnets* (1784).

317 *Verses*, p. 33.

318 *Verses*, pp. 39–41.

319 Thomas Park (1759–1834), book collector, bibliographer, and literary editor.

320 Archibald Macdonald.

321 The shoemaker poet Robert Bloomfield (1766–1823) had been one of the bestselling poets of the first decade of the nineteenth century. The bankruptcy of his publishers in 1813 deprived him of royalties owed. This blow, compounded by illnesses, blindness, and a large extended family that depended on his income, left him poor by 1818, when Southey was consulted as to how best to raise money for him. See https://romantic-circles.org/editions/bloomfield_letters.

322 From the Introduction to Thomas Sheridan's *The Life of the Rev. Dr. Jonathan Swift, Dean of St. Patrick's, Dublin*, 2nd edn. (London, 1787), n.p.

323 From a letter of Walter Savage Landor to Southey, 28 November 1828.

324 Thomas Warton was Poet Laureate, as was Southey.

325 The French Revolutionary song.

326 Sir James Robert George Graham, second Baronet (1792–1861) was, when Southey wrote these words, the MP for East Cumberland.

327 In a House of Commons debate on the proposed reform of parliament, held on 19 April 1831, Graham had mentioned with approval Southey's opinion that there were too many MPs. 'Although he (Sir James Graham) could not go that length, yet he agreed with Mr. Southey that, if the number could be diminished, it would be proper.' *Hansard*, third series, vol. III, 4 March–22 April 1831, p. 1,676.

328 Edwin (d. 1801) was born Charles Wyndham, to a family estate at Clearwell Castle, in the Forest of Dean. He took the name Edwin on inheriting his maternal uncle's estates in Wales. He was MP for Glamorgan from 1780 to 1789, when he was succeeded in the seat by his son, Thomas Wyndham (1763–1814), who held it until 1814.

329 A song sheet 'sold at no. 4, Aldermary Church-yard, 1775' and hawked by pedlars.

330 Charlotte Edwin.

331 Sir William Alexander (1755–1842), a lawyer who became Chief Baron of the Exchequer in 1824. His sisters were Bethia (1757–1839), Marianne (1758–1816), Christine (1762–1845), Jane (1765–1843), Isabella (1768–1851), and Joanna (1771–83). Bethia, Jane, and Christine remained unmarried, so it is likely that it was they who resided with their uncle – their maternal uncle, since William Alexander's brother had emigrated to America.

332 When a card party was held, the guests each subscribed a little money to pay for the packs used. Some of or all this money was given to servants as a tip.

333 Thomas Janes, *The Beauties of the Poets; Being a Collection of Moral and Sacred Poetry* (London, 1777, and many later editions).

334 Yorkshire country gentlemen, William Bruere (1751–1836) and William Sadlier Bruere (1783–1852).

Southey's Review of *Mary Colling*

335 Anna Eliza Bray (born Kempe, afterwards Stothard) (1790–1883). Bray was a friend of Southey's. He encouraged her writing, by correspondence, and was instrumental in the publication both of this work – Mary Colling's poems – and of Bray's history of the folklore of the Dartmoor area in which she lived: *A Description of the Part of Devonshire Bordering on the Tamar and the Tavy: its Natural History, Manners, Customs, Superstitions, Scenery, Antiquities, Biography of Eminent Persons, &c. &c.*

ENDNOTES

in a Series of Letters to Robert Southey, Esq. (London, J. Murray, 1836). Reviewing the work here, Southey was puffing his protégé. Southey's letters to Bray concerning Colling can be found in Appendix I.

336 These included *De Foix; or, Sketches of the Manners and Customs of the Fourteenth Century. An Historical Romance* (London, 1826) and *The Talba, or the Moor of Portugal. A Romance* (London, 1830).

337 *Fitz of Fitz-ford. A Legend of Devon* (London, 1830). In this novel, Bray had followed Southey's advice that she should base her writing on the history and legends of her own region, rather than setting her novels abroad.

338 Bray's husband, the Revd Edward Atkyns Bray (1778–1857), was Vicar of Tavistock.

339 From Bray's 17 March 1831 letter to Southey, printed in Colling, *Fables*, pp. 1–2.

340 Edmund Colling (1769/1770–1855), husbandman and assistant to the surveyor of the highways. Her mother was Anne Colling, née Domville (1784/1785–1852).

341 Isaac Watts's *Hymns and Spiritual Songs* (London, 1707) went through many editions in the eighteenth and early nineteenth centuries.

342 *Twelfth Night*, act 2, scene 4.

343 William Shenstone's *The School-mistress. A Poem* (1842) portrayed a veteran teacher – a 'character' – as did Henry Kirke White in 'Childhood. A Poem,' *The Remains of Henry Kirke White*, ed. Robert Southey, 2 vols (London, 1807), I, 279–94.

344 From Bray's 17 March 1831 letter to Southey, printed in Colling, *Fables*, p. 4.

345 From Bray's 17 March 1831 letter to Southey, printed in Colling, *Fables*, p. 7.

346 From Bray's 17 March 1831 letter to Southey, printed in Colling, *Fables*, p. 5.

347 Bray's neighbour in Tavistock.

348 From Bray's 17 March 1831 letter to Southey, printed in Colling, *Fables*, p. 6.

349 Lines 7 and 8 of Charles Lamb's poem 'The Grandame,' first published in *Poems on the Death of Priscilla Farmer: by her Grandson Charles Lloyd* (Bristol, 1796).

350 Line 9 of the 'The Grandame.'

351 From Bray's 17 March 1831 letter to Southey, printed in Colling, *Fables*, p. 6.

352 John Frederick Oberlin (1740–1826), the Alsatian pastor who did much to improve the lives of the poor people of the area. His efforts to educate the poor were assisted by his loyal housekeeper Louisa Scheppler (1763–1837). *Memoirs of John Frederick Oberlin* was published in London in 1829. Southey reviewed it in *The Quarterly Review*, 44 (1831), 342–88.

353 Charlotte Bedford.

354 From Bray's 17 March 1831 letter to Southey, printed in Colling, *Fables*, p. 8.

355 The pagan god of fertility in the Old Testament.

356 From Bray's 17 March 1831 letter to Southey, printed in Colling, *Fables*, pp. 9–10.

357 From Bray's 17 March 1831 letter to Southey, printed in Colling, *Fables*, p. 8.

358 From Bray's 17 March 1831 letter to Southey, printed in Colling, *Fables*, pp. 11–12.

359 From Bray's 17 March 1831 letter to Southey, printed in Colling, *Fables*, pp. 14–15.

360 *King Lear*, act 5, scene 3: 'Her voice was ever soft / Gentle and low – an excellent thing in a woman.'

361 From Bray's 17 March 1831 letter to Southey, printed in Colling, *Fables*, pp. 17–18.

362 Crusoe declares that his father informed him, 'God would not bless me; and I would have leisure, hereafter, to reflect upon having neglected his counsel.' See p. 4 of the London 1826 edition of *The Life and Surprising Adventures of Robinson Crusoe*.

363 *Hamlet*, act 3, scene 3.

364 Benedick in *Much Ado About Nothing*, act 2, scene 3: 'When I said I would die a bachelor, I did not think I should live till I were married.'

365 HMS *Vestal*, a 20-gun, sixth-rate frigate, was launched in 1777.

366 John Jervis, first Earl St Vincent (1735–1823).

367 From Bray's 25 March 1831 letter to Southey, printed in Colling, *Fables*, pp. 22–29.

ENDNOTES

368 The *Vestal* foundered in 1777 with all hands lost.

369 In Thomas Southerne's *Isabella; or, the Fatal Marriage*, act 2, scene 2, Isabella utters these words as she sells her jewels.

370 From Bray's 25 March 1831 letter to Southey, printed in Colling, *Fables*, pp. 31–37.

371 From Bray's 25 March 1831 letter to Southey, printed in Colling, *Fables*, pp. 38–41.

372 From a letter of Eliza Bray to Southey, 1832.

373 Southey's persona in his *Sir Thomas More, or, Colloquies on the Progress and Prospects of Society*, 2 vols (London, 1829). The effects of education and the spread of cheap print are discussed in vol. II, 420–23.

374 Ebenezer Elliott (1781–1849), an iron founder by trade, was a largely self-taught poet who had frequently sought Southey's advice on his poems, commencing in 1808. Increasingly politically radical, Elliott published in 1831 *Corn Law Rhymes*, a volume indebted to *Lyrical Ballads*, of whose poetical merits Southey and Wordsworth thought highly, although they opposed its politics. For Southey's view of it, see his letter of 29 March 1832: *New Letters*, II, 375. Wordsworth commented in 1836, 'None of us have done better than [Elliott] has in his best, though there is a deal of stuff arising from his hatred of existing things. Like Byron, Shelley, &c., he looks on much with an evil eye. . . . Elliott has a fine eye for nature. He is an extraordinary man.' Henry Crabb Robinson, *Diary, Reminiscences, and Correspondence* (London, 1870; 1872), II, 171.

375 John Struthers (1776–1853), a shoemaker and author of *The Poor Man's Sabbath* (1804), *The Peasant's Death* (1806) and *Poems, Moral and Religious* (1814). Struthers was assisted into publication by Joanna Baillie, who had known him as a child, and by Walter Scott. In 1827, he published a *History of Scotland* and, in 1832, became the librarian of the Stirling Library, Glasgow. *The Poetical Works of John Struthers, with Autobiography* was published in 1850.

376 Crocker (1797–1861) was another shoemaker poet who received encouragement from Southey, who visited him in Chichester in December 1830 and declared 'his poems are of very considerable merit' (*Life and Correspondence*, VI, 126). Crocker's *The Vale of Obscurity, The Levant, and Other Poems* was published by Longmans in 1830.

377 Millhouse (1788–1839) worked as a framework knitter in a Nottingham workshop and later as a clerk in a savings bank. His publications included *Vicissitude, a Poem in Four Books and Other Pieces* (1821), *Blossoms. Being a Selection of Sonnets*. 2nd edn. (1823), *The Song of the Patriot, Sonnets, and Songs* (1826), and *Sherwood Forest, and Other Poems* (1827).

378 Southey derives his information from the narrative prefacing Crocker's *Vale of Obscurity*, pp. x–xi. John Thelwall (1764–1834) was a political radical whose oratory at mass meetings was so feared by the government of the 1790s that he was arrested and charged with treason. After acquittal, he pursued poetry, befriending Coleridge and Southey, and then became a lecturer on the art of public speaking (using passages of verse to exemplify his ideas and to help his audience master rhythmic utterance).

379 William Collins (1721–59).

380 From the narrative prefacing Crocker's *Vale of Obscurity*, p. ix.

381 Alexander Pope, 'The Epistle to Dr. Arbuthnot,' line 129.

382 William Fitzhardinge Berkeley, Viscount Dursley (1786–1857), the illegitimate son of the fifth Earl of Berkeley, styled himself 'Colonel Berkeley.' He was made Baron Seagrave in 1831 as the reforming Whig ministry sought to increase its number of supporters in the House of Lords. Southey's remarks reflect Tory disapproval both of this procedure and of Berkeley himself. He was a notorious hard-drinking rake, while his and his father's long campaign to have him recognised as the sixth Earl was widely thought to have involved the forgery of a marriage register.

ENDNOTES

383 Cambridge and Oxford.

384 "Grief" and 'joy': an abbreviated form of the titles of the volumes of encomiastic verse produced by the universities upon the death of one monarch and accession of his successor, as in *Academiæ Cantabrigiensis luctus in obitum serenissimi Georgii I. Euergetou Magnæ Britanniæ, &c. Regis: et gaudia ob potentissimi Georgii II. patriarum virtutum ac solii hæredis successionem pacificam simul et auspicatissimam* (Cambridge, 1727).

385 'Praiseworthy man.'

386 Mixing English and Latin – as in Franglais.

387 'A worthy lorded man.' 'Lorded' rather than 'lauded': Southey's pun indicates his distaste for Colonel Berkeley's elevation to the peerage.

388 Southey's sarcasm implies that Berkeley's character is widely known for the wrong reasons.

389 Cardinal Arnaud d'Ossat (1537–1604): 'Whatever Fortune seems to give to my left hand, I take with the right.' From a letter of 4 January 1595 in *Lettres du Cardinal d'Ossat avec des notes historiques & politiques de M. Amelot de La Houssaie* (Amsterdam, 1728), I, 329.

390 King George IV (b. 1762) died in 1830.

391 George IV was succeeded by King William IV (1765–1837).

392 Arthur Wellesley, first Duke of Wellington (1769–1852), was Prime Minister from 1829 to November 1830.

393 Sir Robert Peel (1788–1850) was Home Secretary from 1828 to 1830.

394 That is, as a response to the official announcement of William IV's accession to the throne, in November 1830.

395 *Bell's Life in London, and Sporting Chronicle*: a weekly broadsheet that heavily featured sports news, especially boxing and horse racing. It was edited by Vincent George Dowling (1785–1852). The title was given to Alford in the issue of 28 March 1830 in a spirit of irony: 'We must decline the sublime poetical effusions of Mr. John Alford, the Poet Laureate of Trowbridge.'

396 John Benett (1773–1852), of Pythouse, Wiltshire, MP for Wiltshire from 1819 to 1832.

397 Sir John Dugdale Astley, first Baronet (1778–1842), was MP for Wiltshire from 1820 to 1832.

398 George Crabbe (1754–1832) had been Rector of Trowbridge since 1814.

399 William Everett Waldron (c. 1770–1833) was the owner of a textile mill in Trowbridge.

400 'K.' in Mortimer's initials is possibly a misprint for 'H.' Edward Horlock Mortimer (1786–1857) was Trowbridge's most prominent businessman – an owner of woollen mills.

401 Charles Grey (1764–1845) was Prime Minister from 1830 to 1834. A Whig, he ensured the Reform Bill passed during his period in office.

402 William Lamb, second Viscount Melbourne (1779–1848), was Home Secretary from 1830 to 1834.

403 *The Keepsake*, beginning in 1827, was one of the new, popular literary annuals. It was renowned more for the luxury of its paper, bindings, and engravings than for the quality of its verse – although Southey contributed two slight poems to it in 1829 (Wordsworth and Coleridge also contributed verse). It was owned and edited by the engraver Charles Heath (1785–1848).

404 'There are,' 'There is,' 'It is,' or 'It was.' Coleridge used this construction, imitating the common speech of West Country people, in 'The Ancient Mariner' (line 1): 'It is an ancient mariner, and he stoppeth one of three.'

405 Southey means an agreed written version of rural dialect, such as the written version of northern Scottish speech known as Doric.

ENDNOTES

406 John Cunningham (see note 116 earlier).

407 'The Birth of Envy,' Colling, *Fables*, pp. 44–45.

408 The Dartmoor legends of Lady Howard's coach made of human bones and of the terrifying hound that roamed the moor (later developed by Arthur Conan Doyle in *The Hound of the Baskervilles* after a visit to the area) feature in Eliza Bray's *Fitz of Fitzford* and *A Description of the Part of Devonshire Bordering on the Tamar and the Tavy*.

409 Colling, *Fables*, pp. 73–75.

410 Pierre Carlet de Chamblain de Marivaux (1688–1763).

411 From *La Paysanne parvenu ou Les Memoires de Madame la marquise de L** V*** (1735–38), now attributed not to Marivaux but to Charles de Fieux, Chevalier de Mouhy (1701–45). The phrases quoted appear in Part One – p. 3 of the La Haye, 1736 edition.

412 A civil war involving revolt by the lower classes.

413 During the reign of Edward III (1312–77), Jacob van Artevelde (c. 1295–1345), 'Captain General,' aligned Flanders with England and against France. When he proposed to recognize as sovereign Edward III's eldest son, Edward the Black Prince, rather than the Count of Flanders, a revolt occurred in which he was killed. One of his sons, Philip (b. 1340), led an unsuccessful revolt against the Count of Flanders in 1382.

414 The peasant revolt of 1358 in northern France.

415 A peasant revolt of 1524–25 in Germany provoked by changes brought about by the Reformation.

416 Samuel Johnson quoted these lines to James Boswell while in Nairn, on a tour of the Scottish Highlands, on 27 August 1773. They are from 'Contemplation,' by the Revd Richard Gifford (1725–1807). They appear on p. 222 of vol. II of the London 1821 edition of *The Life of Samuel Johnson, LL. D.*

417 From p. 29 of vol. I of the London 1821 edition of *The Life of Samuel Johnson, LL. D.*

418 National poets of Italy: Ludovico Ariosto (1474–1533), author of *Orlando Furioso*, and Torquato Tasso (1544–95), author of *Gerusalemme Liberate*.

419 The serial publication that gave the biographies of criminals condemned to death at Newgate Prison.

420 Domingo dos Reis Quita (1728–70) and Francisco Dias Gomes (1745–95). Southey considered himself an expert on Portuguese literature, having studied it first when living in the country in 1795–96 and 1800–01. He wrote *History of Brazil* (1810–19) and began, but never completed, a history of Portugal. He discussed Iberian literature extensively in the second, revised, edition of his *Letters Written During a Short Residence in Spain and Portugal* (London, 1799). See the editors' introduction and notes to *Letters Written During a Short Residence in Spain and Portugal*, ed. Jonathan González and Cristina Flores (London, 2021).

421 *Hamlet*, act 1, scene 2: from the prince's famous soliloquy beginning 'O that this too solid flesh would melt.'

422 James Townley's farce *High Life Below Stairs* (1759) mocked pretentious servants aping their masters' manners.

423 Mary Anne Hughes (c. 1770–1853). The daughter of the Anglican clergyman George Watts (d. 1810), she married another cleric, Thomas Hughes. In the late 1810s, she became a friend and correspondent of Southey. She was also on excellent terms with Walter Scott, and her *Letters and Recollections* of the latter was published in 1904.

424 The 'learned pig' was a fairground show of the 1780s: the animal had been trained so that it seemed to be able to answer arithmetical questions and spell out words by picking up cards in its mouth. It was superseded by more junior porkers after its death in 1788.

ENDNOTES

425 James Hogg (1770–1835), the poet, novelist, and ballad collector who had been a shepherd at Ettrick, near Yarrow.

426 John Murray (1782–1845), Southey's regular publisher, who did indeed publish *Lives of Uneducated Poets*.

427 Poet Laureate.

428 A street near Paternoster Row, St Paul's, London, where Southey's publisher Longman and Rees had premises.

429 Grosvenor Charles Bedford (1773–1839). Bedford, a civil servant, was a schoolfriend of Southey's.

430 Both the new Mechanics' Institutes and University College London were established on secular and utilitarian principles in the 1820s. The knowledge they inculcated was to be 'useful' rather than religious – bookkeeping and engineering rather than classical poetry.

431 Margaret Holford Hodson (1778–1852), poet and translator, lived with her husband, Septimus Hodson (1768–1833), at Ripon, within 20 miles of the Brueres at Kirkby Hall.

432 Charles Hodson (1793–1829), Mrs Hodson's stepson.

433 William Otter (1768–1840) edited *The Life and Remains of the Rev. Edward Daniel Clarke, LL.D.* (London, 1824).

434 Charles Watkin Williams Wynn (1775–1850). Wynn was a schoolfriend of Southey's. Later an MP and a minister, he obtained a government pension for Southey that superseded the £160 annuity he had previously given him from his personal wealth.

435 A joke: Wynn was Welsh; Monmouthshire was, in Southey's time, assumed to be in England.

436 William Van Mildert (1765–1836) was Bishop of Durham from 1826 to 1836.

437 John Neville White (1782–1845) was the elder brother of Henry Kirke White, whose works Southey edited in 1807 to great popular success.

438 Southey's *History of the Peninsular War* was published in three volumes, from 1823 to 1832.

439 Colling's poem 'To R. Southey, Esq' appeared on pp. 50–51 of *Fables*.

440 An engraving of a sketch of Colling by William Patten Jr appeared as the frontispiece of *Fables*.

441 Here Southey is commenting on the three letters that Bray addressed to him telling Colling's life story. These were published as the introduction to Colling's *Fables*.

442 Bray's Tavistock neighbour in whose house Colling was a servant.

443 That is, in Southey's review of *Fables* in *The Quarterly Review*.

444 Bowles (1762–1850), a poet whose sonnets were a major influence on Coleridge and Southey in the mid-1790s. Southey reviewed Bowles's poem *The Spirit of Discovery* (1804).

445 Southey reviewed James Grahame, *British Georgics*, in *The Quarterly Review*, 3 (1810), 456–61. His review of James Montgomery, *Poems*, appeared in *The Quarterly Review*, 6 (1811), 405–19, and of *The World Before the Flood* appeared in *The Quarterly Review*, 11 (1814), 78–87. His review of Walter Savage Landor's *Count Julian: A Tragedy* was published in *The Quarterly Review*, 12 (1812), 86–92.

446 Southey's daughter (1810–1864).

447 *A Description of the Part of Devonshire Bordering on the Tamar and the Tavy: its Natural History, Manners, Customs, Superstitions, Scenery, Antiquities, Biography of Eminent Persons, &c. &c. in a Series of Letters to Robert Southey, Esq.* (London, 1836).

448 Edward Atkyns Bray.

449 John Russell, sixth Duke of Bedford (1766–1839), who owned large amounts of property in Tavistock and the surrounding area.

450 'Godlike mind.'

451 Probably meant to allude to Robert Burns. Burns had acquired a reputation for drinking and womanizing after the biography included in James Currie's four-volume edition of his works (1800) – this went into its eighth edition in 1820.

ENDNOTES

452 The pro-revolutionary play of Southey's radical youth, which he had written in 1794 and left unpublished, was published in a pirate edition in 1817, intended to expose the hypocrisy of his current conservative arguments in favour of the arrest and detention of radicals.

453 See note 211.

454 Referring to Frederick Bryant's use of rhyme to mock people in his social circle. See p. 166.

455 Bellman's verses were the doggerel poems by which beadles – local officials responsible for dealing with minor offenders – sought tips from the well-to-do populace at Christmastime.

456 Dugald Stewart remembered this remark by Robert Burns in a letter to Burns's biographer Currie, printed in James Currie's *The Works of Robert Burns; With an Account of His Life*, 4 vols (London, 1800), I, 143.

457 'Everything knowable.'

458 [Note in review:] N. B. A Frenchman's libel on the greatest of English philosophers, in which, inter alia, it is insinuated that his mental faculties had lost their vigour before he thought of writing on theological subjects, has been literally translated, and published as the 'Life of Newton,' by the Society for the Diffusion of *Useful Knowledge*.

459 'They are without a sacred bard': Horace, Odes. Book IV, IX. 25.

460 John Wright (1805–44), a weaver by trade, was a self-taught poet whose *The Retrospect, or Youthful Scenes* (1825) attracted favourable notices.

461 'the more divine mind/spirit.'

462 Lines 15–20 of Charles Lamb, 'The Ballad Singers' (translated from the Latin of Vincent Bourne), in Lamb's collection *Album Verses, with a Few Others* (London, 1830), p. 57.

463 James Grahame (1765–1811), whose *British Georgics* Southey had reviewed in *The Quarterly Review*, 3 (1810), 456–61, had published *The Sabbath, with Sabbath Walks and Other Poems* in 1808.

464 A lightly fictionalized James Hogg was the naïve, boozy butt of humorous sketches in *Blackwood's Magazine*. By 1831, Hogg was afflicted by debts, some a consequence of the bankruptcy of Constable, his Edinburgh publisher. In London in 1832, the publisher of his *Altrive Tales* also went bankrupt, when only 1 of a projected 12 volumes had appeared.

465 In 1831, Allan Cunningham was in the midst of publishing his biographies of artists: *Lives of Eminent British Painters, Sculptors, and Architects* (1829–1833).

466 Elizabeth Sophia Lawrence (1761–1845). Lawrence owned Studley Park, a large estate containing a landscape garden and the ruins of Fountains Abbey.

467 That is, Elizabeth Sophia Lawrence of Studley Park.

468 J. Tourle, a farmer of Langport, died in 1801.

469 That is, in the Forest of Dean, where stood the oak trees that were used to build the warships that allowed 'Britannia' to 'rule the waves' and preserved her from invasion.

470 Charlotte Smith, 'Sweet violets! From your humble beds,' lines 9–10. From Smith's *Conversations Introducing Poetry: Chiefly on Subjects of Natural History* (London, 1804), pp. 78–79.

471 The then-current Lord of Alnwick Castle was Hugh Percy, third Duke of Northumberland (1785–1847).

472 The river Laver runs through Studley Park, Yorkshire – scene of Jones's poems, 'Lines Addressed to Mrs. Lawrence' and 'A Voice from Ripon.'

473 Probably one of the daughters of the Bruere household – Harriet Louisa Sadlier Bruere (1816–1884).

474 Harriet Louisa Sadlier Bruere's younger sister was Julia Sophia Sadlier Bruere (1818–1894).

475 Anna Maria Bruere.

476 Harriet Louisa Sadlier Bruere.

ENDNOTES

477 Nancy Bruere, née Sadlier (1760–?).
478 Harriet Louisa Sadlier Bruere. 'T.' Sadlier Bruere is likely a misprint for 'J.' – Julia Sophia Bruere.
479 Harriet Louisa Sadlier Bruere.
480 Nancy Bruere, née Sadlier.
481 Albert Sadlier Bruere (1820–?).
482 Anna Maria Sadlier Bruere (1806–1828), one of the daughters of Jones's employer William Sadlier Bruere.

INDEX

Note: Page numbers followed by n indicate text found in a note.

'Address to a Dead Cat, An' (Jones)
    243–246
'Address to a Violet, An' (Jones) 261–262
Alford, John 193–195
Amir Khan, and other Poems 23
Anderson, Robert 11, 26
Anniversary, The 23
Arnold, Matthew 10
*Attempts in Verse, by John Jones, an Old
    Servant* (Southey) 2, 25; introduction to
    101–139; review of in *The Edinburgh
    Review* 211–214; review of in *The
    Quarterly Review* 223–226
'Author to His Book, The' (Jones) 232

Bacon, Francis 109
bad criticism 173
bad poetry 173
Barber, Mary 11
Barnfield, James 192–193
'On the Battle of Waterloo' (Jones) 293–295
Bedford, Grosvenor C. 203
'On Being Confined to School' (Kirke
    White) 60–61
Bennet, John 29, 156–157
Blacklock, Thomas 11, 12
Bloomfield, Robert 4, 5, 13, 28, 30, 32,
    172, 307n50, 317n321
Booth, Charles 8
Boswell's Life of Johnson 199
Bowles, William Lisle 209
Bray, Eliza 32, 33, 317n325, 318n338;
    on Colling 179–188; correspondence
    about Colling 206–209; correspondence
    about Davidson 208; correspondence
    about Jones 206–207; *Fitz of Fitzford, a
    Legend of Devon* 179

Browning, Robert 15
Bruce, Michael 11
Bryant, John Frederick 20, 30–31; death
    of 172; life of 161–172; selections of
    poetry 169–172
Bryan, William 20, 37n25
Burke, Tim 34
Burns, Robert 230, 306n29, 322n451,
    323n456
'Butterfly to His Love, The' (Jones) 248

capitalism 7
Carlile, Richard 35
'Cemeteries and Catacombs of Paris'
    (Southey) 20–21
Chantrey, Francis 4
Chatterton, Thomas 2, 12, 14, 36n2, 36n5,
    37n20, 59, 307n66
'Children's Dirge, The' (Jones) 282–283
Clare, John 4, 5
class distinctions 106–107, 198–199, 200
Clifton Grove (Kirke White) 13, 71–72
'From a Cobler to B.' (Jones) 300–301
Coleridge, Samuel 14
Collected Poems (Bloomfield) 5
Collected Poems (Chatterton) 12
Colling, Mary Maria 32–33;
    correspondence about 206–210; 'On the
    Death of My Maternal Grandmother'
    188–190; grandparents 184–188;
    language 195; 'Letter to My Sister
    Anne, A' 196–198; life of 179–188;
    selections of poetry 196
Collins, William 3, 191, 318n379
'Contemplation' (Kirke White) 62–63n1
Corn Law Rhymes (Elliott) 17, 191
Cotton, Charles 26, 103, 203, 309n116

INDEX

Cowper, William 3, 191
Crocker, Charles 2, 191, 319n376, 319n378
'Cruel the hand' (Yearsley) 160
Cunningham, Allan 3, 4, 23, 230
Cunningham, John 11, 104, 195, 202, 309n116
Curse of Kehama, The (Southey) 17, 36n6

Davidson, Lucretia Maria 24–25; correspondence about 208; death of 98–99; life of 89–100; selections of poetry 92, 93–94, 94–95, 97–98; 'To a Star' 95–96
'Deep in the Dell' (Jones) 243
Dermody, Thomas 10–11, 14, 305n2; *Extravaganza* 54; life of 40–58; *Peace, a Poem* 56; 'Rights of Justice, The' 51
Description of the Part of Devonshire Bordering on the Tamar and the Tavy, A (Bray) 32
Dickens, Charles 7
Dodsley, Robert 11, 152, 314n262
Duck, Stephen 27, 27–28, 36n1, 219–220, 228; death of 151; life of 140–152; selections of poetry 142, 151; Swift epigram 150; 'Thresher's Labour' 143–149

Ecclesiastical Sketches (Wordsworth) 116n2
Edinburgh Review, The 9, 211–223
education 6–7, 190, 192, 201
Eliot, T. S. 26
Elliott, Ebenezer 15–17, 191, 319n374
Ellis, George 11
'Epistle from Robert Southey, Esq. to Allan Cunningham' (Southey) 23
'Epitaph on Philip and Mary Jones, An' (Jones) 302
'Excuse to a Young Lady, A' (Jones) 283
Extravaganza (Dermody) 54

Fables, and other Pieces in Verse, by Mary Maria Colling (Southey's review of) 32, 179–201
Falconer, William 11, 310n141
'Fanciful Description of a Passage Down part of the River Wye, A' (Jones) 266–272
Farmer's Boy, The (Bloomfield) 5, 13, 307n50
Fennor, William 136–137
Fitz of Fitzford, a Legend of Devon (Bray) 179
'Friend of My Heart, The' (Jones) 257

Goldsmith, Oliver 3, 24, 90, 191, 308n104
Gomes, Francisco Dias 200, 321n420
Gradgrind (Dickens) 7
Grahame, James 209, 229, 322n445, 323n463
Grierson, Constantia 11
Groom, Nick 36n5

'Hark! Hark! &c.' (Jones) 255–256
Harrison, Tony 7
Heaney, Seamus 7
Hill, Thomas 5, 6
history 8
Hodson, Margaret Holford 204, 205–206
Hogg, James 5, 23, 230, 322n425, 323n464
'Home' (Jones) 260–261
Hone, William 35
Hughes, Mary Anne 202–203, 205, 321n423

Introductory Essay to the Lives and Works of Our Uneducated Poets (Southey) 23, 31, 32, 101–178

'Jane Barnaby' (Jones) 262–264
Jeffrey, Francis 36n6
Johnson, Samuel 1, 11, 37n12, 199–200, 321n416
Jones, Henry 11
Jones, John 25, 31, 173–174; 'Address to a Dead Cat, An' 243–246; 'Address to a Violet, An' 261–262; 'Author to His Book, The' 232–233; 'Butterfly to His Love, The' 248; 'Children's Dirge, The' 282–283; 'From a Cobler to B.' 300–301; correspondence about 202–207; 'Deep in the Dell' 243; in *The Edinburgh Review* 211–223; 'Epitaph on Philip and Mary Jones, An' 302; 'Excuse to a Young Lady, A' 283; 'Fanciful Description of a Passage Down part of the River Wye, A' 266–272; 'Friend of My Heart, The' 257; 'Hark! Hark! &c.' 255–256; 'Home' 260–261; 'Jane Barnaby' 262–264; 'Journey of Life, The' 233–234; 'Laver's Banks' 273–275; letters from 101–102, 104–105; life of 174–178; 'Lines Addressed to Mrs. Lawrence' 241; 'Lines Addressed to the Misses L. and T. Sadlier Bruere' 290–291; 'Lines Occasioned by Reading the Following Printed Bill' 295–296;

326

INDEX

'Lines, Occasioned by Walking over Some Fallen Leaves' 246–247; 'Lines on Parting from Miss H.' 284–285; 'Lines on the Death of Miss Sadlier Bruere' 302–303; 'Lines Written for Miss L. S. B.' 291; 'Lines Written for Miss L. S. Bruere' 290; 'Louisa to Julia' 286; 'By Love We Were Led, Jane' 265–266; 'Mary Killcrow' 257–260; 'Mary St. Clair' 279; 'My Mary Is No More!' 275; 'My Nose' 299–300; 'Old Mawley to His Ass.' 249–251; 'On the Battle of Waterloo' 293–295; 'On the Death of Gaffer Gun' 297; 'On the Death of Lord Byron' 292–293; 'Orran and Bertha' 279–281; 'Poor Kitty' 295; 'A Prayer in Affliction' 302; in *The Quarterly Review* 223–231; 'Red-Breast, The' 102–103, 225; 'Reflections on Visiting a Spring at different Seasons of the Year' 213–214, 276–279; 'Sally Roy' 264; selections of poetry 176, 177; 'Snowball, The' 234–239; Southey's relationship with 101–105; 'Thou Tell'st Me, My Love, &c.' 285–286; 'To a Friend of Early Life' 287–289; 'To a Gentleman Who Married a Second Wife' 297–299; 'To A Wild Heath Flower' 248; 'To Eliza' 256–257; 'To Lydia' 255; 'To Maria on Her Birthday' 286–287; 'To Our Worthy Shepherd, Mr. Way' 304; 'To The Tongue' 251–255; 'Verses Written for a Boy to Learn and Repeat' 301–302; 'Voice from Ripon, A' 242; 'Why That Sigh, &c.' 240; 'World's Like a Tyrant, &c., The' 273; 'Written for A. S. B. On His Birth-Day' 291–292; 'Written for a Young Lady' 283–284; 'Written in Alnwick Castle' 272–273; 'W. Stevenson' 296–297
Jonson, Ben 26, 113, 122, 310n128, 311n151, 312n201
'Journey of Life, The' (Jones) 233–234

Keats, John 13, 15
Keepsake, The 5, 195, 320n403
Kirke White, Henry 2, 7, 13–15, 20, 28, 37n22, 97, 98; admonitory sentences 83–84; *Clifton Grove* 13, 71–72; 'Contemplation' 62–63n1; death of 85; life of 59–88; 'Lines Written in Wilford Church-Yard' 78–80; 'My

Own Character' 73–74; 'Ode on Disappointment' 76–78; 'On Being Confined to School' 60–61; *Remains of Henry Kirke White, The* (Southey) 13, 17, 59–88, 309n109; 'To the Herb Rosemary' 68; 'To the Morning' 69–70
Knowles, Herbert 20–22

Lamb, Charles 18, 34, 229, 310n139
language 106–107, 195–196
'Laver's Banks' (Jones) 273–275
Lay of the Last Minstrel (Scott) 5
Leapor, Mary 11–12
'learned pig' 321n424
Leavis, F. R. 10
'Letter to My Sister Anne, A' (Colling) 196–198
Life and Lucubrations of Crispinus Scriblerus, The (Woodhouse) 29
Life of Chatterton (Southey) 12
Life of Kirke White (Southey) 13, 25
Life of Thomas Dermody, The (Raymond) 10, 40–58
'Lines Addressed to Mrs. Lawrence' (Jones) 241
'Lines Addressed to the Misses L. and T. Sadlier Bruere' (Jones) 290–291
'Lines Occasioned by Reading the Following Printed Bill' (Jones) 295–296
'Lines, Occasioned by Walking over Some Fallen Leaves' (Jones) 246–247
'Lines on Parting from Miss H.' (Jones) 284–285
'Lines on the Death of Miss Sadlier Bruere' (Jones) 302–303
'Lines Written for Miss L. S. Bruere' (Jones) 290, 291
'Lines Written in the Churchyard of Richmond, Yorkshire' (Knowles) 20–22
'Lines Written in Wilford Church-Yard' (Kirke White) 78–80
Lives and Works of Uneducated Poets: review of in *The Edinburgh Review* 214–223; review of in *The Quarterly Review* 226–231
Lives of Labouring-Class Poets (Southey) 6
Lives of the Most Eminent English Poets (Johnson) 37n12
Lives of the Poets (Johnson) 1, 11
'Living Sadness, A' (Taylor) 114

327

INDEX

Lofft, Capel 5, 6, 13
'Louisa to Julia' (Jones) 286
Love Letters to My Wife (Woodhouse) 29
'By Love We Were Led, Jane' (Jones)
    265–266
Lyrical Ballads (Wordsworth) 8

Mackenzie, Henry 32, 190
'Maid of Elvar, The' (Cunningham) 3, 23
March of Intellect 8
Marivaux, Pierre Carlet de Chamblain
    de 198
'Mary Killcrow' (Jones) 257–260
'Mary St. Clair' (Jones) 279
Mayhew, Henry 8
Mechanics' Institutes 7
mental crises 34
Millhouse, Robert 2, 191, 319n377
Mill, J. S. 10
Montgomery, James 2, 209, 322n445
Monthly Mirror, The 65
Monthly Preceptor, The 64–65
Monthly Review, The 13, 67, 71–72
More, Hannah 29, 34, 157–159
Morse, Samuel F.B. 24, 89–100
Murray, John 25, 204, 205, 206, 207
'My Mary Is No More!' (Jones) 275
'My Nose' (Jones) 299–300
'My Own Character' (Kirke White)
    73–74
'My Serious Cares and Considerations'
    (Taylor) 108

National Schools 7
'Navy of Ships and other vessels . . .'
    (Taylor) 115
New Poor Law 9

'Ode on Disappointment' (Kirke White)
    76–78
'Old Mawley to His Ass.' (Jones) 249–251
'On the Death of Gaffer Gun' (Jones) 297
'On the Death of Lord Byron' (Jones)
    292–293
'On the Death of My Maternal
    Grandmother' (Colling) 188–190
'Orran and Bertha' (Jones) 279–281

patronage 34, 173, 217, 219–220, 227, 228
Peace, a Poem (Dermody) 56
peasant-poet 36n4
'Pennyless Pilgrimage, The' (Taylor) 122

*Poems and Letters by the Late William
    Isaac Roberts* (Roberts) 18
Poems on Several Occasions (Bennet) 29
Poor Law, New 9
'Poor Kitty' (Jones) 295
'A Prayer in Affliction' (Jones) 302
print culture 4–5
publishing industry 4–5, 190
Purcell, Henry 305n3

Quarterly Review, The: on Bray 179–201;
    on Colling 207; on Jones 223–231; on
    Morse 89–100; review of *Lives and
    Works of Uneducated Poets* 223–231
Quita, Domingo dos Reis 200, 321n420

radical poets 34–35
Raymond, James Grant 10, 40–58, 305n1
'Red-Breast, The' (Jones) 102–103, 225
'Reflections on Visiting a Spring at
    different Seasons of the Year' (Jones)
    213–214, 276–279
Remains of Henry Kirke White, The
    (Southey) 13, 17, 59–88, 309n109
'Rights of Justice, The' (Dermody) 51
Roberts, William 17–19, 20
Rogers, Samuel 20

'Sabbath' (Struthers) 2, 191, 229
'Sally Roy' (Jones) 264
Scott, Walter 5, 23, 200, 319n375,
    321n423
self-education 3, 24, 191–192, 200, 201
self-taught/self-educated/self-instructed
    poets 2
Shelley, Percy 15, 37n22
Shenstone, William 28, 229
shoemaker poets 4, 28, 29, 30, 151, 156,
    229, 317n321
Sir Thomas More (Southey) 7
Smiles, Samuel 8
Smith, Adam 9
'Snowball, The' (Jones) 234–239
social climbing 4
'Soldier's Love, The' (Elliott) 16
*Songs of Scotland, Ancient and Modern,
    The* (Cunningham) 23
Southey, Katharine 210
Southey, Robert: *Amir Khan, and other
    Poems* (review) 24; *Attempts in Verse*
    25; biographical background 1–2, 5–6,
    14, 34; 'Cemeteries and Catacombs

328

INDEX

of Paris' (review) 20–21; *Curse of Kehama, The* 17, 36n6; 'Epistle from Robert Southey, Esq. to Allan Cunningham' 23; *Fables, and other Pieces in Verse, by Mary Maria Colling* (review) 32; *Introductory Essay to the Lives and Works of Our Uneducated Poets* 23, 31, 32; *Life of Chatterton* 12; *Life of Kirke White* 13, 25; moral purpose 9; Poet Laureate 103–104; review of in *The Edinburgh Review* 211–223; review of in *The Quarterly Review* 223–231; *Specimens of the Later English Poets* 11; *Thalaba the Destroyer* 36n6; values of 8–9; *Wat Tyler* 34

Specimens of the Later English Poets (Southey) 11

Spectator, The 141

Spence, Joseph 36n1

Spence, Thomas 35

'Spring' (Woodhouse) 152

'On State Reform' (Alford) 194–195

Sterne, Laurence 312n202

'Storm, A' (Taylor) 119–120

Struthers, John 2, 191, 229, 319n375

Swift, Jonathan 27, 150–151

Taylor, John 26, 27; death of 138; expeditions 121–133; life of 107–116, 138; 'A Living Sadness' 114; 'My Serious Cares and Considerations' 108; 'Navy of Ships and other vessels . . .' 115; 'Pennyless Pilgrimage, The' 122; quatorzains 116; 'Sculler's Travels' 121; 'Storm, A' 119–120; 'Taylor's Motto' 117; 'Taylor's Revenge' 136–137; writings of 110, 111–125, 130, 132–138, 218–219, 313n208

'Taylor's Motto' (Taylor) 117

'Taylor's Revenge' (Taylor) 136–137

Thalaba the Destroyer (Southey) 36n6

Thelwall, John 35

'Thou Tell'st Me, My Love, &c.' (Jones) 285–286

'Three Tabernacles, The' (Knowles) 20

'Thresher's Labour, The' (Duck) 27, 143–149

Tighe, Edward 50–51

'To a Friend of Early Life' (Jones) 287–289

'To a Gentleman Who Married a Second Wife' (Jones) 297–299

'To a Robin Red-Breast' (Jones) *see* 'Red-Breast, The' (Jones)

'To a Star' (Davidson) 95–96

'To A Wild Heath Flower' (Jones) 248–249

'To Eliza' (Jones) 256–257

'To Lydia' (Jones) 255

'To Maria on Her Birthday' (Jones) 286–287

'To Our Worthy Shepherd, Mr. Way' (Jones) 304

'To the Herb Rosemary' (Kirke White) 68

'To the Morning' (Kirke White) 69–70

'To The Tongue' (Jones) 251–255

Traditional Tales of the English and Scottish Peasantry (Cunningham) 23

Tristram Shandy (Sterne) 312n202

uneducated poets 2, 4, 6, 106, 107, 139

Verses (Bryant) 30

'Verses Written for a Boy to Learn and Repeat' (Jones) 301–302

'Voice from Ripon, A' (Jones) 242

Walton, Isaac 202

watermen 108–109

Water Poet *see* Taylor, John

Wat Tyler (Southey) 34

White, John Neville 17

Whitman, Walt 15

'Why That Sigh, &c.' (Jones) 240

Williams, Raymond 10

Wither, George 117

women poets 33

Woodhouse, James 28–29, 34, 229; life of 151–156; selections of poetry 154, 155–156; 'Spring' 152

Wordsworth, William 8, 15, 17, 116n2

working class conditions 198–199

'World's Like a Tyrant, &c., The' (Jones) 273

'Written for A. S. B. On His Birth-Day' (Jones) 291–292

'Written for a Young Lady' (Jones) 283–284

'Written in Alnwick Castle' (Jones) 272–273

'W. Stevenson' (Jones) 296–297

Wynn, C. W. W. 204–205

Yearsley, Ann 20, 29–30, 34; 'Cruel the hand' 160; life of 157–161; poem on her mother 161; writings of 160

Young, Matthew 305n14